LINDA R. WEXLER

A Spot of Tea™

The West Coast Guide to Afternoon Teas

Featuring: California, Nevada, Oregon, Washington, British Columbia, Alaska & Hawaii

Chelsea Street Productions
Altadena, California

Published by:

Chelsea Street Productions
1920 N. Lake Avenue, Suite 108-200
Altadena, California 91001

For inquiries about this and other titles published
by Chelsea Street Productions
Phone: 626-797-4TEA   Fax: 626-794-7387
Toll Free: 800-SPOT OF T   E-Mail: teabooklady@earthlink.net
Please visit our Web Site: www.ASpotOfTea.com

Manufactured in the United States of America
Cover Art & Design Copyright Chelsea Street Productions

Library of Congress Catalog Card Number 97-92413

Wexler, Linda.
     "A spot of tea"; the West Coast guide to afternoon teas;
featuring California, Nevada, Oregon, Washington, British
Columbia, Alaska & Hawaii / by Linda R. Wexler.--2nd. ed.--
Altadena, Calif.: Chelsea Street Productions, c1997.
p. cm.   ISBN 1-888230-02-9
     1. Afternoon teas--California--Guidebooks. 2. Afternoon teas--
Northwest, Pacific--Guidebooks. 3. Teas. I. Title.
TX736 .W48 1997   647 .95794--dc21

A Spot of Tea™ is a trademarked series of tea theme books and fine gifts by Chelsea Street Productions. If your local tea shop, gift shop or bookstore is out of our books, you may call 800-SPOT OF T, to order autographed books directly from the publisher: *A Spot of Tea*™ ($24.95 per book, plus $3.95 postage & handling, and applicable sales tax, U.S.funds) and *My Tea Journal* ($8.95 per book, plus $2.00 postage & handling, and applicable sales tax, U.S. Funds). Please send check or money order to: Chelsea Street Productions at the above address or call to charge on your Visa, MasterCard, or Discover Card. Thank you!

Dedication

To my Mom and Dad
Evelyn and Irving Wexler
with love,
you have been a constant source
of support and love.

Acknowledgement

I want to acknowledge the many gracious tea lovers who write or phone, or visit with me at book signing events. It's always fun and interesting sharing teatime stories and chatting about special tea adventures. Special appreciation must go to all of the proprietors of tea rooms who work so hard to please us. You work long hours preparing and planning, often never knowing for sure, just how many afternoon teas you will be serving. Your time spent washing and ironing and primping and fussing and decorating and serving to our heart's content is **very much** appreciated. I must acknowledge my husband Howard. I'm really fortunate he enjoys tea-traveling with me. My passion has become great fun for him too. Sometimes I think he even welcomes the opportunity to dress-up in a high hat and vest when the vintage mood strikes me. Many of you have met him at various events and tell me how lucky I am, and he likes that. In my first edition, I mentioned my doggies, Barney and Chelsea and got many positive comments. I'm including a photo of them at one of their tea parties. I hope you enjoy reading A Spot of Tea™ , and most of all, discovering and rediscovering many wonderful tea spots. Looking forward to seeing you at tea!

Barney and Chelsea taking tea biscuits

Table of Contents

Many area codes are changing. If a call doesn't go through, please call the operator.

Special Thanks

Thank you to these very special people.

- Norm Abbey, for patient and considerate Macintosh instruction.
- Eric Archer for your helpful suggestions and research.
- Brian Austin, Merrick Baker-Bates, Malcolm Dougal, and Michael Upton for all of your contributions tea insights, and kind words.
- Margaret Burk, for your creative ideas and kind words.
- Debbie, Carole, Esther, Gerry, Gloria, Jan, Joan, Judy, Marie, Nancy, Pam, Pat, Robert, Rosalinda, Ruth, Shirley, Tom, Toni &Val...my good friends who keep up with my tea-adventures.
- Noel Dennis, for your publishing guidance.
- Disneyland® Park for creating "The Mad Tea Party" attraction, and Paula McCance & group for the photograph that says it all.
- Tim Kummerow for our Internet Web Site.
- My Readers, your wonderful letters on stickered and stamped stationary are such fun to receive. Your family recipes, tea memories, ideas, and invitations to tea are truly appreciated.
- Dr. Jerry Nadler and Dr. Irwin Hoffman for healthy advice.
- James Norwood Pratt, your tea books are inspirational, your contributions to the tea world, immeasurable.
- Proprietors of tearooms, gift shops & bookstores for hosting great book signing events and wonderful recipes too.
- Andre Rodriguez, Richard Sears, and Sal Tagavilla for artistic assistance and thoughtful technical support.
- Editors of tea-theme publications, & tea purveyors, for great recipes.
- Matt Virola for your computer guidance with our first book.
- Paul Wallach for enhancing our dining experiences.
- Michael J.Wexler my brother, for working overtime to edit our videos: *"Tea Traveling with Linda."*
- Maureen O.Wilson, Vancouver USA, WA. a dedicated"tea-spotter."

Introduction

Welcome to <u>A Spot of Tea</u>™ THE WEST COAST GUIDE TO
AFTERNOON TEAS. This is our second edition and tea is hotter than
ever! Since the publishing of our first edition at the end of January
1996, one hundred and fifty or so new tea "spots" have opened,
with only a small number closing. You will notice many shops
extending their teatime hours to keep up with increasing demand as
tea awareness grows. We've modified in many ways also to keep up
with your tea interests. This edition includes Alaska and Hawaii and
our sub title is now, THE WEST COAST GUIDE. TO AFTERNOON TEAS. It is my
passion and mission to research and discover new tea spots and
bring you updated information. It is a thrill to discover and pass
along new tea adventures as I share my love of "going to tea".

I've met many of you at booksignings and tearoom or
bookstore grand openings and we've had fun talking about how our
love for tea began. Mine began when I was a little girl. I loved
having tea parties with my little friends. I dressed my dog and
stuffed animals and graciously poured cup after cup of pretend tea.
In those days, I enjoyed my real tea with milk and sugar and chose
my mother's prettiest teacups. One of my fondest childhood
memories was of going to Oppenheim & Collins, or Hengerers'
Tearoom, in Buffalo, New York with my mother and Aunt Jen.
We'd get gussied up in hats and white gloves and go downtown to
tea. I remember tall, thin models sashaying down long runways. We
chatted away about the big-brimmed flowery picture hats and other
important matters of the day while munching on crustless finger
sandwiches. Shopping, my next favorite activity always followed. I
enjoyed picking out that special outfit that I would one day wear to
tea. These are my warm, wonderful memories of carefree times.
Today, many tearooms today invite children and adults to borrow a
vintage hat for tea. My own personal collection just keeps growing!

The inspiration for writing <u>A Spot of Tea</u>™ truly came out
of necessity; for it was in the fall of 1994 that my husband and I
embarked upon what we thought would be, the great "Tea Rush."
Our trip took us up the west coast of the United States through
Northern California, Oregon and Washington into British Columbia.
With a "cupful" of referrals from friends, we looked forward to the
challenge of discovering as many tearooms as possible.

And did we look for tearooms! In phone books, newspaper
food editors, shops, big hotels, small hotels, B&B's, chambers of
commerce and local business associations who would only give out

the names of members. I contacted women's clubs, followed rumors of people in town who thought they heard of a tearoom but couldn't recall the name or location. Ahhhhh! It was so frustrating. We found out the hard way, that most tearooms don't advertise in the yellow pages. The hotels that serve tea are in the phone book, but featured under *hotels.* And so it goes, with the gift shops the antique stores, florists and other unique spots serving Afternoon Tea. Often, the closest thing to a tea heading was *coffee & tea* .

The newest yellow page dilemma for me, arises from the fact that there are number of phone companies, each with their own directory! Many overlap and cover the same geographic area. In my area alone, you have to look at 3 or 4 directories to find where someone may have advertised, I don't even keep them all. Then there's telephone information. Isn't it frustrating? First you have to track down exactly which city or town the tearoom is in, find the area code, then pay for each "out of your area," inquiry. Hmmm.

We did find a few tearooms. One had no reservations available. Another, was closed the day we were in town. One did teas only on Wednesdays, and one served Afternoon Tea only on the first Tuesday of the month. Rumor had it that a great annual benefit tea was not to be missed, but no one had a clue as to who I should contact, or what organization it even benefitted. I was completely baffled. The tearooms seemed impossible to find. Was I the only person on the planet looking for tearooms? I turned to my husband and said, "I will be the great tea-sleuth and write the book." This is the second edition and even more of us are looking for teas!

A Spot of Tea ™ THE WEST COAST GUIDE TO AFTERNOON TEAS, is a truly comprehensive guide for tea lovers living in, and visiting California, Nevada, Washington, Oregon, British Columbia, Alaska & Hawaii. This fun and easy to read guide includes: historical information, newly discovered vintage photos, poems and prized recipes plus updated teatime hours, bill of fare, decor, house specialties, wheelchair accessibility, non-caffeine teas, children's tea parties, reservation policies, parking, credit cards, even where you will find the watercloset. When you drink a lot of tea...you need the W.C! 450 tea spots are featured in this 500 page guide! A Spot of Tea™ includes teahouses, benefit teas, tea boutiques and great "spots" for those times when you've just "gotta hava spotta." From quaint & cozy, to pub-like, to breathtakingly elegant, each proprietor brings his or her unique *something special* to you. Happy Teatimes!

By Malcolm Dougal
British Consul-General
San Francisco, California USA

"Teas origins date back to the 28th century. It is reported that Chinese Emperor, Shen Nung, known as the "Divine Healer," noticed that kinsmen who first boiled their water prior to consumption tended to be healthier than those that did not. One windy day as Emperor Nung was boiling away, some leaves landed in his pot. The Emperor was so taken with the fragrance and taste that the Chinese claim he made the first cup of tea in 2737 BC.

The Honourable Aubrey Franklin wrote in his book, "Tea & Scones...and so much more!" that the Dutch introduced Chinese tea to England in the 17th century. Tea had its first taste of international publicity when on 16/12/1773, a tax sensitive band of colonists chucked 340 chests of perfectly good tea into Boston Harbor. This attempt to monopolize the tea market has served to inspire a number of British exporters.

Today, the tea experience is enjoyed daily by the British while its consumption is reaching record levels in the US. The total US tea market in 1990 was $1.84 billion. In only 6 years, the industry has grown to $4.22 billion, up an amazing 129%. This includes "Ready to drink tea" and the American favorite, "iced tea." And British tea exports to the USA have increased 60% since 1994.

Tea distribution is now as varied as coffee. Tea comes in a variety of forms, types & flavours. Popular teas include herbals, fruit-infused & green while staples such as Earl Grey are top sellers.

The future of tea in the USA seems assured. Industry experts predict tea volume will double in the next five years. Key factors contributing to this growth include:

• Pursuit of a healthy lifestyle and acknowledgement of a greater responsibility for the quality of one's own health.
• Improved knowledge about nutrition and better dissemination of this information to the mass market.

FOREWORD *continued*

• Increasing disposition to de-stress and simplify one's life.
• Greater reliance on natural homeopathic remedies to prevent disease as opposed to invasive procedures to treat disease.
• Continuing appeal of natural products.
• Preference for quality products offering true value.
• Acquisition of affordable luxuries.
• Increasing sense of adventure and appreciation for foreign customs and cuisine.
• A return to simple pleasures associated with family and home.

Perhaps the most important reason for tea's success is its association with warmth, serenity...and the good British way of life! Enjoy your cup of tea."

Malcolm Dougal
British Consul-General
San Francisco

Tea-Tips For Using This Guide

I hope you enjoy many happy teatimes with this, our second edition. I have tried to include helpful information and a few light spots to make you smile. The old family recipes, whimsical original poems, vintage photos and art work are sure to make "A Spot of Tea"™ a fun read as you plan your visits to each tea destination.

Regarding Prices: In every case, with the exception of *tea for two specials,* prices are per person plus applicable regional taxes and gratuity. On occasion, credit card guarantees are imposed. Many establishments serve Afternoon Tea for groups or private parties. Inquire in advance and confirm information regarding room fees, taxes, deposits, monetary guarantees, cancellation policies, dress requirements, handicap accessibility, smoking policies, GST in Canada, and any other of the establishment's policies which apply.

I make it my business to regularly communicate with the proprietors of all of the tea establishments, Directors of Marketing, catering managers, and Food & Beverage Directors regarding a tea spot's current ownership, policies, locations, prices, hours, menus, and various other additions and deletions. In addition, I call everyone **again** before I go to press, to finalize their last minute changes, and mostly to confirm that the establishments are indeed in business! (AT&T *really* likes me!) All said, I still recommend that you call them for verification of information since the inspiration for change can come at any time!

Many spots hold Annual Benefit Teas. Thumb through the book and notice the months when these popular events take place. People look forward to these teas and tend to bring many guests along to support the cause. If an establishment only does teas at holiday time in December, you'll usually see the snowy bow of a fir tree* placed at the bottom of the page to catch your eye. Still other spots enjoy doing Theme Teas. These may occur one or more times throughout the year. Some are scheduled by the season or holiday, others by whim. Call the tearoom to find out what they have planned for the upcoming month. Teas which revolve around Mother's Day and Valentine's Day are very popular and usually sell-outs.

Does your club, troop or "troupe" enjoy discovering new tea spots? You will find that a number of places will gladly cater to you.

Tea-Tips continued

In fact, some places only do tea parties for groups, take note of the required minimum or maximum number of guests. You will find these spots clearly indicated in the guide.

New Addition... indicates a tea spot that is new to **this** edition. We let you know about the new tea spots that plan to open soon too. It is a lot of work to open a tearoom, so if you're near a *New Tea Room Brewing,* stop by and give them a thumbs up!

In California, public dining establishments are non-smoking unless specific areas are otherwise designated. However, please call tearooms ahead of time if smoking & non-smoking environments are of concern to you, particularily in the other states or provinces.

I hope you find the opportunity to enjoy a variety of Afternoon Tea experiences from cozy to grand throughout the year. These are wonderful times for tea lovers. Expand your horizons, try new blends, if you've been a "bag" lady, try "loose." Tea cozies, collectible teapots, tea strainers and modern infusers are all part of the joy of tea, and they make great gifts for your tea friends. Take a few moments to visit with the tearoom proprietors, many will be happy to introduce you to new teas and tea accoutrements from the various tea-loving cultures and countries around the world.

Children really enjoy going for Afternoon Tea. In fact, Children's Dress-Up Tea Parties have become extremely popular. If an establishment has hats & boas, or accessories for youngsters & adults to borrow at tea, we've placed a cute logo on the page for easy spotting. Just hand the book to your child and tell them to look for the little picture of children dressed-up!

The "Autograph Line" is new with this edition. Many of you are already having your books autographed, now it's official!

Last but not least, as many of you know area codes are changing. If no one answers the phone, or you just can't seem to get through, try calling the operator to verify the area code. I truly hope "A Spot of Tea"™ makes your day...and leads you to many wonderful tea spots. Many happy teatimes to you all!

December Holiday Teas....

Dress-Up For Tea

A BRIEF HISTORY OF TEA

By Merrick Baker-Bates
British Consul-General
Los Angeles, California USA

"Teatime, 'with the cup that cheers but not inebriates', has been an important part of the British scene since the custom of tea drinking arrived in London in the mid-seventeenth century. Although today we British are generally regarded as the world's largest consumers of tea- and of the scones and cream, cakes and sandwiches that go with tea, the Portuguese were probably the earliest tea drinkers in Europe.

All successful non-alcoholic drinks contain socially acceptable stimulating drugs, without them, they're no more interesting than hot water. The alkaloid of tea, theine, is the same as that of coffee, but less effective, although stimulating. So when tea arrived in Britain it soon gathered enormous popularity. At first, tea came almost exclusively from the southern Chinese port of Canton; its method of production a closely guarded secret. Surprisingly though, for about one hundred and fifty years a commodity was imported to Europe from halfway across the world, a huge industry grew up around it, yet virtually no one knew how tea was grown, prepared or blended.

It sometimes arrived in curious ways. My wife's family, for example, sent a long case "grandfather" clock to China in the mid-eighteenth century to be lacquered and decorated. According to tradition, it returned full of tea. And, the ships that brought the tea also carried porcelain, china as it became known, principally to act as ballast, which of course included teacups, saucers and pots.

Tea caused trouble in the American colonies when the government of George III tried to kill three birds with one stone. They wanted to sell tea to the wealthy American colonists, thus getting rid of excess supply. They aimed to do that by greatly lowering the duty hitherto charged, thus making the bargain irresistible and putting smugglers out of business. Finally, the imposition of this tiny duty would compel the colonists to admit the right of the British Parliament to tax Americans. All quite sensible in the British eyes, but the Boston Tea Party of 16 December, 1773 was the result. In their immortal parody of British history, "1066 and All That," (published 1930), Walter Sellar and Robert Yeatman described what happened.

"One day George III went insane when he heard that the Americans never had Afternoon Tea. This made him very obstinate and he invited them all to a compulsory tea party in Boston; the Americans however started pouring the tea into Boston Harbor and went on pouring things into Boston Harbor until they were quite independent, thus causing the United States."

By 1801, the English consumed 2.5 lb of tea and 17 lb of sugar (much of it with tea), per head. This cost over $1 billion in today's money and caused a huge trade imbalance with China with the attendant political difficulties. In fact, the Chinese did not really want to import anything or have dealings with foreigners. By the end of the third decade of the nineteenth century, the monopoly of the British East India Company to bring tea from China had come to an end. Prices dropped and the market grew enormously. At the same time, the British started to grow tea of a different variety in India and Ceylon. The rest is history.

When you come to make tea yourself, my mother's method is still the best! Warm the pot, use good quality tea leaves, one teaspoonful for each person and one for the pot, covered with fresh boiling water...all to brew for four minutes. *Happy Teatime !*

Merrick Baker-Bates
British Consul-General
Los Angeles

California

Can you come to my tea party?

FLOWERS & TEA

28871 West Agoura Road
Agoura Hills, California

818-889-3488

New Addition...It's Teatime At...Flowers & Tea. This is a friendly little spot where you'll feel as though you're having tea *with* the proprietors. If Audrey and Susan don't know your name when you walk in, they will surely know your name and tea preferences when you walk out with a bag of the shop's own blend of tea and scone or teabread mix. Drop by for great gifts and the casual Cream Tea. P.S. Susan is a very talented floral artist, so why not bring along your favorite vase for her to fill with beautiful flowers? Voila, a "new" centerpiece.

Cream Teas are served at interesting bistro-style tables with bases of weathered wooden columns. (Unless they're sold!) There are lots fresh flowers all around. Ask Audrey if she still has the pretty rose pattern imported china with the matching teapots. Allow time to browse, Flowers & Tea has unusual and interesting gift items for your perusal. There are tall cabinets filled with tea accoutrements, toiletries, terrific scented "best seller tea lotions & soaps such as cinnamon-orange spice, ginger-peach & passion fruit, jewelry, books, teapots, gifts and other "must have" items. F.Y.I. There are iced as well as hot tea inspirations here too.

$6.95 Friendly Little Cream Tea... Choice of: teapot shaped raspberry-filled cookie, teabread, or scone with cream, lemon curd or preserves and a three cup pot of brewed loose tea.

CREAM TEA: 10am-6pm, Monday-Friday • 11am-5pm, Saturday
• Non-Caffeine Herbal Tea Available
• Watercloset: Same Floor
• **Reservations Are Always Appreciated For Cream Tea**
• Free Parking Lot
• Credit Cards: V,MC&DIS
Proprietor's
*Autograph*_____*Date*_____

ALAMEDA ANTIQUES & TEA

1519 Park Street
Alameda, California

510-523-0895

New Addition...It's Time For A "Spot "While You Shop At...Alameda Antiques & Tea. If you've been sleuthing for that illusive collectible and you're too pooped to poke around, you'll be happy to know that tea is nearby. Alameda Antiques & Tea will be happy to pour you a spotta when you visit their three-story antique "collective" in historic downtown Alameda. Ask Linda, the proprietor to help you make your tea selection. Located on the first floor, the tearoom also known as the "clock room" is also filled with fresh green plants, collectibles & antiques.

Tea is served at tables set with delicate doilies and seasonal centerpieces. Fresh brewed tea is poured from English Chatsford teapots into fine bone china teacups. An interesting and eclectic collection of clocks hang on an exposed natural brick wall making this a fun little spot. And you will always know when it's teatime!

Within the shop's 10,000 square feet you'll find a large variety of antique vendors, a bridal consultant, even a limousine service. P.S. Catered tea parties are available too, for up to 20 guests. F.Y.I. Many of the clocks in the tearoom are for sale. Ask Linda about her special new line of fine premium wines too.

$2.25 Pot of Tea & Biscotti... Two cup pot of fresh brewed loose tea served with two biscotti.

$1.50 Pot of Tea... Two cup pot of fresh brewed loose tea, choose from approximately 24 varieties.

A SPOT OF TEA: 10:00am To 5:30pm • Tuesday Thru Saturday
• 10:00am To 4:00pm • Sunday
• Non-Caffeine/Herbal Tea Available
• Watercloset: Same Floor
• **Reservations: No**
• Metered Street Parking
• Credit Cards: MC,V&AE

Proprietor
*Autograph*_____*Date*_____

18

GARRATT MANSION B&B

(18 Miles From San Francisco)
900 Union Street
Alameda, California

510-521-6796

December Holiday Teas & Private Tea Parties At...The Garratt Mansion B&B. Built in 1893 for Industrialist W.T. Garrat, this terrific 26 room colonial revival mansion is nestled away near the quiet Gold Coast community of Alameda. At one time, this area catered to members of San Francisco's wealthy business community who commuted daily by ferry to their offices.

The Garratt Mansion with its splendid architectural features, is a fine example of what is called, "Victorianna". The original stained glass windows portray potted palms imbedded with jewels, ribbons and spider webs. Huge pocket doors separate a large parlor from the entry hall for an intimate Afternoon Tea. The December Teas are very popular so do call early to reserve your date. F.Y.I. Private tea parties are also available here. Betty, the tea savvy proprietor will be very happy to help you plan your event for 20 to 35 guests. Weather permitting up to 50 guests in the garden.

$15.00 Afternoon Tea... Assorted tea sandwiches, cranberry scone served with cream & jam, assorted desserts and a continuous cup of brewed tea.

DECEMBER HOLIDAY TEAS: Seatings: 1:30pm & 3:30pm
• May Accommodate Some Dietary Needs With Advance Request
• Non-Caffeine/Herbal Tea Available
• Children's Manners Teas
• Watercloset: Same Floor
• **Prepaid Reservations A Must**
• Unmetered Street Parking
• Credit Cards: MC,V,DC&AE

Proprietor's
*Autograph*_____*Date*_____

Two For Two

By Alicia Garcia

"Tea for two" or five or ten
When I think of my brew I get this yen

With cookies, cakes and little tarts
At five o'clock the party starts

Since I was little, now I'm twelve
I get the tea down from the shelves

Hot my cup and brew the toddy
We love it all...me and my body!

Alison's Devonshire Cream

Alison's Espresso Cafe, Huntington Beach, CA.

"This delicious and traditional accompaniment to scones is produced only by cows grazing in the lush green fields of Devonshire, England and is not available outside of Britain. There are several recipes which approximate this rich English cream. We would like to share with you the one we use at Alison's."

Combine one cup heavy cream and one tablespoon buttermilk in a saucepan over medium heat. Heat about 90 degrees. Pour into a glass jar, cover lightly with a piece of waxed paper and set in a warm place (65-70 degrees) for 12 to 20 hours until thickened. Cover with a tight fitting lid and refrigerate for at least six hours.

"Here at Alison's, we like to add a touch of confectioner's sugar and whip slightly. It can be refrigerated for 2 weeks. Enjoy with a freshly baked scone!"

HIGH TEA & COFFEE

1431 High Street
Alameda, California
(Near Lincoln Park)

510-865-1810

New Addition...It's Teatime At...High Tea & Coffee. The island of Alameda boasts some stunning examples of historical Victorian architecture, a lovely stretch of sandy bay beach and an unparalleled view of San Francisco. This friendly, family owned establishment is also located in a turn of the century building. John and Mary, the proprietors of High Tea & Coffee, regularly feature the talents of local artists & musicians in their shop; on weekends you may catch a harpist playing Celtic or Classical music.

Afternoon Tea is presented on a three tiered caddie at tables set with a mis-matched collection cups and saucers, many of which were gifts from friends. A varied menu of specialties is available. Most days, High Tea & Coffee is open from 6:30am or 7:00am to around 6:00pm. F.Y.I. Tea parties are available for groups of 15 to 30 guests. Please call to verify seasonal hours. Ask about picnic tea baskets if you're interested in having a little tea party in the park.

$14.95 Afternoon Tea For Two... Cucumber finger sandwiches, scones served with strawberry butter, tea biscuits with cream cheese & Kiwi, cheese, fresh fruit and a pot of brewed tea.

TEATIME: 4:00pm To 6:00pm • Monday Thru Saturday
• May Accommodate Some Dietary Needs With Advance Request
• Non-Caffeine/Herbal Tea Available
• Children's Tea Parties Welcome
• **Reservations Are Strongly Recommended**
• Watercloset: Same Floor
• Free Parking Lot
• Cash Or Local Check
Proprietor's
*Autograph*_____*Date*_____

21

WEBSTER HOUSE B&B INN

1238 Versailles Avenue
Alameda, California

510-523-9697

It's Teatime At...Webster House. Sometimes referred to as the "best kept" secret in the Bay area, the little island of Alameda in Northern California is home to the Webster House B & B. The Inn is a fine example of Gothic Revival architecture. Designed and fashioned in New York, it was shipped around Cape Horn and assembled in Alameda, California in 1854. This authentic Andrew Jackson Downing home is Alameda's oldest house.

A covered deck allows you to enjoy Afternoon Tea & other menu items outdoors overlooking the waterfall. The large deck seats 44 and wraps around both a lemon and a coastal redwood tree. P.S. Allow time to browse, the gift shop specializes in Native American items & antiques. This is a romantic spot for your special events. Private tea parties are available for up to 75 guests indoors or 150 guests in the garden. Ask Susan to help you plan your tea party.

$17.50 High Tea... Tea sandwiches, scone with Devonshire cream, English banger on a crescent, celery to cleanse the palate, lemon curd tartlet, rum or almond petit four, tea cookie, truffle, strawberries with Devonshire cream & brown sugar to cleanse the palate, pot of brewed loose tea.

$12.50 Afternoon Tea... Three tea sandwiches, scone served with Devonshire cream, slice of tea loaf, rum or almond petit four, tea cookie, truffle and a pot of brewed loose tea.

TEATIME: 1pm-3pm, Monday Thru Saturday • 4pm-6pm. Sunday
• May Accommodate Some Dietary Needs With Advance Request
• Non-Caffeine/Herbal Tea Available
• Children's Tea Parties Welcome
• Watercloset: Same Floor
• **By Advance Reservation Only, Please Call**
• Unlimited Street Parking
• Cash Or Personal Checks
Proprietor's
*Autograph*_____*Date*_____

THREE CORNERS
2555 North Lake Avenue
Altadena, California

626-798-1885

It's Teatime At...Three Corners Dining Room. On a clear day you can see the San Gabriel mountains as you cruise up Lake Avenue on your way to the Three Corners Dining Room. This renovated 1951 restaurant sits adjacent to a small park near the scenic foothills of Altadena. A full menu of homemade specialties is offered in addition to the Afternoon Teas. Debbie, the proprietor is a well-known restauranteur in this lovely Foothill community.

Three Corners is French Provincial in flavor, decorated in tones of soft rose, ivory & white with lacey curtains. Debbie and her friendly staff present the Full Tea on tiered caddies at tables set with pastel tablecloths & toppers, white bone china, and vases of silk flowers. The pretty tapestry upholstered chairs and the "classical to jazz" background music are nice touches. F.Y.I. Private tea parties are available for up to 40 guests, please call to plan. P.S. If it's a clear, beautiful mountain view day, consider dining al fresco.

$9.95 Full Tea... Finger sandwiches, scone with preserves & fruit butters, assorted pastries such as raspberry bars, or a variety of tea breads, a pot of brewed loose tea. $2.00 for a glass of Sherry.

$7.95 Special Tea... Assorted finger sandwiches, scone served with preserves & fruit butters, and a pot of brewed loose tea.

$6.95 Dessert Tea... Cake or tart of the day, pot of tea.

$5.95 Cream Tea... Scone, cream & jam, pot of tea.

TEATIME: 2:30pm To 4:30pm • Wednesday Thru Saturday
• May Accommodate Some Dietary Needs With Advance Request
• Non-Caffeine/Herbal Tea Available
• Children's Tea Parties Welcome
• Watercloset: Same Floor • Wheelchair Accessible
• **Reservations A Must**
• Street Parking
• Credit Cards: MC,DIS&V

Proprietor's
*Autograph*_____*Date*_____

©Disney

DISNEYLAND PACIFIC HOTEL

1717 South West Street
Anaheim, California
(Across From Disneyland® Park)

714-956-6755

New Addition... "Practically Perfect Tea"....At
Disneyland Pacific Hotel. Count on Disney to create magical
and wondrous memories. "Practically Perfect Tea" is just what you'd
expect and more! Tea and other delicacies including precious
"Mickey" shaped currant scones are served to the delight of all on
lovely antique furnishings in an intimate "Victorian" parlour. Servers
in pastel polka dot dresses with plumed hats attentively scurry about
bringing freshly brewed loose tea in a variety of pretty rose pattern
bone china teapots. A "garden" area of the tea room, features
colorful paintings, cushioned white wicker furniture and white lattice.

Adding to the fun, a "practically perfect nanny" sings and
dances as she strolls about the room! For pictures too precious to miss,
don't forget your camera. At the conclusion, guests of all ages are
encouraged to don a feathery boa, vintage or top hat, and pose on a
pretty sofa next to nanny... "say tea." Tea parties for groups up to
50 guests welcome, please call for information.

$18.50 "A Splendid Afternoon Tea"... Apple pillow
and orange scone with sweet cream & raspberry jam, assorted finger
sandwiches, delicious sweet surprises, choice of brewed loose tea.
$12.50 "A Spoonful of Sugar"...*(Children's Afternoon
Tea, ages 4-12 years),* Cheery apple pillow, orange scone with sweet
cream & raspberry jam, finger sandwiches such as: Katie Nanna's
ham & cheese & Tally-ho tuna salad, yummy sweet surprises, and tea.

TEATIME: 10am, 12:30pm, 3pm, Saturday • 12:30pm, 3pm, Sunday
- Weekday Hours Are Seasonal, Please Call For Information
- May Accommodate Some Dietary Needs With Advance Request
- Tea Takes Place On The Second Floor, Elevator Available
- Non-Caffeine/Herbal Tea
- Wheelchair Accessible • Watercloset: Same Floor
- **Reservations Are Recommended**
- Free Parking With Tea Validation
- Credit Cards: AE,V,MC,DC,CB,JCB&The Disney Credit Card

TEA HOUSE OF THE NET

1472 South Euclid Street
Anaheim, California

714-781-2300

New Addition...High Tech Meets Tea At...Tea House Of The Net. The proprietors of this innovative spot were actually planning to open a traditional tearoom but as things progressed it seemed to Charles III, and his dad Charlie Jr., that their plans needed to be modified. They didn't want to give up on tea, so they combined high tech with high tea and came up with something else. Maybe their derailment will to put you on the right track in learning about the Internet.

The Tea House Of The Net is a little cottage of several rooms for folks with varying interests. The living room caters more to tea lovers. The decor includes blue carpeting, antique tables and blue and burgundy upholstered chairs. There's a computer on each table so you can conveniently "browse the web" for $6.00 an hour and includes some coaching. The proprietors are very helpful and interested in educating everyone about the big wide web world. An educated browser is good for their business as they are Internet providers as well. For those of you who have been resisting computers, maybe sugar and tea will ease the lesson.

E-Mail: son@tea-house.com   dad@tea-house.com

$6.00 Per Internet Hour & Complimentary Tea Choice of brewed loose tea, poured from French presses into fine china teacups that were family mementos, milk & sugar cubes too. Approximately 10 varieties of tea, but B.Y.O.Scone.

TEATIME: Noon To 9:00pm • Monday Thru Friday
• 10:00am To 6:00pm, Saturday & Sporadically On Sunday
• Non Caffeine/Herbal Tea Available
• **Reservations: No**
• Watercloset: Same Floor
• Parking: 15 Free Spaces
• Cash Or Check

Proprietor's
*Autograph*_____*Date*_____

26

THE FOX & BEAN
Tea Room & Bistro
8182 E. Santa Ana Canyon Road
Anaheim Hills, California

714-921-4880

New Addition...It's Teatime At...The Fox & Bean Tea Room & Bistro. This interesting tea spot is paired up with a bistro. The "Elizabethan Tea Room," features a number of Afternoon Teas including Lady Hamilton Tea, Shakespeare Tea and Royal Ascot Tea presented Monday Thru Saturday. On Sunday, Leo and Lesley serve Champagne Tea at $25.00 as well as a Victorian Lace Tea, Lady Di Tea and the proprietor's own "Lesley Ann Tea." Afternoon Tea is served on, Andrea by Sadek fine china at tables set with linens & tea lamps, by an attentive tuxedo-clad staff. You can't miss the large shelf which surrounds the tearoom displaying teapots & teacups. F.Y.I. The Fox & Bean has a wine, champagne & fine beer bar too. Private tea parties are available for 8 to 32 guests; "Butler" service may be added for large parties. P.S. Allow time to browse, there is a gift shop as well.

$17.95 The Royal Ascot Tea Service... Selection of tea sandwiches usually include: smoked salmon, cucumber & cream cheese, crab & cress, chives & egg, fresh baked scones with Devonshire cream & preserves, miniature pastries presented on a miniature cake stand such as, fruit tarts, cream horns, eclairs, napoleon, cannoli, cream puffs or petit fours, a decadent truffle, and a pot of brewed loose tea.

TEATIME: 1:30pm-4pm, Monday Thru Saturday, Till 5pm, Sunday
• May Accommodate Some Dietary Needs With Advance Request
• Non-Caffeine/Herbal Tea Available
• Watercloset: Same Floor
• Wheelchair Accessible
• **Reservations Are Requested**
• Free Parking Area
• Credit Cards: V,MC,DIS&AE
Proprietor's
*Autograph*_____*Date*_____

ORPHAN ANNIE'S
Emporium & Tea Garden

1284 South Main Street
Angel's Camp, California

209-736-9086

New Addition...Cream Teas At...Orphan Annie's.
Built in the 1930's as a grocery, this "ugly duckling" commercial building is now home to about 60 antique & collectible vendors. After many hours of sleuthing, hunting and picking, Leanne thought a garden retreat was just what you needed. So, at the back of the store you will now discover Orphan Annie's Tea Garden.

Cream Teas are served at garden tables set with worn teapot centerpieces and vintage teacups. Leanne has created this garden setting in an area that once was just storage. In fact, the old doors have become part of the decor. The trickling water fountain, faux brick path, hunter green accents and nature tapes lend a nice "outdoor" touch. P.S. There are vintage clothing and costume jewelry vendors here too, so adorn yourself with your new purchases and come on over for tea!

$5.95 Daddy Warbuck's Cream Tea... Fresh daily baked scone served with "Annie's" cream & preserves, sweet treat and a pot of brewed loose tea.

TEATIME: 11:00am To 3:30pm • Seven Days A Week
• Non-Caffeine/Herbal Tea Available
• Children's Tea Parties Welcome
• Watercloset: Same Floor
• **Reservations Are Appreciated**
• Free Parking Lot On The Side
• Credit Cards: V,MC,DIS&AE
Proprietor's
*Autograph*_____*Date*_____

ARCADIA HISTORICAL MUSEUM

355 Campus Drive
Arcadia, California

626-446-8512

**It's The Christmas Holiday Tea & Tour At...
Arcadia Historical Museum.** If you love tea, and you love
history, you'll be in for a very pleasant surprise. It's the Arcadia
Historical Museum's Annual Christmas Tea! The event usually takes
place the first Sunday in December.

The Arcadia Historical Museum features exhibits reflecting the
unique and diverse natural and cultural heritage of Arcadia. You will
find a lovely selection of sweet desserts and tea along with an
interesting tour. Please call to verify date and circle your calendar
early. Admission to the museum is free. Donations, artifacts, or
Arcadia memorabilia are always greatly appreciated.

$Donation...Christmas Holiday Tea & Tour
Surprise sweet desserts and a cup of tea served by volunteers.

CHRISTMAS HOLIDAY TEA & TOUR • Call To Verify Date
- Usually Planned For The First Sunday In December
- Watercloset: Same Floor
- Wheelchair Accessible
- **Reservations: No**
- Off-Street Parking And Free Lot
- Donation Requested

Director's
*Autograph*_____*Date*_____

la-Tea-da
21 E. Huntington Drive
Arcadia, California

626-446-9988

   It's Teatime At...la-Tea-da. This a very popular spot for Afternoon Tea. The owner's artistic murals of Earl Grey the cat, a wisteria vine and a natural stone floor complete with weeds & pretty bugs are wonderful. Gayle is musical too, she is likely to break into song if she knows it's your birthday! Afternoon Tea at la-Tea-da is a lot like going to Grandma's house. The decor is warm and inviting in tones of soft eggplant & sage green. Vintage clothing & accessories and unique gift items are nicely displayed throughout.
   You will enjoy many yummy tea treats along with sandwiches tied in bows. Salads, terrific homemade soups and bakery tea-zers such as double-decked toffee, chocolate glazed shortbread, or ginger cake with lemon curd frosted in almond cream cheese will win you over. Save room for the Wishing Well if you love chocolate. F.Y.I. There's a wall full of vintage hats, borrow one that's YOU. Keepsake photos are available for $2.50. Just say "TEA." Private tea parties welcome for up to 49 guests. Allow time to browse!

   $10.75 Full Tea... Assorted tea-ny sandwiches, fruit, dessert, molasses cookie, 60 varieties of tea, or cider or iced tea.
   $7.75 Sandwich Tea... Tea-ny sandwiches, fruit, molasses cookie, pot of brewed loose tea or cider or iced tea.
   $7.75 Dessert Tea... Dessert, fruit, cookie, brewed tea.
   $8.25 Children's Tea...PB&J finger sandwiches, fruit, shortbread, teapot cookie, chocolate cameo, children's "tea."
   $5.25 Tea Tea... Fruit, cookie, chocolate cameo & tea.

TEATIME: 11:00am To 4:00pm*ish* • Tuesday Thru Saturday
• May Accommodate Some Dietary Needs With Advance Request
• Non-Caffeine/Herbal Tea
• Children's Tea Parties Welcome
• Watercloset: Same Floor • Wheelchair Accessible
• **Reservations Are Suggested**
• Plentiful Free Parking In The Rear
• Credit Cards:V&MC
Proprietor's
*Autograph*_____*Date*_____

CAFE NORDSTROM

400 South Baldwin Avenue
Arcadia, California

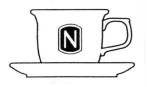

626-821-6363

Afternoon Tea Brewing...At...Cafe Nordstrom. In 1887, at the tender age of 16, John F. Nordstrom left his home in Sweden to come to the United States. He arrived in New York with five dollars in his pocket. A fortuitous meeting years later with Carl F. Wallin a Seattle shoemaker, resulted in the 1901 opening of the first "Wallin & Nordstrom" store on Fourth & Pike Streets in Seattle. Throughout the years, Nordstrom has been guided by its founder's philosophy. "Offer the customer the best possible service, selection, quality and value." I enjoy shopping at Nordstom, the idea of a pianist playing a baby grand piano while I browse for beautiful things suits me to a T. The comfy "oasis" which my spouse calls the "husband waiting area" is appreciated by both of us! When this customer friendly store began serving Afternoon Tea in many of the Cafes at Nordstrom, I wasn't at all surprised.

At teatime, Cafe Nordstrom tables are dressed-up with fresh flowers or plants, fine china, cloth napkins and special teatime silverware. You will be courteously greeted by an enthusiastic cafe manager or their friendly staff. F.Y.I. Outdoor patio dining is available at some of the Cafe Nordstrom locations.

$6.95 Afternoon Tea... Assorted finger sandwiches, scone served with berry-butter, a tasty dessert and a pot of tea.

***ANTICIPATED* TEATIME:** 3pm To 5:00pm • Monday Thru Friday
- Saturday & Sunday By Reservation Only
- May Accommodate Some Dietary Needs With Advance Request
- Non-Caffeine/Herbal Tea Available
- Watercloset: Same Floor
- Wheelchair Accessible
- **Reservations Required For Six Or More**
- Free Parking Lot
- Credit Cards: V,MC,AE&Nordstrom

Manager's
*Autograph*_____*Date*_____

31

CRYSTAL ROSE INN B&B

(South End Of The 5 Cities Area)
789 Valley Road
Arroyo Grande, California

805-481-1854   **1-800-ROSE INN**

It's Tour & Teatime At...Crystal Rose Inn B&B.
Whether you're looking for a little get-away or just passing through town, stop by for tea at the 100 year old Crystal Rose Inn. This Victorian mansion was originally built as a family residence and constructed entirely of redwood at a cost of $10,000. It became the Crystal Rose Inn in 1981, and was purchased by Bonnie, the current owner in 1994. Completely refurbished, the Inn & gardens is now a splendid spot for Afternoon Tea and those special events in your life. Each room of the Inn is named after a type of rose.

Afternoon Tea is served in the dining room at tables set with lace tablecloths, fresh flowers and candles. For an intimate tea setting, consider the third floor turret known as the Queen Elizabeth Tower Room which seats four guests. F.Y.I. A diary in this room reflects guests' sightings by of an unsubstantiated ghost. P.S. Don't miss the Victorian Christmas Tea. Please call for date and times.

$11.50 Afternoon Tea & Tour... Assorted tea sandwiches, chocolate dipped seasonal fruits, home baked currant scone served with Crystal Rose cream & homemade rose petal jam, homemade fruit tart, specialty cake and a pot of fresh brewed tea.

AFTERNOON TEA & TOUR: 2pm-5pm • Monday Thru Sunday
- May Accommodate Some Dietary Needs, 3 Day Advance Request
- Non-Caffeine/Herbal Tea
- Children's Tea Parties Welcome
- Watercloset: Same Floor
- Wheelchair Accessible
- **Reservations Are Requested**
- Free Parking Lot
- Credit Cards: MC,DISV&AE

Proprietor's
*Autograph*_____*Date*_____

COLONY GARDEN
Tea Room

5940 Entrada Avenue
Atascadero, California

805-462-2832

New Addition...It's Teatime At..Colony Garden.
Your hosts Kurt, Debra, Bob & Rick hope you find Afternoon Tea to be as much fun at Colony Garden, as they do. The Rose Friendship Garden is very unique, and a nice spot for tea. It is named for friends who bring a rose tree or rose bush to plant in honor of one of their dear friends.

Afternoon Tea is presented on two or three tierred caddies at English Barley-twist tables much like the ones at Debra's nanna's house. Churchill "Pink Country" china is a nice accent in the mauve & green dining room. The decor includes a rose bouquet pattern carpet with gold scrolls, wainscoted beige walls also with gold scrolls, a Victorian mirror, chandeliers & hand painted framed rose prints. Browse around, there are antiques, imported British foods & gifts, tea accessories & books. F.Y.I. Lots of tasty homemade English specialties too. Private tea parties for up to 50 guests.

$20.00 Royal Tea For Two...(2 Persons, 11am-6pm) Assortment of tea sandwiches, scones served with double Devon cream & preserves, mini sausage rolls, cakes and a pot of tea.
    $6.95 Lite Afternoon Tea... Sandwich of your choice, scone with double Devon cream & preserves, cake and a pot of tea.
    $4.75 Cream Tea... Two homemade scones served with double Devon cream & preserves, and a pot of brewed loose tea.

TEATIME: 8:00am To 6:30pm • Monday Thru Saturday
• May Accommodate Some Dietary Needs With Advance Request
• Non-Caffeine/Herbal Tea Available
• Children's Tea Parties Welcome
• Watercloset: Same Floor • Wheelchair Accessible
• **Reservations Advised For Parties Of Six Or More**
• Unmetered Street Parking Front & Rear
• Credit Cards: V&MC

Proprietor's
*Autograph*_____*Date*_____

GREGORY'S
Historic Restaurant
729 Lincoln Way
Auburn, California

916-823-9993

**New Ownership & New Name...It's Teatime At...
Gregory's Historic Restaurant.** (Advance reservations
required.) The 1881 Historic Landmark Pullen House is the home of
Gregory's Historic Restaurant. Gregory, the new owner has created
a unique atmosphere with three different theme dining rooms. Enjoy
the Magnolia Tea Room with many original paintings featuring the
Afternoon Tea theme. The Crystal Room has a lovely selection of
white moire fabrics and crystal chandeliers. The Mediterranean
Room may tempt you with cobalt blue glassware, real palm trees,
and a "visiting" seascape painting exhibit.

Afternoon Tea is presented on three tiered caddies at tables
set with fine china, linens and fresh flowers. Gregory's is a
romantic spot for weddings & receptions too. Don't miss the
Victorian English Walking Garden with many new sculptures. P.S.
Allow time to browse for tea accoutrements, books & gifts in
Gregory's Tea Shoppe.

$12.95 Afternoon Tea...(Advance Reservation Only.)
Hot savories, finger foods, homemade desserts, cookies & brewed
loose tea. You may change your tea choice to please your palette.

TEATIME: Available: 2:00pm To 3:00pm • Monday Thru Sunday
• May Accommodate Some Dietary Needs With Advance Request
• Non-Caffeine/Herbal Tea Available
• Children's Tea Parties Welcome
• Watercloset: Same Floor
• Wheelchair Accessible
• **By Advance Reservation Only**
• Limited-Time Street Parking
• Credit Cards: MC&V&AE
Proprietor's
*Autograph*_____*Date*_____

34

COUNTRY ROSE TEA ROOM
163 "H" Street
(Off Highway 58)
Bakersfield, California

805-322-5965

Holiday Theme Teas & Tea Parties For Groups At...Country Rose Tea Room. An arbor of seasonally decorated kiwi branches welcomes you to Country Rose. Here you will discover a charming Victorian living room, dining room, sun room & garden. This is a fun spot for holiday theme teas which include St.Patrick's Day Tea, May Day Tea, Harvest Tea, & Friendship Tea. You may hold your own tea party here as well.

Teas are usually scheduled on selected Thursday afternoons, approximately once a month. Please call Lee Anne for dates, times & reservations. Allow time to browse and enjoy the wonderful display of art work, interesting antiques & gift items. F.Y.I. Country Rose does not serve Afternoon Tea in during the summer in June, July or August, but they do however remain open for breakfast and lunch during this time of year.

$16.00 Holiday High Tea... Start with a surprise sweet, assorted finger sandwiches, variety of hors d'oeuvres, fresh seasonal fruit plate, scone with cream & preserves, tea breads, special holiday dessert, and a unique selection of tea for each table.

$12.00 Afternoon Tea... Assorted tea sandwiches, fruit scone with cream & preserves, dessert and a selection of tea.

$4.00 A La Carte Iced Tea & Scone... Served with cream, fresh fruit garnish & preserves.

SELECT HOLIDAY & GROUP TEAS: Please Call For Schedule
- A La Carte Tea & Scone 8am-4pm • Monday Thru Saturday
- May Accommodate Some Dietary Needs With Advance Request
- Alaskan Herb Tea • Children's Back To School Tea
- Watercloset: Same Floor
- Wheelchair Accessible
- **Reservations Are Required**
- Free Unlimited-Time Parking Lot
- Credit Cards: MC&V

Proprietor's
*Autograph*_____Date_____

35

CAMELLIA TEA ROOM
828 First Street
Benicia, California

707-746-5293

It's Teatime At...Camellia Tea Room. Over the years this spot has seen several different retail establishments, but Maryellen has worked diligently to restore this 1897 Historic Italianate Benicia Landmark to become the lovely tearoom it is today. In fact, she received a preservation award recognizing her efforts! Traditional Afternoon Teas are available throughout the day. The tearoom's interior is a showcase. Walls and ceiling are creatively and ornately covered with burgundy & mauve Bradbury & Bradbury Victorian reproduction wallpaper.

Afternoon Tea is presented on a three tiered caddie at tables set with fresh flowers, linens, white bone china, and an eclectic collection of teapots. P.S. Allow time to browse through their cute gift shop with everything from jams & jellies and bulk tea to a full complement of tea accessories. F.Y.I. An extensive lunch menu is also available. This is a must if you're anywhere near Benicia. P.S. Salads & homemade soups are a wonderful special addition!

$12.95 Traditional Tea... Assorted finger sandwiches & savories, two warm scones served with Devon cream & jam, dessert may be lemon streusel cake, and a pot of brewed loose tea.
$6.95 Savory Tea... Assorted finger sandwiches, savories, brewed loose tea, over 30 varieties from which to choose
$5.95 Sweet Tea... Sweets, pot of brewed loose tea.
$3.95 Cream Tea... Scones, Devon cream & jam & tea.

TEATIME: 10:00am To 5:00pm • Tuesday Thru Sunday
- Non-Caffeine/Herbal Tea Available
- Children's Tea Parties Welcome
- Watercloset: Same Floor
- Wheelchair Accessible
- **Reservations Are Recommended**
- Free Parking Lot
- Credit Cards: V&MC

Proprietor's
*Autograph*_____*Date*_____

CAPTAIN WALSH HOUSE

Captain Walsh House

235 East L Street
(2 Blocks from First Street)
Benicia, California

707-747-5653

1 8 4 9
Gracious Gothic Charm
Bed & Breakfast Inn

Tea Parties For Groups At...Captain Walsh House.

The Captain Walsh House is a B&B delightfully serving private Afternoon Teas for the special events in your life. The house has been featured in a number of magazines and newspapers. San Francisco's "Focus" Magazine called the House "witty and imaginative," and Better Homes & Gardens' "Bed & Bath," featured The Captain Walsh House on the front cover. It is a fabulous, lovingly restored 1849 Gothic house designed by prominent architect Andrew Jackson Downing.

The Captain Walsh House was actually built in Boston, Massachusetts, where it was dismantled, shipped around The Horn and erected in Benicia, located approximately 34 miles from San Francisco, & 16 miles from Napa. The current owners have taken it even farther with their design expertise and creative vision towards restoration and interior decoration. Ask about, "Inn Style at The Captain Walsh House" written by the proprietors. Ask about The Jefferson Street Mansion overlooking the Carquinez Strait.

$28.00 Afternoon Tea... Assorted tea sandwiches, homemade scones with creme fraiche & home grown & homemade fig/raspberry curd, mini croissants, "maids of honor," fresh fruit tarts and brewed loose tea. Prices are per person, plus room fee.

PRIVATE AFTERNOON TEAS: 25 To 200 Guests
- Please Call To Plan Your Special Event
- May Accommodate Some Dietary Needs, 1 Week Advance Request
- Non-Caffeine/Herbal Tea Available
- Watercloset: Same Floor
- Wheelchair Accessible
- **Reservations Are A Must**
- Free Off-Street Parking
- Credit Cards: MC,V,DIS&AE

Proprietor's
*Autograph*_____*Date*_____

CHEZ PANISSE
1517 Shattuck Avenue
Berkeley, California

510-548-5049

New Addition...It Time For A Pot Of Tea At...Chez Panisse. My friend Eric just sent me an impressive article on Chez Panisse. One of the people responsible for making this spot so special is "Lady Teasdale" herself, as the staff affectionately refers to Helen Gustafson, the tea buyer and maybe more important, the tea educator. The dedicated staff under the direction of Helen of course, and Alice the innovative proprietor of Chez Panisse, prepares properly brewed exquisite teas. To write about Helen's tea expertise would be another book, so instead, I'll recommend that you read *her* book, *The Agony of the Leaves.*

Chez Panisse, named for Marcel Pagnol French film character of the 30's, is situated in a two-story 1920's Craftsman. A well-known Berkeley landmark, this fine dining spot serves lunch & dinner, but in-between, they have what I would call an un-official teatime. From 3pm to 4pm you can order a divine pot of tea and desserts du jour, like the chocolate souffle tart. Upscale California casual, you'll sit upstairs at tables wrapped in white paper with cloth napkins & white china. The dining area features dim lighting, handsome wood cabinetry and hardwood floors accented with colorful prints & movie posters. P.S. Ask about Afternoon Teas which may become part of the picture. And look for several Chez Panisse cookbooks as well as their annual "Birthday" poster.

$9.00 Special Tea & A Sweet... Sweet du Jour, and a two cup pot of magnificent brewed loose tea.

"IN-BETWEEN" TIME: 3pm To 4pm • Monday Thru Thursday
• Non-Caffeine/Herbal Tea Available • Closed Sundays
• Watercloset: Same Floor
• Wheelchair Accessible On The First Floor By Request
• **Reservations Are Suggested**
• Metered Street Parking
• Credit Cards: V,MC,DIS,DC,AE&JCB
Proprietor's
*Autograph*_____*Date*_____

BARNEY GREENGRASS

9570 Wilshire Boulevard
(Between Camden & Peck)
Beverly Hills, California

310-777-5877

It's Teatime At...Barney Greengrass. An atmosphere of affluence awaits you at Barney Greengrass on the 5th floor of Barney's sophisticated department store in Beverly Hills. A three tiered copper caddie accompanies your savories, sweets & seasonal fresh fruits with raspberry sauce to a perfectly appointed table.

Barney's interior is decorated in tones of beige and white with rich woody accents. There are some pretty unique and artistic touches at Barney's such as the mosaic tile logo, the artistic glass jars which hold the loose tea, and the trickling wall of water. A lovely Afternoon Tea is punctuated by Barney's signature service. P.S. You may also have your Afternoon Tea on the outdoor terrace under a large market umbrella. Enjoy a peek view of busy Beverly Hills while you of course, are partaking of a most leisurely repast. F.Y.I. Private tea parties are available for up to 20 guests.

$20.00 Barney's Afternoon Tea... Indulgent tea sandwiches such as sturgeon & caviar, a divine selection of four tea cakes & cookies, such as black & white checkerboards and mini cranberry scones with lemon curd & Devon cream, seasonal fresh fruit and brewed loose tea served from glass infused pots.

TEATIME: 3:00pm To 5:00pm • Seven Days A Week
• Non-Caffeine/Herbal Tea Available
• Watercloset: Same Floor
• Wheelchair Accessible
• **Reservations Are Advised**
• $4.00 Valet Parking With Tea Validation
• Credit Cards: V,MC,AE&Barneys
Proprietor's
Autograph_____Date_____

I think he's going to propose, over tea!

BEVERLY HILLS HOTEL
9641 Sunset Boulevard
Beverly Hills, California

310-276-2251

It's Teatime At...The Beverly Hills Hotel.
Traditionally known as the place where beautiful people gather, the renovated Beverly Hills Hotel is quite a beauty herself these days. Enjoy Afternoon Tea in the recently renovated Sunset Lounge artistically decorated in soft peach tones. If you prefer al fresco dining, the terrace with pots of flowers and plants is lovely.

The Beverly Hills Hotel's Afternoon Tea is a French Tea Service. It is presented at tables set with linens, fresh flowers and Wedgewood china and silver. A harpist plays daily from 2:00pm to 6:00pm adding to the hotel's ambiance. P.S. You never know who you'll run into here. After tea, Howard and I were meandering around the grounds when he caught an errant tennis ball. He returned it to George Hamilton! P.S. Private tea parties available from 10 to 35 guests.

$23.00 Afternoon Tea... Assorted tea sandwiches including grilled asparagus with Boursin cheese, delectable breads such as apricot poppy seed and chocolate zucchini, marinated seasonal berries, pistachio Madeleine cookies, pastries & sweet surprises with your selection of brewed loose tea. Add $5.50 for a glass of Mimosa or Kir Royale Champagne, Port, or Sherry.

TEATIME: 2:00pm To 6:00pm • Seven Days A Week
• May Accommodate Some Dietary Needs With Advance Request
• Non-Caffeine/Herbal Tea Available
• Watercloset: Same Floor
• Wheelchair Accessible
• **Reservations Are Advised**
• $3.00 Valet Parking With Validation
• Credit Cards: MC,V&AE
L'autograph
*du Concierge*_____*Date*_____

41

NEIMAN-MARCUS
9700 Wilshire Boulevard
Beverly Hills, California

310-550-5900

It's Teatime At...Neiman-Marcus. Wonderful things are brewing at Neiman-Marcus in Beverly Hills. Look for the contemporary butterfly mobile and escalate down to the Mariposa Dining Room on the new Mariposa level for a memorable Afternoon Tea. A "N-M" Afternoon Tea, and a visit to the adjacent Estee Lauder Spa may be just what you need to rejuvenate yourself for more shopping at world famous Neiman-Marcus.

Afternoon Tea is presented on a tiered Mariposa china caddie at tables set with linens, fine china and fresh flowers. Expect the usual gracious attention to detail, and an elegant Afternoon Tea for the discerning palate. If you enjoy being surrounded by beautiful things, treat yourself to Afternoon Tea at Neiman-Marcus. In fact, I'd love to meet you there! Private tea parties may be arranged for up to 110 guests. Please call to plan.

$15.50 Afternoon Tea... Assorted seasonal finger sandwiches, fresh homebaked black currant scones served with fresh cream, strawberry preserves & blackberry jam, savories may include: crab meat & ginger triangles or wild mushroom bouches, petit fours, chocolate-dipped strawberry and a pot of N-M blend, or specialty gourmet brewed loose tea.

TEATIME: 3:00 To 5:00pm • Monday Thru Saturday
• May Accommodate Some Dietary Needs, 2 Weeks Advance
• Non-Caffeine/Herbal Tea Available
• Watercloset: Same Floor
• Wheelchair Accessible
• **Reservations Are Appreciated**
• Validated Self Or Approximately For $3.00 Valet Parking
• Credit Cards: N-M,AE&B-G
Manager's
*Autograph*_____*Date*_____

PADDINGTON'S TEA ROOM

355 S. Robertson Boulevard
Beverly Hills, California

310-652-0624

Paddington's
TEA ROOM

355 So. Robertson Blvd.
Beverly Hills, CA 90211
(310) 652-0624

    It's Teatime At...Paddington's Tea Room..."High Tea catering is our specialty" says owner, Julianne, "but you may also call on us at Paddington's for imported tea-related gifts, gift certificates, tea-lovers custom gift baskets and Afternoon Teas."

    The proprietor of Paddington's says her tearoom is very much like a tearoom in England. The tables are set with fresh flowers, teapot theme tablecloths, Battenburg lace toppers and Royal Albert fine china. A full menu is available in addition to Afternoon Tea. P.S. Allow time to browse around the gift shop. Paddington's carries Paddington Bears, imported teapots, teacups, books, gifts & more. Congratulations to Paddingtons as they start their second decade serving tea lovers!

    $22.00 High Tea... Homemade pate & water crackers, garden vegetables with a scrumptious dip, freshly prepared finger sandwiches: cucumber & whipped cream cheese, watercress & tomato, plain or raisin scone served with real Devonshire cream & selected jams, petite dessert, pot of brewed loose tea.

    $17.00 Afternoon Tea... Freshly prepared finger sandwiches, plain or raisin scone served with Devonshire cream & our selected jams and a pot of brewed loose tea.

HIGH TEA TIME: 2:00pm To 5:30pm • Monday Thru Sunday
• May Accommodate Some Dietary Needs With Advance Request
• Non-Caffeine/Herbal Tea Available
• Children's Tea Parties Welcome
• Watercloset: Same Floor
• **Reservations Are Requested**
• Metered Parking (Sunday Ok)
• Credit Cards: MC,V&AE

Proprietor's
*Autograph*_____*Date*_____

THE PENINSULA HOTEL
9882 Little Santa Monica Boulevard
Beverly Hills, California

310-551-2888　　　　*Reservations* **310-788-2306**

It's Teatime At...The Peninsula Hotel. A pair of white marble lions gently greet you as you enter the main doorway of this magnificent hotel. Straight ahead you will find yourself in the open and airy Living Room Lounge, very much the "showcase" of the hotel, and the spot for Afternoon Tea. The atmosphere is much like a living room, at least ones featured in Architectural Digest!

Afternoon Tea is presented on three tiered caddies at antique tables set with fresh flowers and Bernardaud Limoges china. A fabulous large window overlooks the garden terrace where you may also take tea. The magnificent crystal chandelier and harpist add the elegant touch you might expect. F.Y.I. The Peninsula Hotel has a well established reputation for Power Teas and social Afternoon Teas. P.S. A nice selection of rare and estate teas are offered.

$24.00 The Royal Tea... Glass of Piper Sonoma wine, fresh strawberries & whipped cream, selection of tea sandwiches such as house smoked salmon on basil biscuit, freshly baked raisin and plain scones served with Devonshire cream & preserves, assorted tea cakes, pastries and pot of brewed loose tea.

$18.50 The Full Tea... Selection of tea sandwiches such as Roquefort & walnuts on white bread, freshly baked raisin and plain scones served with Devonshire cream & preserves, assorted Tea cakes, pastries and pot of brewed loose tea.

$14.50 The Lite Tea... Freshly baked raisin and plain scones served with Devonshire cream & preserves, assorted tea cakes, pastries and your pot of brewed loose tea.

TEATIME: Seatings: 3:00pm & 5:00pm • Seven Days A Week
• May Accommodate Some Dietary Needs With Advance Request
• Non-Caffeine/Herbal Tea Available
• Watercloset: Same Floor • Wheelchair Accessible
• **Reservations Are Highly Encouraged**
• $3.00 Valet Parking With Validation
• Credit Cards: DC,V,MC,AE&JCB

L'autograph
*du Concierge*_____*Date*_____

Honey Currant Scones

Courtesy of the National Honey Board

2 1/2 cups all-purpose flour
2 teaspoons grated orange peel
1 teaspoon baking powder
1/2 teaspoon baking soda
1/2 teaspoon salt

1/2 cup butter or margarine
1/2 cup currants
1/2 cup dairy sour cream
1/3 cup honey
1 egg, slightly beaten

Combine flour, orange peel, baking powder, baking soda and salt in large bowl; mix well. Cut in butter until mixture resembles size of small peas. Add currants. Combine sour cream, honey and egg in medium bowl; mix well. Stir honey mixture into dry mixture to form soft dough. Knead dough on lightly floured surface 10 times. Shape dough into 8-inch square. Cut into 4 squares; cut each square diagonally into 2 triangles. Place triangles on greased baking sheet.

Bake in preheated 375 degree F oven 15 to 20 minutes or until golden brown. Serve warm. Makes 8 scones.

 # Honey Cranberry Butter

Courtesy of the National Honey Board

1 cup butter or margarine, softened
1/4 cup honey
1/4 cup chopped fresh cranberries*
1/4 cup prepared cranberry sauce
2 Tablespoons ground walnuts
1 Tablespoon milk
2 teaspoons grated orange peel

Cream butter and honey in medium bowl. Add cranberries, cranberry sauce, walnuts, milk and orange peel. Whip until light pink in color. Serve at room temperature; store in refrigerator, tightly covered. * Substitute frozen cranberries for fresh, if desired; chop before thawing.

REGENT BEVERLY WILSHIRE

9500 Wilshire Boulevard
Beverly Hills, California

310-275-5200

It's Teatime At...The Regent Beverly Wilshire.
Always elegant, always gracious it's the legendary Beverly Wilshire
Hotel known today as the Regent Beverly Wilshire. You can count
on attentive service whether you were born to royalty or just enjoy
being treated as such! Tea is served in the beautiful Lobby Lounge.

Afternoon Tea is presented on three tiered caddies at tables
set with linens, Wedgewood china, & fresh flowers. Or, you may
be seated at comfy upholstered sofas, wingback chairs, and Louis
XVI tables arranged in intimate conversation groups. This is a
perfect spot for a social Afternoon Tea with friends or business
Power Teas with clients. The decor includes dramatic fresh flower
arrangements. P.S. Don't miss the fabulous mural behind the bar.
Stroll through this world famous hotel, it is a treasure. P.S. There
are extraordinary shops in the hotel & nearby Rodeo Drive. Enjoy!

$19.00 The Traditional Afternoon Tea... Assorted
finger sandwiches, home baked scone with Devonshire cream &
strawberry preserves, miniature French pastries, pot of brewed tea.
$23.00 The Royal Tea...A glass of Mumm Cuvee Napa
Brut Prestige added to the Traditional Afternoon Tea.

TEATIME: 3:00pm To 5:00pm • Seven Days A Week
• May Accommodate Some Dietary Needs With Advance Request
• Non-Caffeine/Herbal Tea Available
• Watercloset: Same Floor
• Wheelchair Accessible
• **Reservations For Six Or More Please**
• Complimentary Two Hour Valet With High Tea
• Credit Cards: V,MC,DC,DIS,AE&JCB
L'autograph
*du Concierge*_____*Date*_____

TRUFFLES
43591 Bow Canyon Road
Big Bear Lake, California
(Moonridge Area)
7,000 Ft. Elevation

909-585-2772

Tea Parties For Groups At...Truffles.   Afternoon Tea is very "Inn," especially at Truffles. This country manor style Inn is located on 3/4 of an acre at 7,000 foot elevation! Truffles is a very comfortable spot decorated in traditional and antique furnishings. Your gracious Innkeepers will be happy to help you plan a tea party that is sure to be filled with many special memories.

Afternoon Tea is served at tables that each have their own theme, unique china & unique centerpieces. You are welcome to dress in vintage clothing, hats & gloves, or to plan your own theme tea party, after all, it's part of the fun! A special spot is reserved for your "Tea Time at the Inn." The Afternoon Tea menu has seasonal variations, the following is a sample. F.Y.I. Tea parties are available for groups of 6 to 24 guests. P.S. Allow extra time to peruse the Truffles boutique, there's many unique gifts here.

$12.50 Afternoon Tea... Marvelous fruit cornucopia tea sandwiches on raisin bread, home baked scone with cream & jam, array of sweet surprises which may include fancy cookies and cakes, and always...*truffles* of course, with a pot of tea.

TEA PARTIES FOR GROUPS: 6-24 Guests • Please Call To Plan
- May Accommodate Some Dietary Needs With Advance Request
- Non-Caffeine/Herbal Tea Available
- Watercloset: Same Floor
- **Must Reserve One Week In Advance**
- Free Off-Street Parking
- Credit Cards: V&MC

Proprietor's
*Autograph*_____*Date*_____

LADY PIERREPONT'S
Heirlooms & Edibles

1205 Howard Avenue
Burlingame, California

650-342-6065

It's Teatime At...Lady Pierrepont's Heirlooms & Edibles. A traditional English atmosphere permeates this lovingly restored 1908 Victorian, in downtown Burlingame. An interesting facade welcomes you inside to a lavishly furnished tearoom.

Afteroon Tea is served at tables set with British green tablecloths, white china, fresh flowers & tea strainers. For larger groups, tea is served from two tiered wooden caddies. This beautiful home features heavy wood molding, beams and brass chandeliers. The carpet is green with mauve flowers which perfectly accent the mauve, blue & green Waverly fabric window treatments. There's a lot to see when you look around Lady Pierrepont's. Enjoy tea-theme framed prints & paintings from a local watercolorist amongs other gifts, heirlooms & treasures. The decor may inspire you to find nooks and crannies in your own home to display your new "tea" purchases. Be sure to find the treasured book collection. F.Y.I. There is rich English history at Lady Pierrepont's, most of the wonderful edibles here come from Karen's own family recipes.

$8.50 Traditional Afternoon Tea... Assorted English tea sandwiches, scone fresh cream & preserves, "not too sweet" tea cakes, pastries, a pot of loose brewed Fortnum & Mason Royal tea.
$7.50 Cheese Tea... Assorted English & French cheeses & biscuits, Branston pickle, nuts, fresh fruits, brewed loose tea.
$4.25 Cream Tea... Scones, cream & preserves and tea.

TEATIME: 3:00pm To 4:30pm • Tuesday Thru Saturday
• May Accommodate Some Dietary Needs, 1 Week Advance Request
• Non-Caffeine /Herbal Tea Available
• Watercloset: Convenient
• **Reservations Are Advised**
• Metered Street & Public Parking Lot
• Credit Cards: V&MC

Proprietor's
*Autograph*_____*Date*_____

MOUNT EVEREST
Tea Company
23528 Calabasas Road
Calabasas, California

818-224-8096

New Addition...It's Teatime At...Mt. Everest Tea Company. Old Town Calabasas is home to a terrific new spot of tea. The Mt. Everest Tea Company has actually been in the tea business for more than 200 years in Europe, but this is their first shoppe in the United States. Premium teas, free of chemicals, artificial coloring and flavoring, are imported directly from Europe and sold here in bulk. The expansive shop with nice wood beam ceilings features European crafted murals, tapestries, china and serving ware reminiscent of a turn-of-the-century continental style. The proprietors may even greet you in period costume!

High Teas are served at tables set with linens, fine china & fresh flowers. The shoppe's tearoom is decorated with vibrant original artwork, tapestries and modern teapot sculptures that complement the green and blue tones of the room. Be sure to ask to sample the tea-of-the-day. It is poured from a one-of-a-kind handmade European samovar. Don't miss the collection of rare teacups designed for European royalty. P.S. Private tea parties for children & adults are available. Events & workshops are planned, please call for information. F.Y.I. All products can be mail-ordered.

$20.00 High Tea. Finger sandwiches, scone, Devonshire cream, marmalade & preserves, imported cream pastries cookies & shortbread, pot of brewed loose tea. (Over 100 varieties.)

TEATIME: 2:00pm To 6:00pm • Seven Days A Week
• May Accommodate Some Dietary Needs With Advance Request
• Non-Caffeine/Herbal Tea Available
• Watercloset: Same Floor
• Wheelchair Accessible
• **Reservations Are Suggested**
• Free Parking Lot
• Credit Cards: V,MC&AE Please Call To Verify
Proprietor's
*Autograph*_____*Date*_____

SIMPLY TEA
inside Simply Angels
821 Cornwall Street
Cambria, California

805-927-2824

New Addition...Fun Theme Teas At...Simply Tea.
Looking to put more fun in your life? Enjoy a trip to quaint Cambria and be sure to let Heidi and Starr know you're coming! This mother and daughter are the proprietors of a sweet tearoom & an abundant angel-theme shop, too.

Theme Teas are served for one guest up to 22 at unique hand-painted tables set with white Maryland china & fresh flowers. Heidi is quite artistic, she has stenciled the walls and furnishings and has designs for the floor! Be sure to look down at the stone "patio walkway." The ceiling treatment is cleverly designed too with muslin "clouds." A truly angelic spot! There are a variety of Theme Teas including Nature, Rainy Days, Victorian, Heavenly Angel, Hawaiian, Teddy Bear & Japanese Tea Party Teas. Ask about Starr's two angel books. P.S. Be sure to ask for brewed loose tea.

$9.00 Fun Theme Teas... Open-face puff, baked on premises bagel sandwich, a terrific goodie such as a heavenly brownie with vanilla ice cream, chocolate syrup, carmel sauce, berries & chocolate kisses, party favors and a pot of loose brewed Harney & Son's tea on request. You may want to try chocolate tea!

TEATIME: 8:00am To 6:00pm • Seven Days A Week
• May Accommodate Some Dietary Needs With Advance Request
• Non-Caffeine/Herbal Tea Available
• Children's Tea Parties Welcome
• Watercloset: Same Floor
• Wheelchair Accessible
• **Reserve One Day In Advance For Theme Teas**
• Free Parking Lot
• Credit Cards: V,MC,DIS&AE

Proprietor's
*Autograph*_____*Date*_____

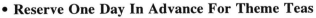

51

THE TEA COZY
4286 Bridge Street
(Off Main St. In East Village)
Cambria, California

805-927-8765

It's Teatime At...The Tea Cozy. This popular English tearoom is located one half block off Main Street in the East Village. The Tea Cozy features traditional Afternoon Teas as well as other English dishes including Ploughman's lunch and Cornish pasties. The Tea Cozy stocks hard to find English groceries as well as imported gifts, antiques, china, silver and royal memorabilia.

Royal Tea is presented on a two tiered caddie at English wooden tables set with fresh flowers. Nearly everything here is homemade or homebaked by Maureen. When she's not preparing food, she enjoys meeting & visiting with her customers. Be sure to invite her out of the kitchen for a visit! F.Y.I. The front garden patio is a popular spot for an informal Cream Tea. Private tea parties are available for groups of 10 or more guests. F.Y.I. Many of the shops items may mail be mail-ordered. Web Site: www.teacozy.com

$30.00 Royal Tea For Two... Tea sandwiches, scone served with Devonshire cream & preserves, lemon curd, cakes and a continuous pot of brewed loose tea.

$5.95 Cream Tea... Two scones with Devonshire cream & preserves, lemon curd and a continuous pot of brewed loose tea.

ROYAL TEATIME: 2:00pm To 4:00pm • Wednesday Thru Sunday
• Cream Tea: 10:00am To 4:30pm • Wednesday Thru Sunday
• May Accommodate Some Vegetarian Needs With Advance Request
• Non-Caffeine/Herbal Tea Available
• Watercloset: Same Floor
• **Reservations: No**
• Free Parking Lot
• Credit Cards: MC&V

Proprietor's
*Autograph*_____*Date*_____

CAMPBELL HISTORICAL
Museum & Ainsley House

300 Grant Street (Bay Area Near San Jose)
Campbell, California

408-866-2119

Seasonal Tea & Tour For Groups, & Annual December Benefit Tea At...Campbell Historical Museum & Ainsley House. The Ainsley House is a designated historic landmark for the city of Campbell. Constructed in 1926, it is a fine example of English Cottage architecture. Surprise! You no longer have to wait until December for the Tea & Tour! Groups of ten or more guests may now enjoy a guided tour and an Afternoon Tea on weekdays during May, June, July, August & September.

The Ainsley House is dressed in its holiday best for the Annual Benefit Tea thanks to the efforts of many local Interior Designers and volunteers from the Campbell Historical Museum & Ainsley House. For added fun, one of the bedrooms becomes a holiday boutique and features many interesting and festive gifts.

$25.00 Weekend December Benefit Tea, Fashion Show & Tour. Finger sandwiches, scone with cream & jam, tea.
$15.00 Weekday December Benefit Tea & Tour..A variety of finger sandwiches, scone with cream & preserves and tea.

$12.95 Weekday Tea & Tour For Groups Of 10 Or More Guests. Finger sandwiches, sweets, & a pot of brewed tea. Available April through September, in the beautiful garden.

GROUP TEA & TOUR: Weekdays As Scheduled For 10+ Guests
Annual December Benefit Tea: Usually On Monday, Tuesday & Wednesday, The First Two Weeks Of December & One Weekend
• Please Call For Dates • Non-Caffeine/Herbal Tea Available
• Watercloset: Same Floor • Wheelchair Accessible First Floor Only
• **Reservations Are Required**
• Large Parking Lot
• Cash Or Check

Volunteer's
*Autograph*_____*Date*_____

LISA'S TEA TREASURES

1875 South Bascom Avenue Suite 165
(The Prune Yard)
Campbell, California

408-371-7377

New Addition...It's Teatime At...Lisa's Tea Treasures. Tea lovers will delight in tea and treats from around the world in an atmosphere of Old World elegance at Lisa's Tea Treasures. Dale Ann & her attentive staff attired in pink or traditional black & white tea-length Victorian maid outfits welcome you.

The Afternoon Tea menu features a variety of savories, finger sandwiches, homemade soups, salads, delicate tea cakes, scones & delicious pastries. A wall of gourmet teas in canisters is quite impressive. The decor is lovely, and pretty Victorian furniture is featured throughout. Allow time to browse in the gift parlour which features fine china, tea accessories and imported gourmet items that are certain to please. Private tea parties are available for up to 25 guests. There are four fabulous tea selections, sample below.

$13.95 My Lady's Respite... Assorted tea sandwiches such as: egg salad supreme, chicken tarragon and cucumber mint, petite savory, dessert, and a pot of connoisseur full-leaf tea.

$9.95 Court Jester's Surprise... Tea or flavored milk, freshly baked scone, peanut butter & jelly tea sandwiches, pigs-in-a-blanket, fresh fruit, an assortment of mini cupcakes. (Child's Special)

$4.25 To $7.95 A La Carte Specials... Delectable specialties from soups & scones to salads & sweets.

TEATIME: 10am-6pm • Monday Thru Saturday •12-5pm Sunday
• May Accommodate Some Dietary Needs With Advance Request
• 99.6% Caffeine Free & Herbal Tea Available
• Children's Tea Parties Welcome
• Watercloset: Same Floor • Wheelchair Accessible
• Parking: Unlimited Free Parking
• **Reservations Are Appreciated & Required For Weekends**
• Credit Cards: V&MC Checks Ok

Proprietor's
*Autograph*_____*Date*_____

CAFE NORDSTROM
6602 Topanga Canyon Boulevard
Canoga Park, California

818-884-7900 *Ask For Cafe Nordstrom*

Afternoon Tea Brewing...At...Cafe Nordstrom. In 1887, at the tender age of 16, John F. Nordstrom left his home in Sweden to come to the United States. He arrived in New York with five dollars in his pocket. A fortuitous meeting years later with Carl F. Wallin a Seattle shoemaker, resulted in the 1901 opening of the first "Wallin & Nordstrom" store on Fourth & Pike Streets in Seattle. Throughout the years, Nordstrom has been guided by its founder's philosophy. "Offer the customer the best possible service, selection, quality and value." I enjoy shopping at Nordstom, the idea of a pianist playing a baby grand piano while I browse for beautiful things suits me to a T. The comfy "oasis" which my spouse calls the "husband waiting area" is appreciated by both of us! When this customer friendly store began serving Afternoon Tea in many of the Cafes at Nordstrom, I wasn't at all surprised.

At teatime, Cafe Nordstrom tables are dressed-up with fresh flowers or plants, fine china, cloth napkins and special teatime silverware. You will be courteously greeted by an enthusiastic cafe manager or their friendly staff. F.Y.I. Outdoor patio dining is available at some of the Cafe Nordstrom locations.

$6.95 Afternoon Tea...Assorted finger sandwiches, scone served with berry-butter, a tasty dessert and a pot of tea.

ANTICIPATED **TEATIME:** 3pm To 5:00pm • Monday Thru Friday
- May Accommodate Some Dietary Needs With Advance Request
- Non-Caffeine/Herbal Tea Available
- Watercloset: Same Floor
- Wheelchair Accessible
- **Reservations Please, For Six Or More**
- Free Parking Lot
- Credit Cards: V,MC,AE&Nordstrom

Manager's
*Autograph*_____*Date*_____

THE TEA COZY

18517 Canyon Square
(Soledad Canyon)
Canyon Country, California

805-252-8617

New Addition....It's Teatime At...The Tea Cozy. Described by the proprietor as a contemporary Victorian English tea cafe, this new tea spot features many homemade English specialties in addition to Afternoon Tea. Linda & her mom Lily enjoy spending time with their guests, many of whom hail from across the "pond." The Tea Cozy is decorated in warm tones of burgundy and green with cabbage-rose pattern wallpaper and burgundy carpet. Lacey half-curtains accent the burgundy colored box-framed windows.

High Tea is presented on three tiered silver caddies at tables set with tablecloths, floral pattern china and small silk flower arrangements. Classical background music and friendly proprietors are what make The Tea Cozy, a cozy spot for your Afternoon Tea. Allow time to peruse the shop which specializes in British foods & gifts, books, gift baskets & handmade crafts. P.S. Private tea parties are available for groups up to 25 guests. Linda is an English tea party specialist and she will be happy to cater a tea party for you!

$7.50 High Tea... Selection of English tea sandwiches, savory pastries, homemade fancy cakes & a pot of hot English tea.
$5.50 Traditional Cream Tea... Freshly made scone, real Devonshire cream & English jam, and a pot of hot English tea.

TEATIME: 11:00am To 6:00pm • Tuesday Thru Saturday 11-5 Sun
• May Accommodate Some Dietary Needs With Advance Request
• Children's Tea Parties Welcome
• Non-Caffeine/Herbal Tea Available
• Watercloset: Same Floor
• **Reserve For Six Or More Guests**
• Free Parking Lot
• Credit Cards:V,MC,&AE
Proprietor's
*Autograph*_____*Date*_____

56

THE COUNTRY COURT
Tea Room

911-B Capitola Avenue
Capitola, California

408-462-2498

New Addition...It's Teatime On Sundays At...The Country Court Tea Room. Quaint carriage houses do seem to make wonderful tearooms, and this carriage cottage with blooming planter boxes is no exception. The heart, or main part of The Country Court Tea Room is located in the 150 year old part of the house, but several other rooms were added in later years. Donna the proprietor, credits her late husband's woodworking artistry for most of the furnishings in the tearoom.

Donna wants her customers to feel quite at home and relaxed here. Afternoon Tea may be served outside in the lovely Magnolia Courtyard weather permitting, or in the dining room if you prefer. Tables are set with ivory tablecloths, white china and silver bowls of fresh flowers. Browse around, there are "tea" prints and tea theme accessories to purchase along with cozies & cookbooks. Breakfast, brunch & lunch are offered in addition to Afternoon Tea. Please call for days and hours. F.Y.I. Donna can cater a tea party for you too.

$12.95 Afternoon Tea... Variety of canapes & tea sandwiches, a warm apricot/cherry/currant scone served with lemon curd & fresh fruit, special dessert and a "cozy" pot of brewed tea.

TEATIME: 4:30pm To 5:30pm • Sunday
• May Accommodate Some Dietary Needs With Advance Request
• Non-Caffeine/Herbal Tea Available
• Children's Tea Parties Welcome, Ages 8+
• Watercloset: Same Floor
• **Reservations Are Requested**
• Free Parking Lot
• Cash Or Check

Proprietor's
*Autograph*_____*Date*_____

"TICKY BOO" TEA SHOPPE

2957 State Street
Carlsbad, California

760-720-7800

New Addition...It's Teatime At... "Ticky Boo" Tea Shoppe. "Is everything "Ticky Boo ?" Asked the server at this adorable new tea spot. "Oh yes, one guest replied, and that's a whole lot better than codswallop!" The proprietor Beverly is a hoot, she along with daughters Stefeni and Tifeni run this sweet tea shop.

Afternoon Tea is presented on a three tiered caddie by servers wearing black & white aprons and small white "things" stuck on their heads, as Beverly describes them. Tables are set with linens, fresh flowers and candlelit teapot warmers. The decor includes four crystal chandeliers, a decorative fireplace, a wall village, and a surprise floor. Private tea parties are available for 21 to 25 guests. A tailor made menu is also offered at around $20.00 per guest. Browse around a bit, there are over 80 English & Scottish teas for sale along with British foods and gifts which may be mail-ordered. P.S.Be sure to look down! E-Mail: tickyboo@earthlink.net Web Site: www.geocities.com/NapaValley/3194

$12.50 High Tea... Assorted tiny tea sandwiches, scrumptious sweets, and a pot of brewed loose tea.
$4.25 Scones A La Carte... Served with butter, clotted cream, lemon curd, English strawberry jam or marmalade.
$2.50 Tea Sandwiches A La Carte... Choose radish, watercress, chicken salad, egg & olive, cream cheese or cucumber.
$2.50 Tea For One... Two cup pot of brewed loose tea.

TEATIME: 11:00am To 4:00pm • Thursday Thru Monday
• May Accommodate Some Dietary Needs With Advance Request
• Non-Caffeine/Herbal Tea Available
• Watercloset; Same Floor
• **Reservations Are Advised**
• Unmetered Street Parking
• Credit Cards: V,MC&AE
Proprietor's
*Autograph*_____*Date*_____

Tea Talk Lemon Curd

*Courtesy of **TEA TALK**, a newsletter on the pleasures of tea,
Diana Rosen, Editor   Sausalito, California*

2 large eggs, plus 2 large yolks, whisked together
3/4 cup granulated sugar
2 Tablespoons grated lemon peel
2/3 cup freshly squeezed lemon juice (about 3 medium lemons)
1/3 cup unsalted butter, chilled and cut into pieces

In a heavy-bottomed 1 1/2 quart saucepan, whisk the eggs and yolks together and add sugar, juice and peel. Sprinkle in a few grains of salt. Add butter pieces. Cook mixture on low heat, stirring constantly while cooking until it thickens enough to heavily coat the back of a spoon, about 8 minutes. DO NOT LET MIXTURE BOIL, or the egg yolks will curdle. **Pour** mixture into glass dish, cover with plastic wrap and refrigerate at least four hours before serving. Keeps in the refrigerator up to one month. Use directly on scones like a jam, or use as a filling for tarts. Makes about 1 1/2 cups.

Coconutea Cookies

*Courtesy of **T.J. Lipton Co.***

1/2 cup boiling water
2 Lipton® Flo-Thru® Tea Bags
1-3/4 cups all-purpose flour
1/2 teaspoon baking powder
1/2 teaspoon baking soda
1/2 teaspoon salt

12 Tablespoons butter, softened
1/2 cup light brown sugar
1/3 cup sugar
1 egg
1/2 teaspoon vanilla extract
1-1/4 cups shredded coconut

Preheat oven to 350 degrees F. In teapot, pour boiling water over tea bags, cover and brew 5 minutes. Cool. In small bowl, combine flour, baking powder, baking soda and salt; set aside. In large mixer bowl, with electric mixer beat butter and sugars until well blended. Add egg, vanilla and tea until just blended. At low speed, gradually beat in flour mixture. Stir in one cup coconut. On greased cookie sheet, drop mixture by tablespoons. Sprinkle tops with remaining 1/4 cup coconut. Bake 12 minutes or until golden. Cool slightly; remove from cookie sheet and let cool on wire rack. Makes about 30 cookies.

Sometimes you can take your best friends to tea!

CYPRESS INN HOTEL

Corner of Lincoln & 7th Street
Carmel, California

408-624-3871

New Addition...It's Teatime At...Cypress Inn Hotel. Built in 1929, this wonderful Mediterranean style Inn now serves Afternoon Tea. The Inn is located in the heart of downtown Carmel, about six blocks from the beach.

Many features set the Cypress Inn apart from others, but for me, a woman who named her publishing company after her doggie, the fact that your beloved pooch is welcome at teatime, is the most marvelous! And why not? Progressive hospitals now have devoted pets as part of their volunteer staff. This pooch-friendly attitude should come as no surprise when I mention that the Inn is co-owned by none other than Doris Day. Her pet rescue efforts are nearly as well known as her movie and theatrical career.

Afternoon Tea is served on fine imported china in the courtyard, in the Living Room under the beamed ceiling, or in the Library Bar. The decor is elegant with tiles, hardwood floors, and clean off-white furnishings. Jazzy big band sounds are piped-in and will put you in good rhythm. French doors lead out onto a beautiful courtyard which has its own fireplace. A la carte tea specialties are also offered. P.S. Look for Miss Day's terrific theatrical posters behind the Library Bar.

$9.50 Complete Tea Service... Tea sandwiches, homemade scone, berries with cream, tea cookies, and a pot of G.H. Ford "teaball" tea.

TEATIME: 3:00pm To 4:30pm • Monday Thru Friday
• May Accommodate Some Dietary Needs With Advance Request
• Non-Caffeine/Herbal Tea Available
• Watercloset: Just Up A Small Flight Of Stairs
• **Reservations: Not Necessary**
• 90 Minute Unmetered Street Parking
• Credit Cards: V,MC&AE

L'autograph
*du Concierge*_____*Date*_____

DOROTHY MARIE'S
Tea Company
Dolores & Ocean
Carmel, California

408-373-8463

New Addition...Dorothy Marie's Tea Company. Dorothy Marie's Afternoon Teas have been so popular that she has opened a second location! Welcome to her new Carmel tearoom. The shop and tearoom have been planned to look very much like her Pacific Grove spot with the addition of a tea bar.

Afternoon Tea is served on a pretty pastel palette of antiques & fine linens. The tea service is a collection of new and old English bone china, some pieces belonging to Dorothy Marie's grandmother; and as always, classical music in the background. The gift shop continues to specialize in things that go with tea. Look for the whimsical handmade tea cozies made by her mom, and Dorothy Marie's own label teas. The delectable menu from Dorothy Marie's Pacific Grove tearoom is featured at this location as well. F.Y.I. Children's Etiquette teas are planned along with informal tea classes.

$13.25 Dorothy Marie's Tea Ceremony. Homemade scone served with Devonshire cream & preserves, assorted finger sandwiches, delectable French pastries, pot of brewed loose tea.

$6.95 Cream Tea.... Fresh homemade scone served with Devonshire cream & preserves, seasonal fruit and a pot of tea.

TEATIME: 10:00am To 5:00pm • Tuesday Thru Saturday
• May Accommodate Some Dietary Needs With Advance Request
• Non-Caffeine/Herbal Tea Available
• Children's Tea Parties Welcome
• Watercloset: Same Floor
• **Reservations Are Recommended**
• Street Parking Limited, City Lots
• Credit Cards: V,MC&AE

Proprietor's
*Autograph*_____*Date*_____

PATISSERIE

On Mission Between 7th & Ocean
(Part of Carmel Plaza)
Carmel, California

408-624-5008

Tea & Scones At...Patisserie. Take a well-deserved tea break and try a really yummy scone too. If you've never been to Carmel put it on your list of places to go. It's a terrific city and one of my favorite get-away places in California.

The heart of the shopping district contains streets with neat cottage-type shoppes specializing mostly in lovely goods of all kinds. Patisserie is located in this lovely and lively area of town which attracts many people. On a cool day when the fog rolls in, you can find a comfy spot in front of the fireplace to enjoy your pot of tea and Patisserie's famous scones. Try tea and see why.

$3.25 Tea & Scone... Pot of tea, (20 choices of tea,) and a wonderful fresh baked blueberry oatmeal scone with fresh homemade raspberry puree & butter.

TEA & SCONES: 11:30am To 4:30pm • Monday Thru Friday
- 9:00am To 9:00pm, Saturday & Sunday
- Non-Caffeine/Herbal Tea Available
- Watercloset: Nearby
- Wheelchair Accessible
- **Reservations For Six Or More Please**
- Parking Garage Below, 1/2 Hour Validated
- Credit Cards: V,MC&AE

Proprietor's
*Autograph*_____*Date*_____

THE TUCK BOX
Tea Room

Dolores Street
(Between Ocean & 7th. Street)
Carmel, California

408-624-6365

New Proprietor...It's Teatime At...The Tuck Box Tea Room. This fascinating "fairy-tale" cottage is not to be missed if you have the good fortune to find yourself in the lovely seacoast village of Carmel. This adorable and incredibly unique cottage was designed by Hugh Comstock in the early 1920's. The Tuck Box Tea Room is under new ownership but there still familiar friendly faces around. Tuck Box now serves lunch & dinner in addition to Tea.

Afternoon Tea is quite casual here, served at small tables with place mats and white, blossom-pattern Syracuse china. Tea & scones with wonderful ollieberry jam is memorable, but don't forget your camera. You'll want photo memories of this spot!

$5.25 Afternoon Tea... Tuck Box scone or English muffin served with whipped cream & ollieberry preserves and Tuck Box Ceylon black brewed loose tea.

$3.00 Dessert Of The Day

TEATIME: 12:30pm To 4:30pm • Seven Days A Week
• Watercloset: Same Floor
• Non-Caffeine/Herbal Tea Available
• Limited-Time Street Parking
• **Reservations: No**
• Cash Or Check
Proprietor's
*Autograph*_____*Date*_____

PATRICIA'S VICTORIAN TEA CO.

21409 and 214 07 Devonshire Street
(Hughes Shopping Center)
Chatsworth, California

818-341-2162

It's Teatime At...Patricia's Victorian Tea Co.
Here's a spot with a very appropriate "Devonshire" Street address. Patricia has just pushed out the walls for a newly expanded tearoom. It is decorated in a Victorian garden motif with wicker accessories, a garden rose wall mural, and burgundy and green accents.

Afternoon Tea is presented on tiered caddies at tables set with tablecloths, lace toppers, fresh flowers and Royal Albert fine china. Patricia is known for her homebaked treats including English muffins, blueberry and raisin scones and her cinnamon crumb cake with chocolate chips. F.Y.I. There's an antique piano in the tearoom which you are invited to play. Patricia says she probably won't sing along however. Catering, custom gift baskets, and private tea parties for up to 50 guests are available.

$12.99 Duchess Of Devonshire High Tea.. Assorted finger sandwiches, hot meat pie or sausage rolls, and brewed tea.
$10.99 Lady Chatsworth Tea... Assorted finger sandwiches, scone, assorted pastries, pot of brewed tea.
$5.99 Devonshire Cream Tea.. Scone with Devonshire cream & preserves and a pot of brewed tea.
$3.75 Pot Of Tea... Two cup pot of tea with cookies.

TEATIME: 2:00pm To 4:30pm • Monday Thru Saturday
• May Accommodate Some Dietary Needs, 1 Week Advance Request
• Non-Caffeine/Herbal Tea Available
• Children's Tea Parties Welcome
• Wheelchair Accessible • Watercloset: Same Floor
• **Reservations Required For Duchess & Lady Chatsworth Teas**
• Free Parking Lot
• Credit Cards: MC&V
Proprietor's
*Autograph*_____*Date*_____

A Spot of Tea

ROSES & IVY
853 Manzanita Court
Chico, California

530-891-1085

It's Teatime At...Roses & Ivy. This ranch style home built in 1953, became Roses & Ivy in 1995. The lovely English Country Garden ambiance is thanks in part to a profuse rose garden. The interior of the shop is attractively decorated in a palette of spring florals. The rooms are informally referred to as the Rose Room with a pink blush, and "rose" theme items, and the Iris Room with a cheerful morning sunshine glow.

Tea Luncheon is served at mahogany antique tables set with green depression glass plates & serving pieces, complimented by edible flowers, pink tablecloths and fresh flower centerpieces. A very nice gift shop will enhance your tea experience. P.S. Be sure to stop at Mr. McGregor's Garden Gift shop located adjacent to Roses & Ivy for tea & scones & gifts & delectable sweets such as the Raspberry Chantilly cake. Private tea parties are also available for 2 to 200 guests on Saturdays. Please call Kathleen for details.

$9.95 Tea Luncheon... Assorted tea sandwiches, gourmet green salad, quiche, fresh baked scone of the day, such as: strawberry, or currant/pecan, or apricot/strawberry, served with lemon curd, mock Devonshire cream & honey or wildflower berry butter, desserts featuring the signature Godiva chocolate mousse torte or poached pear and a pot of tea. Changes Daily

TEATIME: 11:00am To 3:00pm • Monday Thru Saturday
• May Accommodate Some Dietary Needs With Advance Request
• Non-Caffeine/Herbal Tea Available
• Watercloset: Same Floor
• Wheelchair Accessible
• **Reservations Are Recommended**
• Free Parking Lot
• Credit Cards: V&MC
Proprietor's
*Autograph*_____*Date*_____

ELEGANT CLUTTER
Tea Room, Gallery Of Art
& Boutique

4200 Chino Hills Parkway Suite #610
Chino Hills, California

909-393-5282

      New Location...Special Event Teas...At Elegant Clutter. This well-known spot of tea has not only a new address, but a new direction. The shop's primary new focus is their Gallery of Art, and appearances by known artists and authors. Artist events are planned to coincide with Special Event Teas.

      Special Event Tea menus will continue to be innovative as before, with colorful unique place settings and delicious goodies. Sometimes, the Event Tea will be more of a luncheon tea, while at other times, a Dessert Tea. The proprietors have always been inspired by the seasons and holidays of the year. The flavor of the shop and the tea events will continue along this festive line. Please call to see what's brewing on the upcoming schedule. Fashion Teas are planned too. Allow browsing time in the Gallery & gift shop.

      $10.50-$16.50 Special Event Teas... Ranging from Dessert Teas...To Afternoon Teas with finger sandwiches, pinwheels, seasonal soup or seasonal fresh fruit platter, petit fours, scone served with cream & preserves, shortbread, desserts, brewed loose tea. (Price is approximate, menus are inspired by events.)

SPECIAL EVENT TEAS: Please Call For Event Schedule
- Non-Caffeine/Herbal Tea Available
- Watercloset: Same Floor
- **Reservations Are Required**
- Free Off-Street Parking
- Credit Cards: MC,V&DIS

Proprietor's
*Autograph*_____*Date*_____

BAMBOO TEA HOUSE

221 Yale Avenue
Claremont, California

909-626-7668

New Addition...Monthly Tea Tastings & More At...Bamboo Tea House. "Tea as a way of life," is well communicated at the Bamboo Tea House. Tranquility, serenity and a collection of fine teas and accessories from around the world await you. Steps away from the hustle & bustle of Yale Avenue discover the ancient & modern Oriental pleasures and treasures of tea.

Yixing pots, fine imported loose teas, batik wall-hangings, orchids in baskets, and Chinese scholar brush stroke painting supplies are available at the Bamboo Tea House. The intimate tea house is decorated in creamy beige tones with bamboo fixtures and columns. An old Japanese chest, rock garden and fountain add to the ambiance. Anna has an extensive collection of teas, Japanese, Chinese greens and oolong as well as English teas. She is warm and friendly and always happy to visit and talk "tea" with her customers. Ask about the handsome custom-made tea canisters which come in approximately 3.5 or 6 ounce sizes depending on the tea's volume. They are the perfect accessory for the tea you give as a gift. Monthly tea-tastings & special events are planned. Please call for schedule, prices & to reserve your spot. Don't miss the bamboo fountains. Please call for the prices of the monthly Tea Tastings.

$.95 To $9.45 oz. A Variety Of Over 100 Teas

LOOSE TEA & MORE: 10am To 6:00pm • Monday Thru Saturday
• 12:00Noon To 5:00pm, Sunday
• Non-Caffeine/Herbal Tea Available
• Watercloset: Same Floor
• **Reservations: No**
• Limited Time Street Parking & Rear Lot
• Credit Cards: V,MC&AE

Proprietor's
*Autograph*_____*Date*_____

SOME CRUST TEA ROOM

115 Yale Avenue
Claremont, California

909-621-1946 *Tearoom*
909-621-9772 *Bakery*

New Addition...It's Teatime At...Some Crust Tea Room.(On Fridays & Saturdays) What a pleasant surprise we had while walking down Yale Avenue, by happenstance we stumbled upon Some Crust Tea Room. It was early evening, but by sheer luck, the proprietor Dorothy was still in. She graciously invited us in for a look about. What a delightful tour it was. We went through her wonderful immaculate bakery, a well known spot in Claremont and her innovative, artistic tearoom. Afternoon Tea is served at tables set with tablecloths and fresh flowers. Small hand-painted accent tables complement the modern art theme. The walls and high ceilings are painted white and display large modern paintings.

Some Crust is certainly non-traditional in decor, when compared to Victorian style tearooms. But, I thought the modern art feeling was quite interesting. It was like being in an art museum tearoom, if there were such a thing. Dorothy could surely give museums some good ideas! She sent us home that evening with a sample of her signature baked goodies. Absolutely delicious!

$12.50 Afternoon Tea... Assorted tea sandwiches, basketful of warm currant scones, Devonshire cream & strawberry jam, variety of petit sweets, a pot of brewed loose tea.

TEATIME: 2:00pm To 5:00pm • Friday & Saturday
• Afternoon Tea For Groups Of 6+ Daily By Reservation Only
• May Accommodate Some Dietary Needs With Advance Request
• Non-Caffeine/Herbal Tea Available
• Watercloset: Same Floor
• **Reservations Are Appreciated**
• Limited Time Street Parking
• Credit Cards: V,MC&DIS

Proprietor's
*Autograph*_____*Date*_____

THE GARDEN ESCAPE
Tea & Gift Shop
250 W. First Street, Suite 152
Claremont, California

909-626-2271

New Addition...It's Teatime At...The Garden Escape Tea & Gifts. Everything's coming up flowers at The Garden Escape Tea & Gifts. The shop is conveniently located next door to the historic Claremont train depot used today by Metro Link. This is an informal little gift and tea shop with three tables indoors and four on the covered brick patio. The garden decor features nice grass green hardwood floors, violet walls, a large garden mural and two fountains. The Garden Escape is a dream come true for Canadian born Marlene, who gave up a nursing career to open her shop. Her mom Mary, also a nurse, helps out when she's in town.

Afternoon Tea is presented with care on a two tiered cake stand, at white wrought iron tables with floral cushions. The floral theme continues with imported Pansy Pattern china by Pacific Rim and pretty floral paper napkins tied with raffia. Marlene enjoys visiting with her customers, in fact she says she visits more than she works! "Socializing is good for the soul!" Enjoy a leisurely tea here with nice instrumental background music. P.S. Unique gifts & tea accessories are displayed on attractive floor to ceiling shelves. F.Y.I. Intimate tea parties are available for up to seven guests.

$7.95 Afternoon Tea... Nine assorted tea sandwiches, cream scone, fresh fruit, cream & lemon curd, tea cake, cookie, and a pot of brewed loose Republic of Tea served with honey stick.

TEATIME: 8:00am To 6:00pm • Monday Thru Friday
- 9:00am To 5:00pm, Saturday
- Watercloset: Same Floor
- Wheelchair Accessible
- Two Hour Free Parking
- **Reservations Preferred**
- Credit Cards: V,MC&AE

Proprietor's
*Autograph*_____*Date*_____

70

PRIMROSE COTTAGE

356 Pollasky Street
(Near 4th. Street)
Clovis, California

209-297-5257

It's Teatime At...Primrose Cottage. If you love traditional old world charm, pack your bags and head to Clovis, a city with lots of "Old Town" personality. The Primrose Cottage is located in an historic building, a hotel back at the turn of the century. Primrose Cottage is reminiscent of the Victorian period with loads of charm, antiques and exquisite wall coverings.

Afternoon Tea is presented on a three tiered caddie accented with flower garnishes, at tables set with damask tablecloths and white Austrian bone china. Nearly everything here is homemade by Teresa, the proprietor and is served in rooms throughout the cottage. P.S. Allow time to browse, the boutique has lovely gifts & imported English items such as Hobnobs, and chocolate covered digestives. Tea parties are available for up to 50 guests. P.S. You may now enjoy Sunday Brunch & Tea. Enjoy! Ask about the newsletter.

$12.50 Full Traditional English Tea... Three finger sandwiches, homemade scone with cream, lemon curd & jam, selection of tarts & treats, and a pot of brewed loose tea.
$8.95 The Daily Luncheon Tea... Two petit finger sandwiches homemade scone, petit green salad, special tea cakes, pot of brewed loose tea of the day.
$3.95 Tea & Scone... Homemade scone with Primrose Cottage cream, lemon curd & jam and a pot of brewed tea.

TEATIME: 11:00am To 5:00pm • Tuesday Thru Friday
• 11:00am To 4:00pm, Saturday • 10:30am To 3:00pm, Sunday
• May Accommodate Some Dietary Needs With Advance Request
• Non-Caffeine/Herbal Tea Available
• Children's Tea Parties Welcome
• Watercloset: Same Floor
• **Reservations Are Appreciated Especially On Weekends**
• Two Hour Street Parking
• Credit Cards: DIS,V,MC&AE
Proprietor's
*Autograph*_____*Date*_____

ASHLEY HOUSE

736 North La Cadena Drive
Colton, California

909-370-4480

It's Teatime At...Ashley House, Once-A-Month Theme Teas Too. Built in 1890, the Ashley House is a beautiful Queen Anne Victorian with a wraparound front porch and distinctive half-moon vent in the front gable. The house was carefully moved to its current location around 1950. Over the years there have been five owners and in 1988 Judy purchased the Ashley House and added many of the lovely Victorian touches you see today. Theme Teas are usually featured on the third Wednesday of the month and include Renaissance Tea, Teddy Bear Tea, Adventure In Paradise Tea and Dress-Up Tea. The Christmas Tea also features a holiday boutique.

Tea is served at tables set with tablecloths, linen napkins, fresh flowers or centerpieces and burgundy Buffalo China. Please call for calendar of Theme Teas. The Christmas Tea & Boutique is usually the first week in December. P.S.Private tea parties available.

$13.00 Monthly Buffet Theme Teas Warm savory, cucumber sandwiches, scone bread, Devonshire cream & preserves, fresh fruit, dessert, and a pot of loose brewed tea. ($7.00 Children)

$9.95 Summer Afternoon Tea.. Mini quiche, cucumber sandwiches, scone, cream & preserves, fruit, dessert, a pot of tea.

$9.95 High Tea... Warm savory, cucumber sandwiches, scone bread with Devonshire cream & preserves, pot of brewed tea.

$6.95 Victorian Tea... Cucumber tea sandwiches, scone served with Devonshire cream & preserves, sweets, a pot of tea.

TEATIME: 11:00am To 2:00pm • Tuesday Thru Friday
• Call For Schedule Of Once-A-Month Theme Teas
• May Accommodate Some Dietary Needs With Advance Request
• Non-Caffeine/Herbal Tea Available
• Children's Tea Parties Welcome
• Watercloset: Same Floor
• **Reservations Are Required**
• Street Parking Available & Nearby Lot
• Cash Or Check

Proprietor's
*Autograph*_____*Date*_____

Rose Petal Sugar

"Miz Tea," Everyone's Cup Of Tea, Santa Rosa, CA.

"A delicate and delightful way to flavor your tea."

Pick the petals from your most fragrant "spent" rose blossoms.
Make sure they are insect and pesticide free.
In a glass container with tight fitting lid, layer granulated white
sugar with rose petals.
Make several layers.
Stir occasionally. Taste the sugar.
After 3 weeks sugar will have a delicate rose flavor & fragrance.
Brown, crystallized, or colored sugar are not suitable
for Rose Petal Sugar.

Too Many Teacups

By T. Potts

Teacups here and teapots there
everywhere I turn

Some on tables, more on shelves
others dangling in the air

To think it began with one chipped pot
with little pink roses from an antique spot

Now, teapot gifts are flowing in
my house is like the Smithsonian!

When going to tea is your thing...
You just can't stop bringing them in!

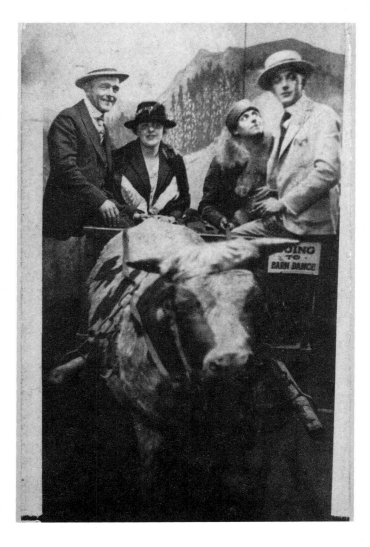

Go West, the road to tea is paved with gold!

SIERRA GOLD TEA COMPANY

22727 Columbia Street
(Off Highway 49 Gold Rush Trail)
Columbia, California

209-588-9370

New Addition...It's Time For A Spot Of Tea At...Sierra Gold Tea Company. Hold yer horses...it's time for tea! C'mon in and meet Mary and Connie they're awfully nice ladies and it's mighty cute here at Sierra Gold Tea Company!

The town of Columbia is very interesting as it is part of an historic park owned by the state. All shops and businesses are posed in circa 1870 venues right down to their "gold rush" clothing. Afternoon Tea had not yet technically come to California, so tea and afternoon sweets from old family recipes are served in its stead.

Everything at this cozy spot is fresh, homemade and baked on premises. They don't even own a freezer. Tables are set with tablecloths, fresh flowers in mason jars, early California mismatched china, mom's teacups and English bone china teapots. The shop is located in the old bright red Dondero Barn made of pecky cedar wood. I couldn't make this up, it's really called that because of real woodpecker holes. Like barn ads of old, a teapot is painted on the side. The interior is creme, blue and maroon with oriental rugs, a wood burning stove & staff in period costumes. Sierra Gold sells bulk teas by the ounce, tea accessories, handcrafted glass teapot jewelry & more. P.S. Garden seating & tea parties for up to 20 guests. F.Y.I. You can pan for gold & go for stagecoach rides.

$1.50 Or $3.50 Pot Of Tea.. With rock crystal swizzle.
$2.25 Osogood Pie Or Gram's Apple Pie
$1.00 Mom's Bonanza Bread... 5 jams & spreads too.

TEATIME: 7:00am To 5:00pm • Closed Wednesday
• May Accommodate Some Dietary Needs With Advance Request
• Non-Caffeine/Herbal Tea Available
• Watercloset: Same Floor
• **Reservations Are Recommended**
• Free Parking Lot Nearby
• Credit Cards: MC,V&DIS

Proprietor's
*Autograph*_____*Date*_____

SHERMAN LIBRARY & GARDENS

presents **Cafe Jardin**
2647 East Coast Highway
Corona del Mar, California

Reservations **714-673-0033**
714-673-2261

It's Teatime At...Sherman Library & Gardens. A new tea experience created by Wakao in association with Cafe Jardin is proudly presented at Sherman Library's Tea Garden. Now, a visit to the beautiful 2.2 acre Sherman Library & Gardens may include a memorable, unique and relaxing three course tea which combines cultural influences from England, Asia & France.

"Our Discovery Garden is designed especially, though not exclusively, for blind visitors. It's island-like shape can be circumnavigated by wheelchairs. In the Discovery Garden, the emphasis is on plants whose essential appeal, rather than the eye, is to the senses of touch or smell." In addition to beautiful grounds and a fern grotto, you will also discover the Sherman Research Historical Library. The garden & gift shop are open daily 10:30am-4:00pm. Library hours: 9:00am to 4:30pm Monday through Friday. Admission to the gardens is $3.00, exact change is appreciated. F.Y.I. General membership is $35.00, $25.00 for Seniors, includes entrance to the gardens. P.S. Private tea parties for 2 to 20 guests.

$25.00 "Tea Infusion"... Savories such as: Seared seabass in rice paper, and salmon & cucmber, presented with Shiso tea; whole wheat/dried mulberry scone and a poppyseed/cardamon scone served with Devonshire cream, seasonal berry compote, presented with an essence of rose tea; chocolate mascarpone cake, apple rosemary tart, fresh strawberry with chocolate & ginger, fruit tart, pistachio toffee, presented with vanilla almond tea.

TEA IN THE GARDEN: One Seating: 2:30pm, Monday Thru Friday
• Non-Caffeine/Herbal Tea Available
• Watercloset: Same Floor
• Wheelchair Accessible
• **Advance Reservations Are Necessary**
• Required Admission $3.00, Free Parking Lot
• Credit Cards: V,MC,DC&AE

Director's
*Autograph*_____*Date*_____

TASSELS TEA ROOM
inside Elizabeth Benefield
3127 East Coast Highway
Corona del Mar, California

714-673-7714

New Addition....It's Teatime At...Tassels Tea Room. Surround yourself with stylish home furnishings, beautiful antiques and an array of gifts while enjoying tea at Elizabeth Benefield. Laury's tearoom is artfully designed to please. A full luncheon menu is available in addition to Afternoon Tea.

Afternoon Tea is served at tables set with tablecloths, fresh flowers or centerpieces, fine china, and silver tea strainers. Tea specialties are presented on silver three tiered caddies. The decor of the room is ever changing as are the decorating trends, but there is a distinctive antique pine fireplace & a sign above it from a tearoom in England also named "Tassels", old French doors and chandeliers. Private tea parties are available for 20 to 30 guests. F.Y.I. Elizabeth Benefield is Laury's grandmother, how honored she must be.

$19.00 Quarterly Theme Tea... These special events teas usually include a sweet little gift from Tassels. Menu as below.
$15.00 Afternoon Tea... Assorted sandwiches such as: herb cheese & cucumber, chicken tarragon, turkey with apples & almonds, and tomato & watercress, scones, cookies, lemon curd tarts, chocolate tarts & truffles, fruit tarts, brewed loose tea.

TEATIME: 11:30 To 4:30 • Monday Thru Saturday
• May Accommodate Some Dietary Needs With Advance Request
• Non-Caffeine/Herbal Tea Available
• Children's Tea Parties Welcome
• Watercloset: Same Floor
• **Reservations Are Appreciated**
• Free Parking Lot In The Back
• Credit Cards: V,MC&AE

Proprietor's
*Autograph*_____*Date*_____

HOTEL DEL CORONADO

1500 Orange Avenue
Coronado, California

800-HOTEL DEL   619-435-6611

It's Teatime On Sundays & Daily In December At...Hotel Del Coronado. Reserve your place well in advance for Afternoon Tea at the world famous Hotel Del Coronado. Built in 1888, this is the only ocean front hotel in California. The hotel is Internationally renowned and often visited by the world's royalty. The Hotel Del is frequented by Hollywood film makers too. "Some Like It Hot" was one unforgettable movie filmed here. In recent years episodes of "Baywatch" and other shows were filmed here.

Afternoon Tea is graciously served in The Palm Court on the lobby level of the Hotel Del. It is a wonderful spot with a panoramic view of the hotel's gardens. The Palm Court is elegantly decorated in off-white & celery green, and accented with large potted palms. The hotel's own royal tea service is a classic white china with a accented with crown. P.S. Make your reservations early for these popular December Holiday Teas. F.Y.I. During the month of December, Afternoon Tea is served everyday except Christmas Day.

$14.95 The Del Tea... Assorted tea sandwiches, such as bay shrimp & celery salad on puff pastry, French Brie cheese with pippin apple & grape slices sprinkled with walnuts, homebaked mini pastries may include, rich butter cookies, mini creme puffs, petit lemon meringue, Swiss chocolate truffles, pot of brewed loose tea.

SUNDAYS & DECEMBER TEAS
- Seatings: 12:00Noon, 12:30pm, 2:00pm, 2:30pm, 3:30pm
- December Teas Daily, Except Christmas Day • 12Noon To 3:30pm
- May Accommodate Some Dietary Needs With Advance Request
- Non-Caffeine/Herbal Tea Available
- Watercloset: Same Floor
- Wheelchair Accessible
- **Reservations Are Required**
- Validated For One Hour Of Self-Parking
- Credit Cards: V,MC,DIS,DC,CB,AE&JCB

Proprietor's
*Autograph*_____*Date*_____

LITTLE WOMEN
191 East 16th Street
Costa Mesa, California

714-646-7212

Little Girls Tea Parties At...Little Women. Tea parties have become quite the fashion, little girls ages 5 years old and up can have fun and memorable, dress-up tea parties at Little Women. The proprietors opened their doors in 1992 for what has become a very entertaining way to celebrate a little girl's birthday or special event. The children are treated to an afternoon of playing "grown-up". Miss Beth and Miss Sarah have indeed found what brings glee to little women's hearts!

The children are greeted in a darling Victorian-style parlor and escorted to the dressing area where they select feathery boas, hats, purses, gloves and sparkling costume jewelry for their day of glamour. This includes "make-up," nail polish, and just the right hairdoings. Miss Sarah and Miss Beth seem to have as much fun as the girls do. The teatime meal is served from silver tiered trays; all rather elegant and lady like. A tea party runs about two hours and can accommodate 8 to 20 young ladies. A keepsake photo of each child is a nice touch. Ask about the Teddy Bear Tea in December, and Dolly & Me Tea in May and Etiquette Teas. F.Y.I. Host parents are welcome to stay.

$295.00 Tea Party For 8 Girls...($22.00 Each additional child) Tea sandwiches, Birthday Girl's take-home personal cake, assorted fancy desserts and red raspberry "tea."

LITTLE GIRL'S TEA PARTIES: Minimum 8 Guests
• May Accommodate Some Dietary Needs With Advance Request
• Red Raspberry Caffeine Free "Tea"
• Watercloset: Same Floor
• **Please Call To Reserve Your Party Date**
• Metered Street Parking
• Cash Or Check

Proprietor's
*Autograph*_____*Date*_____

TEA & SYMPATHY

369 East Tustin Street
(East 17th Street & Tustin)
Costa Mesa, California

714-645-4860

It's Teatime At...Tea & Sympathy. If a cup of hot tea & a little sympathy is what you need, you're certainly in the right place. Tea & Sympathy hits the spot with tea and English delicacies. Tea &Sympathy features a large selection of Scottish, Irish and Welsh books, plus antiques, gifts and imported foods. Elle magazine included Tea & Sympathy in their feature, "100 Secret Addresses" from around the world.

Afternoon Tea is served at antique tables set with "Blue Willow," Wood & Sons china. A silver teapot remains on the table for your convenience and is attentively refilled. P.S. Private tea parties for up to 45 guests, and a tea party catered at your home are also available. F.Y.I. If you haven't experienced Toad in the Hole, Shepherd's Pie or Bangers & Mash, they are house specialties and you may want to give these English dishes a try.

$12.95 Victorian Tea... Tea sandwiches, currant scone, raspberry jam & Devon cream, dessert, PG Tips English Tea.

$10.00 Afternoon Tea... Tea sandwiches, warm scone with raspberry jam & whipped cream, pot of PG Tips English tea.

TEATIME: 11:00am To 6:00pm • Monday Thru Saturday
- 11:00am To 4:00pm • Sunday
- May Accommodate Some Dietary Needs With Advance Request
- Children's Tea Parties Welcome
- Non-Caffeine/Herbal Tea Available
- Watercloset: Same Floor
- **Reservations Are Suggested**
- Free Parking Lot
- Credit Cards: MC,V,AE,DC&DIS

Proprietor's
*Autograph*_____*Date*_____

THE GARDEN BISTRO

Crystal Court of South Coast Plaza
(Second Level)
Costa Mesa, California

714-546-6004

It's Teatime At...The Garden Bistro. A relaxing, impromptu Afternoon Tea is just what you need after a day of adventure, covering all the stores in the South Coast Plaza and The Crystal Court. This is world class, endurance shopping and you deserve a break!

The Garden Bistro is a "garden" of sorts, located inside of the busy Crystal Court Mall. This garden atmosphere may help to take your mind off sale signs and the other busy shoppers. There is even a blue sky ceiling mural to help with your visualization; the weather is always great in this Garden Bistro. F.Y.I. Private tea parties are available for 10 to 150 guests; perfect for a tour bus of shoppers. If you're a tour guide, remember to call ahead first however, that's a whole lot of finger sandwiches!

$15.95 Full Afternoon Tea... Assorted finger sandwiches such as caviar on French bread, salmon with dill & caper, cucumber, and basil feta-tomato, scone with preserves, seasonal fresh fruit, cookies, cake, and a pot of brewed loose tea.

$9.95 Lite Afternoon Tea... Fruit scone with preserves, seasonal fresh fruit, cookies, cake and a pot of brewed loose tea.

TEATIME: 2:30pm To 5:30pm • Seven Days A Week
• May Accommodate Some Dietary Needs With Advance Request
• Children's Tea Parties Welcome, Ages Six Years Up
• Non-Caffeine/Herbal Tea Available
• Watercloset: Same Floor
• Wheelchair Accessible
• **Reserve For Five Guests Or More Please**
• Crystal Court Parking
• Credit Cards: MC,V&AE

Proprietor's
*Autograph*_____*Date*_____

81

COVINA HERITAGE HOUSE — 1908

COVINA VALLEY
Historical Society

Call For Reservations & Street Address
(Please Leave A Message)
Covina, California

626-332-1429

It's Teatime Once A Month At...Covina Valley Historical Society Heritage House. What a treat to have Afternoon Tea and tour this terrific 1908 Craftsman home. Owned for generations by the Nash family, it is now the Covina Heritage House owned by the Covina Valley Historical Society and managed through the volunteer efforts of its members. Tea is graciously served in the library, sun room, dining room and living room.

Afternoon Tea is served at tables set with cherished old linens, cloth napkins, fresh flowers and an eclectic collection of Oriental fine china. Everything is homemade; the scones that very morning. You'll enjoy touring this charming spot and visiting with the friendly volunteers who share the history and relocation details of the house. P.S. If you have lovely family heirlooms that are going under-appreciated, consider donating them to The Covina Historical Society. You can be sure they will be displayed, loved and well cared for. F.Y.I. The Afternoon Tea & Tour takes place once a month from October to June. Sorry, no Afternoon Teas in July, August or September.

$10.00 Donation Tea & Tour... Assorted open-face tea sandwiches, scone, Devonshire cream & preserves, English Trifle with or without Sherry, a continuous cup of lovely brewed tea.

TEA & TOUR ONCE A MONTH: 1:00pm • Please Call For Dates
• Non-Caffeine/Herbal Tea Available Upon Request
• Watercloset:Same Floor
• **Reservations Are Required**
• Free Parking Lot
• Cash Or Check

Director's
*Autograph*_____*Date*_____

GRANDMA'S TEA GARDEN

117 North Citrus Avenue
Covina, California

626-966-7363

New Addition...It's Teatime At...Grandma's Tea Garden. The white teapot on the green awning is your first sign that something good is brewing inside. Grandma's Tea Garden is certainly a welcome addition to the busy Covina business district on quaint Citrus Avenue. A warm and friendly atmosphere awaits as mother and daughter busily prepare tasty treats for Afternoon Tea.

The tearoom is decorated in colorful cheery hues with hand-painted flowers and delicate "visiting" fairies. A flowery picket fence and arbor add to the indoor garden setting. Tea is served at tables set with fresh flowers, tablecloths & an eclectic collection of fine bone china. The tea sandwiches are quite colorful, served tied in ribbons on pretty pastel colored bread. And they taste as good as they look. Be sure to peek into the gift cabinets for nice take home treats. Private tea parties are also available, please call to plan. Ask about children's Teddy Bear Teas too.

$9.25 Afternoon Tea... Five assorted tea sandwiches, fruit with cream, shortbread, dessert, pot of brewed loose tea.

$9.25 Grandma's Garden Tea... Cup of soup, petite salad, fresh bread, sliced cheese, fruit, dessert, brewed loose tea.

$6.95 Dessert Tea... Scone served with fresh seasonal fruit & cream, choice of dessert and a pot of brewed loose tea.

$5.50 Children's Tea Party...PB&J or cheese sandwich, fresh fruit, cookie and "tea."

TEATIME: 10:00am To 5:00pm • Tuesday Thru Saturday
• May Accommodate Some Dietary Needs With Advance Request
• Non-Caffeine/Herbal Tea Available
• Children's Tea Parties Welcome
• Watercloset: Same Floor
• Wheelchair Accessible
• **Reservations Are Appreciated**
• Credit Cards: V,MC&DIS

Proprietor's
*Autograph*_____*Date*_____

THE MULBERRY TREE

23794 Lake Drive
Crestline, California

909-338-2793

New Addition....It's Teatime At...The Mulberry Tree. One can hardly think of a Mulberry tree without thinking of memorable childhood tunes. Afternoon Tea served in the unique setting of this turn of the century Victorian, will no doubt make wonderful new memories for you. Mother & daughter Marlis and Jennifer invite you to visit and share good times with them at their full service restaurant & tearoom. P.S. Wear that beautiful hat!

Afternoon Tea is served at tables set with linens, fresh flowers and a collection of mis-matched china & silver. Tea is served in The Alcove on the first floor which can cozily accommodate 6 or 7 guests, and upstairs as well, for larger groups. The Alcove, with bay windows and a chandelier is a very popular spot. The house is decorated in teal, mulberry & rosey tones, and classical music plays in the background. F.Y.I. Private tea parties are available for 2 to 20 guests. P.S. Don't miss the neat gift & antique cottage next door called The Mulberry Tree Cottage. It has a a sweet little garden and patio too.

$10.50 Afternoon Tea... Assorted finger sandwiches, white chocolate basket of scones served with lemon curd, cream & preserves, delectable desserts, and a pot of brewed tea.

TEATIME: 2:00pm • Wednesday Thru Saturday
• May Accommodate Some Dietary Needs With Advance Request
• Non-Caffeine/Herbal Tea Available
• Watercloset: Same Floor
• Wheelchair Accessible First Floor
• **Reservations Are Appreciated**
• Free Parking Lot
• Credit Cards: V,MC,DIS&AE
Proprietor's
*Autograph*_____*Date*_____

84

RITZ CARLTON
Laguna Niguel
1 Ritz Carlton Drive
Dana Point, California

THE RITZ-CARLTON®

714-240-2000

It's Teatime At...Ritz Carlton Laguna Niguel. The Library Lounge at the beautiful Ritz-Carlton may be just your cup of tea. The lounge has comfortable sofas, wingback chairs, a fireplace, handsome antiques, beautifully designed fresh flower arrangements and a fabulous view of the Pacific Ocean.

Afternoon Tea is presented on tiered caddies at tables elegantly set with classic Wedgewood china. Count on Ritz Carlton signature attentive service. Live music is generally a part of the tea service and enhances the experience. F.Y.I. There are usually three Afternoon Tea seatings in December, followed by a return to the regular schedule of open seating in January. P.S. Monday through Friday open seating is from 2:00pm to 4:00pm, Saturday and Sunday seatings are at 2:00pm and 4:30pm. F.Y.I. Christmas Teas book up about two months in advance, plan early for next year!

$28.50 Royal Tea... Kir Royal Cocktail with Chambord, and strawberries with Grand Marnier & Devonshire cream added to the Traditional Tea.

$21.00 Traditional Tea... Assorted tea sandwiches such as smoked Atlantic salmon with Russian caviar; currant scone served with Devonshire cream & boutique fruit preserves, Scottish shortbread, Chelsea Bun, tartlet, fruit breads and a bittersweet chocolate Mignardise with a pot of brewed loose tea.

$16.50 Light Tea... Currant scone with Devonshire cream & boutique fruit preserves, Scottish shortbread, Chelsea Bun, tartlet, fruit breads, chocolate Mignardise, pot of brewed loose tea.

TEATIME: 2:00pm To 4:00pm • Monday Thru Sunday
• May Accommodate Some Dietary Needs With Advance Request
• Non-Caffeine/Herbal Tea Available
• December Children's Teddy Bear Teas
• Watercloset: Same Floor • Wheelchair Accessible
• **Reservations Are Required**
• $9.00 Sorry No Parking Validation
• Credit Cards: V,MC,DC,DIS,AE&JCB

L'autograph
*du Concierge*_____*Date*_____

TRADITIONS

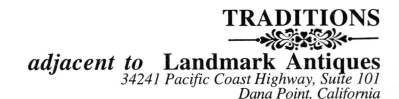

adjacent to Landmark Antiques

34241 Pacific Coast Highway, Suite 101
Dana Point, California

714-248-7660

New Addition...It's Teatime At...Traditions. Start a new tradition by visiting Judy & Ken's "Traditions" for Afternoon Tea. The Victorian style, main floor parlor is decorated with antique furnishings, green & pink floral carpeting, dark green walls, and a carved mantel; the upper level easily accommodating larger parties. Gilded mirrors reflecting various historic periods and styles cover the walls, along with an abundance of artwork & stained glass. Breakfast, lunch & Afternoon Teas are prepared on premises. F.Y.I. Ken was executive chef at Clint Eastwood's Hogsbreath in Carmel. Make his day, come for tea!

Kathy, will greet you for Afternoon Tea and seat you at tables set with pink tablecloths, cloth napkins & fresh flowers. Allow time for browsing as there are 65 antique vendors at their adjacent shop Landmark Antiques. P.S. Private tea parties are available for 12 to 50 guests with a $100.00 room fee.

$18.95 "Traditions Tea"... Canapes including: shrimp salad, smoked salmon, scones served with Devon cream & lemon curd, bread pudding, chocolate torte, creme puffs, pot of tea.

$11.95 English Country Tea... Canapes, freshly baked orange/cranberry scones served with Devonshire cream & lemon curd, mini tart, blueberry muffins, and a pot of brewed loose tea.

$8.95 Cream Tea.. Orange/cranberry scones, Devonshire cream & lemon curd, surprise, and a pot of brewed loose tea.

TEATIME: 11:00am To 4:00pm, Daily, Friday & Saturday Till 10pm
- May Accommodate Some Dietary Needs, 1 Day Advance Request
- Non-Caffeine/Herbal Tea Available
- Children's Tea Parties Welcome
- Watercloset: Main Floor • Wheelchair Accessible, Main Floor
- **Reservations Are Recommended**
- Free Three Level Parking Structure
- Credit Cards: V&MC

Proprietor's
*Autograph*_____*Date*_____

FURNACE CREEK INN
& Ranch Resort
Highway 190
Death Valley National Park, California

760-786-2345

New Addition...It's Teatime From Mid-October Thru April At...Furnace Creek Inn & Ranch Resort. "Tea is Hot!" and nowhere could this be more true than at the Furnace Creek Inn in Death Valley. This four Diamond resort does everything in *cool* style. Believe it or not, Furnace Creek has been serving traditional Afternoon Teas for over 70 years. Not iced tea, hot tea! Toni is the busy proprietor, she's hard to catch up to but do try to say hello. Don't miss the garden oasis with a cascading creek, ponds & palm trees; quite an accomplishment when you think of the heat in this area.

Afternoon Tea is served from tea carts in the elegant Lobby Lounge, a spot which overlooks Panamint Mountains and the desert floor. Tables are set with "Palermo" by Villeroy & Boch and cloth napkins. The decor is classic 1930's, from the blue & green slate floors to the complementary overstuffed couches, chairs and gold accent pieces. Photos reveal some of the resort's highlights over the past 70 years. P.S. When you call to confirm teatime, they may think you mean tee-time as they're very golf-minded here. Maybe tea 'n tee is just what you have in mind. F.Y.I.This is a lovely resort with hotel & motel type accommodations & a nice gift shop. Enjoy!

$8.95 Afternoon Tea... Miniature tea sandwiches, fresh baked date scones served with Devonshire cream, petit tarts & pastries, fresh seasonal fruit and a pot of tea.

- **TEATIME:** 4pm-5pm, Monday-Saturday, Mid-October Thru April
- May Accommodate Some Dietary Needs With Advance Request
- Non-Caffeine/Herbal Tea Available • Watercloset: Same Floor
- **Reservations Are Not Required**
- Free Parking Lot
- Credit Cards: V,MC,DIS,DC,AE&JCB

Proprietor's
*Autograph*_____*Date*_____

THE VILLAGE GREEN

89 Avenue Portola
El Granada, California

415-726-3690

It's Teatime At...The Village Green. This establishment's name, The Village Green Tea Room was taken right out of history. The term "greens" originated from feudal days when English bowmen practiced their archery on the green stretches of nature close to their homes in the small English villages. Even though the villages grew, the "greens" were preserved. A "Green" is known today as a setting for cricket matches, church fetes, flower shows festivals, sports days and May Day celebrations.

At The Village Green, the Tea Plate is served at tables set with white English china. The windows covered with lacey white curtains are the focal point of the room. There are windows on three walls for a terrific view of the Pacific Ocean. Royal family pictures & memorabilia and prints of the English countryside cover the available space. Chris & Susan are the proprietor of The Village Green which offers a variety of traditional English dishes such as Cornish Pastie, Bubble & Squeak, Treacle Tarts, and Hot Fruit Crumble in addition to the traditional tea plate.

$7.95 Tea Plate... Cucumber & cream cheese sandwich, scone & jam, shortbread, crumpet, sausage, cake, jam tart, orange bread and a pot of brewed tea.

$4.50 Cream Tea... Two scones served with clotted cream & jam and a pot of brewed tea.

TEATIME: 9:00am To 3:00pm • Monday Thru Friday
- 9:00am To 4:00pm, Saturday & Sunday • Closed Wednesday
- Non-Caffeine/Herbal Tea Available
- Children's Tea Parties Welcome
- Watercloset: Same Floor
- **Reservations: No**
- Unmetered Street Parking
- Credit Cards: V&MC

Proprietor's
Autograph _____*Date*_____

TEA TIME 1889
9092 Elk Grove Boulevard
Old Towne Elk Grove, California

916-686-6030

New Addition...It's Teatime At...Tea Time 1889.
A pink Victorian is home to Tea Time 1889. Since the house was built in 1889, Bettyjean commemorated the event in the name of her tearoom. A pretty flowering garden and fountain lead the way to the tearoom. In fact, weather permitting, you may take tea outdoors.
Afternoon Tea is served at antique tables set with turn of the century china and crystal. Each table has a unique vintage European theme with pictures and fresh flowers that match. The serene music, soft lights, and vintage attired servers help us feel part of Victorian times. Theme Teas are historically inspired and date prior to 1889. They include The Children's Medieval Forest Tea, Alice In Wonderland Tea and The Children's Princess Tea. F.Y.I. The detailed 20 page menu decoratively explains the history of the area, and is Bettyjean's own artistic creation. Ask about seasonal teas, private teas & catering. Allow time to peruse their gift shoppe too.

$12.95 Full Tea... Veggie-friendly finger sandwiches, scones, cream & jam, crumpets, tea breads, pastries, berry tarts as available, something chocolate, brewed loose tea paired to the menu.
$9.75 Light Tea... Trio of tea sandwiches, a scone served with cream & jam, crumpet, petit four and a pot of loose tea.
$6.50 Cream Tea...(Available 3pm-5pm only) Two scones, cream & jam, crumpet & pot of brewed loose tea

TEATIME: 11:30am To 5:00pm • Wednesday Thru Saturday
• & The Second Sunday Of The Month
• May Accommodate Some Dietary Needs With Advance Request
• Non-Caffeine/Herbal Tea Available
• Children's Tea Parties Welcome
• Watercloset: Same Floor
• **Reservations Are Required Friday, Saturday & Sunday**
• **Appreciated, On Wednesday & Thursday**
• Unmetered Street Parking
• Credit Card: V

Proprietor's
*Autograph*_____*Date*_____

EL MONTE HISTORICAL
Society Museum

3150 North Tyler Avenue
El Monte, California

626-444-3813

Tea & History In January, March, September & November At...El Monte Historical Society Museum. The town of El Monte was "born" when people came looking for gold and stayed on to live and farm the land. A visit to the museum is an opportunity to learn about the rich history of the town of El Monte and "meet" the brave wagon train pioneers who built the first public school in Southern California in the year 1851. The El Monte Historical Museum was built as a tribute to this, the oldest settlement in the San Gabriel Valley. The museum encompasses 8,500 square feet of history and is filled with unusual and interesting artifacts.

Generally, these teas take place on the third Sunday of the month in September, November, January & March and are prepared and presented by many of the local women's service organizations including: The American Legion Auxiliary, Business & Professional Women, The Republican Women, The Soroptomists, United Methodist Women's Organization & The Women's Club. Tentative Tea & History dates: November 16, 1997, January 18, 1998, March 15, 1998, September 20, 1998, November 15, 1998, January 17, 1999, March 21, 1999 & September 19, 1999. Please call to confirm dates. P.S. Membership in the El Monte Historical Society is welcomed & encouraged.

$ Complimentary Tea & History... Tea sandwiches, cake & cookies, mints, tea graciously poured by from silver urns.

TEA & HISTORY: As Scheduled
• Watercloset: Convenient
• Wheelchair Accessible
• **Reservations Please**
• Free Off-Street Parking
• Donations Are Appreciated

Curator's
*Autograph*_____*Date*_____

90

EURO CAFE
411 1/2 Main Street
El Segundo, California

310-322-0400

It's Teatime At...Euro Cafe. Look for a unique mural of the British Lion & Unicorn and you will soon discover a neat little spot that specializes in traditional English fare. Tasty treats such as Shepherd's Pie, and Beans On Toast, are all homemade. On the weekend evenings Euro Cafe adds the extra special English treat, roast beef & lamb. The decor of the Euro Cafe has been described as elegant English, with lovely flowery accents and lace curtains.

Afternoon Tea is served at tables set with bone china crockery, the traditional English way according to the Jaquie the proprietor. Tea parties for groups and children's tea parties are quite welcome, and Jaquie can now cater a tea for you at home or your place of business. F.Y.I. With advance reservations, your Afternoon Tea can become an intimate Evening Tea served on the cafe's fairy lit outdoor patio. The patio can accommodate approximately 15 guests. P.S. Cheesecake is a house specialty, if you order ahead, your favorite will be ready to take home after tea.

$7.99 Traditional Afternoon Tea... Delicate finger sandwiches, freshly baked scone served with Devonshire cream, fruit cake, and a pot of piping hot English tea.
$4.99 Cream Tea... Scone served with Devonshire cream & preserves and a pot of piping hot English tea.

TEATIME: 2:00pm To 6:00pm • Tuesday Thru Sunday
• Non-Caffeine/Herbal Tea Available
• Watercloset: Same Floor
• **Reservations Are Recommended**
• Free Parking Lot
• Credit Cards: MC,DIS,DC,CB,V&AE
Proprietor's
*Autograph*_____*Date*_____

91

TEA BERRIE COFFEE & TEA

162 S. Rancho Santa Fe Road Ste. E 70
Encinitas, California

760-633-1400

New Addition...It's Teatime At...Tea Berrie. Look for a burgundy awning and lots of potted plants to discover Mary's new spot called Tea Berrie. Both a coffee house & tearoom, Tea Berrie is many things to many people. Mary serves a variety of lovely Afternoon Teas along with other Tea Berrie specialties.

Afternoon Teas are presented on tiered caddies at tables set with doilies, fresh flowers & Blue Willow china by friendly servers in long pinstripe floral aprons. A dark green fan pattern carpet nicely offsets the high back upholstered floral chairs, comfortable green sofas and elegant draperies. Allow time to browse a bit, Tea Berrie carries collectible tea ware, tea theme gifts, and custom tea gift baskets. F.Y.I. Tea & live music are available Friday & Saturday evenings. P.S. Ask about the Holiday Teas. Tea parties are available for up to 18 guests, please call to plan.

$13.95 Victorian Tea... Tea sandwiches, scone, lemon curd, Devonshire cream & jam &, desserts, pot of brewed loose tea.
$10.95 Afternoon Tea... Assorted tea sandwiches, assorted desserts and a pot of brewed loose tea.
$5.95 Cream Tea Or Dessert Tea... Scone, lemon curd, Devonshire cream & jam or cakes & cookies and a pot of tea.
$5.95 Children's Tea... Assorted tea sandwiches, assorted cookies, choice of tea, hot chocolate or milk.

TEATIME: 7:00am To 7:00pm • Sunday Thru Thursday
• Till 11:00pm, Friday & Saturday • Call For Seasonal Hours
• May Accommodate Some Dietary Needs With Advance Request
• Non-Caffeine/Herbal Tea Available
• Children's Tea Parties Welcome
• Watercloset: Same Floor • Wheelchair Accessible
• **Reservations Strongly Suggested**
• Free Parking Lot
• Credit Cards: V,MC,DIS,DC,JCB&AE
Proprietor's
*Autograph*_____*Date*_____

92

VINTAGE TEA ROOM
inside Gilded Lily Antiques
217 E. Grand Avenue
Escondido, California

760-743-1292

New Addition....It's Teatime At...Vintage Tea Room...Inside Gilded Lily Antiques. This spot of tea is located in a 100 year old state historical monument. Gilded Lily is a well-known antique & vintage clothing shop with something new added, tea. Eleanor thought a tearoom would add a nice touch and I believe she was right. The shop, somewhat like a museum, houses a collection of fine clothing from the mid 1800's thru the 1970's.

Stroll under the rose arbor towards the back of the shop & voila, the Vintage Tea Room. Afternoon Tea is served at tables set with coordinating print tablecloths and a collection of new & antique china, each piece with a silver accent somewhere. Antique furnishings and gold accent pieces are on display throughout the shop, decorated in tones of hunter green & burgundy. Why not gild yourself! Don a vintage hat & accessories for old-fashioned teatime fun. Allow time to browse, treasures & gifts abound. Private tea parties for 15 to 45 guests. Several teas are offered, as an example:

$8.95 Coronation Tea... Assorted tea sandwiches, freshly baked scone served with Devonshire cream & jam or lemon curd, a sinfully delicious dessert of the day and a pot of brewed loose Taylor's of Harrogate English Tea.

TEATIME: 11:00am To 4:00pm • Tuesday Thru Saturday
• May Accommodate Some Dietary Needs With Advance Request
• Non-Caffeine/Herbal Tea Available
• Watercloset: Same Floor
• Wheelchair Accessible
• **Reservations Are Recommended**
• Free Three Hour Parking
• Credit Cards: V,MC,AE&DIS
Proprietor's
Autograph_____Date_____

CHANTILE LACE
Antiques, Collectibles & Tea Spot

435 Santa Clara Avenue
Fillmore, Californa

805-524-0727

New Tiny Tea Spot Brewing... It's **Time For A Tiny Spot Of Tea At..Chantile Lace.** Leave it to Rosemary, she has her fingers in so many pots that I shouldn't be surprised now that she's taken on a Caboose. Welcome to Chantile Lace, located close to Fillmore's new City Hall. This girl is going places, in a matter of speaking anyway...you see Chantile Lace is located in a now stationary 1930's ish Southern Pacific red Caboose.

For those passengers waiting to ride the rail to Santa Paula, Chantile Lace offers a neat spot to shop or linger over tea while waiting for the "All aboard whistle!" But make advance reservations if you want to enjoy your repass on-board. You'll be dining as the conductor & engineer did, in a little spot that can accommodate four guests from a rolling tea cart table with white linens & flowers.

The interior of the Caboose features hand painted red roses & ivy, a red carpet, and antiques, vintage clothing, hats & accessories. Cream Teas will be served on "American Rose" by Homer-Laughlin china. Al fresco sipping is planned too, Rosemary ordered red & white polka dot umbrellas and an awning. Don't miss the nearby Baggage cars which are also now antique shops!

$5.00 Cream Tea... Fresh baked scone served with cream & marmalade, Danish treat, and brewed loose or iced tea.

ANTICIPATED **SPOT OF TEA TIME:** High Noon, Friday
- 11:00am, Saturday • 1:00pm, Sunday
- Non-Caffeine/Herbal Tea Available
- Watercloset: Nearby Common Area
- **Reservations Are Required**
- Free Adjacent Parking Lot
- Credit Cards: V&MC

Proprietor's
*Autograph*_____*Date*_____

COURTHOUSE CAFE
24406 Main Street
Foresthill, California

916/530-367-4848

High Tea For Groups Of Six Guests Or More At... Courthouse Cafe. The Courthouse Cafe was built in 1863 as both the residence and Courthouse for the officiating judge, and has been lovingly renovated by the current proprietors. The interior is cream and white with Battenburg lace touches and rose colored floor coverings. The interesting windows are authentic and were salvaged from the town's old mill. Sound great? You be the Judge!

High Teas are served at tables set with pink or white linens, cloth napkins, "flowers of month" china, or Judith's set of English cottage-scene fine china. Renovation is still underway, so stop by and see what's brewing. Ask Judith about Teddy Bear Teas for up to 12 children, and other theme teas which are being planned. Tour groups are very welcome here and generous parking is available for the tour buses. Courthouse Cafe can now serve up to 40 guests for High Tea in the garden. Please call one week in advance and let Judith know that your group is on the way!

$10.00 High Tea...Assorted tea sandwiches are served on herb bread and usually include curried chicken salad, tarragon egg salad, and mint cream cheese with cucumber, seasonal fresh fruit, golden scone served with a selection of jams, lemon curd & Devonshire cream, dessert and "Courthouse" blend tea.

$6.00 Dessert Tea...Scones, sweet surprises, pot of tea.

HIGH & DESSERT TEA : Six Guest Minimum • May Be Scheduled Seven Days A Week From 11:00am To 4:00pm
• Herbal Tea Available By Advance Request
• Children's Tea Parties Welcome
• Watercloset: Same Floor
• Wheelchair Accessible
• **One Week Day Advance Reservation Required**
• Move The Horses For Plentiful Parking
• Credit Cards: V&MC

Proprietor's
*Autograph*_____*Date*_____

Take your cheerful staff to tea!

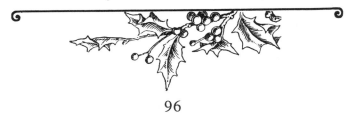

TYME FOR TEA
inside Ma Mere, Int'l.

37501 Niles Boulevard
Fremont, California

510-790-0944

New Addition...It's Teatime On Saturday & Sunday At...Tyme For Tea. Rumor had it that Diane & Darla's shop existed but it was like searching for fortunes in cookies. I finally found their tearoom that comes to life on weekends, hidden inside Ma Mere, Int'l. It was my good fortune to meet these ladies.

The Niles area of Fremont was sleepy for years but is now considered an up & coming antique area. The tearoom & antique store are located in what once was The Wesley Hotel where Charlie Chaplain's cast & crew stayed in the early 1900's while filming The Tramp, for Essanay Studios. P.S. This is great movie trivia in case we all wind up on Jeopardy! Over 400 movies were filmed in Niles, or Niles Canyon including those starring Bronco Billy.

Tea is served by the proprietors Diane & Darla, with help from apron-clad husbands. Tables are set with tablecloths, fresh flowers and mismatched old & new china. An old radio or Victrola croons tunes from the 1930's, so wear a vintage hat and fit right in! Peek about, gift items are tucked here & there. Parties for 15 to 26.

$12.50 Victorian Tea... Scone, creme & lemon curd, tea sandwiches such as: chicken pecan on hazelnut poppy seed bread dipped in crushed pecans, dessert may include: mocha chocolate mousse and almond cookie, and a pot of brewed loose tea.

$6.95 Tyme For Tea & Pastries... Delicious!

SATURDAY & SUNDAY TEAS: 11am To 5pm, Ask About Fridays
- Non-Caffeine/Herbal Tea Available
- Children's Tea Parties Welcome
- Wheelchair Accessible • Watercloset: Same Floor
- **Reservations Are Recommended**
- Unmetered Street Or Parking Lot
- Credit Cards: V&MC

Proprietor's
Autograph _____*Date*_____

97

THE OLDE SHIP
709 North Harbor Boulevard
Fullerton, California

714-871-7447

The Olde Ship
British Pub and Restaurant

Afternoon Tea Brewing...At...The Olde Ship. The Olde Ship has been known for years as a traditional English pub complete with dark wood-beamed ceilings and a dart board. In addition to their well-known English dishes, the proprietors Doug and his daughter Leanne are planning to start Afternoon Teas. Doug has been collecting different sets of antique Victorian bone china on his many trips back to England while visiting family in Epsom-Surrey, just south of London. Plans are still formulating so do give him your opinion "mate," when you drop by for Rhubarb Crumble, Sherry Trifle or other English delectables.

Afternoon Tea will be served at tables set with tablecloths & fresh flowers, a bit more formal than the usual fare here. Servers in black trousers or black skirts and aprons will present tea specialties on silver trays. Doug wants this to be a special experience for you and your impressions are important to him. Doug and Leanne enjoy visiting with their customers, you won't feel like a stranger for long.

$11.95 Lady Hamilton Tea... Assorted finger sandwiches, homemade scone with Devonshire cream & strawberry jam, choice from the dessert tray, pot of brewed loose tea.

$5.95 Dorset Cream Tea... Homemade scone served with Devonshire cream & preserves and a pot of brewed loose tea.

ANTICIPATED **TEATIME:** 2pm-4:30pm • Monday Thru Saturday
• Watercloset: Same Floor
• Wheelchair Accessible
• **Please Drop By**
• Unmetered Street Parking & Small Lot
• Credit Cards: V,MC,DIS&AE
Proprietor's
*Autograph*_____*Date*_____

BENBOW INN
445 Lake Benbow Drive
Garberville, California

707-923-2124

Tea & Scones At...Benbow Inn. If you haven't yet discovered the Benbow Inn and you're fortunate enough to find yourself in Garberville between late April and January 2, you owe yourself a treat. Stop by for English tea and fresh baked scones which are served daily at 3:00pm in the lobby during these months. This fabulous stone and wood English Tudor-style hotel Inn was designed by architect Albert Farr in 1926, and is a must see.

The Lobby of the Benbow is quite wonderful with French doors and handsome carved redwood beams. There are lots of overstuffed couches, antiques and artwork for your comfort and aesthetic pleasure. Did I mention it overlooks the Inn's beautiful gardens? Outdoor terrace seating is also available weather permitting. Stopping by for a "spotta" & a scone, is a very nice way to "meet" the Inn and it's friendly proprietors. You may even want to consider spending the night here sometime. (I know I'm ready!)

$5.00 Tea & Scones... Freshly baked scones served with cream & jam and tea served from a unique tea urn.

"SPOTTA" TEA AND A SCONE: Usually 3:00pm, Please Call
- Daily From The End Of April Thru January 2nd.
- Non-Caffeine/Herbal Tea Available
- Watercloset: Lobby Floor
- **Reservations: No**
- Free Off-Street Parking
- Credit Cards: V,MC,DIS&AE

Proprietor's
*Autograph*_____*Date*_____

COUNTRY ROSE INN B&B

COUNTRY ROSE INN
bed & breakfast

Please Call For Address & Directions
Gilroy, California

408-842-0441

Tea Parties For Groups At... Country Rose Inn B&B. Nestled between Morgan Hill, California and Gilroy, you will discover the Country Rose Inn, a romantic 1920's Dutch Colonial farmhouse manor and B&B. The scenic area is considered the heart of California's pastoral central coast. Tea is lovingly served in a most pleasing atmosphere with lots of fresh flowers and a nice collection of antique & contemporary furnishings.

Afternoon Tea is served for groups of 20 to 40 guests. Tables are set with tablecloths, home grown fresh flowers, linen napkins, and Rose's collection of floral pattern pottery, often with depression glass accent pieces. There are two dining rooms at Country Rose. The main dining room has a picture window framed in pink netting. The second dining room was originally the chandelier lit piano room. Both rooms have soft country rose pink walls which seem to reflect the spectrum of the day. One of the rooms still has the original wooden floors, the other, dusty rose carpeting. Smaller groups may choose to dine in the parlour which opens on to the deck. P.S. Don't miss the eye-catching sideboard in the main dining room, and the baker's rack. F.Y.I. Mary will be happy to arrange for a pianist or other local musician if you choose.

$24.00 Afternoon Tea... Assorted tea sandwiches, salad such as: cabbage sesame crunch or tossed greens with almonds & mandarin oranges, scone with cream & jam, sweets may include: peanut butter hugs, Russian Wedding cakes, cinnamon/buttermilk or orange/poppy seed tea bread or Dreyer's ice cream on a chocolate brownie topped with raspberry puree, and a pot of brewed tea.

PRIVATE TEA PARTIES: Please Call To Schedule
• May Accommodate Some Dietary Needs With Advance Request
• Non-Caffeine/Herbal Tea Available   • Watercloset: Same Floor
• **By Prepaid Reservation Only**
• Parking In The Meadow
• Cash Or Check
Proprietor's
*Autograph*_____*Date*_____

LISA'S TEA TREASURES
Glendale Galleria Salon
Glendale, California

818-247-2186

It's Teatime At...Lisa's Tea Treasures. A beautiful escape & most welcome respite from strenuous galleria shopping, Lisa's Tea Treasures on the 2nd floor of the Galleria is truly elegant. The wall & ceiling treatments are a vision of artistic genius.

If you love tea and you love to shop, Lisa's Tea Treasures really does have treasures for you. Fine china, unique tea ware, books, gourmet food items & more are all here. The tea canisters, with a wide variety of Lisa's teas will delight you. The gracious proprietor Fancy, keeps surprising me with wonderful new and innovative menu specialties. Afternoon Tea is beautifully served on tall tiered caddies by a friendly & attentive staff. The special touches include covered jars full of ginger cookies on each table. Enjoy!

$14.95 Monthly Theme Teas, Treasure Hunt Tea Plate. Example: Island Gem scone, Devonshire cream & tea gele, tropical tea sandwiches with exotic chicken, mango & macadamia nuts on Hawaiian bread, mermaid's jewel souffles, tropical fruit sorbet, key lime cheesecake & candy lime, Lisa's brewed loose tea.

$8.95-$12.00 Tea Plates Around The World. Tea sandwiches, miniature scones, Devonshire cream & tea geles. Add $3.00-$3.50 for a pot of brewed tea,

$7.50 Tea & Tea Sandwiches... Your choice of tea served with a combination of different tea sandwiches.

TEATIME: 10:00am To 9:00pm • Monday Thru Friday
• 10:00am To 8:00pm, Saturday • 11:00am To 7:00pm, Sunday
• May Accommodate Some Dietary Needs With Advance Request
• 99.6% Caffeine-Free Tea Available
• Children's Tea Parties Welcome
• Wheelchair Accessible • Watercloset: Same Floor
• **Reservations Are Suggested**
• Mall Parking
• Credit Cards: MC,V&JCB
Proprietor's
*Autograph*_____*Date*_____

101

THE VILLAGE FLORIST
& Tea Cottage

116 West Foothill Boulevard
Glendora, California

626-857-7264

It's Teatime At...The Village Florist & Tea Cottage. This sweet tea "cottage" is situated inside of a working flower shop. Georgina is the artistic proprietor & floral designer. I particularly like some of the whimsical touches here like the faux, painted-on-the-floor "rugs" and the "experienced" teapots which now reside atop the dividing wall. Allow time to browse in the gift shop. I discovered treasures cleverly displayed in a vintage suitcase.

Georgina will makes you feel right at home. Her Afternoon Teas are served at tables set with mismatched everything from vintage tablecloths & napkins to fresh flowers in well-worn teapots. The shop is conveniently laid out and quite conducive to private tea parties for up to 25 guests. Ask about the Holiday Open House in November with complimentary confections. The village business district participates with a tree lighting ceremony & horse drawn carriage rides, please call for date. F.Y.I. Senior discounts offered.

$9.95 Full Tea... Six assorted finger sandwiches, homemade buttermilk scone with cream & jam, butter cookie with boysenberry filling, fresh fruit, dessert & pot of brewed loose tea.

$5.50 Tea & Scone... Seasonal fresh fruit, buttermilk scone served with cream & jam and a pot of brewed loose tea.

TEATIME: 11am-5pm • Monday-Saturday • Last seating 2:30pm
- May Accommodate Some Dietary Needs, 2 Day Advance Request
- Non-Caffeine/Herbal Tea Available
- Children's Tea Parties Welcome
- Watercloset: Same Floor
- **Reservations Are Required**
- Free Off-Street Parking
- Credit Cards: V,MC&D

Proprietor's
*Autograph*_____*Date*_____

THE PICKET FENCE
Tea Room & Gift Shop
18121 Chatsworth Street
(Granada Village Shopping Center)
Granada Hills, California

818-831-0037

New Tearoom Brewing... **It's Teatime At The Picket Fence.** "From the white picket fence to the front porch & French doors, the ambiance at The Picket Fence is strictly American" says Linda, the proprietor of this new tearoom. Linda has owned a gift shop for years, and we've been talking about her dream of adding a tearoom for quite sometime.

Afternoon Tea will be presented from tiered caddies at tables set with Battenburg tablecloths, cloth napkins, custom-made china & fresh flowers. Garden murals, hunter green carpeting, porch posts & white lace will transport you to a leisurely summer day! Allow time to browse, the work of local artists and tea treasures are everywhere. Private tea parties available for up to 30 guests.

$16.00 High Tea... Quiche or Pastie, tea sandwiches, tea cakes, scone, Devon cream, mini pastries, pot of brewed loose tea.

$13.00 Afternoon Tea... Assorted finger sandwiches, scone with Devon cream, mini pastry, a pot of brewed loose tea.

$10.00 Spa Tea... Fresh fruit, salad or soup, sugar-free cookie, and a pot of brewed loose tea.

$6.00 Cream Tea... Scone, Devon cream & jam & tea.

ANTICIPATED **TEATIME:** 10:00am-4pm, Monday Thru Saturday
- 12Noon To 4:00pm, Sunday
- Non-Caffeine/Herbal Tea Available
- Children's Tea Parties Welcome
- Watercloset: Same Floor • Wheelchair Accessible
- **Reservations Are Suggested**
- Free Parking Lot
- Credit Cards: MC,V,DIS&AE

Proprietor's
*Autograph*_____*Date*_____

CAMELLIA INN B&B

211 North Street
(North of Santa Rosa)
Healdsburg, California

707-433-8182   **1-800-727-8182**

Special Event & Benefit Teas At...Camellia Inn B&B. Special event teas take place four times a year at this award winning historic Italianate Victorian House, built in 1869. One of the popular benefit Afternoon Teas assists Canine Companions for Independence (C.C.I.). 100% of the proceeds goes directly to the organization. Other ongoing benefit teas are for H.E.L.P., and The Historical Society. Look for the Children's Fashion Tea in April, and a Mother's Day Tea in May, do call for dates and reservations.

Afternoon Tea is presented from silver trays and a silver tea service, buffet style in the Inn's large double parlor. Tables are set with tablecloths, fresh flowers, and Delmas's personal collection of fine china. The room is beautifully filled with antiques,Victorian couches and warm family mementos. If you have time, ask for a tour of the Inn and the grounds too. They are graced with the beauty of more than 50 varieties of camellias and azaleas. Tea trivia: Did you know that the tea plant is taxonomically known as Camellia Sinensis? P.S. Private tea parties are available for your own special events for up to 40 guests.

$10.00 Camellia Afternoon Tea...($6.00 Children under 12) Selection of tea sandwiches such as chicken salad in puff shells with Kiwi chutney, signature sweets, which often include lemon bars and mints, and a pot of brewed loose tea.

SPECIAL EVENT & BENEFIT TEAS: Please Call For Schedule
- Children's Tea Parties Welcome
- Watercloset: Same Floor
- **Reservations Are Required**
- Parking Area And Street Park
- Cash Or Check

Proprietor's
*Autograph*_____*Date*_____

HEALDSBURG INN
On The Plaza

110 Matheson Street
Healdsburg, California

707-433-6991   **800-431-8663**

New Addition...It's Time For Tea & A Tour On Fridays, Saturdays & Sundays At...Healdsburg Inn On The Plaza. You'll step back in time when you enter this charming B&B hotel located in Healdsburg's turn of the century Wells Fargo Express Building. Genny the proprietor will be happy to point out many of the Inn's architectural details which include vaulted skylights, arches, corbels and turn of the century chandeliers.

Afternoon Tea is served on the second floor up two flights of stairs, in the Solarium Tea Room. Tea service includes fresh flowers, linen tablecloths, English "Crown" teacups, a lovely silver tea service, and Irish or classical music. Private tea parties for adults and children are welcome for up to 20 guests. A special children's menu is available. Please call for general information, room fee, and to reserve your special event date. P.S. Allow time to browse through the gift shop located on the first floor.

$9.50 Afternoon Tea... Savory sandwiches, homemade scones served with Devonshire cream, lemon curd & jam, lemon curd, assorted tasty desserts, and a pot of brewed loose tea.

TEATIME: 2:30 To 4:30pm • Friday, Saturday & Sunday
• May Accommodate Some Dietary Needs With Advance Request
• Non-Caffeine/Herbal Tea Available
• Children's Tea parties Welcome
• Watercloset: Same Floor
• **Reservations Are Required**
• Limited Time Street Parking, Nearby Lot
• Credit Cards: V&MC

Proprietor's
*Autograph*_____*Date*_____

Have you and your sister dreamed of opening a tearoom?

SISTERS' SECRET GARDEN
1312 West Florida Avenue
Hemet, California

909-658-6461

New Addition...It's Teatime At...Sisters' Secret Garden. It's no secret that these sisters enjoy reminiscing about the late nineteenth century. The walls are adorned with old family photographs, fabulous outfits & flamboyant hats. And do they have hats! Some have appeared in movies like Gigi, & A Streetcar Named Desire. Rosalind Russell's hat from, His Girl Friday is here too.

Afternoon Tea is attentively served from three tiered caddies at tables set with tablecloths, fresh flowers and beautiful menus. June and Marlene take great pride in their homemade specialties tastefully named to honor some of their Victorian ancestors. There are many a la carte delectables as well. June's sweet husband of some 40 years, emphasizes that gentlemen are very welcome here. Private tea parties are available for 7 to 37 guests indoors, or outdoors weather permitting. Allow time to browse through the gift shop. P.S. Look for the "sisters' parlour."

$9.75 Grandmother Tinnie's Tea... Soup of the day, crisp green salad with Sisters's secret dressing, tea sandwiches, scone with berries & Devonshire cream, and a pot of brewed tea.

$8.75 Aunt Clementine's Collection... Crisp garden salad with Sister's secret dressing, assortment of tea sandwiches, scone with berries & Devonshire cream, and a pot of brewed tea.

TEATIME:11am-3pm • Monday-Friday • 11am-3pm,Saturday
• May Accommodate Some Dietary Needs With Advance Request
• Non-Caffeine/Herbal Tea Available
• Children's Tea Parties Welcome
• Watercloset: Same Floor • Wheelchair Accessible
• **Reservations Are Required**
• Free Parking Lot
• Cash Or Check Only
Proprietor's
*Autograph*_____*Date*_____

VICTORIAN DAWN MANSION
13567 Main Street
Hesperia, California

760-949-2055

New Addition..It's Teatime At...Victorian Dawn Mansion. "Please have a seat and relax over our delectable Afternoon Teas." There are many interesting theme teas here, ask about "Queen for a Day Tea" complete with dazzling borrowed tiara, velvet cape & throne or, host your own tea tyme party. Business associations, women's ministries, organizations and dear friends will find Victorian Dawn a neat place to meet.

Afternoon Teas are served at tables set with lace tablecloths, vintage mis-matched china and unique centerpieces which often include flower-filled purses & vintage teapots. The tearoom is beautifully decorated by Janie and her manager Linda. Victorian Dawn includes a lovely gift & antique shop. F.Y.I. Expansion plans are underway and will more than double seating. Monthly Theme Teas, "Garden Party Fashion Show," and "Nation's First Ladies' Tea," are very popular so call for the schedule and reserve your spot early. Private tea parties and special events are available in the Victorian Gazebo Garden. P.S. Bring your camera.

$13.50 Afternoon Tea Tyme... Tea sandwiches, scone, Devonshire cream & preserves, fruit, dessert, brewed loose tea.
$10.95 Fairy Princess "Dress Up" Birthday Tea Party... Per Child. (Birthday Girl $17.95, receives a fairy halo & wand.) Dress-up accessories, tea-etiquette lessons, British party favors, tea sandwiches, fresh fruit, dessert or custom birthday cake.
$5.95 Dessert Tea. Fresh fruit, dessert, brewed loose tea.

TEATIME: 10:00am To 5:00pm • Tuesday Thru Saturday
• May Accommodate Some Dietary Needs With Advance Request
• Non-Caffeine/Herbal Tea Available
• Watercloset: Same Floor • Children's Tea Parties Very Welcome
• **24 Hour Advance Reservation Required**
• Free Parking Lot
• Credit Cards: MC,V&DIS
Proprietor's
Autograph _____Date_____

ALISON'S ESPRESSO CAFE

5930 Warner Avenue (Shopping Plaza)
Huntington Beach, California

714-377-2028

**New Addition...It's Teatime On Mondays At...
Alison's Espresso Cafe.** (By Reservation Only) This quaint
establishment is an unexpected surprise neatly tucked away in a
shopping plaza. Enjoy Victorian style ambiance at Alison's with
soothing classical background music, green wicker, floral cushioned
chairs, potted palms, antique furnishings, family heirlooms, framed
teapot & teacups prints and a neat "copper" ceiling treatment. Pop in
for a "spotta," & a scone, sweet dessert or light gourmet specialty
Monday thru Sunday, but do plan for the Monday Afternoon Tea.
      Monday...is teatime! The four course Afternoon Tea is
served at tables set with fresh flowers, antique silver, and unique
china pieces from Alison's own family collection. Everything here is
homemade down to the adorable white or milk chocolate tea mints.
F.Y.I. Tea parties for groups may take place after 1:00pm on
Saturdays & Sundays for 15 to 30 guests. P.S. Alison's also caters
tea parties for adults and children. "Just Ask Alison!"

$14.50 Four Course Afternoon Tea... Assorted tea
sandwiches tied in ribbons & flowers, tea breads such as: chocolate
chip scone or heart-shaped nutmeg scone with Devonshire cream &
preserves, petite cranberry walnut muffin or carrot bread, a small
mixed green salad tossed with raspberry vinaigrette, fresh pears,
walnuts & feta cheese, lemon curd tartlet, petite pecan-rum cake,
chocolate dipped strawberries, mint, and a pot of brewed loose tea.

TEATIME MONDAY: Seatings: 10:30am & 2:00pm
- May Accommodate Some Dietary Needs With Advance Request
- Non-Caffeine/Herbal Tea Available
- Children's Tea Parties Welcome
- Watercloset: Same Floor
- **Reservations Are Required**
- Free Parking Lot
- Cash Only

Proprietor's
*Autograph*_____*Date*_____

WILDFLOWER TEA ROOM
inside The Bread Basket

54710 North Circle Drive
Idyllwild, California
(5,500 Ft. Elevation)

909-659-3506 Or 909-659-2070

New Addition...It's Teatime At...The Bread Basket's Wildflower Tea Room. On the second & fourth Wednesday of the month, Santy & David's Wildflower Tea Room awaits your discovery. It's a cheery spot decorated with honey-colored wood wainscoting, petite flower wallpaper & colorful framed prints. Tea may also be served outside weather permitting, on the patio shaded by several creamy colored market umbrellas.

Afternoon Teas reflect seasonal themes and are presented on three tiered caddies at tables set with print and solid tablecloths, toppers, silver tea strainers, lacey cloth napkins and a flowery collection of antique china and silver. F.Y.I. Private tea parties are available for 20 to 60 guests; The Breadbasket can also cater tea parties. You may want to stop by the bakery before leaving and take home some of Tut's famous scones, breads and fancy desserts.

$14.95 Sweet William... Glass of Champagne, tea sandwiches, soup or salad, fresh fruit, two scones with sweet cream & raspberry preserves, two petit fours, surprise sweet, and a pot of Fortnum & Mason or P.G. Tips brewed loose tea.

$7.95 Sweet Pea... Children under 10 years. Assorted sandwiches, soup or salad, fresh fruit, two scones with sweet cream & raspberry preserves, a petit four, surprise sweet, lemonade or tea.

TEATIME: 4:00pm • Second & Fourth Wednesday, Monthly
• May Accommodate Some Dietary Needs With Advance Request
• Non-Caffeine/Herbal Tea Available
• Children's Tea Parties Welcome, Ages 4+
• Watercloset: One Flight Up
• **Reservations Are Required**
• Free Parking Lot
• Credit Cards: V,MC,DIS&AE

Proprietor's
Autograph _____*Date*_____

JULIAN TEA & COTTAGE ARTS
(60 Miles NE Of San Diego, Elevation 4200 Feet)
2124 Third Street
Julian, California

760-765-0TEA(0832)

New Addition...It's Teatime At...Julian Tea & Cottage Arts. The Bailey-King house built in 1898 is the home of Julian Tea & Cottage Arts. Edie has diligently restored this 100 year old house built by Clarence King on the site of the city's old Town Hall. F.Y.I. Julian is modeled after gold towns that beckoned men west in search of glittering opportunities. P.S. King is credited with discovering The Golden Chariot Mine.

Please make reservations for Afternoon Tea, but "Drop In For Tea", is just that. Both are served in the first floor tearoom with trees in view and the sounds of horse-drawn carriages clip-clopping to the rhythmic chimes of nearby church bells. The room is predominately white, with accents of hunter green & rose. Beautiful antique linens are used at tea along with a collection of fine china, silver, and fresh seasonal centerpieces. The second floor is a gallery reserved for artists. The proprietors is herself a weaver and has created a spot for other local artisans to exhibit their work. P.S. Private tea parties are available for up to 10 guests.

$7.95 Afternoon Tea... Finger sandwiches, homemade scones with cream & just-picked homemade fruit jam, fresh baked dessert such as: apple/walnut cake, date-nut pudding, or peach shortbread and a continuous cup of brewed Yorkshire Gold tea.

$5.25 "Drop In For Tea"... Homemade sweet of the day or scone or muffin or English biscuits & continuous cup of tea.

TEATIME: 12-3:00pm, Thursday-Monday
- May Accommodate Some Dietary Needs With Advance Request
- Non-Caffeine/Herbal Tea Available
- Children's Tea Parties Welcome
- Watercloset & Tea Room: First Floor
- **Reservations Are Appreciated For Afternoon**
- Front & Rear Parking
- Credit Cards: MC,V&AE

Proprietor's
*Autograph*_____Date_____

TURNABOUT TEA CUP

1432 Foothill Boulevard
La Canada, California

818-790-3342

It's Teatime At...Turnabout Tea Cup. They say, it's like having tea in the garden when you visit this darling antique & tea shop. Long time friends Ann & Lou created a wonderful warm & friendly atmosphere here, and they have welcomed Sharon, their dear friend and now proprietor with all their hearts. Sharon always has a friendly smile for you, and is pleased to help you with all of your tea party plans from invitations & tea-favors to a custom menu.

Afternoon Teas are served in a bright & cheery light-filled room at tables set with collectible vintage tablecloths, fresh flowers, & lovely Noritake fine bone china. Allow time to browse, there are wonderful collectibles & antiques at the shop, I always find something I can't live without. The shop is extra pretty at Christmas time, I love the Victorian teacup tree, and was even inspired to make my own. Alas, my little tree doesn't hold a teacup to Lou's! F.Y.I. You'll enjoy Turnabout's own blend of tea & other specialties, they're quite good & make great gifts. Special event teas and classes are held throughout the year, call for schedule. P.S. Private tea parties are available on Sundays for 15 to 40 guests. Enjoy!

$12.95 High Tea... Four assorted tea sandwiches, scone with cream & jam, two sweets, pot of brewed loose tea.
$9.25 Afternoon Tea... Two assorted tea sandwiches, a scone served with cream & jam, a sweet & a pot of brewed tea.
$2.50 Pot of Tea... Add a sweet too for $1.75
$5.50 Cream Tea... Two scones & a pot of brewedtea.

TEATIME: 10:30am To 4:00pm • Tuesday Thru Saturday
• May Accommodate Some Dietary Needs With Advance Request
• Non-Caffeine/Herbal Tea Available
• Children's Tea Parties Welcome, Ages Six years up
• Watercloset: Same Floor
• **Reservations Are Advised**
• Small Rear Lot & Unmetered Street Parking
• Credit Cards: MC,V&DIS

Proprietor's
*Autograph*_____*Date*_____

LISA'S TEA TREASURES
71 Lafayette Circle
Lafayette, California

510-283-2226

It's Teatime At...Lisa's Tea Treasures. This 75 year old cottage with an attractive burgundy awning is home to Lisa's Tea Treasures. Tea lovers enjoy fine tea & treats here in an atmosphere of old world elegance. A wide selection of teas may accompany your Morning, Afternoon or Evening Tea meal. Allow time to browse, the shop's gift parlour has an extensive selection of fine china, tea ware and gourmet food items, many of which are exclusively imported by Lisa's Tea Treasures.

Doreen serves Afternoon Tea in the beautifully decorated Parlour Room, Garden Room, Hunt Room or Rose Room. Lisa's Tea Treasures' menus feature savories, finger sandwiches, delicate tea cakes, scones & delicious pastries. P.S. There are many lovely and unique gifts here, some created by the proprietor herself as well as other local artisans. These teapots, teacups, jams, fruit curds and of course tea, make elegant yet practical gifts that are certain to please. Ask about the monthy Afternoon Tea special at $14.95.

$12.00 To $13.95 Traditional Afternoon Tea Includes a pot of connoisseur full-leaf tea, tea sandwiches, savories and sweets. Nine fabulous selections.

$5.50 To $12.85 Light Afternoon Delights Tea Includes a pot of connoisseur full-leaf tea, with a sampling of scones, savories and sweets. Nine fabulous selections.

TEATIME: 11am-5:30pm, Monday-Saturday • 12-5:30pm, Sunday
- Monday Hours Are Seasonal, Please Call To Confirm
- 99.6% Caffeine-Free Tea Available
- Children's Tea Parties Welcome
- Watercloset: Same Floor
- **Reservations Are Suggested**
- Limited-Time Street Parking
- Credit Cards: V&MC

Proprietor's
*Autograph*_____*Date*_____

TEA FOR TWO
424 Forest Avenue
Laguna Beach, California

714-494-7776

New Addition...Tea Symposiums, Theme Teas, Tea Tastings & Tea Gifts At...Tea For Two. Welcome to a lovely gift shop that will suit you to a T. The proprietor does everything in an impressive fashion. This bright and cheerful spot has elegant treasures and tea accoutrements from all over the world.

You'll enjoy speaking with Pat and her friendly staff who are more than happy to help you pick out that something special from over 1,000 tea-related items. They are knowledgeable about fine teas in fact, Tea For Two now has its own handsomely packaged blend of tea along with a number of other exclusive Tea For Two, specialty items. Drop by for a tasting, ask about the white chocolate teapot and the Earl Grey bonbons.

Educational and entertaining tea symposiums usually include Afternoon Tea and take place quarterly on scheduled Saturdays or Sundays at various locations in Laguna Beach. Please call for information, location and reservations. Tea experts, authors and other specialists are often featured guests. Look for forthcoming products on their web site: teafortwo.com

$35.00ish...Tea Program & Afternoon Tea... As Scheduled...Afternoon Tea presented in three courses, fresh baked scones served with lemon curd, cream and preserves, tea sandwiches, specialty desserts, chocolate truffle and a continuously poured cup of Tea For Two's own blend. (Per person plus tax)

TEA GIFTS & MORE: 10:00am To 6:00pm • Seven Days A Week
- Please Call For Extended Seasonal Hours
- Tea Symposiums, As Scheduled
- **Advance Reservations And Prepay Required For Tea Events**
- Watercloset: Same Floor
- Free Parking Behind Store
- Credit Cards:V,MC,DIS&AE

Proprietor's
*Autograph*_____*Date*_____

JANE'S SECRET GARDEN CAFE

8384 La Mesa Boulevard
La Mesa, California

619-464-0611

New Addition...It's Teatime At...Jane's Secret Garden. If it was a secret, it won't be a secret any more. Jane's is a wonderful cafe with a gourmet kitchen & bakery on premises. They create a full menu of delicacies in addition to the Teas. The Victorian High Tea is served in the dining room, while the entertaining Saturday Theme Teas are served on the second floor, one flight up in the Tearoom. An arbor, fountain & hand painted mural along the back & side walls set the mood for the fun ahead. Wear a hat or borrow one if you like on the way to the tearoom.

Unique Saturday Theme Teas are served at tables set with tablecloths, fine china & fresh flowers. Something fun is always going on here. Private tea parties are available for up to 60 guests. Jane's is located in a quaint shopping area so you can stroll off the sweets! F.Y.I.There really is a secret garden & there really is a Jane, see if you can find them both! P.S. A harpist plays on Sundays.

$14.95 Children's Tea Parties. (Price is per child, minimum 10 children.) Sandwiches, fresh fruit, scone, cream & jam, muffin & decorated birthday cake. Games, prizes & favors!
$11.95 Saturday Theme & Victorian High Teas Tea sandwich, petite quiche, fresh fruit, delicious muffin, scone served with cream & jam, surprise dessert, and a pot of brewed loose tea.
$8.95 Children's High Tea...12 Years & under.

TEATIME: 7:00am To 2:00pm • Victorian High Tea, Daily
- 11:00am & 2:00pm • Saturday Theme Teas • Call For Schedule
- May Accommodate Some Dietary Needs With Advance Request
- Non-Caffeine/Herbal Tea Available
- Children's Tea Parties Welcome
- Watercloset: First Floor On The Main Dining Room Level
- Wheelchair Accessible First Floor Only
- **Reservations Are Required For All Teas**
- Metered Street Parking
- Credit Cards: V&MC

Proprietor's
*Autograph*_____*Date*_____

WHISTLE STOP
Cafe & Tea Room

412 West Avenue "J" Suite B
Lancaster, California

805-726-7214

New Addition...Tea Parties For Groups At... Whistle Stop Cafe & Tea Room. Here's a spot you'll be glad you stopped at! It's ok to "toot" your own whistle Amanda, you're doing a fine job. Dress-Up Birthday Tea Parties for adults & children are the tearoom's specialty. Boys & girls find "costumes" in the Dress-Up Room where they borrow hats, gloves, high heeled shoes & jewelry for their dramatic entrance to tea. P.S. Adults are invited to borrow hats & accessories too at fun-filled tea parties.

Afternoon Teas are presented on three tiered caddies at tables set with mis-matched vintage china. The tearoom is decorated with roses and Amanda's favorite rosy tones. Miss Amanda serves, and entertains with memorable stories. She credits Emily Post for her proper etiquette and passes along many helpful tips to her guests. Tea parties are available for 6 to 36 guests. B.Y.O.Birthday cake. F.Y.I. A you may want to purchase a video of the event for $15.00.

$12.50 Adult Birthday Teas... Tea sandwiches, scone, whipped butter & jam, dessert, pot of tea, a handmade doll as a gift.
$12.50 Bear Necessity Tea Party.. Sandwiches, fruit, scone, whipped butter & jam, punch or tea & handmade doll gift.
$10.00 Queen's Full English Tea... Tea sandwiches, scone, whipped butter & jam, dessert, pot of brewed loose tea.

TEA PARTIES FOR GROUPS: Please Call To Plan
- Usually Scheduled On Saturdays & Sundays
- May Accommodate Some Dietary Needs With Advance Request
- Non-Caffeine/Herbal Tea Available
- Children's Tea Parties Welcome, Ages 7+
- Watercloset: Same Floor • Wheelchair Accessible
- **24 Hour Advance Reservation Required**
- Free Parking Lot
- Cash Or Check Only

Proprietor's
*Autograph*_____*Date*_____

LA QUINTA RESORT & Club

49499 Eisenhower Drive
La Quinta, California

760-564-4111

It's Teatime In The Desert At...La Quinta Resort & Club. This legendary hideaway is regarded as one of the most distinctive resorts in the Palm Springs area. Built in 1926, it is also happens to be the oldest resort. La Quinta was a favorite retreat for the stars of Hollywood's "Golden Era" and served as an inspiration for Frank Capra's, "It Happened One Night".

Afternoon Tea is a seasonal experience at La Quinta. Tea season usually starts in October and runs through May. A delightful, casual Afternoon Tea is served in the Santa Rosa Room with its comfy country Spanish decor. The room has white walls with soft turquoise & peach tone accents, a large archway, and an authentic, original hotel window. On a chilly afternoon, you may enjoy tea by the two-way fireplace. P.S. Peek into the teapot buffet which houses terrific collectible teapots for your viewing pleasure.

$9.75 Afternoon Tea... Assorted tea sandwiches such as smoked Scottish salmon or egg mousse, Scottish brandied currant scone with sweet cream butter & preserves, tea breads, French pastries, and an individual pot of brewed loose tea.

TEATIME: 2:00pm To 5:00pm • Wednesday Thru Sunday
- In Season, Usually October Thru May, Please Call For Dates
- May Accommodate Some Dietary Needs With Advance Request
- Non-Caffeine/Herbal Tea Available
- Watercloset: Same Floor
- Wheelchair Accessible
- **Reservations Are Recommended**
- Validated Parking
- Credit Cards: MC,V&AE

L'autograph
*du Concierge*_____*Date*_____

CHAI OF LARKSPUR
25 Ward Street
Larkspur, California

415-945-7161

New Addition...It's Teatime At...Chai Of Larkspur. Betty is the knowledgeable and friendly proprietor of Chai, located adjacent to a California historic preservation district. She has re-invented Afternoon Tea to the delight of tea lovers who voted Chai the best Tea Salon in a 1996 "San Francisco Focus" critics restaurant poll.

Chai Of Larkspur enjoys a rich yet serene ambiance thanks to the "weaving together" of colorful European and exotic Chinese motifs. Eggplant-tone rattan chairs and large shade umbrellas will beckon you outdoors to dine in the flowering courtyard. Or if you wish, dine in the parlor surrounded by a cache of tea treasures from around the world. Chai is many things to many people, an exotic romantic spot, a comfortable place for meeting friends, and an inspiring spot for individuals taking tea alone with Betty. Private tea parties are available for 8 to 50 guests, please call for information. F.Y.I. Chai's menu is quite varied, this is just a taste.

$23.00 The Blues & Jazz With Tea...A delicious Chai sampler tray, tax & gratuity included. Presented on the fourth Saturday of the month. Dine at 7:00pm, concert at 7:30pm.

$17.00 Chai Classic...A selection of tea sandwiches featuring cucumber, pear, toasted walnuts, and smoked salmon with seasoned spreads, scone served with Devonshire cream, lemon curd & preserves, lemon curd squares, spiced apple bread, shortbread cookies and a continuous pot of brewed loose tea.

TEATIME: Noon To 7:00pm • Sunday Thru Thursday
• Noon To 10:30pm • Friday & Saturday • Closed Monday
• May Accommodate Some Dietary Needs With Advance Request
• Non-Caffeine/Herbal Tea Available
• Wheelchair Accessible
• **Reservations Welcomed**
• Free City Parking Lot
• Credit Cards: MC&V
Proprietor's
*Autograph*_____*Date*_____

BRISTOL FARMS

2080 Bellflower Boulevard
Long Beach, California

562-430-4134

   New Addition...Host A Tea Party With Help From Bristol Farms. Teas, as we all know are fun & popular events for any or no occasion at all! I'm often asked at book signings about my own tea parties. Afternoon Teas at home are especially fun for me because I get a chance to be creative and bring out my pretty vintage plates, teacups, teapots, vases & Victorian lace. I keep my list of guests to eight friends for ease of conversation. Setting the table the day before really saves time. I also set a tea strainer for each guest.
   Early in the day I pick dewy garden flowers, plunge them into squeaky clean vases of water and head to Bristol Farms in South Pasadena. I buy one large container each of tuna, chicken & seafood salads. Next, a stop at their bakery for 24 pre-ordered mini, or 8 large scones, 3 different loaves of bread for cookie-cutter shaped tea sandwiches and a dozen mini chocolate eclairs and cream puffs. I choose two 16 oz. jars of preserves & 3 small jars of lemon curd. I make my own cream, but they usually have clotted cream if you like. Edible blossoms, strawberries, grapes, kiwi, bananas & star fruit are a must. An extra bunch of flowers, and I'm off! To make your tea party more fun & "interactive" ask each of your guests to bring a different small package of tea. With individual teapots, it encourages tea-tasting & is a neat conversation facilitator. (But that's another book!) With 8 guests it's easier to have plates preset with 3 tea sandwiches, edible flowers, melange of fruit and a "teacup" of soup, made from 4 packages of creamy asparagus soup to which I add pre-cooked fresh asparagus bits. Scones are on individual plates. My bread pudding made from bread crusts is great! F.Y.I.If you prefer, pick-up a catered tea from Bristol Farms.

TEATIME SHOPPING: 8:00am To 10:00pm • Seven Days A Week
• May Accommodate Some Dietary Needs With Advance Request
• Tins Of Non-Caffeine/Herbal Tea Available
• Wheelchair Accessible • Watercloset: Same Floor
• Large Free Parking Lot
• Credit Cards:V,MC,DIS&AE
Manager's
*Autograph*_____*Date*_____

Vermont   Pleasure

From Tetley USA, Inc.

5 Tetley tea bags   1teaspoon Ground cinnamon
4 cups of water   3/4 cup vanilla ice cream
2-3 Tablespoons Maple syrup

Place tea bags, syrup and 3/4 teaspoon
Cinnamon in teapot. Pour in 4 cups
boiling water. Steep, covered, 5 minutes.
Remove tea bags, pour into mugs, and
top with small scoop of ice cream and
dusting of cinnamon. Serves 5

Afternoon   Tea-cher

By Thea Tyme

All day long I dream of tea
and tearooms yet to visit

I watch the clock and wait for three
my bag is in hand, I'm ready to flee!

A teacher's job is most rewarding
exhausting, challenging, never boring

By Friday I'm plum out of steam
to pooped to participate, only to dream

of Afternoon Tea, and a lottery scheme!

ELISE'S TEA ROOM & Gifts

3930 Atlantic Avenue
Long Beach, California

562-424-2134

New Addition...It's Teatime At...Elise's Tea Room & Gifts. A coral & teal colored awning welcomes you to Elise's dream, her lovely and comfortable tearoom which she invites all to enjoy. This sweet proprietor takes great pride in her pretty tearoom and hopes to delight your senses with her charming teas.

Afternoon Tea is graciously served at tables set with fresh flowers, floral topped tablecloths, cloth napkins and English bone china from Elise's personal collection. The tearoom is decorated with soft pink colored walls, pink floral wallpaper, antique chairs, some with tapestry seats and an elegant mint green drapery swag. Classical music too. A full menu of specialties is also available. There are many tea treasures in the boutique for your gift giving pleasure, so do allow extra time. P.S. Private tea parties for adults and children are welcome for up to 40 guests. Ask about Tea Dance classes on Sundays with Elise's husband Dr. Marcos.

$9.50 Afternoon Tea... Twelve finger sandwiches, scones with cream & jam, fancy dessert, pot of brewed loose tea.
$8.50 Alice In Wonderland Tea... Two large finger sandwiches, scone with cream & jam, dessert, brewed loose tea.
$5.50 Light Tea... Three assorted finger sandwiches, two scones with cream & jam, petite dessert, brewed loose tea.

TEATIME: 10am-6pm • Tuesday Thru Saturday • 12-4pm, Sunday
• May Accommodate Some Dietary Needs With Advance Request
• Non-Caffeine/Herbal Tea Available
• Children's Tea Parties Welcome
• Watercloset: Same Floor
• Wheelchair Accessible
• **Reservations For Five Or More Recommended**
• Free Parking Lot In Rear
• Credit Cards: V,MC&DIS

Proprietor's
*Autograph*_____*Date*_____

VINTAGE TEA LEAF
969 East Broadway
Long Beach, California

562-435-5589

New Addition...It's Teatime At...Vintage Tea Leaf. How nice to hear about Vintage Tea Leaf, and Beverly's many creative ideas and signature touches such as the optional "meet new people over tea" tables. Another novel idea was to use an antique bank counter for a tea bar. Before tea, guests are invited to select a vintage teacup for their Afternoon Tea service.

Afternoon Tea is presented from two or three tiered caddies at antique tables set with linens, English bone china teacups, & centerpieces of fresh flowers arranged in teacups, creamers & sugar bowls. The Vintage Tea Leaf has stately decor with dark burgundy walls and gold-leaf wallpaper. Beverly calls it "antique-eclectic" not frilly. The shop carries a wide variety of tea books, brewing accessories, jewelry, tea-theme gifts, wedding accessories, "one-of-a-kinds," the works of local artists, even fresh flowers. A full menu is offered in addition to several Afternoon Teas selection. Ask about tea classes, tea-tastings and private tea parties for 15 to 50 guests. P.S. Approximately 70 International teas are sold here. F.Y.I. Your pots of tea are infused with mountain spring water. Theme Teas too!

$16.00 Vintage Rose Tea... Four assorted tea sandwiches, scone with Devonshire cream & lemon curd, tea bundt cake, vintage chocolate treat, pot of brewed tea.
$9.00 Vintage Petit Tea.. Two assorted tea sandwiches, scone, Devonshire cream & lemon curd, small pot of brewed tea.

TEATIME:11:30am To 6:00pm • Saturday, Sunday & Monday
• 11:30am-7pm, Wednesday, Thursday & Friday • Closed Tuesday
• Non-Caffeine/Herbal Tea Available
• Children's Tea Parties Welcome
• Wheelchair Accessible • Watercloset: Same Floor
• **Reservations For Groups Of Six Or More**
• Free Street Parking
• Credit Cards: MC,V,DIS&AE

Proprietor's
*Autograph*_____*Date*_____

THE BUTLER'S PANTRY

305 Second Street
Los Altos, California

415-941-9676

New Proprietor...It's Teatime At...The Butler's Pantry. This tearoom was once again voted one of the top five restaurants in the Bay Area by the San Jose Mercury Daily News. Enjoy an English country home atmosphere with Rosina, the shop's new proprietor. The creamy textured walls striped in blue, burgundy & green, nicely accent the rotating collection of local artists.

Afternoon Tea is presented from three tiered caddies at tables set with fresh flowers, linens and "Memories" English bone china. The Butler's new Gift Pantry is located in the lobby and features imported foods & gifts. Ask about children's etiquette classes, and the December Holiday Tea with Santa and carolers. Private tea parties and catering are also available. Please call to plan.

$14.95 High Tea... Tea sandwiches, scone with cream & preserves. Or, The Butler's Savory Pastry Plate & scone with Devon & preserves, salad & a pot of the special tea room blend.
$7.95 Light Morning Or Afternoon Tea...10-Noon & 3:00pm Daily. Sandwich, hors d'oeuvres, 2 mini fruit scones, Devon cream & preserves, petit four and a pot of brewed loose tea.
$7.95 Children's Tea. Peanut butter & jelly sandwiches, scone, teddy cookie, petit four, raspberry tea or black-currant fizz.
$6.95 Cream Tea... English fruited scone with choice of preserves & Devon cream and a pot of brewed loose tea.

TEATIME: 9:00am To 5:00pm • Monday Thru Friday
• 10:00am To 5:00pm, Saturday •10:00 To 4:00pm, Sunday
• May Accommodate Some Dietary Needs, 3 Day Advance Request
• Non-Caffeine/Herbal Tea Available
• Watercloset: Down The Hall
• Wheelchair Accessible
• **Reservations Are Recommended**
• Free Limited-time Parking Lot Nearby
• Credit Cards: V,MC,DIS&AE
Proprietor's
Autograph_____Date_____

123

BLOOMINGDALES
59th & Lex
(Century City)
10250 Santa Monica Boulevard
Los Angeles, California

bloomingdale's

Extension 7189 **310-772-2100**

New Addition...It's Teatime At...Bloomingdales.
Leave it to Bloomingdales to discover my favorite things, shopping and Afternoon Tea. I was delighted to discover that not only did Bloomies come to California, but thanks to savvy management, they're now serving Afternoon Tea. I guess I can have it all!

Afternoon Tea is served in the restaurant known as "59th & Lex," an interesting crescent shaped room decorated in an unusual combination of soft muted colors. Comfy velvet banquettes & chairs upholstered in blue, gray green, yellow & purple designer fabrics pull up to tables designed with natural inlaid woods in a checkerboard effect. Black paper makes for an interesting table covering. The walls are colorfully adorned with framed cartoon prints from the New Yorker. Nicely coordinated, are the "Bloomie" attentive servers in Nicole Miller, or other trendy ties & aprons.

$9.50 Tea Time... Assorted petite finger sandwiches including, cucumber, tuna or chicken salad & turkey, chocolate ganache, and a pot of Tao Tea.

TEATIME: 2:30 To 5:00pm • Seven Days A Week
• May Accommodate Some Dietary Needs With Advance Request
• Non-Caffeine/Herbal Tea Available
• Watercloset: Ladies Same Floor, Gents One Floor Up
• Wheelchair Accessible
• **Reservations Not Required**
• Century City Parking, Three Hours Free
• Credit Cards: Bloomies, V,MC,DIS&AE
Manager's
*Autograph*_____*Date*_____

124

<u>S c o n e s</u>

Recipe by Chef Darin Sehnert, The Restaurant at Kellogg Ranch

2 Cups Flour
1 1/2 Teaspoons Baking Soda
2 Teaspoons Cream of Tartar
1 Tablespoon Sugar
1/4 Teaspoon Salt
4 Ounces Unsalted Butter
6 Ounces (3/4 Cup) Milk

Sift together all dry ingredients. Cut in butter until only small lumps remain. Make a well in the center, pour in milk and mix until just combined. Turn onto a floured board abd press enough to just pull dough together. Roll out to a thickness of 1/2" to 3/4". Cut out with cutters of desired shape. Place on heavy sheet pan. Brush with water and sprinkle with sugar. Bake in a 450 degree F. oven for 15 to 20 minutes until light brown in color.
Optional additions:

Cranberry Orange:
Mix into dry ingredients the minced zest of 2 oranges. Add 1/2 lb. chopped cranberries.

Raisin:
Mix 1/2 cup of raisins or dried currants into dough while stirring after adding the milk.

CHADO
8422 1/2 West Third Street
Los Angeles, California

213-655-2056

It's Teatime At...Chado... And Now A New Chado Tea Shop Too. A wall of canisters at Chado contains an impressive 250 Chado teas! Welcome to Chado, a neat spot for tealovers tea indulgence seeking "calm" in their hectic lives. Chado is located in the middle of a busy Los Angeles business and residential district close to the Beverly Center, and serves as an "island of tranquility" away from the area's hustle and bustle.

Chado sells all kinds of teas and tea accouterments. The proprietor also happens to be a tea importer and travels around the world bringing back an extraordinary selection of elegant teas. Devon is very interested in tea education and will be happy to familiarize you with the essence and varieties of teas. I have found my visits with him to be quite informative, and no doubt you will too. F.Y.I. Special Chado blend teas can be mail-ordered, please call for their catalog. Private tea parties are available on Sundays for up to 20 guests. P.S. No coffee here! **New Addition...**Visit the new **Chado Tea Shop** in the famous Farmer's Market in Los Angeles, stall #750. Approximately 100 bulk loose teas are available along with of course, a wonderful hot cuppa to go.

$15.00 Chado Afternoon Tea... Assorted finger sandwiches, fresh scone with clotted cream & preserves, fresh fruit, pastries and a pot of brewed bulk tea from Chado's 250 choices.

TEATIME: 11:30am To 5:00pm • Monday Thru Saturday
- Non-Caffeine/Herbal Tea Available
- Watercloset: Same Floor
- Wheelchair Accessible
- **Reservations Very Much Appreciated**
- Metered Street Parking
- Credit Cards: MC,V&AE

Proprietor's
*Autograph*_____*Date*_____

DUTTON'S
Brentwood Books

11975 San Vicente Boulevard
Los Angeles, California

310-476-6263   800-286-7323

Tea & Scones & Good Books Too At...Dutton's.
Some people know it as the bookstore with the red door, and this red door opens to reveal an eclectic independent bookstore with a spacious open-air courtyard. Vintage teapots & crockery are displayed along with over 300,000 books. Dutton's is a fun spot that features poetry readings and author book signing "teas."

The owner of the store prepares homebaked scones from his grandmother's recipe for those very special book events. Doug told me that when his grandmother moved to California she discovered a love for cooking with oranges. She especially liked the Mandarin variety that grew in their front yard. This particular scone recipe is what she served when her friends came to tea. Doug reconstructed his grandmother's scone recipe from lovingly well-worn notes and is pleased to feature it for special events at Dutton's Brentwood. P.S. You may want to call and ask to be on the mailing list for the bimonthly newsletter of events.

$5.00 Tea For Two... Share a pot of tea and a big heart-shaped blueberry scone. (Or, look for the tasty lemon cake.)

$3.00 Tea & A Scone... Cup of tea and a flower-shaped buttermilk scone.

TEA & SCONES & A GOOD BOOK: 11am To 5pm • Sunday
• 9am To 9pm, Monday Thru Friday • 9am To 6pm, Saturday
• Non-Caffeine/Herbal Tea Available
• Watercloset: Same Floor
• Wheelchair Accessible
• **Just Drop By**
• Free Parking Lot
• Credit Cards: V,MC&AE

Proprietor's
*Autograph*_____*Date*_____

FOUR SEASONS HOTEL

300 South Doheny Drive
Los Angeles, California

310-273-2222

It's Teatime At...Four Seasons Hotel. The elegant Four Season Hotel is located just a short distance to Beverly Hills. As one would expect the decor is beautiful with marble accented furnishings, grand exotic flower arrangements and a courteous staff. Afternoon Tea is served indoors in The Gardens Cafe, not to be confused with the adjacent dining room of similar name, The Garden's Restaurant. The Gardens Cafe is lovely casual room which offers an intimate, bright & airy setting.

Afternoon Tea is served at tables set with print floral skirts & white toppers, white Limoges china, and fresh flowers. The tearoom is decorated in creamy beige tones with arm chairs, banquettes, creamy colored drapes and two white columns. Parties of 16 or more guests may enjoy Afternoon Tea in the Garden Court, a private dining room at $22.00 per person plus a 20% service fee. Please call catering to plan your special event tea parties for larger groups. P.S. Here's a fun idea. Leave your cars parked at the hotel and grab a cab for the short ride to Rodeo Drive. You and your friends will have even *more* to talk about over tea!

$17.50 Traditional English Afternoon Tea. Open-faced tea sandwiches, English tea breads and pastries, freshly baked scones served with Devonshire cream & lemon curd and a pot of brewed loose tea. (Royal Tea: Add $5.50 for a glass of Louis Roederer Champagne.)

TEATIME: 3:00 To 4:30pm • Monday Thru Saturday
• May Accommodate Some Dietary Needs With Advance Request
• Non-Caffeine/Herbal Tea Available
• Wheelchair Accessible
• Watercloset: Same Floor
• **Reservations Are Required**
• Vaidated Self-Parking Or Valet Park $3.00
• Credit Cards: V,DC,MC,AE&JCB
L'autograph
*du Concierge*_____*Date*_____

HOTEL BEL-AIR
701 Stone Canyon Road
Los Angeles, California

310-472-1211

It's Teatime At...Hotel Bel-Air. Retreat up Stone Canyon Road to the Hotel Bel-Air. Long considered one of LA's "best kept secrets," the hotel is quite fabulous. Only 10 miles from the finest Beverly Hills shops, entertainment and offices, the secluded Hotel Bel-Air is surrounded by 11.5 acres of unhurried "Shangri-la." The hotel's main building is a two-story pink stucco 1920's mission-style structure crowned by a bell tower, and covered by lacey red-flowering trumpet vines.

Afternoon Tea is served in The Restaurant at the end of one of the graceful arcades. Tea is beautifully served from a three tiered caddie with blue and silver glass plates. Tea tables are covered in pink tablecloths with mint-green checkered skirts, pink cloth napkins, fresh flowers, and fine imported white china. If you're in a romantic mood, the terrace overlooking the hotel gardens and the beautiful Swan Lake is quite inspiring. This bougainvillea draped terrace features a heated floor for your year round comfort.

$16.50 Afternoon Tea... Assorted finger sandwiches, two warm currant scones served with Devon cream, strawberries & preserves, Bel-Air assorted pastries, and your selection of brewed loose Harney & Sons Tea presented with a strainer.

TEATIME: 3pm-5pm, Monday Thru Friday • 3:30-5pm, Saturday
• May Accommodate Some Dietary Needs, 3 Day Advance Request
• Non-Caffeine/Herbal Tea Available
• Watercloset: Same Floor
• Wheelchair Accessible
• **Reservations Are Advised**
• Complimentary Valet Parking
• Credit Cards: V,MC,AE&DC

L'autograph
*du Concierge*_____*Date*_____

CAFE NORDSTROM

10830 West Pico Boulevard
Los Angeles, California

310-470-6155

New Addition...It's Teatime At..Cafe Nordstrom.
In 1887, at the tender age of 16, John F. Nordstrom left his home in Sweden to come to the United States. He arrived in New York with five dollars in his pocket. A fortuitous meeting years later with Carl F. Wallin a Seattle shoemaker, resulted in the 1901 opening of the first "Wallin & Nordstrom" store on Fourth & Pike Streets in Seattle. Throughout the years, Nordstrom has been guided by its founder's philosophy. "Offer the customer the best possible service, selection, quality and value." I enjoy shopping at Nordstom, the idea of a pianist playing a baby grand piano while I browse for beautiful things suits me to a T. The comfy "oasis" which my spouse calls the "husband waiting area" is appreciated by both of us! When this customer friendly store began serving Afternoon Tea in many of the Cafes at Nordstrom, I wasn't at all surprised.

At teatime, Cafe Nordstrom tables are dressed-up with fresh flowers or plants, fine china, cloth napkins and special teatime silverware. You will be courteously greeted by an enthusiastic cafe manager or their friendly staff. F.Y.I. Outdoor patio dining is available at some of the Cafe Nordstrom locations.

$6.95 Afternoon Tea... Assorted finger sandwiches, scone served with berry-butter, a tasty dessert and a pot of tea.

TEATIME: 2:30pm To 5:00pm • Monday Thru Friday
• May Accommodate Some Dietary Needs With Advance Request
• Non-Caffeine/Herbal Tea Available
• Wheelchair Accessible • Watercloset: Same Floor
• **Reservations Required Six Or More**
• Free Parking Lot
• Credit Cards: V,MC,AE&Nordstrom
Manager's
*Autograph*_____*Date*_____

PACIFIC DINING CAR

1310 West Sixth Street
Los Angeles, California

213-483-6000

It's Teatime At...The Pacific Dining Car. This 75 year old restaurant has been described as, "sort of an oasis" near bustling downtown Los Angeles. The Pacific Dining Car was built to the scale of a real dining car. Never destined for life on the rails, it was pulled to its Sixth Street location on real train wheels and exists solely for your dining pleasure. The train has a dark mahogany interior and is comfortably elegant.

Afternoon Tea is served with tablecloths, fresh flowers and Villeroy Beaulieu china, at tables with big comfortable club chairs. Private tea parties are also available. Please call Mike; he will gladly help you plan a great event. Have Afternoon Tea on the train, instead of taking the "A" train, you can take the "TEA" train!

$10.00 Afternoon Tea... Assorted tea sandwiches, home made scone, sweets, choice of Sherry or glass of wine and a pot of brewed loose tea.

TEATIME: 3:00pm To 5:30pm • Monday Thru Sunday
• May Accommodate Some Dietary Needs With Advance Request
• Non-Caffeine/Herbal Tea Available
• Watercloset: Same Floor
• Wheelchair Accessible
• **Reserve For Larger Parties Please**
• Private Parking Lot, Approx. $2.50
• Credit Cards: MC,V,DC&AE
Proprietor's
*Autograph*_____*Date*_____

PARK HYATT LOS ANGELES
At Century City
2151 Avenue Of The Stars
Los Angeles, California

310-277-2777

It's Teatime At...Park Hyatt Los Angeles. (By Advance Reservation) Park Hyatt Hotels often stand out from the crowd, particularly this hotel since it is the only hotel in Century City to offer a formal Afternoon Tea. Century City is located on the west side of Los Angeles near Beverly Hills. It's is a pretty neat area with movie theaters, the fabulous Schubert Theater, shopping, restaurants, even Twentieth Century Fox Film Studio!

Afternoon Tea is served in the elegant and inviting, open and airy Garden Room. The room, which overlooks the garden and gazebo is decorated in peach tones accented with celery green in the tapestries. A large fresh flower arrangement and dramatic chandelier truly catch your eye. Tea is presented on a three-tiered caddie and served at tables set in off-white linens, cloth napkins, Royal Doulton china, and fresh flowers. P.S. The Garden Room is separate but actually part of The Park Grill. On a beautiful day, consider taking Tea outdoors in The Gazebo Garden.F.Y.I. Powers teas are quite popular here. Tea parties for groups & special events are available.

$15.00 Traditional Afternoon Tea... Assorted finger sandwiches, fresh fruit, scone with Devonshire cream & preserves, pastries, gateau, tea breads and a choice of brewed Harney Teas.

TEATIME: 3pm To 5pm • Monday Thru Saturday • No Holidays
- May Accommodate Some Dietary Needs With Advance Request
- Non-Caffeine/Herbal Tea Available
- Children's Tea Parties Welcome
- Watercloset: Same Floor
- Wheelchair Accessible
- **Advance Reservations Are Required**
- Three Hour Gratis Valet Parking With Validation
- Credit Cards: V,MC,DIS,DC,AE&JCB

L'autograph
*du Concierge*_____*Date*_____

REGAL BILTMORE HOTEL

506 South Grand Avenue
Los Angeles, California

213-624-1011

It's Teatime At...The Regal Biltmore Hotel. The Biltmore Hotel originally opened its beautiful doors on October 1, 1923. Afternoon Tea is served in the area that was originally the hotel lobby, now called the Rendezvous Court. The beautiful cathedral-like carved ceiling accented in 24-karat gold, the travertine pillars, Italian bronze chandeliers, and a multi-tiered fountain of Tennessee rose marble, are captivating. Classical background music and comfortable upholstered chairs are always a nice touch.

Afternoon Tea is presented on a three-tiered caddie at wrought iron tables set with super bone Hankook china. P.S. While at the hotel, make a point to notice the vaulted ceilings in the Main Galleria, the pair of 1930's art deco carved murals in the Cognac Room, and the historic photos from the academy awards circa 1930's and 40's. (They are hanging on the walls in the gallery bar adjacent to the Cognac Room.) Enjoy Afternoon Tea and history!

$18.95 Biltmore Tea. Add a glass of Domaine Chandon, Harvey's Bristol Cream or Dry Sack Sherry to Traditional Tea.

$14.95 Traditional Tea... Tea sandwiches, such as brioche with watercress, cucumber/cream cheese; freshly baked scone with Devonshire cream & preserves, fruit tarts, chocolate truffles, banana nut bread, raspberry pound cake, pot of brewed tea.

$5.50 Rendezvous Tea... Raspberry pound cake & tea.

TEATIME: 2:00pm To 5:00pm • Seven Days A Week
- May Accommodate Some Dietary Needs, 3 Day Advance Request
- Non-Caffeine/Herbal Tea Available
- Watercloset: Few Steps Up
- Wheelchair Accessible, Lift Available
- **Reservations Are Highly Recommended**
- Reduced-Price Parking With Validation
- Credit Cards: MC,V,DIS&AE

L'autograph
*du Concierge*_____*Date*_____

RENAISSANCE LOS ANGELES

9620 Airport Boulevard
Los Angeles, California

Please Call Catering **310-337-2052**
Hotel **310-337-2800**

Tea Parties For Groups Of 25 Or More Guests At...Renaissance Los Angeles Hotel. Plush furnishings and sophisticated surroundings along with close proximity to the Los Angeles airport make this a great spot for meetings with coast-hopping "jet-set!" business executives. Arrange an Afternoon Power Tea, it might just put that positive spin on your next big deal.

Afternoon Teas are served at tables set with tablecloths, cloth napkins, Villeroy & Boch fine china and the hotel's silver tea service. The hotel can accommodate 25 to 400 guests in different banquet rooms, but the intimate Library with a faux fireplace and splendid paintings, bookcases full of books, and antiques is quite special for 30-40 guests. And, the black & white tuxedo clad servers are quite attentive. P.S. The chef at the Renaissance is pleased to customize your Tea. Browse around, the Director of Catering told me there's around $18 million dollars worth of magnificent artwork!

$9.75 Afternoon Tea.. Assorted finger sandwiches, fruit tarts, fresh baked scone served with strawberries, brown sugar & Devonshire cream, and pot of brewed loose tea. (Price is per person plus applicable room fee if any, 18% service charge and sales tax.)

TEA PARTIES FOR GROUPS: Please Call Catering Office
• 25 Guest Minimum
• May Accommodate Some Dietary Needs, 2 Week Advance Request
• Non-Caffeine/Herbal Tea Available
• Watercloset: Same Floor
• Wheelchair Accessible
• $10.00 Self Park Or $14.00 Valet, With Validation
• **Reserve Two Weeks In Advance, Please**
• Credit Cards: V,MC,DIS,AE&JCB

L'autograph
*du Concierge*_____*Date*_____

WESTWOOD MARQUIS
Hotel & Gardens
930 Hilgard Avenue
(Between Beverly Hills & Westwood)
Los Angeles, California

310-208-8765 *Ask For Catering*

Private Tea Parties For Groups At...Westwood Marquis Hotel & Gardens. (Minimum of 15 guests) The luxurious Westwood Marquis was one of the first spots to present Afternoon Teas over 10 years ago. Afternoon Tea is now served only to groups by advance reservation. Please call the **catering** department to plan a tea party for your special event.

Afternoon Tea parties may take place in the Erte Room, Marquessa Room or the Sierra Room, each with their own decor and personality. F.Y.I. Minimum of 15 guests is required. Add 18% gratuity, sales tax and server fee. The server fee of $75.00 is imposed for less than 20 guests. Please call for revised details and to plan your tea party. Weather permitting, up to 200 guests may be accommodated in the garden. P.S. If you miss the regular Afternoon Teas, let the hotel know. Maybe we can encourage its return!

$18.95 Afternoon Tea... A glass of Sherry, delicate finger sandwiches, golden caviar garnished with finely chopped onion & egg on rounds of dark rye bread, scone served with Devonshire cream & marmalade & jam, cookies, petit fours, pate and a pot of brewed loose tea.

TEA PARTIES: Please Call Catering • Minimum 15 Guests
• May Accommodate Some Dietary Needs With Advance Request
• Non-Caffeine/Herbal Tea Available
• Watercloset: Same Floor
• Wheelchair Accessible
• **Reservations Are Required**
• Two Hour Valet Park With Validation Is $5.00
• Credit Cards: MC,V,DIS,DC,AE&JCB

L'autograph
*du Concierge*_____*Date*_____

WYNDHAM CHECKERS HOTEL

Checkers Restaurant

535 South Grand Avenue
Los Angeles, California

213-624-0000

It's Teatime At...Wyndham Checkers Hotel. This European style hotel is situated only steps away from many downtown Los Angeles office buildings and high-rises. It was the recipient of the Los Angeles Conservancy Preservationist Award. Consider taking your clients to tea, it could be a wise business move, and you will surely stand out from the crowd.

Afternoon Tea is served in the Lobby Lounge at tables set with "Katani Crane" by Wedgewood, white linens, cloth napkins and a single rose. It is a comfortable spot with overstuffed chairs and marble tables. P.S. The hotel has a nice collection of fine art, so if the office can wait while you browse around, take a little tour. F.Y.I. Reservations are limited to 20 guests.

$18.50 The Traditional Afternoon Tea... Assorted finger sandwiches, freshly baked warm scone served with Chantilly Cream & homemade preserves, delightful miniature pastries, and a selection of house teas.

TEATIME: 3:00pm To 5:00pm • Seven Days A Week
- May Accommodate Some Dietary Needs, 3 Day Advance Request
- Non-Caffeine/Herbal Tea Available
- Watercloset: One Floor Up
- Wheelchair Accessible
- **Reservations Are Recommended**
- Parking: Self Or Valet Available For Nearly The Same Price, Approximately $1.75 Every 20 Minutes
- Credit Cards: V,MC,DC,DIS,AE&JCB

*L'autograph
du Concierge*_____*Date*_____

136

LISA'S TEA TREASURES

330 North Santa Cruz Avenue
Los Gatos, California

408-395-8327

    It's Teatime At...Lisa's Tea Treasures. Tea lovers will delight in tea & treats from around the world in an atmosphere of Old World elegance at Lisa's Tea Treasures. You'll find a wide selection of teas to accompany the tea menu which features savories, finger sandwiches, homemade soups and salads, delicate tea cakes, scones, and delicious pastries. The selection of teas is impressive.

    Afternoon Tea is served in the sunny Victorian Room or the Hunt Room with its decorative fireplace. Pat & her attentive servers are attired in black or pink, tea-length Victorian maid's outfits.

    The gift parlour features a fine selection of china, tea ware and imported gourmet items that make elegant yet practical gifts. P.S. The four o'clock hour is Children's Tea Party time complete with a special menu. Please call to reserve a tea party "play date" for up to 30 children. Please call for special holiday hours as well. Ask about the the monthly Afternoon Tea specials around $15.95.

    $12.00 To $15.95 Traditional Afternoon Tea. Pot of connoisseur full-leaf tea, tea sandwiches, savories & sweets. Eight fabulous selections.

    $12.00 The Court Jester's Surprise... Child's festive fruity watermelon-berry tea, peanut butter & jam tea sandwich, scone, fresh fruit, playful cookie and a "mouse-a-four" petit-four.

    $6.50 To $7.95 A La Carte Specials... Crumpets or scones or tea sandwiches, includes a pot of connoisseur full-leaf tea with a sampling of scones, savories & sweets. Four selections.

TEATIME: 11:30am, 2:00pm & 4:00pm • Tuesday Thru Sunday
• May Accommodate Some Dietary Needs With Advance Request
• 99.6% Caffeine-Free Tea Available
• Children's Tea Parties Welcome
• Wheelchair Accessible • Watercloset: Same Floor
• **Reservations Are Suggested**
• Limited-Time Street Parking
• Credit Cards: V&MC

Proprietor's
*Autograph*_____*Date*_____

BARNABEY'S HOTEL

3501 North Sepulveda Boulevard
Manhattan Beach, California

800-552-5285   **310-545-8466**

It's Teatime Tea At...Barnabey's Hotel. "Barnabey's is hospitality in the true 19th Century European tradition. The hotel & restaurant abound with Victorian charm, romance & antiques." One of the premier hotels in the South Bay, Barnabey's has loads of charm and a caring attitude towards guests.

Afternoon Tea is now served five days a week in the Garden Terrace at tables set with white tablecloths and fresh flowers. You'll find the Tea Captain to be very thoughtful and attentive. Private tea parties are available for 30 to 150 guests; and depending on the size of the group, you may take tea in The Veranda Room, The Library or The Garden Room, all attractively decorated. Please call for details and to reserve your tea party date. "Put some glorious past in your future...at Barnabey's."

$14.00 Afternoon Tea...A selection of finger sandwiches, English tea breads & pastries, fresh baked scones served with Devonshire cream & preserves, petit fours, brewed tea.

TEATIME: 2:00pm To 5:00pm • Tuesday Thru Saturday
- May Accommodate Some Dietary Needs With Advance Request
- Non-Caffeine/Herbal Tea Available
- Children's Tea Parties Welcome
- Watercloset: Same Floor
- Wheelchair Accessible on The First Floor
- **Reservations Are Recommended**
- Gratis Valet Or Self Park For Tea Events
- Credit Cards: MC,V,DC,DIS&AE

L'autograph
*du Concierge*_____*Date*_____

BRISTOL FARMS

1570 Rosecrans Avenue
Manhattan Beach, California

What The World Is Coming To.

310-643-5229

New Addition...Host A Tea Party With Help From Bristol Farms. Teas, as we all know are fun & popular events for any or no occasion at all! I'm often asked at book signings about my own tea parties. Afternoon Teas at home are especially fun for me because I get a chance to be creative and bring out my pretty vintage plates, teacups, teapots, vases & Victorian lace. I keep my list of guests to eight friends for ease of conversation. Setting the table the day before really saves time. I also set a tea strainer for each guest.

Early in the day I pick dewy garden flowers, plunge them into squeaky clean vases of water and head to Bristol Farms in South Pasadena. I buy one large container each of tuna, chicken & seafood salads. Next, a stop at their bakery for 24 pre-ordered mini, or 8 large scones, 3 different loaves of bread for cookie-cutter shaped tea sandwiches and a dozen mini chocolate eclairs and cream puffs. I choose two 16 oz. jars of preserves & 3 small jars of lemon curd. I make my own cream, but they usually have clotted cream if you like. Edible blossoms, strawberries, grapes, kiwi, bananas & star fruit are a must. An extra bunch of flowers, and I'm off! To make your tea party more fun & "interactive" ask each of your guests to bring a different small package of tea. With individual teapots, it encourages tea-tasting & is a neat conversation facilitator. (But that's another book!) With 8 guests it's easier to have plates preset with 3 tea sandwiches, edible flowers, melange of fruit, and a "teacup" of soup, made from 4 packages of creamy asparagus soup to which I add pre-cooked fresh asparagus bits. Scones are on individual plates. My bread pudding made from bread crusts is great! F.Y.I.If you prefer, pick-up a catered tea from Bristol Farms!

TEATIME SHOPPING: 8:00am To 10:00pm • Seven Days A Week
• May Accommodate Some Dietary Needs With Advance Request
• Non-Caffeine/Herbal Tea Available
• Wheelchair Accessible • Watercloset: Same Floor
• Large Free Parking Lot
• Credit Cards:V,MC,DIS&AE

Manager's
*Autograph*_____*Date*_____

139

THE RITZ-CARLTON®

THE RITZ CARLTON
Marina Del Rey
4375 Admiralty Way
Marina Del Rey, California

310-823-1700

It's Teatime On Weekends At...The Ritz Carlton, Marina Del Rey. Something magical happens when you take tea at The Ritz Carlton in Marina Del Rey. Maybe it has something to do with the fact that The Library Lounge overlooks the ocean and a marina with beautiful yachts. You see, The Ritz Carlton is at the water's edge of the world's largest man-made marina. Some people are no doubt looking at their own yacht! Our preference is to take tea around 3:30pm during the winter months when the sun sets early. After Tea, we walk directly outside from the Library Lounge and watch the divine sunset from the veranda.

Afternoon Tea is attentively and elegantly presented from a three tiered cake stand at tables set with Rosenthal "Classical" china. I have found the food & service at this Ritz Carlton to be particularly excellent. A harpist or pianist usually entertains at teatime. F.Y.I. Parties of six or more may schedule an Afternoon Tea for any day.

$20.00 Full Service Tea... Tea sandwiches, scone with Devonshire cream & strawberry preserves, English & Irish tea cakes, fruit tart, cookie, shortbread and a pot of brewed loose tea.
$25.00 Royal Service Tea... Add a glass of Perrier-Jouet NV, Brut & a plate of fresh strawberries with whipped cream.

TEATIME: SATURDAY & SUNDAY: 2:00pm To 5:00pm
- Call For Possible Extended Days
- May Accommodate Some Dietary Needs With Advance Request
- Non-Caffeine/Herbal Tea Available
- Children's Tea Parties Welcome
- Watercloset: Same Floor • Wheelchair Accessible
- **Reservations Are A Must**
- Valet Parking $5.00 With Validation
- Credit Cards: V,MC,DIS,DC,AE&JCB

L'autograph
*du Concierge*_____*Date*_____

McCLOUD HOTEL B&B

408 Main Street
(At The Foot Of Mt. Shasta)
McCloud, California

916-964-2822

Special "Day" Teas And Tea & Savories On Saturdays At...McCloud Hotel. The McCloud Hotel was originally built in 1916 to provide housing for mill workers, school teachers & visitors to the McCloud area. Drop-in and meet Marilyn, the gracious innkeeper of this terrific Historic Landmark, and while you're there be sure to notice the hotel's original registration desk.

Cozy up on an overstuffed chair or a 1930's style bold print sofa in front of the lobby fireplace to enjoy tea & scones. The McCloud Hotel is a wonderful place for you to just relax, whatever the season. And, you don't have to be an overnight guest to enjoy a "cuppa." Ask the proprietors about the awards which have been bestowed upon their hotel. Special teas such as Springtime Tea at the end of March, Mother-Daughter Tea at the beginning of May, Late Summer Tea in late September and Great Christmas Cookie Exchange & Afternoon Tea in December, are always lots of fun.

$8.00 Special "Day" Teas... Call for schedule. Sample Christmas Menu: Assorted finger puff sandwiches, four layer Harlequin sandwiches, open faced rye rounds with shrimp, scone with cream & lemon curd & marmalade, chocolate dipped orange & kiwi slices, chocolate peanut meringue kisses, chocolate truffle, etc.

$4.00 Tea & Savories... Fresh baked scone of the day, or Mrs. Pettygrew's lemon pecan cake, or savories and a cup of brewed loose tea.

SATURDAY TEA & SAVORIES: 3:30pm
- Special "Day" Teas As Scheduled On Selected Sundays
- Non-Caffeine/Herbal Tea Available
- Wheelchair Accessible • Watercloset: Same Floor
- **Reservations Suggested For Six Or More Please**
- Parking Lot And Street Parking
- Credit Cards: V,MC&DIS

Proprietor's
*Autograph*_____*Date*_____

ALLIED ARTS GUILD
Restaurant
75 Arbor Road
Menlo Park, California

415-324-2588

Annual Valentine's Day Tea At...Allied Arts Guild. In 1929, Garfield and Delight Merner bought 3.5 acres of land through a Spanish land grant on which they planned to build a guild for artists & craftsmen. An old barn and sheds were preserved and several new Spanish Colonial buildings were erected. Beautiful tiles and objects of art imported from the Mediterranean countries were used to decorate the walls. Today, the lovely Allied Arts Guild is operated solely to benefit the Lucille Salter Packard Children's Hospital at Stanford. Allow time to have tea and browse here.

The Valentine's Day Tea is served at tables set with pink linens, fine china, silver service, and a fresh camellia on each plate. A harpist plays soothing background music. Be sure to visit their Traditional Shop which features a nice selection of china, silver, antiques & gifts. F.Y.I. The Valentine's Day Tea is very popular so plan ahead. P.S. Christmas Teas are now being planned, call for info. Ask about Samantha's Ice Cream Socials, usually in the fall.

$17.50 Christmas Tea... Please call for November date.
$16.00(Approx.)**Annual Valentine's Day Tea...**Finger sandwiches, savories, sweets, and a continuous cup of tea.
$5.00ish "Tea & Philanthropy"... Homemade dessert of the day and a pot of tea. Patio dining is also available.

VALENTINE'S DAY TEA: 2:00pm & 3:30pm • 2/13/98, 2/12/99
- Tea & Philanthropy 1:00pm To 2:30pm • Monday Thru Friday
- Non-Caffeine/Herbal Tea Available
- Ask About Children's Easter Bunny Lunches
- Watercloset: Same Floor • Wheelchair Accessible
- **Reservations Are Recommended**
- Reserve & Pre-pay For Valentine's Day Tea
- Parking Lot & Street Parking
- Cash Or Check

Director's
*Autograph*_____*Date*_____

BATTERIE DE CUISINE
presents Polly Put The Kettle On
(*inside* The Allied Arts Guild Complex)
75 Arbor Road
Menlo Park, California

415-322-8127

New Addition...Tea Tasting & Sweet Saturday At...Batterie De Cuisine. Whisk yourself away to the wonderful circa 1929 Spanish Colonial Allied Art's Guild and to Batterie de Cuisine for a Saturday of shopping & tea tasting. Linda, the proprietor of the shop, and Sally, of Polly Put The Kettle On, have created a lovely little tea escape for you on Saturdays. Linda and Sally are always open to suggestions for new and creative baked specialties, so please feel free to share a favorite recipe with them.

Batterie de Cuisine is already familiar to most of you. It is a charming shop that sells nearly everything needed for the kitchen along with a full complement of tea accoutrements. In fact, the cozy parlor tearoom is completely devoted to tea and tea accoutrements including china, tea linens, teapots, tea cards, tea books, tea infusers, etc.etc.! Allow time to stroll around the gardens, courtyards, shops, studios and galleries too, in this peaceful place. F.Y.I. Ask about the new tea classes which are planned.

$Complimentary... Assorted homebaked cakes or cookies & a cup of brewed loose tea. Each week you will sample a new tea.

TEA TASTING & "SWEET SATURDAY": 10am-2pm, Saturday
• Non-Caffeine/Herbal Tea Available
• Watercloset: Same Floor
• **Please Drop By**
• Free Parking Lot
• Credit Cards: V,MC&JCB
Proprietor's
*Autograph*_____*Date*_____

143

LISA'S TEA TREASURES

1145 Merrill Street
(Across From Train Station)
Menlo Park, California

415-326-8327

It's Teatime At...Lisa's Tea Treasures. "Lisa's Tea Treasures" is located in a turn-of-the century Victorian home directly across from the city's CalTrain depot. Relax with a steaming pot of freshly brewed tea and a meal of succulent savories, sandwiches and sweets taken in the comfort & charm of the Victorian era.

This gracious home with a professionally landscaped garden is available for your special occasion tea parties too. It provides an unique venue for business meetings as well. A treasure trove for tea connoisseurs, Roberta's gift parlour is filled with numerous specialty teas & accoutrements including strainers, cozies, books, imported fine bone china, porcelain & ceramic tea service pieces. A gourmet pantry boasts an array of edible specialties. F.Y.I. Afternoon Tea is served on the garden patio weather permitting.

$13.00 To $17.95 Traditional Afternoon Tea. Pot of connoisseur full-leaf tea, tea sandwiches, savories & sweets. A great selection of Afternoon Teatimes From Around The World.
$7.00 To $8.50 Light Afternoon Tea Delights. Pot of connoisseur full-leaf tea, with a sampling of either scones, savories, sweets or tea sandwiches.Four Varieties Available.

TEATIME: 10:00am To 5:30pm • Tuesday Thru Sunday
• Tea Seatings: 11:30, 2:00 & 4:00pm • Closed Holidays
• May Accommodate Some Dietary Needs With Advance Request
• 99.6% Caffeine-Free Tea & Herbal Tisanes Available
• Children's Tea Parties Welcome
• Watercloset: Same Floor
• Wheelchair Accessible
• **Reservations Recommended** • **Seating Based On Availability**
• Free Parking Lot
• Credit Cards: V&MC
Proprietor's
*Autograph*_____*Date*_____

144

STANFORD PARK HOTEL
100 El Camino Real
Menlo Park, California

415-322-1234 *Please Call The Catering Office*

Tea Parties For Groups At...Stanford Park Hotel.

The Stanford Park Hotel is a relatively new hotel built in the early 1980's. A thoughtful blend of yesterday and today, it was designed with copper-clad gabled roofs, dormer windows, balconies, red brick pillars and carved oak staircases. A collection of handsome antiques and fine art nicely rounds out the picture.

Tea parties may take place in a variety of dining areas or banquet rooms. The Private Dining Room nicely suits 10 to 14 guests, while The Woodside Room can accommodate up to 130 guests. Afternoon Teas may be presented either buffet style or individually served. Weather permitting during the summer months, The Garden Courtyard is a popular spot. F.Y.I. This is a Four Star & Four Diamond hotel with many amenities. Have fun!

$18.00 Afternoon Tea... Open face & traditional finger sandwiches such as watercress/chopped egg, cucumber & salmon, dates-nuts-cream cheese, English scone and crumpets with butter, Devonshire cream & jam, variety of sweets, including mini tarts, petit fours & mini chocolate eclairs and an assortment of teas. (Price is per person, plus applicable room fee, tax and service fee).

TEA PARTIES FOR GROUPS: Please Call Catering To Plan
- May Accommodate Some Dietary Needs With Advance Request
- Non-Caffeine/Herbal Tea Available
- Children's Tea Parties Welcome
- Watercloset: Same Floor
- Wheelchair Accessible
- **Please Call To Plan Your Tea Party**
- Watercloset: Same Floor
- Complimentary Parking With Tea Party
- Credit Cards: MC,V,DC,DIS&AE

L'autograph
*du Concierge*_____*Date*_____

THE GARDEN GRILL

1026 Alma Street
Menlo Park, California

650-325-8981

It's Teatime At...The Garden Grill. The Garden Grill is owned by a gentleman considered to be a real enthusiast of all things British including quite naturally, Afternoon Tea. This is quite a popular spot in town and many people seem to have heard about Jose Louis. He's difficult to catch up with, but do try to say hello. He and Jessica are the friendly proprietors of The Garden Grill.

Afternoon Tea is attentively served at tables set with linens, white china & fresh flowers in the peach-tone Bay Window Room. In season, enjoy a casual Afternoon Tea outdoors under the oak tree on the patio.F.Y.I. The pastry chef prepares everything from scratch here including the scones, breads, jams and even the clotted cream. His mini cheese scones are incredibly popular and available baked or frozen for take home. Look for their adjacent gourmet shop called The Rock Of Gibralter for British & Spanish specialties. Jessica told me that The Merienda is the Spanish equivelant of Afternoon Tea!

$16.75 The Tea Party...(Per person, for four or more guests) Mini Cornish Pasty, tea sandwiches, homemade scone with clotted cream & jam, mini cheddar & tomato tartlet, mixed dressed field greens, assorted tea cakes & a pot of brewed loose tea.

$13.50 The Complete Tea... Finger sandwiches on homemade bread, scone with clotted cream & "Garden Grill" jam, assorted tea cakes, and a pot of brewed loose tea.

$9.00 The Cream Tea... Homemade scone served with clotted cream & "Garden Grill" jam and a pot of brewed loose tea.

TEATIME: 3:00pm To 5:00pm • Monday Thru Saturday
• May Accommodate Some Dietary Needs With Advance Request
• Non-Caffeine/Herbal Tea Available
• Children's Tea Parties Welcome
• Watercloset: Same Floor • Wheelchair Accessible
• **Reservations Are Required**
• Free Street Parking
• Credit Cards: V,MC,DC&AE

Proprietor's
*Autograph*_____*Date*_____

FRILLS VINTAGE TEA
Parlour & Boutique
504 South Myrtle Avenue
Monrovia, California

626-303-3201

    It's Teatime At...Frills Vintage Tea Parlour & Boutique. Frills is a unique and fun spot for Afternoon Tea and tea parties. It is a truly fine place to wear a terrific flamboyant picture hat! Can't find a hat? Borrow one of Frill's vintage chapeaus. They have hats for the monsieur as well. Don't forget your camera, there are many treasured photo opportunities here.

    Everything at Frills is homemade down to the tasty cameo chocolates. Kathy is the gracious tea parlour proprietor, she will make you feel like family for that precious time you share. P.S. Catering is Kathy's specialty, ask about teapot cakes. Allow plenty of time to explore at Frills as there is a fine collection of vintage clothing, jewelry & accessories plus walls of neat hats. The artistic talents of designers are here too. Tara's beautiful one-of-a-kind jewelry pieces & hats are works of art, like my aqua feather brooch.

    $11.50 King's Tea... Meat pie, fruit, tea sandwiches, teapot cookie, dessert, pot of brewed loose tea, chocolate cameo.

    $10.50 Peasant Tea... Tin cup of soup, green salad, fruits, cheese, loaf bread, slice of shortbread, brewed loose tea.

    $9.50 Queen's Tea... Tea sandwiches, fresh fruit, teapot cookie, choice of dessert, pot of brewed loose tea, chocolate cameo.

    $7.00 Children's Tea... Peanut butter & jelly sandwich, short bread, fresh fruit, molasses teapot cookie and tea.

TEATIME: 11:00am To 4:00pm • Tuesday Thru Saturday
- Plus Evening Tea On *"Happening"* Old Town Friday Nights
- May Accommodate Some Dietary Needs, 1 Week Advance Request
- Non-Caffeine/Herbal Tea
- Children's Tea Parties Welcome
- Watercloset: No, Visit A Nearby Store
- **Reservations Are Recommended**
- Limited Time Off-Street Rear Parking
- Credit Cards: V,MC&DIS (No Checks)

Proprietor's
*Autograph*_____*Date*_____

BORDERS BOOKS & MUSIC

5055 South Plaza Lane
Montclair, California
(Montclair Plaza)

909-625-0424

New Addition...It's Teatime At...Borders Books & Music. And you thought you could only get great books at Borders! Enjoy tea and a scone at Border's Cafe Espresso. I'm not sure whether it's the tea that enhances the enjoyment of a good book or the other way around, but at Borders you are invited to walk about with a cup of the relaxing brew while hunting for a good book or two!

The bright and upbeat cafe offers comfortable dining tables where you can sip, and get to know your new book. Be sure also to pick-up a monthly event schedule. Borders often has interesting lectures, children's story hours and author signings. This is a happening spot for a weekend date too. On Friday & Saturday evenings there is live music from around 7:30 or 8:30pm, and from 6:00pm on Sundays. Jazz to rock to pop! Groovy!

$2.75 Scone... Fresh daily, choose from raisin, cranberry and my favorite, chocolate chip scone with butter & preserves.
$1.50 Pot of Tea... Loose brewed Republic of Tea or a bagged pot of Tazo.

TEATIME: 9:00am To 11:00pm • Monday Thru Thursday
• 9:00am To Midnight, Friday & Saturday • 9am To 10pm, Sunday
• Non-Caffeine/Herbal Tea Available
• Watercloset: Same Floor
• Wheelchair Accessible
• **Please Drop By**
• Free Parking Lot
• Credit Cards: V,MC,DIS&AE
Manager's
*Autograph*_____*Date*_____

148

LONDON BRIDGE
Pub & Tea Rooms

Fisherman's Wharf II
(10 Paces From The Water)
Monterey, California

408-655-2879

It's Teatime At...London Bridge Pub & Tea Room. "Thank-you for joining us for Afternoon Tea at The London Bridge Tea Rooms, just 10 paces from the water. Tea is a time honored English tradition which we are happy to share with you."

Afternoon Tea is casually served at tables set with linens, mis-matched china, (Bunny buys teacups that she loves on a whim), and sometimes fresh flowers. You'll enjoy visiting with this friendly proprietor and shopping for antiques, gifts, English groceries, dart supplies & teapots in her gift shop. P.S. Private Afternoon Tea Parties are available for up to 38 guests. F.Y.I. If you or your mate has a hankering to play darts after tea, this is the place!

$7.95   Afternoon Tea... Assorted finger sandwiches, such as tomato & cucumber, boiled egg, dessert sweet or scone served with cream strawberry jam, and a pot of brewed loose Yorkshire Gold or Typhoo Tea.

$5.95 Devonshire Cream Tea... Fresh scone served with jam & cream, Yorkshire Gold Tea and a hot water jug so you can make your tea as strong or weak as you like.

$5.95 Tea &Cookies... Variety of fancy cookies & tea.

TEATIME: Cream Tea: 11:30am To 10:00pm • Seven Days A Week
• Afternoon Tea: 2:00pm To 4:30pm • Seven Days A Week
• May Accommodate Some Dietary Needs, 2 Day Advance Request
• Watercloset: Same Floor
• **Reservations For Larger Parties Only**
• Metered Parking And A Proper Lot
• Credit Cards: V,MC&DIS

Proprietor's
*Autograph*_____*Date*_____

LUCY'S TEA HOUSE

180 Castro Street
Mountain View, California

415-969-6365

New Addition..It's Teatime At...Lucy's Tea House. Originally from Taiwan, Lucy who was then an English teacher, dreamed of opening a teahouse. In her country teahouses were very prevalent, often several on a block as people sought refuge from the hectic daily pace. Lucy's "someday" dream became a reality. Lucy's Teahouse is a relaxed, unhurried retreat. Her teaching continues as she educates customers in the "ways of tea."

Tea specialties at Lucy's Tea House include a variety of blended teas and fruit juice tea drinks with intriguing names such as Forest Rain Drops, Molly Honey, Purple Violet, Oriental Beauty & Jealous Lover. The teahouse is decorated in rattan and batik with comfortable high back rattan cushioned chairs or sofas and accented with decorative potted plants. Plan to spend some time here, even "relaxing" can sometimes take a concerted effort! Lucy has added interesting iced teas which include grapefruit, guava & mango teas served over ice. P.S. Ask Lucy about her pig passion. Enjoy!

$4.99 Vegetarian Rice Plate
$4.99 Tea House Sandwiches... Choose from turkey, chicken, beef, ham or tuna sandwich served with a petite salad and a pot of brewed loose house blend tea or tea ice cream.
$3.50 Tea Ice Cream Or Refreshing Tea Float
$2.50-$3.99 Pot Of Tea... Teas #2 through #16 are exotic additions to Green, Black and Oolong. Lucy's and her staff will be happy to help you decide on your brewed loose tea selection.

TEATIME: 11am-10pm, Monday-Thursday, Till 12am Fri. & Sat.
- May Accommodate Some Dietary Needs With Advance request
- Non-Caffeine/Herbal Tea Available
- Children's Tea Parties Welcome
- Watercloset: Same Floor
- **Reservations: No**
- Free Parking Lot
- Cash

Proprietor's
*Autograph*_____*Date*_____

THE EMMA NEVADA
House B&B
528 East Broad Street
Nevada City, California

530-265-4415　　　800-916-EMMA

New Addition...It Teatime For Groups At...The Emma Nevada House. Enjoy a gracious getaway at this charming 1856 Victorian B&B located about 60 miles northeast of Sacramento. This restored house is the childhood home of opera star Emma Nevada. "Nevada" as she was known, performed for Queen Victoria, and sang in many of Europe's major opera houses. Ruth Ann offers Afternoon Teas and Theme Teas including an Edible Flowers Tea and a Mother-Daughter Tea in May. Tea is served in three rooms, The Dining Room, The Sun Room with floor to ceiling antique windows overlooking the garden, or on the serene deck.

Afternoon Tea is served at tables set with fresh flowers or nosegays, tablecloths and antique china. Do you need a little pampering? Ask about "A Victorian Ladies Weekend," with two night's stay and of course, Afternoon Tea. For around $360, two guests enjoy a get-acquainted party, breakfast, massage, facial, mani-pedicure and theater event. Sound great? I'll meet you there!

$11.00 Afternoon Tea... Array of tea sandwiches, scones such as lemon cream or orange almond scone served with lemon curd, cream & jam, delectable desserts and a continuous cup of loose brewed tea.

TEATIME: 6-16 Guests • 3:30pm, Sunday-Thursday, As Scheduled
- May Accommodate Some Dietary Needs With Advance Request
- Non-Caffeine/Herbal Tea Available
- Children's Tea Parties Welcome, Ages 6+
- Watercloset: Same Floor
- **Reservations Are Required**
- Free Parking Lot
- Credit Cards: V,MC,DC&AE

Proprietor's
*Autograph*_____*Date*_____

THE RED CASTLE
Historic Lodging
109 Prospect Street
Nevada City, California
(Between Reno & Sacramento)

800-761-4766   **530-265-5135**

Tea Parties For Groups At...The Red Castle. The discovery of gold in Deer Creek near Nevada City in 1849 made a thriving metropolis from a rustic little mining camp. This finding enabled Judge John Williams a mine owner himself, to realize his long held dream of building a mansion. Soon, a four-story, Gothic Revival mansion overlooking Deer Creek and the city beyond was completed. Christened, "The Castle," it was completed in 1860 and is one of only two brick homes of this style on the west coast. Today, this architectural landmark is an award winning 21 room B&B on a peaceful tree-lined street with other stately Victorians.

Afternoon Tea is presented by Mary Louise in elaborate buffet style, with lit candelabras, crystal, blue & white floral china, ornate & whimsical 19th century American Victorian silver service, an epergne, and footed cake plates. Parlour seating is at antique tables or by tea carts as in Victorian times. P.S. Weather permitting, the garden is quite wonderful for large groups. F.Y.I. It's just beautiful here in Autumn when the trees are in brilliant color.

$8.50 Windsor Tea & Tour. Finger sandwiches, cream scone with strawberry preserves, mushroom palmiers, Swiss cheese gougeres, fudge, pecan tassies, lemon tarts, espresso cheesecake or Gold Nugget cake, Banbury tarts, a continuous cup of tea plus an historic overview & guided tour of The Red Castle. (Sample Menu)

TEA PARTIES FOR GROUPS: As Scheduled For 6 To 100 Guests
• Available Weekdays • It's OK To Join A Group, Please Call
• Non-Caffeine/Herbal Tea Available
• Watercloset: Same Floor
• **Reservations Are A Must, Please Call To Plan Your Event**
• Street Parking & Private Off-Street Lot
• Credit Cards: V&MC

Proprietor's
*Autograph*_____*Date*_____

OLIVIA'S DOLL HOUSE
Tea Room
22700 Lyons Avenue
Newhall, California

805-222-7331

New Addition...Children's Dress Up Tea Parties At...Olivia's Doll House Tea Room. Catered dress-up tea parties for 6 to 20 children are a delight for so many little girls. They are invited to have their hair styled, have makeup and nail polish applied, and play dress-up. They may borrow gowns, hats, boas and costume jewelry and participate in a fashion show. Little boys are not excluded, with costumes for them as well, and young guests receive a photo button of themselves in their attire.

Birthday attendees sit at a big heart shaped table with the honoree sitting at the "royal" throne. He or she as host, gets to ring the bell for service. To the delight of parents and guardians, the favors, food and birthday or special occasion cake is included. Children attending receive a favor, while the honoree receives a handmade doll as gifts from Olivia's. Olivia's also prepares a record of all gifts received. Hosting and guest parents or guardians are welcome to stay and enjoy the festivities. Parties are two hours and one party is scheduled per time period. Please call for further details.

$225.00 Children's Dress Up Party For 6 Children...(Each additional child $25.00) Fruit & dip platters, tiny pizzas, cocktail wieners, sandwiches, candy, heart shaped brownies, cake, lemonade or iced tea.

TEATIME: As Scheduled, Please Call To Plan
• May Accommodate Some Dietary Needs With Advance Request
• Non-Caffeine Beverages
• Watercloset: Same Floor
• Wheelchair Accessible
• **Reserve At Least Two Weeks In Advance**
• Free Parking Lot
• Cash Or Check, Deposit Required

Proprietor's
*Autograph*_____*Date*_____

A SECRET AFFAIR
3441 Via Lido
Newport Beach, California

714-673-3717

New Addition...It's Teatime At...A Secret Affair.
"Our unique English tea parlour is quite authentic, we're English!" Cheryl and Linda are the proprietors of A Secret Affair in Newport Beach, California. Quite creative, they've named their Afternoon Tea selections to appropriately complement the "secret" theme in the shop's name. But it is no secret that they have a charming tearoom!

Afternoon Tea is served at tables set with silk floral teacup centerpieces, Battenburg lace, Dickens china, floral teapots, black & gold flatware and crystal stemware. Tapestry arm chairs and a circa 1700 French chandelier add to the ambiance. The trellised indoor garden, filled with the sounds of a grand piano is a delightful spot for Afternoon Tea. P.S. Lunch is also offered. Allow time to shop, there are greeting cards, hats, jewelry & gifts. Private tea parties are available for 20 to 40 guests, please call to plan your special event.

$29.95 Tea For Two. Scones, Devon cream & raspberry preserves, tea sandwiches for two, tea cakes or English Trifle, gratis glass of Harvey's Bristol Cream Sherry, a pot of brewed loose tea.

$15.95 Scandalous Tea... Warm scone, Devon cream & preserves, petite tea sandwiches, tea cakes or English Trifle, complimentary glass of Harvey's Bristol Cream Sherry, pot of tea.

$9.95 Romantic Tea... Warm scone with Devon cream & raspberry preserves, petite tea sandwiches, brewed loose tea.

$5.95 Gossip Tea. Scone, cream & preserves, pot of tea.

TEATIME: 11:00am To 5:00pm • Monday Thru Thursday
* 10:00am To 5:00pm, Friday & Saturday
* Sundays Are Reserved For Private Parties Of Ten Or More Guests
* Non-Caffeine/Herbal Tea Available
* Children's Tea Parties Welcome
* Watercloset: Down A Few Steps
* **Reservations Are Requested**
* Metered Street Parking & Nearby Parking Lot
* Credit Cards: V&MC

Proprietor's
*Autograph*_____*Date*_____

FOUR SEASONS
Newport Beach
690 Newport Center Drive
Newport Beach, California

714-759-0808 *Ask For The Gardens Restaurant*

It's Teatime On Saturdays & Sundays For Groups At...Four Seasons. Gracious hospitality awaits you at the Four Seasons, the only Five Diamond hotel in Newport Beach. The Garden's Cafe & Lounge at this prestigious hotel is a beautiful setting for their weekend Afternoon Teas and the annual Holiday Teas as well, which take place in December usually starting from after Thanksgiving and continuing almost daily thru December 24.

Afternoon Tea is attentively served at tables set with Limoges china & fresh flowers. Be sure to stroll around and take in the gardens. F.Y.I. There are 4.7 landscaped acres! You may want to allow extra time since Fashion Island shopping is nearby. Afternoon Teas are available for groups of 10 to 28 guests.

$16.50 Full Tea... Assorted tea sandwiches, currant scone served with Devonshire cream & lemon curd, selection of pastries and a choice of brewed tea.

$21.00 Royal Tea... The above plus of a glass of Champagne or Sherry.

TEA PARTIES FOR GROUPS: 2pm-4:30pm •Saturday & Sunday
• Call For Extended December Afternoon Tea Hours
• May Accommodate Some Dietary Needs, 3 Day Advance Request
• Non-Caffeine/Herbal Tea Available
• Children's Tea Parties Welcome
• Watercloset: Same Floor
• Wheelchair Accessible
• **Reservations Are Required**
• Complimentary Valet Parking
• Credit Cards: V,MC,AE&JCB

Proprietor's
Autograph _____*Date*_____

155

TEA TIME MEMORIES

615 East Balboa Boulevard
Newport Beach, California

714-723-6480

New Addition...It's Teatime At...Tea Time Memories. Why not make a delightful day of tea and shopping on Balboa Peninsula starting with a visit to Teatime Memories? The shop is decorated in forest green and burgundy. A lush artistic floral spray with magnolias, ivy and twinkle lights is quite an eye-catcher. When you make reservations be sure to let Barbara know if it's a birthday, a balloon and gift will wing its way to the honoree!

Afternoon Tea is served at tables set with tablecloths & lace, exceptional fresh flowers, delicate fine china, linen napkins tied with bows, & liquid "candle" luminaries. The plush antiquey tapestry chairs are quite wonderful. Barbara and staff are just a ring away. A bell on each table invites you to ring for service, or your next course. Bring a favorite hat or borrow one of the many placed throughout the shop and pose for a complimentary photo. Allow time to browse, there are Victorian gifts, heritage lace accessories, jewelry, books, baskets, paintings and teapots & teacups beautifully displayed in the little gift shop. Tea parties too, for up to 24 guests. Ask about the Mother & Daughter teas. P.S. $1.off with this book!

$15.95 Afternoon Tea... Scones with cream, lemon curd, raspberry jam & orange marmalade, five finger sandwiches, fresh fruit, a generous dessert, and a pot of brewed loose tea.

$11.95 Pauper's Tea... Scones with cream, lemon curd & preserves, finger sandwiches, fresh fruit, a pot of brewed tea.

$5.95 Tea & Scone

TEATIME: 10:00am To 5:00pm • Wednesday Thru Monday
• May Accommodate Some Dietary Needs With Advance Request
• Non-Caffeine/Herbal Tea Available
• Children's Tea Parties Welcome
• Wheelchair Accessible • Watercloset: Same Floor
• **Reservations Are Suggested**
• Metered Street Parking & Nearby Pay Lot
• Credit Cards: V,MC&AE, Checks OK

Proprietor's
*Autograph*_____*Date*_____

Celebrate beautiful memories with Afternoon Tea!

TEACUPS & TULIPS
400 Westminster Avenue
Newport Beach, California

714-650-5223

New Tearoom Brewing...Its Teatime At...Teacups
& Tulips. Think pink when you look for this new tea spot located
in a 1940's pink & white house. Justine, the new proprietor has
expanded the shop previously known as Crafter's Corner to include
two tearooms. Her Tea Rose Room is especially for grandmothers,
mothers & children, and is decorated in lilac & pink with cabbage
rose prints & ribbons. Special attention will be given to youngsters.

Afternoon Tea will be presented on tiered caddies at tables
set with tablecloths, an assortment of fine china, both cloth & paper
napkins, & fresh flowers arranged in Justine's personal prized
collection of vases. The main tearoom is bright and airy with floral
& lattice pattern wallpaper accenting the bright salmon walls and
white lacey curtains. Allow time to browse, the T &T has clothing &
accessories, a vintage kitchen room, children's room, garden path,
hand-painted furnishings, antiques & more. Outside dining & light
lunches are planned. Tea parties too, for 18-20 guests.

$16.95 Tulips Tea. Finger sandwiches, salad, fruit, petite
desserts, scones, Devon cream & preserves & brewed loose tea.
$13.95 Justine's Tea...Finger sandwiches, scones,
cream & preserves, fruit, dessert & brewed loose tea.
$6.95 Demi Tea...Scones, Devon cream & brewed tea.

ANTICIPATED **TEATIME:** 10am-5:30pm • Tuesday Thru Saturday
• Sunday & Monday By Advance Reservation Only
• May Accommodate Some Dietary Needs With Advance Request
• Non-Caffeine/Herbal Tea Available
• Children's Tea Parties Welcome, Ages 5+
• Watercloset: Same Floor
• **Reservations Are Requested**
• Free Rear Parking Lot
• Credit Cards: V,MC,DIS&AE
Proprietor's
*Autograph*_____*Date*_____

FLICKERING FLAMES
& Special Things

2085-A River Road At Second Street
Norco, California

909-371-1034

New Addition...It's Teatime At...Flickering Flames & Special Things. Something of a General Store, Flickering Flames is located in a rural Southern California community. For more than 10 years, a United States Post Office has been located here along with an ever expanding gift & candle shop. Kim, the proprietor is very happy to bring Afternoon Teas to town.

Afternoon Tea with a frequently changing menu, is served on "Duchess" by Arthur Wood, English bone china. The tearoom has a pastel Victorian garden look with soft hued tablecloths, white furniture, floral wallpaper and a waterfall. Allow time to browse around, there's a lot to see. P.S.Why not bring along your address book. You can pick out pretty note cards and drop a few lines to friends while you're having tea. Your envelopes will have a Norco U.S. Mail postmark, and you can't beat the convenience! F.Y.I. Private tea parties are available for 2 to 24 guests.

$14.95 Enchanted Tea... English tea sandwiches, petit quiche, scone with Devonshire cream & raspberry preserves, fresh fruit, special sweets, a pot of tea. And it's ok to change tea choice.
$7.95 Pot Of Tea & Dessert

TEATIME: 11:30am To 3:00pm • Tuesday Thru Saturday
• Sundays May Be Available For Groups By Special Request
• May Accommodate Some Dietary Needs With Advance Request
• Non-Caffeine/Herbal Tea Available
• Children's Tea Parties Welcome
• Watercloset: Same Floor
• **24 Hour Advance Reservation Required**
• Free Parking Lot
• Credit Cards: V,MC,DIS&AE

Proprietor's
*Autograph*_____*Date*_____

TOUCH OF BRITAIN

5712 Watt Avenue
(Near McClellan A.F.B.)
North Highlands, California

916-344-8472

New Addition..It's Teatime On Saturdays At...Touch of Britain. Visit an authentic English tearoom right here in North Highlands. Lilian and Jean are on their second decade of serving the community with British delicacies and imported foods & gifts. "High Teas" are usually served in May and September.

I somehow get the feeling that these proprietors are looking at the world through proverbial, rose-colored glasses. Cream Teas are served in the quaint pink tearoom at tables set with pink tablecloths & small pink floral centerpieces. The curtains are pink and white striped, the binds are pink, and the proprietors and staff wear pink and white outfits. Private tea parties are available for 20 to 40 guests. If you're feeling "in the pink" you now know where to go! F.Y.I. They are also are well known for their tasty fish & chips.

$12.95 Touch Of Britain High Tea... Assorted finger sandwiches, small scones served with Devonshire cream & preserves, assorted pastries, and a pot of tea.

$4.50 Cream Tea... Homemade raisin scone served with Devonshire cream & preserves and a pot of tea.

$2.75 Pot Of Tea... Brewed English bagged or loose tea.

$2.00 Crumpets... Yummy & homebaked.

TEATIME: 11:00am To 3:00pm • Monday Thru Saturday
• 12Noon To 3:00pm, Sunday
• Non-Caffeine/Herbal Tea Available
• Watercloset: Same Floor
• Wheelchair Accessible
• **Reservations Are Required**
• Free Parking Lot
• Credit Cards: V&MC

Proprietor's
*Autograph*_____*Date*_____

THE MAYFLOWER CLUB, INC.

11110 Victory Boulevard
North Hollywood, California

818-760-9367

Benefit Afternoon Tea Dances...And A Christmas Tea At...The Mayflower Club. The Afternoon Tea Dances and the Christmas Tea are festive and popular events for The Mayflower Club. The Tea Dance features live music, often with an appearance by a former member of the R.A.F.Orchestra. Much of the money raised from these entertaining teas goes towards a very special children's event which The Mayflower Club holds annually.

Since 1972, nearly 200 special needs children have been invited annually to the club to enjoy "The Mayflower Players" perform their English pantomime. The youthful audiences gleefully participate as The Mayflower Players bring each colorful storybook character to life. Children receive gifts and a good time is had by all.
December 7, 1997.$8.00 Christmas Afternoon Tea Program. 2:00 To 4:30 Tea sandwiches, scone with cream & jam, English Christmas cake, tea and Christmas Carols by the choir.

June 7, 1998...$8.00 Afternoon Tea Dance. 2:30 To 5:30, Tea sandwiches, scone with cream & jam, dessert and tea.
August 23, 1998. $8.00 Afternoon Tea Dance. 2:30-5:30 Tea sandwiches, scone, cream & jam, dessert and tea.
December 6, 1998...$8.00 Christmas Afternoon Tea Program. 2:00 To 4:30 Tea sandwiches, scone with cream & jam, English Christmas cake, tea and Christmas Carols by the choir. Please call for the 1999 schedule of events.

FUNDRAISER TEAS & TEA DANCE: As Scheduled
• Watercloset: Same Floor
• **Reservations Are Required, Please Call To Confirm Dates**
• Parking Lot And Street Parking
• Prepay By Check & Ticket Will Be Sent
Director's
*Autograph*_____*Date*_____

(Circa 1879
Paddison Farm

PADDISON FARM
Victorian Estate
11951 Imperial Highway
Norwalk, California

562-863-4567

Theme Tea Parties For Groups At...Paddison Farm. Paddison Farm is listed on the National Register of Historic Places. Established as an agricultural farm in 1879, it is owned by the 4th and 5th generation descendants of John Paddison. The Eastlake Victorian architecture, gazebo, rose arbor, and six acre country setting make a charming backdrop for TV, movies & private tea parties for the special events in your life, for 20 to 200 guests.

The proprietor has designed an Anne of Green Gables Tea & a Secret Garden Tea. Either may be scheduled for your private tea party. Non-theme teas or your own theme teas are welcome too. Parties are usually scheduled on Friday or Sunday afternoons. Please call to plan, and reserve your event date well in advance.

$26.00 Secret Garden Private Theme Tea Party...(20+ Guests) Citron & current scone with jam & creme fraiche, savories including walnut bread with almond chicken salad, garnished with edible flowers, lemon pound cake with fresh berries, chippers, sugar and spice heart, apple-cinnamon tea. (Menu varies)

$26.00 Anne Of Green Gables Private Theme Tea Party...(20+ Guests) Avonlea scone, preserves & cream, egg salad pastry cups, tea sandwiches, lemon tartlets, gingersnaps, "Anne's" chocolate goblin cake, raspberry cordial, kindred spirits Blackberry tea, Victorian bottle centerpieces. The pourer is beloved "Anne", ready to engage in lively poetic conversation. Piped-in "Anne" music & collectibles boutique, library too. (Menu varies)

PRIVATE TEA PARTIES ONLY: Call To Plan Your Tea Party
- May Accommodate Some Dietary Needs, 7 Day Advance Request
- Non-Caffeine Tea On Request
- Watercloset: Same Floor
- **Reservations Are Required, Please Book Your Date Early**
- Complimentary Park In Adjacent Lot
- Cash Or Check

Proprietor's
*Autograph*_____*Date*_____

VICTORIAN HILLTOP HOUSE
(Between San Bernardino and Hesperia)
Oak Hills, California

760-956-1243

A Tea & Victorian Fashion Tour At...Victorian Hilltop House. A very special experience awaits you at Victorian Hilltop House. The proprietor is a social & fashion historian who writes and speaks on Victorian lifestyles, clothing, customs, etiquette and the ritual of Afternoon Tea. You will be invited to the proprietors home much as in Victorian times when friends visited friends for Afternoon Tea. Barbara's home is a Queen Anne style new Victorian, built in 1992. You are all invited to wear your finest Victorian attire for tea. Hats and gloves are encouraged but optional.

Tea guests will be treated to a tour of vintage fashion memorabilia in the Carriage House Studio Museum. You are invited to view fashions and accessories from the 1860's to the 1960's including Victorian and Edwardian wedding gowns and Flapper and Civil War Era dresses. P.S. This talented tea expert has written a lovely gift book entitled, "Angel Victorian Tea Book". F.Y.I. The gates open at 1:45pm for your convenience, however please note, guests will be greeted at the door at 2:00pm.

$15.00 Victorian 3 Course Afternoon Tea... Start with warm savories and tea sandwiches, fresh homemade scone usually orange/nutmeg or apple/pecan served with Devon cream & fresh homemade lemon curd courtesy of the backyard lemon tree, fresh homemade jam & jelly, fresh seasonal fruit, specialty dessert such as: chocolate truffle torte with raspberry sauce garnished with kiwi & fresh garden grown mint, dessert tray, and brewed loose tea.

TEA & FASHION TOUR: Call For Monthly Schedule
- 2:00pm To 4:30pm Usually, Or As Scheduled • Up To 16 Guests
- Weekdays & Saturdays As Scheduled
- Non-Caffeine/Herbal Tea Available
- Watercloset: Same Floor
- Unlimited-Time Off-Street Parking Area
- **Reservations Are Required**
- Check Or Money-Order, Prepay Two Weeks In Advance

Proprietor's
*Autograph*_____*Date*_____

DUNSMUIR
House & Gardens
2960 Peralta Oaks Court
Oakland, California

510-615-5555

Christmas Tea & Tour...At...Dunsmuir House & Gardens. Annually, for two magical weeks in December it's holiday time at the beautiful 37 room, 1899 Colonial Revival Dunsmuir Mansion. Floral designers and more than 100 volunteers decorate the mansion to create a breathtaking turn of the century holiday masterpiece. Meander through the first and second floor rooms filled with elegant Edwardian era decorations and antique furnishings. Enjoy horse drawn carriage rides reminiscent of the mid 1800's, fabulous holiday entertainment, a soiree, artistic decorations, period costumes, unique gifts, and wonderful weekend Holiday Teas!

The elegant weekend Christmas Teas served on fine china and silver at The Dinkelspiel House is a must! Be sure to also visit The Dunsmuir Gift Shop which carries tea-related gifts. Advance reservations are highly recommended for the Christmas Tea & Tour. Seatings are usually at 11:30am, 1:30pm, & 3:30pm on scheduled Fridays, Saturdays & Sundays during this period, please call for dates. F.Y.I. This fabulous spot may be rented for your special events for 75-300 guests indoors and up to 4,000 guests outdoors. Ask Roselyn for info & to reserve a date. P.S.Scheduled events take place throughout the year in addition to the Christmas Tea & Tour.

$25.00 (Approx.) Holiday Tea & Tour... Freshly baked scones with whipped sweet butter, lemon curd & fruit jam, tea sandwiches, fresh fruit, mini desserts may include tea cookies, cranberry nut bread, chocolate mousse pastry cups, lemon & apricot bars and a pot of Dunsmuir blend tea. Price includes entrance fee.

DECEMBER CHRISTMAS TEA & TOUR: Please Call For Dates
- Usually The First Two Weeks In December
- Seatings: 11:30am, 1:30pm & 3:30pm
- Watercloset: Same Floor • Wheelchair Accessible
- **Reservations Are A Must**
- Free Street Parking
- Credit Cards: MC&V

Director's
*Autograph*_____*Date*_____

MENDIPS-A TEA PARLOUR

305 West Ojai Avenue
Ojai, California

805-640-8327

New Addition...It's Teatime At...Mendips. Three generations of ladies are likely to greet you at this new tearoom in Ojai. Carol the proprietor, actually owned a tearoom on the east coast at one time, but returned home to Ojai to open Mendips with her mother Virginia and her daughter Sydney. Mendips is a petite tea parlour decorated in a deep Victorian palette and style with oriental rugs and upholstered sofas. Everything is antiquey including the teacups & teapots. Carol has collected teapots since high school.

Afternoon Tea is served at tables set with lace tablecloths, the family collection of translucent bone china teacups, and fresh flowers. Everything is homemade and baked fresh daily at Mendips with ingredients like plugre, which is European pure butter. The cream scones as well as most of the other baked goods herald from old family recipes. The bread is made from a circa 1730 recipe. Ask about Mendips' own blend of tea. P.S. Did you notice the Victorian gazing ball? Anyone curious about the name of this tearoom?

$15.00 Victoria Tea... Tea sandwiches, cream scones, afters, and a pot of brewed loose tea.

$7.00 Earl Of Sandwich Trey... Seven assorted tea sandwiches on homemade bread, a pot of brewed loose tea.

$7.00 Albert's Cream Tea... Cream scones baked to order served with jam & cream and a pot of brewed loose tea.

TEATIME: 12:00 To 5:00pm • Wednesday Thru Sunday
• May Accommodate Some Dietary Needs with Advance Request
• Non-Caffeine/Herbal Tea Available
• Watercloset: Same Floor
• **Reservations: No**
• Free Street Parking
• Cash Only

Proprietor's
*Autograph*_____*Date*_____

THE PLAZA PANTRY

221 East Matilija
Ojai, California

805-646-6325

Wednesday Once-A-Month Teas At...The Plaza Pantry. (By advance reservation) The Plaza Pantry is an informal British restaurant and English goodies shop where you can enjoy a proper pot of tea and many homebaked English "afters". If you're a large group do "ring" Beryl up and let her know you're on the way.

Afternoon Tea is served on the first Wednesday of the month. The proprietor gussies thing up a bit with tablecloths and fresh flowers. Each guest is served from a pretty platter. The teacups are Beryl's own collection of assorted English china. Individual Brown Betty teapots are used exclusively. F.Y.I. You may purchase a varity of English gift & food items at Plaza Pantry including Beryl's homemade Christmas cake at holiday time. Ask about International Dinners complete with entertainment. Private tea parties are available for 8 to 20 guests.

$5.00 Wednesday Tea... Assorted tea sandwiches, scone with cream & preserves or crumpet with homemade lemon curd, three assorted fancies, and a pot English tea, of course.

WEDNESDAY TEAS: First Wednesday Of Month
- May Accommodate Some Dietary Needs With Advance Request
- " Spot of Tea And..." 8am To 4pm • Monday Thru Saturday
- Non-Caffeine/Herbal Tea Available
- Watercloset: Same Floor
- Wheelchair Accessible
- **Reservations Requested For Wednesday Afternoon Teas**
- Free Parking Lot With Two Hour Limit
- Cash Or Check

Proprietor's
*Autograph*_____*Date*_____

Apricot Ginger Bread

*Courtesy of **Celestial Seasonings***

1 cup water
4 Apricot Ginger tea bags
1 cup softened butter
1 cup brown sugar

1 cup honey
3 eggs
2 1/2 cups flour
1/2 teaspoons baking powder

Bring the water to a boil in a heavy saucepan. Add the tea bags and continue to boil for 5 minutes. Remove and discard the bags. Place the butter, sugar, and honey in a large mixing. Pour the tea over, and whisk and whisk until the butter is belted and slightly cooled. Beat the eggs, and add. Then stir in the dry ingredients and beat until smooth. Pour into a buttered (or any non-stick sprayed) 9x13-inch pan, and bake at 350 degrees F. for 50 to 60 minutes until done.

Mango Ceylon Sorbet

*Compliments of **The Republic of Tea***

"This most flavored tea is light, sweet, and intoxicatingly fragrant. Mango and marigold blossoms are blended with superior black leaf teas to produce an uplifting cup. A favorite retreat for coffee lovers, this tea is great hot or iced. Here is a quick tropical recipe for the summertime."

4 teaspoons Republic of Tea Mango Ceylon Tea
1 1/2 cups of boiling water
3 teaspoons of raw sugar
Half a beaten egg white
Springs of mint for garnish

Infuse the tea for 3-4 minutes in freshly boiled water. Pour the in a bowl and melt the sugar in the hot tea. Cool, then put in the freezer till half frozen. Carefully mix in the egg white and leave to freeze completely. Serve the sorbet, which should be soft, in pre-cooled glasses. Garnish with mint. Serves 4.

A special Afternoon Tea is worth waiting for!

TOTTENHAM COURT LTD.

242 East Ojai Avenue
Ojai, California

805-646-2339

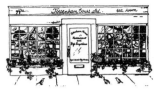

It's Teatime At...Tottenham Court Ltd. Tottenham Court is a favorite of Afternoon Tea lovers. The cheery atmosphere invites you to forget time and just enjoy the day. Tottenham Court is the recipient of the Fortnum & Mason award for excellence in tea service, a tribute marking the first time this award has been presented to a dining establishment outside of Great Britain! You'll be tea-totally inspired here, great shopping is accompanied by the lively tunes of a pianist, the shop is brimming with treasures.

Afternoon Tea is presented on tiered caddies at tables set with rose pattern tablecloths, "Summer Chintz" English china & either mini rose topiaries or glowing tea lamps. The attentive servers are attired in pinafores. Allow time to shop, the antique apothecary cabinets are full of glorious gifts. F.Y.I. The terrific mural is by Suzanne Miller of Empire State Building fame. P.S. Andi will be happy to help you create a unique and memorable tea party for about 30 guests. P.S. Champagne, wine & imported beer available too.

$12.50 The Queen's Own Tea... Array of finger sandwiches, scone, imported Devonshire cream, preserves or lemon curd, trio of sweets, Cream Sherry, and a pot of brewed loose tea.
$8.50 Children's Princess Tea...A smaller version of the Queen's Own Tea, for children under 12 years old only.

TEATIME: 11:00am To 5:00pm • Thursday Thru Tuesday
• Tuesday & Wednesday Are Now Reserved For Private Tea Parties
• May Accommodate Some Dietary Needs, 1 Week Advance Request
• Non-Caffeine/Herbal Tea Available
• Children's Tea Parties Welcome
• Watercloset: Same Floor
• Wheelchair Accessible
• **Reservations Advised For Weekends**
• Two Hour Free Park On Ojai & Rear Lot
• Credit Cards: V,MC&AE

Proprietor's
Autograph _____*Date*_____

BEST OF FRIENDS
Tea Room
1051 North Meads
(Ridgeline Country Club)
Orange, California

714-633-4710

It's Tee & Tea Time At...Best Friends Tea Room.
What a pleasant surprise to discover Best Friends Tea Room situated inside The Ridgeline Country Club's Club House. This is truly an unexpected spot for Afternoon Tea. Kathy's tearoom is beautifully appointed with careful attention to Victorian detail.

Afternoon Tea is served at pretty antique tables with fresh flowers, linens, pretty china and classical music. On a cool late afternoon or evening, the fireplace and candlelit atmosphere make for a warm and charming Afternoon or Evening Tea. "Be ready to enjoy an hour of friendly chatter & delicate tasty treats and treasures while sipping a perfectly brewed cup of tea". Private tea parties are available for 15 to 28 guests. Please call to plan your special event.

$15.00 Good Morning Tea At 10am... Scone, jam & cream, wild rice & pecan pancakes with hot spiced fruit, tearoom eggs, fresh fruit, sweet treasures and an a pot of brewed loose tea.
$15.00 Best Of Friends Tea At 1pm... Scone, jam & cream, soup, tea sandwiches, fresh fruit, sweet treats, pot of tea.
$18.95 Evening Teas At 4:00pm... Scone with jam & sweet cream, tea sandwiches, fresh fruit, Victorian stew, sweet treats, pot of tea. For groups of 15 or more by advance reservation.

TEATIME: 10am & 1pm • Friday, Saturday, Sunday & Monday
- May Accommodate Some Dietary Needs, 1 Week Advance Request
- Non-Caffeine/Herbal Tea Available
- Children's Tea Parties Welcome
- Wheelchair Accessible • Watercloset: Same Floor
- **One Week Advance Reservation For Weekends**
- Free Parking Lot
- Cash Or Check

Proprietor's
*Autograph*_____*Date*_____

BUTTERCUP COTTAGE
269 North Glassell
Old Towne Orange, California

714-997-5895

New Addition...It's Teatime At...Buttercup Cottage. Do you remember when friends would hold a fresh-picked buttercup under your chin to see if you liked butter? Well you'll be all aglow again on your way up the steps to the adorable Buttercup Cottage! The outside is as cute and inviting as the inside. Not only are there precious hand-painted "scenes" perfectly perched, but the surrounding white picket fence and gate are crowned by cut out teapots and teacups. It is obvious that the proprietors Janette and Tamara were creative and worked diligently on their tearoom.

Afternoon Tea is served with colorful tablecloths, fresh flowers and eclectic English bone china at this cheerful spot decorated in buttercup yellow, periwinkle & teal. Borrow a vintage hat from Janette's fab vintage collection. Allow time to browse in the gift shop which features romantic clothing, unique gifts, hats, vases, linens & more. Tea parties are available for up to 32 guests.

$16.95 Buttercup Tea... Assorted tea sandwiches, homebaked scone with jam & sweet creme, homemade soup, petite salad, freshly baked sweets and a pot of brewed loose tea.
$9.95 Sunflower Tea...(Children 7&Under) Scone, jam & creme, tea sandwiches, fruit, sweet surprise and tea or lemonade.
$5.50 Tea &Scone. No reservation needed for this repast.

TEATIME: 11:00am To 2:30pm • Wednesday Thru Friday
• Two Seatings On Saturday, 11:00am & 3:00pm
• May Accommodate Some Veggie Needs, 1 Day Advance Request
• Non-Caffeine/Herbal Tea Available
• Children's Tea Parties Welcome
• Watercloset: Same Floor
• **Reservations Required For Buttercup & Sunflower Teas**
• Free Parking Lot & Two Hour Street Parking
• Credit Cards: V&MC
Proprietor's
*Autograph*_____*Date*_____

171

SOMEPLACE IN TIME
Tea Room

132 South Glassell
(Antique Mall, Historic Old Town)
Orange, California

714-538-9411

It's Teatime At...Someplace In Time Tea Room. This spot of tea offers a welcome respite to a hectic "tour of shopping". After visiting 45 dealers on three floors all with cleverly displayed collectibles & antiques, a pick-me-up tea may be just the ticket. After all, think of the calories you've just burned!

Afternoon Tea is served adjacent to the antiques, or outside on the patio at tables set with tablecloths, and enchanting "memorabilia under glass," cloth napkins, fresh plants, edible flowers and a mis-matched collection of china. I really enjoyed "reading" my table. The proprietors Cheryl & Vicki welcome you to borrow a vintage hat & boa if you like, to complete your Afternoon Tea ensemble. P.S. Lunch is available in addition to Afternoon Tea. Someplace In Time is available for private tea parties for your group too. F.Y.I.Special occasion teas are planned throughout the year, please call for schedule. Gift certificates too.

$13.95 The Queen Elizabeth Tea... Tea sandwiches, fresh fruit, scone with Devonshire cream & jam, a lovely dessert, pot of brewed loose tea. (Reservations are recommended & must be guaranteed by credit card. Walk-ins may be accommodated.)
$5.25 Anne Boleyn Tea. Dessert or scone & brewed tea.

TEATIME: 11:00am To 4:00pm • Tuesday Thru Sunday
• May Accommodate Some Vegetarian Needs With Advance Request
• Non-Caffeine/Herbal Tea Available
• Watercloset: First Floor
• **Reservations & Guarantee Required For Queen Elizabeth Tea**
• Free Parking In The Rear
• Credit Cards: MC&V
Proprietor's
*Autograph*_______*Date*_____

THE FRENCH INN
248 South Batavia
Orange, California

714-997-5038

New Owner..High Tea For Groups Of 12 Or More Guests At...The French Inn. The time honored tradition of "meeting for tea at The French Inn" continues. The Mediterranean Revival style French Inn, built in 1892 is on the National Register of Historic Places. Attractive grounds surround the home which Sarah, has recently redecorated. The heritage rose garden near the vine covered arbor is also a fine spot for a summer tea. A full menu of homemade specialties is offered at The Inn in addition to High Teas & International Theme Teas. Sarah's eclectic heirloom collection of clear & green depression glass & vintage teacups is a nice addition.

Afternoon Tea is presented buffet style from the historic dining table. Guests are seated on comfortable chairs in the parlour, where they may wander about and chat with friends or peruse the many collectible books placed throughout. P.S. A vintage Steinway piano is available for musical guests. Please call for date & details. Sarah will help you plan a "tailor-made" tea party for up to 175 guests. F.Y.I. Sarah can provide speakers for an additional fee. P.S. A new gift shop is opening. Ask about Holiday Boutique Teas.

$15.00 The French Inn High Tea... Assorted tea sandwiches, homebaked scones served with Devonshire cream & preserves, a special hot savory dish or chilled salad an assortment of confections, pots of brewed loose tea. (Per person plus tax & fees.)

HIGH TEA FOR GROUPS: 12 To 175 Guests • As Scheduled
• Available Seven Days A Week • Please Call To Plan
• May Accommodate Some Dietary Needs With Advance Request
• Non-Caffeine/Herbal Tea Available
• Watercloset Same Floor
• **Reserve Your Group's Date Early**
• Unmetered Street Parking
• Cash Or Check
Proprietor's
*Autograph*_____*Date*_____

RONALD McDONALD HOUSE
Benefit Tea *at* The Center Club

650 Town Center Drive
(Adjacent To The Performing Arts Center) Costa Mesa, California

714-639-3600 *Invitation*   **714-662-3415** *Directions*

New Addition...October Annual Ronald McDonald House Benefit Tea & Fashion Show At...The Center Club. What a wonderful opportunity to enjoy tea at a really special private club and help support the outstanding efforts of The Orange County Ronald McDonald House. The House is a "home-away-from-home" for families of children undergoing treatment for life threatening illnesses at nearby Children's Hospital of Orange County, or any of the nine hospitals in Orange County with pediatric care centers. Since 1989, over 3,000 families have been served.

A wonderful Tea & Fashion Show are elegantly presented in The Center Club's Garden Court, a small ballroom with floor to ceiling windows overlooking a Japanese water garden. Chandeliers, handsome wood paneling, landscape oils by renowned California artists, dusky rose and blue carpet, and The Center Club silver service contribute to the beautiful old world grandeur here. You're golden efforts to support this fine organization are truly appreciated. A Fashion Show and opportunity tickets add to the festivities!

$50.00 The Center Club Tea.. Finger sandwiches such as curried chicken with almonds & apricot chutney, raisin scones, Devonshire cream & strawberry preserves, Victorian poppy seed cake, banana pound cake, mini tarts, double chocolate brownies, chocolate dipped strawberries, and a continuous cup of tea.

ANNUAL BENEFIT TEA: 3pm To 5pm, As Scheduled Mid-October
- Non-Caffeine/Herbal Tea Available
- Watercloset: Same Floor • Wheelchair Accessible
- **Early Reservations Are Suggested**
- Gratis Valet Parking Included
- Credit Card: MC

Director's
*Autograph*_____*Date*_____

174

THE ROSE COTTAGE
Antiques
254 South Glassell Street
Orange, California

714-516-1472

The Rose Cottage
Antiques
Collectibles • Gifts • Tea • Etiquette

*New Tearoom Brewing...*It's Teatime At...The Rose Cottage Antiques. Janie and Olga have exciting ideas for their new antique store & tearoom situated in a century old Victorian cottage. The cottage is painted blush rose with green trim and a green roof. There are beautiful gardens with roses everywhere, and a wonderful white picket fence. Tea Etiquette classes, along with Theme Tea events are planned. Olga is a restauranteur, Janie an antique specialist, their talents combine beautifully.

Afternoon Tea will be presented on tiered caddies at tables set with three petticoats, fresh flowers, and a matching color palette of china by servers attired in lace pinnies. The Victorian dining room is appointed with antique furnishings, a fireplace, crystal chandelier and rosy hand-stenciled walls. Allow plenty of time to browse in The Gift Room, Children's Room & Ladies' Boudoir for unique gifts, American & English teaware, jewelry, linens & books. Parties soon for 20-24 guests. Intimate teas in the Ladies' Boudoir too.

$14.95 Lady Di's Afternoon Tea... Tea sandwiches, tea breads, assorted desserts, handmade truffles, brewed loose tea.
$9.95 Fergie's Cream Tea... Fresh fruit & seasonal berries, scone, cream & preserves, pot of brewed loose tea.
$4.95 Light Afternoon Tea... Freshly baked scone with cream & preserves, pot of brewed loose tea.

TEATIME: 11:30am To 3:00pm • Wednesday Thru Sunday
• May Accommodate Some Dietary Needs With Advance Request
• Non-Caffeine/Herbal Tea Available
• Children's Tea Parties Welcome, Ages 10+
• Watercloset: Same Floor
• **Reservations Are Appreciated**
• Small Rear Parking Lot & Unmetered Street Parking
• Credit Cards: V,MC&AE

Proprietor's
*Autograph*_____*Date*_____

THE VICTORIAN MANOR
Tea Rooms & Garden
204 North Olive Street
Old Towne Orange, California

714-771-4044

New Addition...It's Teatime At...The Victorian Manor Tea Rooms & Garden. If you see a turn of the century lilac Victorian mansion with a wrap porch trimmed in white & deep pink, it must be The Victorian Manor. Carol & Kelly's tearoom offers Afternoon Tea and lunches which are served in four rooms throughout the mansion. You may choose to take tea in The Rose Room, the lavender hued Elizabeth Ann Room, the yellow Magnolia Room or on the second floor, in the blue Wedgewood Room.

Afternoon Tea is served at tables set with pastel tablecloths, fresh flowers & mismatched fine china. Hand painted chairs are a nice touch. The servers are attired in black uniforms, with white Battenburg lace aprons or vests and teapot name pins. A Cordon Bleu trained chef supervises the kitchen and all delectables are made on premises. F.Y.I. A full lunch menu is available in addition to Afternoon Tea. P.S. Private tea parties too, please call to plan.

$14.98 Princess Anne Tea... Signature heart shaped scone, cream & assorted jams, soup, tea sandwiches, lemon parfait & fruit, truffles, Victorian Manor confections, brewed loose tea.

$12.98 Duchess Tea... Heart shaped scone served with "manor" cream & assorted jams, tea sandwiches, lemon parfait & fruit, truffles, Victorian Manor confections, pot of brewed loose tea.

TEATIME: 10:00am To 5:00pm • Seven Days A Week
- May Accommodate Some Dietary Needs With Advance Request
- Non-Caffeine/Herbal Tea Available
- Children's Tea Parties Welcome
- Watercloset: Same Floor
- Wheelchair Accessible First Floor
- **Reservations Are Recommended**
- Ample Free Parking Lot
- Credit Cards:V,MC,DIS&AE

Proprietor's
*Autograph*_____*Date*_____

THE HOLIDAY HOUSE
750 South "B" Street
(In Heritage Square)
Oxnard, California

805-483-4542

Private Tea Parties At...The Holiday House. "Our pride and pleasure is our customers," says Rosemary the proprietor of the adorable Holiday House in Oxnard's unique Heritage Square. Holiday House is a historic house which was actually re-located along with others to make a "village" called Heritage Square. The house was lovingly renovated by the artistic proprietor and offers many interesting nooks and rooms in which to wander about. Discover beautiful artwork, an adorable tearoom and more.

Several theme teas are planned throughout the year and include Valentine's Tea, St.Patrick's Day Tea, Spring Tea, Mother's Day Tea, Summer Tea, Autumn Tea and Holiday Tea. Please call for dates and information. Private tea parties by appointment only.

$12.50 Tea Luncheon... Umbrella sandwiches, Heritage Squares, fruit platters and tea. (Price is per person for a party of 10 guests with advance reservation.)

$7.50 A Tea Party For Young Ladies... Mini tea cakes, condiments and fruited tea. (Price is per person for a party for 10 guests by advance reservation.)

PRIVATE TEA PARTIES: Up To 10 Guests By Appointment
- May Accommodate Some Dietary Needs With Advance Request
- Non-Caffeine/Herbal Tea Available
- Children's Tea Parties Welcome
- Watercloset: Same Floor
- Wheelchair Accessible
- **Teas By Appointment Only**
- Free Parking Lot
- Credit Cards: MC&V

Proprietor's
*Autograph*_____*Date*_____

177

DOROTHY MARIE'S
Tea Company

716 Lighthouse Avenue
Pacific Grove, California

408-373-8463

It's Teatime At...Dorothy Marie's Tea Company. This early 1900's former courthouse is the home of Dorothy Marie's Victorian tearoom. The shop and tearoom are decorated in a pretty pastel palette of antiques and fine linens. Tea is served from a collection of new and old English bone china teacups, some actually belonged to Dorothy Marie's grandmother. A local harpist often plays during Afternoon Tea. F.Y.I. An informal history of tea class usually takes place on the last Saturday of the month.

The gift shop specializes in all things that go with tea as well as carrying Dorothy Marie's own blend of tea. You'll especially like the whimsical handmade tea cozies made by the proprietor's mom. Ask about Children's Etiquette Teas. P.S. Watch for the new Dorothy Marie's Tea Company in Carmel, California.

$13.25 Dorothy Marie's Tea Ceremony... Assorted finger sandwiches, homemade scone served with Devonshire cream & preserves, delectable French pastries, pot of brewed loose tea.

$6.95 Cream Tea... Fresh homemade scone served with Devonshire cream & preserves, seasonal fruit and a pot of tea.

TEATIME: 11:30am To 3:30pm • Tuesday Thru Saturday
- May Accommodate Some Dietary Needs With Advance Request
- Non-Caffeine/Herbal Tea Available
- Children's Tea Parties Welcome
- Watercloset: A Few Steps Up
- **Reservations Are Recommended**
- Street Parking
- Credit Cards: V,MC&AE

Proprietor's
*Autograph*_____*Date*_____

A LA TARTE PATISSERIE
& Salon De The

1037 Swarthmore Avenue
Pacific Palisades, California

310-459-6635

New Tearoom Brewing At...A La Tarte Patisserie
& Salon De The. Bonnie lived in France for many years before
moving here to open her bakery. Together, she and Bert are the
proprietors of this simply lovely French Normandy patisserie &
soon to be salon de the. Plans are brewing to knock out a wall and
create a beautiful new tea salon. Now that's a "grand opening!"
    Afternoon Tea will be presented at antique tables set with
fresh flowers and mis-matched fine china & silver by servers
wearing white tabliers as in France. The shop is artfully decorated
with terra cotta tile floors, a fountain, antique lace curtains, antique
European furnishings and just a few of Bonnie's favorite "frogs."
There are also "country chic" wicker baskets, copper pots &
wonderful handmade ceramics by Susan, Bonnie's sister-in-law.
P.S. Enjoy al fresco terrace dining under a market umbrella. F.Y.I.
Lunch and tres magnifique French pastries auci. Bon Appetit!

    $16.00 Tea Time... Freshly prepared canapes, scones
served with Devon cream, lemon curd & cranberry-pear preserves, a
variety of petit fours such as mini-operas, French macaroons, fresh
fruit tarts or almond tuiles, and a pot of brewed loose tea.

ANTICIPATED **TEATIME:** 2pm To 5pm • Tuesday Thru Saturday
• Expansion Plans Brewing, Call For Extended Hours & Days
• May Accommodate Some Dietary Needs With Advance Request
• Non-Caffeine/Herbal Tea Available • Very Vegan Friendly
• Watercloset: Same Floor
• **Reservations Are Appreciated**
• Small Rear Parking Lot & Metered Street Parking
• Credit Card: V
Proprietor's
*Autograph*_____*Date*_____

TEA TIME

542 Ramona Street
(In The Heart Of Downtown)
Palo Alto, California

650-328-2877

It's Teatime At...Tea Time. This tea lover's shop is "dedicated to the enjoyment of fine quality teas from around the world." Tea Time is a casual California style tea shop located in an interesting old stone building in the heart of downtown Palo Alto. Molly and Michael's emphasis is on personal service and tea education, including the proper preparation of a pot of tea. You may choose from over 100 varieties of fine quality teas, tisanes and herbal blends. All teas are brewed in Chatsford teapots with built-in mesh infusers. Tea is measured in grams for each size teapot and after proper brewing, is served in tea glasses. Tasty cream scones with lemon curd are the most popular accompaniment to tea.

Shelves are filled with exquisite blue and white Lomonosov porcelain tea sets from Russia as well as fine tea accouterments including tea tins, tea strainers, electric tea kettles and vintage fine bone china teacups. Look for the gold canisters which hold their precious teas, and explore the world of tea through "smelling cups." F.Y.I. Mail-order now available, please visit Tea Time's new website: www.tea-time.com

$5.95 Plate Of Tea Sandwiches
$2.00, $3.25 Or $4.75 Pot Of Tea... Small, medium or large pot of brewed loose tea.
$2.00 Cream Scone... Served with lemon curd.

TEATIME: 10:30am To 6:00pm • Monday Thru Friday
- 11:00am To 6:00pm,Saturday
- Non-Caffeine/Herbal Tea Available
- Watercloset: Nearby Establishment
- **Reservations Please For Parties Of Four Or More**
- Parking Garage & Two Hour Street Parking
- Credit Cards: V&MC

Proprietor's
*Autograph*_____*Date*_____

ELIZABETH F. GAMBLE Garden Center

1431 Waverley Street
Palo Alto, California

415-329-1356

      Once-A-Month, Wednesday Garden Tea & Tour At...The Elizabeth F.Gamble Garden Center. This Colonial Georgian revival style house was built for Edwin Percy Gamble in 1902. Elizabeth F. Gamble later added the Tea House and the surrounding gardens to the estate. "Our Teas at the Gamble Garden Center are very elegant yet personal." It is quite a delight to relax with Afternoon Tea while gazing out onto the well manicured gardens. The Docent Tour of the garden starts at 3:30pm.

      Please call for the schedule of ongoing special events and education classes, and to verify the once-a-month Afternoon Tea dates. F.Y.I. Often in December, there are three Afternoon Teas dates plus a Children's Tea Event. Membership and volunteer opportunities are are available.

      $12.50 Tea &Garden Tour... Assorted tea sandwiches such as fresh asparagus roll, orange cream with strawberries, spring hat cookie, chocolate almond torte, crystallized orange peel and tea.

ONCE-A-MONTH GARDEN TEA & TOUR: Wednesday
- Third Wednesday Of The Month • 2:00pm To 4:00pm
- Non-Caffeine/Herbal Tea Available
- Watercloset: Same Floor
- Wheelchair Accessible
- **Reservations Are A Must**
- Unlimited-Time Free Parking Lot
- Pre-Pay Please By Cash Or Check

Proprietor's
*Autograph*_____*Date*_____

GIVENCHY HOTEL & SPA

4200 East Palm Canyon Drive
Palm Springs, California

800-276-5000   760-770-5000

New Addition...It's Teatime   At...Givenchy. If the ultimate in French pampering is just the respite you need from your hectic lifestyle, then a visit to the Givenchy Hotel & Spa is for you. I'm referring not only to the Afternoon Tea which is tres magnifique but to the wonderful Spa Packages designed on request, to range from A Day of Splendor to the Ultimate French Pampering Package.

Afternoon Tea is prepared by their award winning chef, and beautifully presented in The Garden Room which looks out onto the manicured rose and citrus gardens. Tables are set with linens, fresh flowers, tea lamps and "Artois Blue" fine china made for the famous French Chateau Bagatelle, home of Marie Antoinette. P.S. Don't miss the spa boutique which carries unique gifts and the Givenchy line of cosmetics. F.Y.I. The porcelain manufacturer Bernardaud produced this china pattern in 1776 for the Comte d'Artois. It was crafted to compliment the many gardens at Bagatelle. In the design, one can see the flowers that bloom seasonally at Chateau Bagatelle.

$15.00 Afternoon Tea... Assorted finger sandwiches, fresh baked scones served with Devonhire cream, strawberries & preserves, assorted pastries and a pot of brewed tea.

TEATIME: 3:00pm To 5:00pm • Seven Days A Week
• May Accommodate Some Dietary Needs With Advance Request
• Non-Caffeine/Herbal Tea Available
• Watercloset: Same Floor
• Wheelchair Accessible
• **Reservations Are Appreciated**
• Free Self Parking Or Courtesy Valet
• Credit Cards: V,MC,DIS,DC,AE&JCB
Proprietor's
*Autograph*_____*Date*_____

DOUBLETREE HOTEL

191 North Los Robles Avenue
Pasadena, California

626-792-2727 *Please Ask For Catering*

It's Teatime For Business & Social Gatherings At...Double Tree Hotel. The Double Tree Hotel in Pasadena is a refreshing spot for your group's business or social tea party. There are lovely banquet rooms, but I especially like the patio area with the mosaic tile fountain, and large market umbrellas.

The Double Tree "High Tea" is served buffet style, and would be quite wonderful for a professional meeting of 25 or more guests or a large bridal shower tea party. Personally, I have always found the food and ambiance at the Double Tree to be quite nice. And, I do love those chocolate chip cookies! Please call catering for details, and to plan your group's party. P.S. I would be remiss if I neglected to mention their fabulous Sunday brunch.

$17.95 Double Tree "High Tea"... Assorted finger sandwiches such as walnut chicken salad, dilled egg salad, cucumber & cream cheese, scone, Devonshire cream, strawberry preserves & marmalade, fresh fruit tarts, shortbread cookies and assortment of freshly brewed loose teas. (Price is per person, plus appropriate sales tax, predetermined gratuity & room fee.)

BUSINESS TEAS FOR GROUPS: 25+ Guests, Please Call Catering
- May Accommodate Some Dietary Needs With Advance Request
- Non-Caffeine/Herbal Tea Available
- Watercloset: Same Floor
- Wheelchair Accessible
- **Call Catering Early To Hold Your Date**
- Non-Validated Self Parking $2.50 Per Car Maximum Weekends
- $6.75 Maximum On Weekdays
- Credit Cards: Most Majors

L'autograph
du Concierge _____*Date*_____

ELEGANCE DESIGNER YARNS
presents Ragtime Gourmet
Tea, Coffee & Desserts

696 East Colorado Boulevard, Suite 8
Playhouse District Pasadena, California
(Arcade Lane)

626-792-2404

New Addition...It's Time For Yarn & Tea At Elegance Designer Yarns. Knit one, purl two, sip of tea...sounds like a novel pattern for a cozy little Afternoon Tea. In fact, you might want to ask Ashley for a tea cozy pattern so you can stitch away while taking tea. Why not bring a teacup from your tea set and match the yarn? Tea & specialties will be served either inside the lovely Elegance Designer Yarns shop or outside in the arcade's Tuscany style historic brick courtyard, main and veranda levels.

Afternoon Tea is presented at tables set with tablecloths, cloth napkins, fresh flowers and Royal Doulton china. Allow time to browse, the shop is nicely decorated with colorful gifts, gift baskets, beautiful yarns, and a rotating exhibit of artist's & photographer's works. Ask about knitting & crochet classes and custom designed patterns. F.Y.I. Private tea parties for groups may be arranged for Sundays, please call to plan. P.S. You could have a Madame LaFarge Tea Party for your knitting group!

$12.95 Afternoon Tea... Finger sandwiches, scone with Devonshire cream & jam, dessert, & a pot of brewed loose tea.
$5.95 Cream Tea... Scone or dessert and a pot of tea.

YARN & TEATIME: 10:00am To 6:00pm • Tuesday Thru Saturday
• May Accommodate Some Dietary Needs With Advance Request
• Non-Caffeine/Herbal Tea Available
• Children's Tea Parties Welcome
• Watercloset: Up One Flight Of Stairs
• **Reservations Are Required For Teas**
• Park Behind The Arcade On Green Street, East Of El Molino
• Credit Cards: V,MC,DIS&AE

Proprietor's
*Autograph*_____*Date*_____

FINE THINGS COFFEE
Collectibles & Tea Room

30 South Oakland Avenue
Pasadena, California

626-585-8307

New Addition...It's Teatime At...Fine Things Coffee Collectibles & Tea Room. A peek behind the lace curtains reveals a new spot of tea that looks more like a tearoom than the name "coffee" would imply. Fine Things appeals to the early a.m. coffee crowd but as afternoon draws near...Voila, a tearoom! Fine Things specializes in Children's "Dress-Up" Tea Parties with fancy dresses, hats, makeup & jewelry for children to borrow during these memorable events. Please call for the party details.

Afternoon Tea is served from silvers platters at tables set with lacey white tablecloths & toppers, fresh flowers and violet floral pattern fine china. Christine, originally from Birmingham, England welcomes you to her shop. Almost everything here is for sale, I had my eye on the teacup chandelier!

$16.50 Children's Dress-up Tea Parties...(Per child, minimum 8-15 young guests) PB&J or PB&B sandwiches, fruit, Teddy Bear or angel shaped cookies, raspberry decaf tea.

$7.50 Children's Tea... Above menu, no dress-up.

$14.95 High Tea... Assorted tea sandwiches, scone with cream & jam, two special sweets, pot of loose PG Tipps tea.

$11.25 Afternoon Tea... Tea sandwiches, scone with cream & jam, sweet of the day, pot of loose PG Tipps tea.

$6.75 Cream Tea... Two scones, cream & jam & tea.

TEATIME: 10:30am To 4:00pm • Monday Thru Saturday
• Non-Caffeine/Herbal Tea Available
• Children's Tea Party Specialists, Ages 5+
• Watercloset: Same Floor
• **Reservations Are Advised**
• Limited Time Street Parking
• Cash Or Check

Proprietor's
*Autograph*_____*Date*_____

185

THE JOHN BULL
Restaurant & Pub
958 South Fair Oaks Avenue
Pasadena, California

626-441-4353

It's Teatime At...The John Bull Restaurant & Pub. This English Pub is an unexpected treat not far from Old Town Pasadena. Dark wood beamed ceilings, wooden booths, dart board and expansive bar, are all part of the English pub atmosphere at The John Bull. This is a great spot to introduce someone who is reticent around ruffles, lace, flowers & bows, to Afternoon Tea! Make yourself comfortable in a booth, pick-up a local British newspaper, and enjoy a sporty Afternoon Tea.

The menu at The John Bull includes excellent traditional English fare in addition to Afternoon Tea. They are very well-known for their delicious beer battered Fish & Chips. I'm told that people come from all over the land for this dish.

$8.50 Afternoon Tea... Thin tea sandwiches, sausage roll, pub chutney, two tea tarts, with your choice of a steaming teapot of Brook-Bond P.G. Tips or glass of Sherry or house wine.

TEATIME: 3:00pm To 5:00pm • Monday Thru Sunday
• Watercloset: Same Floor
• Wheelchair Accessible
• **Reservations: No**
• Free Parking Lot
• Credit Cards: V,MC,DIS&AE, No Checks
Proprietor's
*Autograph*_____*Date*_____

186

LIPTON TEAHOUSE
124 East Colorado Boulevard
Pasadena, California

626-568-8787

New Addition...Lipton Teahouse. It is still "soothing and invigorating," but this is definitely not your grandmother's Lipton! Sir Thomas Lipton an expert in the exotic leaf, would be proud of the 90's direction that tea has taken. Welcome to the new trendy, contemporary and relaxing spot of tea on the block...Lipton! The teahouse is located in a renovated historic brick building. The wonderful original pressed-tin ceiling is juxtaposed against clean, contemporary designs with curves, beautiful light woods, and hand-painted murals. An information rail winds its way around the counter to tea-educate while you wait and vintage Lipton Tea advertisements from The Book Of Tea, add a touch of nostalgia.

Outdoor tables provide Colorado Boulevard ambience while inside, comfortable banquettes and tables invite you to linger over tea with your newspaper or laptop. Must-try special tea drinks include Chai Latte & Chills, and Tea Spritzers & Frappes, perfect accompaniments to Lipton breakfasts or lunches. Hot chocolate Chai & cookies baked on premises always hit the spot for me on chilly Pasadena evenings. Great collectible teapots & tea accessories too.

$2.25 Pot Of Estate Blend Tea... Brewed loose private Estate blend teas with exotic names like, Silver Tip and Dragonwell.

$1.25 Tea To Go... 16 oz. Cup of new method brewed tea, 4 daily selections or choose your own; bagged teas available.

$.95-$1.60 Bakery Treats. Bakery-fresh scones, *or* rich chocolate tea brownies, *or* crumpets, *or* muffin-tops, *or* bagel swirls *or* cookies to accompany your delightful spotta tea.

$1.95-$4.95 Lipton Lunches... Daily selection.

SOOTHING & INVIGORATING TIME: 7:00am To 9:00 • Daily
• Non-Caffeine/Herbal Tea Available • Fri. & Sat. Till Midnight
• Wheelchair Accessible • Watercloset: Same Floor
• Metered Street, Pay Parking Lot Nearby
• Credit Cards: V&MC
Manager's
*Autograph*_____*Date*_____

LUCKY BALDWIN'S

17 South Raymond Avenue
Old Town Pasadena, California

626-795-0652

New Addition..It's Teatime At...Lucky Baldwin's. This spot of tea is located in Old Town Pasadena just a few steps from the route of the famous Rose Parade. Lucky Baldwin's presents a tasty, casual Afternoon Tea in addition to a full menu of traditional English and American favorites.

Afternoon Tea is served either up a flight of stairs in the second floor dining room overlooking Raymond Boulevard, or on the first floor outdoor patio. Pink tablecloths, matching napkins, fresh flowers and "Blossom Time," Royal Albert china are part of Afternoon Tea at Lucky Baldwin's. You'll enjoy visiting with the friendly staff who take great pride in their yummy homebaked fruit and cream scones and lemon curd. Private tea parties are available for up to 12 guests, please call Peggy to plan.

$12.95 The Park Lane... Selection of fresh made to order finger sandwiches, a warm scone served with fresh cream & jam, assortment of cakes and pastries and a continuous cup of brewed, loose "Taylor of Harrogate" tea.

$8.95 The Knightsbridge... Selection of fresh made to order finger sandwiches, choice of warm scone served with cream & jam or hot buttered crumpets served with homemade lemon curd, and a continuous cup of brewed, loose "Taylor of Harrogate" tea.

$5.95 The Picadilly... Choice of warm scone with cream & jam or hot buttered crumpets with homemade lemon curd, and a continuous cup of brewed, loose "Taylor of Harrogate" tea.

TEATIME: 2:00pm To 5:00pm • Seven Days A Week
- May Accommodate Some Dietary Needs With Advance Request
- Non-Caffeine/Herbal Tea Available
- Watercloset: First Floor
- **Reservations Are Required**
- Metered Street Parking And Nearby Lot , No Validation
- Credit Cards: V,MC&DIS

Proprietor's
*Autograph*_____*Date*_____

188

PASADENA
Historical Museum

470 West Walnut Street
Pasadena, California

626-577-1660

PASADENA
HISTORICAL
MUSEUM

New Addition...A Victorian Luncheon Tea & Tour **On The First & Third Wednesday Of The Month, October Thru July At...Pasadena Historical Museum.** A gracious volunteer offering a glass of wine will greet you at the front door of the Fenyes Mansion. Built in 1905, this interesting home has most of its original furnishings. They are well preserved and artistically displayed throughout the mansion. My favorite spot is the theater-music-artist salon which always beckons me to linger awhile. The estate was donated to the Pasadena Historical Museum, dedicated to educating visitors about the rich history of Pasadena.

The Luncheon Tea is served in the foyer at tables set with vintage tablecloths, fine china and fresh flowers. Everything is homemade on premises and served by the volunteers. The tour is a real treat; there are lovely Victorian treasures everywhere. Allow extra time for a visit to the gift shop and the rotating gallery exhibit. Ask Ardis about the new series of Victorian Theme Luncheons featuring interesting guests; also hat decorating classes and other activities. F.Y.I. The grounds may be available for private parties.

$15.00 Luncheon Tea & Tour... Homemade selection of the day such as a hot chicken breast or a special quiche, a salad, an inspired dessert, and a continuous cup of brewed tea poured from gorgeous embossed Victorian silver teapots.

LUNCHEON TEA & TOUR: 12:15pm • First & Third Wednesday
• The First & Third Wednesday Of The Month • October Thru July
• Groups Of 20-60 Guests May Schedule A Private Tea & Tour
• Watercloset: Same Floor
• **Reservations And Pre-Pay A Must**
• Free Parking Lot
• Credit Cards: V&MC
Proprietor's
*Autograph*_____*Date*_____

PEET'S COFFEE & TEA

605 South Lake Avenue
Pasadena, California

626-795-7413

New Addition...It's Teatime At...Peet's. A vine covered brick landmark on fashionable South Lake is now home to Peet's Coffee & Tea and represents Peet's first venture into Southern California. Those of you who enjoy buying loose tea for your personal pleasure will appreciate Peet's, and find their staff very helpful and informative. I visited the shop for the first time shortly before it opened, and had an informative visit with Eliot, one of Peet's knowledgeable tea buyers. We looked at, and compared many different kinds of teas but I particularly liked the Golden Dragon Oolong. Some of the teas are only available thru the catalog.

Petit green marble tables complement the dark mahogany tone cabinets in Peet's roomy interior. If you prefer, there is outdoor patio seating too. A large green board on the wall behind the counter is a handy reference to Peet's currently featured, traditional and exotic teas. Peet's entered the tea and coffee biz over 30 years ago in Northern California. Their Intergalactic Headquarters is in Berkeley, call 1-800-999-2132 for their many locations.P.S.Browse around, Peet's carries a nice selection of teapots, cups, mugs and infusers.

$1.00 Tall "Spotta"... Relax a while with a wonderful glass mug of fresh brewed tea. This is great opportunity to try new blends in pursuit of favorite teas for your home teapot.
$2.00ish Sweet Tea Treats...A variety, fresh daily.

LOOSE TEA & A SPOTTA: 6:00am-11pm • Monday Thru Friday
• 6:00am To 11:00pm Saturday • 7:00am To 9:00pm Sunday
• Tea Education Classes Available
• Watercloset: Same Floor
• Free Parking Lot • Wheelchair Accessible
• Peet's Debit Card Available
• Credit Cards:V,MC&DIS
Manager's
*Autograph*_____*Date*_____

THE RAYMOND

1250 S. Fair Oaks Avenue
(At Columbia Street)
Pasadena, California

626-441-3136

It's Teatime At...The Raymond. The charming Raymond Bungalow was built in 1901 by Walter Raymond, the same gentleman who built the grand Raymond Hotel. The Raymond is not only a fine example of a Craftsman style cottage, but a tribute to preservationist visionaries who restored this landmark so it could become the restaurant we know today. Leaded glass, beamed ceilings and three flowering outdoor brick garden patios will no doubt enhance your enjoyment of a wonderful Afternoon Tea.

Afternoon Tea is served at wooden craftsman style tables and booths indoors or under umbrella tables with colorful directors chairs on the East, West or South patios outdoors. The Raymond is quite condusive for tea parties too. The Bar Room with a view of the East "Wisteria" patio is my choice. In March or April the picturesque purple wisteria tree is in bloom. How nice...in time for my birthday!

$15.00 Afternoon Tea... Glass of champagne or sherry, petit sandwiches of sliced radish on buttered black bread, smoked salmon & fresh dill on rye bread, shaved ham with mustard sauce on white bread, phyllo pastry triangle stuffed with sweet sausage, seasonal fresh fruit, choice of cakes and sweets and your choice from a selection of English brewed loose teas.

$8.00 Cream Tea... Choice of cakes & brewed loose tea.

TEATIME: 12:00Noon To 4:00pm • Tuesday Thru Sunday
• May Accommodate Some Dietary Needs With Advance Request
• Non-Caffeine/Herbal Tea Available
• Children's Tea Parties Welcome
• Watercloset: Same Floor
• Wheelchair Accessible
• **Reservations Are Suggested**
• Free Parking Lot
• Credit Cards: V,MC,CB,DC,DIS,AE&JCB

Proprietor's
*Autograph*_____*Date*_____

191

THE RITZ-CARLTON°

RITZ CARLTON
Huntington Hotel
1401 South Oak Knoll Street
Pasadena, California

626-568-3900

It's Teatime At...Ritz Carlton Huntington Hotel.

A magnificent view of the gardens awaits when you indulge in Afternoon Tea at the Ritz Carlton. This fabulous spot was at one time known as the historic Huntington Hotel built in 1926. Afternoon Tea is served in the Lobby Lounge with its lovely paintings, gilded mirrors, sconces and antiques. Expect the usual "Ritz" attentive service in this handsomely furnished lounge. Even if you're a local resident, you'll feel as though you are on holiday when you visit this Ritz Carlton.

Afternoon Tea is presented on a two or three tiered caddie at tables set with fine china, silver tea service, and fresh flowers. A lounge pianist adds to the elegant ambiance. The Lobby Lounge can accommodate a tea party for up to 50 guests.

$23.75 Royal Tea... Kir Royale Champagne Cocktail, finger sandwiches, English scone, Devonshire cream & preserves, assorted pastries, tea cakes, mini fruit tarts, petit fours, Grand Marnier or Chambord berries & cream, pot of hot or iced tea.

$16.75 Traditional Afternoon Tea... Tea sandwiches, scone with Devonshire cream & preserves, assorted pastries, mini fresh fruit tarts, petit fours and a pot of hot or iced tea.

TEATIME: 2:00pm To 5:00pm • Wednesday Thru Friday
- 1:00pm To 5:00pm • Saturday & Sunday
- May Accommodate Some Dietary Needs With Advance Request
- Non-Caffeine/Herbal Tea Available
- Watercloset: Same Floor • Wheelchair Accessible
- **Reservations Suggested, A Must For Six Or More**
- Self Park, Or Valet Park For $3.00 With Validation
- Credit Cards: V,MC,DC,DIS,AE&JCB

L'autograph
*du Concierge*_____*Date*_____

ROSE TREE COTTAGE

828 East California Boulevard
Pasadena, California

626-793-3337

It's Teatime At...Rose Tree Cottage. Turn off your beepers and cellular phones and get ready to relax and enjoy a delightful & traditional Afternoon Tea at the very charming Rose Tree Cottage. Attention to every detail is quite evident here. There are floral print double tablecloths on tables arranged in comfortable intimate settings. The decor is a colorful variety of florals complementing the lovely Royal Albert "Blossom Time" and Royal Dalton English china.

Lots of treasured gifts abound, so allow time to browse. You'll find an extensive collection of Beatrix Potter and a library of books to add to your own collection. Servers in black and white starched embroidered aprons are part of the traditional ambiance. Ask Mary and Edmund about Sunday afternoon "Travel Teas, Holiday Teas and Children's Story Time Teas." This is a wonderful spot for your special event parties of 24 to 36 guests. Please reserve early for Mother's Day and special event teas.

$19.50 Full Afternoon Tea... Selection of finger sandwiches, traditional rich currant scone served with double Devon cream & jam of the day, delicious sweets, and a continuous cup of Rose Tree Cottage blend tea.

$10.50 Cream Tea... Choice of scone or cake of the day with cream & jam, continuous cup of Rose Tree Cottage blend tea.

TEATIME: 1pm, 2:30pm, 4:00pm • Tuesday Thru Sunday
- May Accommodate Some Dietary Needs With Advance Request
- Non-Caffeine/Herbal Tea Available
- Watercloset: Same Floor
- Wheelchair Accessible
- **Ring One Day In Advance For Reservations**
- Limited-Time, Unmetered Street Parking
- Cash Or Check Only In The Tea Room

Proprietor's
*Autograph*_____*Date*_____

TEA ROSE GARDEN
28 South Raymond Avenue
Old Town Pasadena, California

626-578-1144

It's Teatime At...Tea Rose Garden. What a pleasant surprise to walk into a fragrant full service florist and discover Afternoon Tea. This is a unique spot with lots of Victorian gifts, tea theme specialties, fresh flowers arrangements and Afternoon Tea.

Afternoon Tea is served English courtyard style at wrought iron bistro tables & chairs. There's even a fountain and lovely hand painted "sky." Tea is graciously served by Grace and her helpful staff on Regency's Angelic and Summertime Rose English bone china. Guests are served on personal, silver three tiered caddies adorned with edible flowers and petals. Ask about High Tea as well as Mother's Day, Valentine's Day and Christmas Teas priced around $17.95. The outdoor "secret garden" is accessed through the back of the shop. It is quite wonderful for larger tea parties from 20 to 40 guests. The per person price for these private tea parties is approximately $15.00. F.Y.I. A la carte items are also offered.

$9.95 English Afternoon Tea. Tea sandwiches, scone served with cream & preserves, fresh fruit, shortbread cookie, an individual pot of brewed loose tea served with a strainer.

$9.95 French Afternoon Tea... Croissant sandwich, choice of some yummy dessert possibilities such as cheesecake, chocolate ganache, chocolate mousse cake or other surprises, fresh seasonal fruit and a pot of brewed loose tea.

$8.95 Chinese Afternoon Tea... Two Chao Sui Bao, sui mai, fresh fruit, cream, Chinese pastry, pot of brewed loose tea.

TEATIME: 9:00am To 6:00pm • Seven Days A Week
- High Tea By Reservation Only From 4:00pm To 6:00pm
- Non-Caffeine/Herbal Tea Available
- Children's Tea Parties Welcome
- Watercloset: Same Floor • Wheelchair Accessible
- **Reservations Are Requested**
- Parking Structure Nearby, First Hour Free
- Credit Cards: MC,V&AE

Proprietor's
*Autograph*_____*Date*_____

Easy Fresh Lemon Ice Cream

Courtesy of Sunkist Growers, Inc.

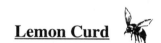

2 cups heavy cream, whipping cream or half-and-half
Grated peel of 1 Sunkist® lemon   1 cup sugar
1/3 cup fresh squeezed lemon juice
6 to 10 lemon boats or shells (optional)

In large bowl, combine cream and sugar; stir to dissolve sugar. Blend in lemon peel and juice. (The mixture will thicken slightly.) Pour into shallow pan and freeze until firm, about 4 hours. Serve in lemon boats or shells, or in dessert dishes. Garnish with fresh mint leaves and strawberries, if desired. Makes 6 to 9 servings (about 3 cups). **To make lemon boats,** cut large lemon in half length-wise. Carefully ream out juice (save for use in other recipes). Scrape shells clean with spoon. Edges may be notched or scalloped with kitchen shears or paring knife. To prevent tipping, cut a thin slice from bottom of shell.

Lemon Curd

Compliments of The TeaTime Gazette, St.Paul, MN.

"Throughout the United Kingdom, Lemon Curd ranks as an all-time, old-time favorite. Besides being a scrumptious tart filling, it is delicious as a spread for toast & scones.

2/3 cup strained, fresh lemon juice (approximately 4-6 lemons)
1/2 cup sugar plus 2 Tablespoons   3 Tablespoons butter
4 large or 5 medium eggs   1/2 teasp.unflavored gelatin

Place juice & sugar in top of a double boiler over, not in, boiling water. Stir until the sugar has dissolved. Remove from heat and stir in the beaten eggs. When well mixed, return to heat. Add the butter 1 T. At a time, stirring constantly and making sure each piece has melted before adding the next. Continue cooking and stirring, scraping the sides and bottom of the pan from time to time until the curd has the consistency of thick cream. Sprinkle gelatin over 1 T. Cold water and let set for about 5 minutes. Add to hot lemon curd and mix well. Pour into jars and refrigerate. Eat within 4 weeks. Yield: 1-2/3 cups.

Put on your flamboyant hat, and let's **tea** party!

TEA WITH THE AUTHOR
Surprise "Event" Location To Be Announced
Pasadena Vicinity, California

626-797-4TEA

New Addition...First Annual Fanciful Fashion, And Tea Party Event With Me. Enjoy a spot of tea & more with the author. We'll chat about tearooms, meet new people and just have fun. Over the last couple of years many of you have said that you would love to get together for Afternoon Tea, so let's do it! Dig out that favorite hat or vintage outfit, gloves, and sparkly rhinestone jewelry that you've been saving...this is the place to wear it! A vintage fashion show, door prizes & more surprises planned.

Bring ideas for at-home tea parties and extra copies of your favorite recipes to exchange, as well as great photos of memorable tea parties. This group will really appreciate looking at them. Please remember to put your name, or identifing sticker on the back of each photo or album since photos of tearooms can be quite similar. We will also be viewing the video, *"Tea Travels With Linda,"* as well as looking through my personal photo albums of tearoom visits. By the way, if you have written a tea poem or painted a tea-picture, bring it along. Sound like your cup of tea? Please join us. Please also, make your reservations early as space is limited.

$35.00 Afternoon Tea... Assorted finger sandwiches, scones served with creme & preserves, fresh fruit, surprise dessert, and brewed loose tea.

TEATIME: 2:00pm, Sunday, November 8, 1998
- *And* November 7, 1999
- Non-Caffeine/Herbal Tea Available
- Watercloset: Same Floor
- Please Call Re: Wheelchair Accessibility
- **Advance Reservations & Prepay Required**
- Free Parking Lot
- Credit Cards: V,MC&DIS

My
*Autograph*_____*Date*_____

ZELI COFFEE BAR
at Vroman's Bookstore

695 East Colorado Boulevard
Pasadena, California

Vroman's **800-769-BOOK**   *Zeli* **626-356-9901**

New Addition...It's Time For A Spotta & More At... Zeli Coffee Bar. Zeli is a beautifully decorated, jewel-like oasis located on Colorado Boulevard at the southwest entrance of the remodeled Vroman's Bookstore. Sit with your new book and sip al fresco on famous Colorado Boulevard, or plant yourself on a comfortable and terrific looking love seat inside, as I like to do.

The interior of Zeli is very appetizing and looks like it popped right out of Architectural Digest. You won't forget why you're there however, the scones & sweets are delicious and artfully presented. Zeli Coffee Bar is its own company, but a pass through door into Vroman's is very convenient. Vroman's is one of the most innovative bookstores anywhere. Not only do they courteously attend to their customers, but they also attract the most famous authors in the world who come to sign books and meet book lovers. When you see a line of people wrapped around the block you'll understand what I mean. Vroman's is two floors of great books and gifts for the entire family. Stop by Zeli to see what's brewing and pick-up Vroman's monthly newsletter for lots of book lover info.

$5.00ish Tea & A Scone... An a la carte selection of gourmet scones may include cranberry, peach-walnut or chocolate served with preserves or butter & three cup pot of brewed loose tea.

TEATIME: Seven Days A Week • 6am-10pm, Monday-Thursday
• 6am-11pm, Friday • 7am-11pm, Saturday • 7am-7pm, Sunday
• Non-Caffeine/Herbal Tea Available
• Watercloset: Elevator To The Second Floor Of Vroman's
• Wheelchair Accessible
• **Please Drop By**
• Limited Time Street Parking Or Vroman's Lot
• Credit Cards: V&MC

Proprietor's
*Autograph*_____*Date*_____

MARIA OF LONDON
English Tea Room

2 Liberty Street
("A"Street Victorian District)
Petaluma, California

707-762-5251

Private Tea Parties At...Maria of London Visiting Maria of London is a lot like visiting England. The tearoom is located in The Palms, which was built 100 years ago around the *other* turn of the century. Maria is quite an expert on tea history and Victorian trivia including that, about which Victorians gossiped. Petalumans are quite familiar with Maria because she enthusiastically participates in many of the City's civic and community events. She was even featured in the April 1996 issue of Sunset magazine.

Afternoon Tea is served on English bone china in one of two parlors in Marie's heritage Petaluma home. In addition to serving an authentic English Afternoon Tea, Maria chats about tea, her favorite subject. Ask about fun-filled tea & shopping trips to England with Maria and her daughter Susan. Also, about the origin of the tea-caddie spoon, now custom made for the shop. F.Y.I. Entertaining theme teas are being planned, please call for details.

$20.00 The Palm Room Tea. Tea sandwiches, English scone served with cream & jam, selection of cakes such as Victoria sponge cake,"Queen Mum's Cake", English Christmas cake and Sherry trifle and a pot of brewed loose tea.

$15.00 Maria Of London High Tea... Traditional sandwich, followed by cream cracker with English cheese, fruit bread topped with cream cheese/tomato chutney and radishes with a pickled onion; wheatmeal biscuit, scone with cream & jam, crumpet; cakes such as, Bakewell tarts & Eccles cakes, and brewed loose tea.

$12.00 Victorian Cream Tea. Cucumber sandwich, scones with cream & jam, and a pot of brewed loose tea.

PRIVATE TEA PARTIES: As Scheduled • 2 To 30 Guests
• Call For Available Dates & Times
• Watercloset: Same Floor
• **Reservations Are Required**
• Free Two Hour Parking Lot Nearby
• Cash Or Check

Proprietor's
*Autograph*_____*Date*_____

PETALUMA HISTORICAL
Library & Museum
at Masonic Hall

Corner of Petaluma Boulevard & Western Avenue
Petaluma, California

Reservations Ask For Kareen **707-778-0123**

The Annual Victorian Benefit Holiday Tea & Tour At...For The Petaluma Historical Library & Museum. During museum renovation, the traditional Holiday Tea will take place at the historic iron-front Masonic Hall and will include a visit to the nearby Historical Museum.

Step into enchanted Victorian Petaluma where tables are graced by fine china, holiday centerpieces, linens & lace. Tea is served by volunteers attired in black & white with Battenburg lace aprons and maid's caps. Sweets are selected from the dessert buffet. P.S. An Antique Store open house takes place the same afternoon, and later in the evening there are Victorian Parlor Tours. Please call the Petaluma Historical Museum 707-778-4398 for Parlor Tour and general information regarding these holiday events on the first Sunday in December. Reserve tickets by sending a self-addressed, stamped envelope, note first seating choice: 1pm or 3pm and $25.00 check payable to: Petaluma Museum Association: 20 Fourth Street, Petaluma, CA. 94952. F.Y.I. More theme teas may be brewing.

$25.00 Victorian Holiday Tea & Tour... Tea sandwiches, scones with preserves & vanilla cream pudding, English liqueur trifle, tiny mincemeat tarts, chocolate madeleines with powdered sugar & continuous cup of tea. Sample menu.

HOLIDAY TEA: First Sunday In December • 1:00pm & 3:00pm
• Watercloset: Same Floor
• Wheelchair Accessible By Elevator To The Third Floor
• **The Event Is By Paid Reservation Only**
• Metered Street Parking, Sundays Ok
• Send Check And S.A.S.E.

Director's
*Autograph*_____*Date*_____

TEA IN THE GARDEN

366 Main Street
Placerville, California
(Historic Gold Rush Country)

530-626-4946

New Addition...It's Teatime At...Tea In The Garden. A painted teapot in the window of an historic turn of the century Victorian announces Tea In The Garden, a "must" spot! This cheery unique gift shop & American style tearoom is gleefully gingham, right down to the green gingham gift bags & yellow tissue that match the green gingham wallpaper with yellow watering cans. Lynne is a designing woman, and everything is just "so."

Afternoon Tea is presented on a three tiered Spode caddie at hand painted willow tables set with fresh flowers, custom made decorated sugar cubes, cloth napkins, Spode china, and French gingham hunter green & yellow silverware. The chintz chair cushions match and so do the servers attired in gingham costumes. Private tea parties are available for 8-16 guests. P.S. Allow plenty of time to browse, Lynne is a specialist at buying outstanding items for her gift shop. Crabtree Tree & Evelyn, fine teas, gourmet foods, books, garden hats, toiletries and fine artwork to mention a few. F.Y.I. Cool glasses of mint julep iced tea in season. Ask about Sweet Alyssum, Rose Arbor, English Ivy & Dickens's Teas too!

$12.50 Afternoon Tea... Assorted finger sandwiches, Champagne sorbet, scones served with homemade herb & fruity butters & rose petal jam, surprise desserts, pot of brewed loose tea.

TEATIME: 11:30am & 2pm, Tuesday To Saturday • Sweets, 3-5pm
• May Accommodate Some Dietary Needs With Advance Request
• Non-Caffeine/Herbal Tea Available
• Children's Tea Parties Welcome, Ages 7+
• Watercloset: Same Floor
• **Reservations Are Required**
• Free Parking Structure Nearby
• Credit Cards: V,MC&DIS

Proprietor's
*Autograph*_____*Date*_____

SPECIAL TEAS & HEIRLOOMS

(East Bay) 520 Main Street
Pleasanton, California

510-484-9829

It's Teatime At...Special Teas & Heirlooms. This historic building was a first class livery more than 160 years ago. Today, much of the original structure remains, even the windows. Interestingly enough, the brick courtyard yielded a pleasant surprise when Mary cut back an overgrowth of greenery. Voila! A 30 year old hand painted mural was discovered!

Afternoon Tea is served at tables set with handmade mauve, burgundy & green linens, and a collection of European fine china and silver. "While sipping your tea be sure to keep an eye out for Special Teas & Heirloom's very own Victorian ghost. They say she appears from time to time in a long dress, seeming a little lost. Not to be alarmed, she's just looking for a cup of tea and good conversation, not unlike yourself." Ask about the Blue Room which is a cute, cozy spot for two guests. P.S. Be sure to say hello to Erica, she often helps out in the tearoom on weekends or during the summer months. Allow time to browse at heirlooms, gifts & collectibles. Private tea parties for 25-50 guests.

$14.95 Special Tea Fare... Assorted finger sandwiches, savory, petits four, madeleines, cookies, tea cake, scone with Devonshire cream, strawberry jam & lemon curd, brewed loose tea.

$8.95 Cream Tea... Two scones served with Devonshire cream & strawberry jam & lemon curd, pot of brewed loose tea.

$8.95 Tea & Dessert... Tea sized desserts & a pot of tea.

$8.95 Children's Tea... Peanut butter & jam finger sandwiches, petit fours or madeleines, cookie and Tutti Fruitti tea.

TEATIME: 11:00am To 4:00pm • Tuesday Thru Saturday
• Sundays Are Reserved For Ten Or More Guests
• Non-Caffeine/Herbal Tea Available
• Watercloset: Same Floor
• Wheelchair Accessible
• **Reservations Are Recommended**
• Limited-Time Unmetered Parking
• Credit Cards: MC,V,DIS&AE

Proprietor's
*Autograph*_____*Date*_____

COZY KETTLE
5649 Pony Express Trail #7
Pollock Pines, California

530-644-0360

It's Teatime On Wednesday, Saturday & Sunday At...Cozy Kettle. Here's a perfect place to stop off Highway 50 on your way to Lake Tahoe. This cozy spot was voted 1996 Pollock Pines Business of the Year by the local Chamber. Cozy Kettle has a charming atmosphere with pretty table cloths, mix 'n matched china, lace curtains, classical background music and pink faux finish walls. Mary bakes scones and breads including a pretty pastel colored loaf. This proprietor has a loyal following of customers who take tea and bring her lots & lots of vintage hats which she invites you to borrow at tea. She calls this spot the tiniest tearoom you've ever seen.

The Cozy Kettle is also a gift shop with teacup paper lined shelves full of teapots, tea clocks, tea picture frames, tea magnets and other tea theme things that you can't live without. F.Y.I. Pollock Pines is a lovely and scenic one hour drive from Sacramento as you head east. Cozy, intimate tea parties are available for your special events. Ask about theme teas which are presented monthly.

$7.00 Afternoon Tea... Finger sandwiches, fresh fruit, scone with cream &strawberry jam, pot brewed loose Xanadu tea.

$3.75 Cream Tea... Scone served with strawberry jam & cream and a pot of brewed loose Xanadu tea.

$2.50 Desserts... Bread pudding with carmel sauce, or angel food cake served with fresh fruit and whipping creme.

TEATIME: 11:00am To 3:00pm • Wednesday Thru Saturday
• Call For Possible Extended Summer Hours & Days
• May Accommodate Some Dietary Needs With Advance Request
• Non-Caffeine/Herbal Tea Available
• Children's Tea Parties Welcome
• Wheelchair Accessible • Watercloset: Same Floor
• **Reservations Are Recommended**
• Free Unlimited-Time Parking Lot
• Cash Or Check

Proprietor's
Autograph_____Date_____

CAL POLY POMONA
School Of Hotel &
Restaurant Management

3801 West Temple Avenue
Pomona, California

Reservations **909-869-4471**

New Addition...The Annual Benefit "Friends & Tea" At...Cal Poly Pomona University. Enjoy first hand the talents of gifted students enrolled in the School of Hotel & Restaurant Management. It is fascinating to peer behind the glass and view epicurean works of art in progress. All profits from this event which was created by the, Friends of the Restaurant at Kellog Ranch, are used to enhance the food and beverage program here, one of the nation's leading hospitality management programs. Uniformed apprentice chefs under the supervision of talented instructors feature recipes which they have developed and prepared for your Afternoon Tea pleasure.

Did you know that the public may enjoy lunch and dinner prepared by student chefs periodically throughout the year? Meet the student chefs who will be creating the fabulous dishes of the future. Please call: 909-869-4700 for schedule of lunches and dinners. P.S. Membership in the "Friends" is welcome and encouraged.

$15.00 Friends' Afternoon Tea... Assorted delicious mini-scones served with a unique cream & preserves, assorted tea sandwiches with very creative spreads, freshly prepared sweet desserts and a pot of tea. Price is approximate, call to confirm.

TEATIME: Please Call For The May Date, Hours & Reservations
• P.S. A Fall Tea May Be Added, Please Call For Information
• Non-Caffeine/Herbal Tea Available
• Watercloset: Same Floor • Wheelchair Accessible
• **Advance Reservations Required**
• Prepaying Insures Your Spot
• Parking Lot Up The Hill Near The Entrance
• Credit Cards: V,MC&AE

Director's
*Autograph*_____*Date*_____

THE GARDEN
presents Tea Under The Tree
with White Gloves
& Party Manners

845 North Geary Avenue
Pomona, California

909-629-2062

New Addition...Annual Mother's Day Tea At...The Garden. Does an old fashioned Afternoon Tea in the garden capture your mother's romantic heart? If so, reserve your spot for a Mother's Day Tea, Under The Tree at The Garden. The Garden, is a nursery located in a two story Transitional style home with a wonderful wrap around porch. They specialize in old fashioned, hard to find cottage perennials & herbs, gifts & bulk tea.

Mother's Day Tea is served under the 60 year old English Walnut tree. Dawn, the owner of The Garden presents a catered Mother's Day Tea by White Gloves & Party Manners. Karen and her staff attired in floral bonnets and matching Empire-style dresses present a lovely and delicious tea at tables set with linens, English rosebud china & fresh flowers. Wear a flowery chapeau, bring your camera and say "tea." P.S. Why not bring along mom's favorite chipped teapot to fill with a new plant? A sweet memento of the day!

$16.95 Mother's Day Tea... Finger sandwiches, homemade mini quiche, fresh seasonal fruit, scones with cream & preserves, teapot cookie and a continuous cup of brewed loose tea.

MOTHER'S DAY TEA: 11:00am, 1pm & 3pm • Sunday
- Non-Caffeine/Herbal Tea Available
- Children's Tea Parties Welcome
- Watercloset: First Floor
- **Prepaid Advance Reservations Required**
- Unmetered Street Parking
- Credit Cards: V&MC

Proprietor's
*Autograph*_____*Date*_____

THE RITZ-CARLTON®

RITZ CARLTON
Rancho Mirage
68-900 Frank Sinatra Drive
Rancho Mirage, California

760-321-8282

It's Teatime, In Season, At...Ritz Carlton.
"Season" is usually from the end of September thru June at the fab Ritz Carlton Hotel situated high on a plateau in the Santa Rosa Mountains. On your way up the hill to the hotel you'll drive past a wall of rushing water and soon reach their circular entrance. Bronze statues of mountain rams seem to welcome you. Keep your eye out, real ones could be just on the other side of the mountain!

The Lobby Lounge is an elegant spot for Afternoon Tea. The Ritz Carlton Hotels are quite wonderful, decorated with handsome furnishings, comfortable seating, and offer impeccably attentive service. Harpists or pianists usually entertain in the afternoon at teatime. On Wednesdays, local merchants and models dazzle you with the latest in desert fashions. Please remember that Afternoon Tea is served in season only, please call for dates.

$14.50 Full Tea... Tea sandwiches, scone with cream, English & Irish tea cakes & breads, mini fresh fruit tart, chocolate dipped strawberry, shortbread cookie and a pot of brewed loose tea.

$22.00 Royal Tea Service... Add berries in Grand Marnier & a glass of Ritz Carlton selection of Champagne to above.

$11.00 Light Tea... Scone served with Devonshire cream & fruit preserves, English & Irish tea cakes & breads, mini fresh fruit tart, chocolate dipped strawberry, pot of brewed loose tea.

$7.00 Children's Tea... Selection of sandwiches, scone, fresh fruit tart, chocolate chip cookie and a choice of tea or chocolate. Ask about Children's Teddy Bear Teas in December.

TEATIME: 2:30pm To 4:30pm • Tuesday Thru Saturday In Season
• May Accommodate Some Dietary Needs With Advance Request
• Non-Caffeine/Herbal Tea Available
• Wheelchair Accessible • Watercloset: Same Floor
• No Tea Service In July & August
• **Reservations Are Requested**
• Complimentary Valet With High Tea
• Credit Cards: V,MC,DIS,DC,AE& JCB

L'autograph
*du Concierge*_____*Date*_____

MOREY MANSION B&B
presents Dodi of Redlands High Tea

1900 Terracina Boulevard
Redlands, California

909-793-7970

New Addition...It's Teatime On Wednesdays & Saturdays At...Morey Mansion. The distinctive Morey Mansion is a grand example of turn of the century Victorian architecture. The mansion, situated on three acres in the Inland Empire was built by David Morey in 1890 as gift for his accomplished wife Sarah. Over the years, the house has been featured in movies and advertisements and is easily distinguished by its French Mansard roof and sculptured onion shaped dome, similar to domed buildings in eastern Europe & Russia. The interior is wonderful too, accented with beveled glass Victorian Belgian Bay windows and French Tiffany style stained glass. Larry, the Innkeeper can fill you in on much of its history. F.Y.I. Gable and Lombard stayed here when her aunt & uncle owned the mansion! It's interesting to note that no 2 wood carvings in the home are alike.

Afternoon Tea is presented by Dodi of Redlands High Tea. It is served in the Living Room, Library & Dining Room, at turn of the century tables set with white lace linens, fine china & garden roses. On Saturdays, a harpist usually entertains under the beautiful golden oak archway hand carved by Morey himself, between the main rooms. P.S. Private parties are available, please call for info.

$12.00 On Wednesdays Or $15.00 On Saturdays.. Victorian Tea Afternoon... Tea sandwiches such as cream cheese & celery walnut garnished from the herb garden, scone with Redland's cream & preserves, dessert, Harney & Son's loose tea.

TEATIME: 12Noon-4pm, Wednesday • 12Noon-3pm, Saturday
• Reduced Caffeine Tea Available
• Watercloset: Same Floor • Children's Tea Parties Welcome
• **Reservations Are Highly Recommended**
• Free Parking Lot
• Credit Cards: V,MC&AE

Proprietor's
*Autograph*_____*Date*_____

CAFE NORDSTROM

1835 Hawthorne Boulevard
Redondo Beach, California

310-542-9440

New Addition...It's Teatime At...Cafe Nordstrom. In 1887, at the tender age of 16, John F. Nordstrom left his home in Sweden to come to the United States. He arrived in New York with five dollars in his pocket. A fortuitous meeting years later with Carl F.Wallin a Seattle shoemaker, resulted in the 1901 opening of the first "Wallin & Nordstrom" store on Fourth & Pike Streets in Seattle. Nordstrom has been guided by its founder's philosophy ever since. "Offer the customer the best possible service, selection, quality and value."

I delight in shopping at Nordstom. The idea of a pianist playing a baby grand piano while I shop for beautiful things suits me to a T. The comfy "oasis" which my spouse calls the "husband waiting area" is appreciated by both of us. Because the store enjoys a reputation for being customer friendly, I wasn't surprised when they began serving Afternoon Tea in many Cafes at Nordtrom.

Afternoon Tea is served at tables set with fresh flowers, fine china, cloth napkins and special teatime silverware. The cafe managers are enthusiastic & friendly as is the courteous staff. F.Y.I. Outdoor patio dining available at some locations.

$6.95 Afternoon Tea... Assorted finger sandwiches, scone with berry-butter, dessert, pot of brewed bagged tea.

TEATIME: 3:00pm To 5:00pm • Seven Days A Week
• May Accommodate Some Dietary Needs With Advance Request
• Non-Caffeine/Herbal Tea Available
• Watercloset: Same Floor
• Wheelchair Accessible
• **Reservations Are Required For Six Or More Guests**
• Free Parking Lot
• Credit Cards: V,MC,AE&Nordstrom
Manager's
*Autograph*_____*Date*_____

THE ROYAL-TEA ROOM

3567 Main Street
(In The Old Main Emporium Mall)
Riverside, California

909-369-5867

New Addition...It's Teatime At...The Royal-Tea Room. The Royal-Tea Room is nestled in the cozy Old Main Emporium Mall, across the way from the historic Riverside Mission Inn. Azeb's goal is "to provide a quiet, relaxed atmosphere where tea lovers can enjoy a traditional tea with elegance and charm. This is a serene tearoom, where guests delight in sharing a pot of tea with a friend, acquaintance or business partner."

Afternoon Tea is beautifully served in two courses at tables set with doilies, fresh flowers and an eclectic collection of English fine bone china and crystal. Private tea parties are welcome for 8 to 20 guests with a small room fee. Ask about Children's Tea Parties too. The bill-of-fare is expected to change from time to time. P.S. Browse about, there are wonderful tea-theme gifts & accessories.

$12.95 Royal Afternoon Tea. Assorted tea sandwiches, savories, salad, tea breads, scones served with cream & preserves, fruit in season, dessert and a pot of brewed bag or loose tea.
$9.25 Royal Tea Special... Assorted tea sanwiches, savories, salad, seasonal fruit, tea biscuits, brewed bag or loose tea.
$8.50 Royal Dessert Tea... Scones, tea bread, cream & preserves, fruit in season, dessert, a pot of brewed bag or loose tea.
$5.75 Royal Garden Tea. Scone, tea bread, fruit & tea.

TEATIME: 11:30am To 4:00pm • Tuesday Thru Friday
• Sunday & Monday Are Reserved For Parties Of Eight Or More
• May Accommodate Some Dietary Needs With Advance Request
• Non-Caffeine/Herbal Tea Available
• Children's Tea Parties Welcome7+
• Watercloset: Same Floor • Wheelchair Accessible
• **Reservations Are Preferable**
• Two Hour Free Parking
• Cash Or Check
Proprietor's
*Autograph*_____*Date*_____

BRISTOL FARMS

What The World Is Coming To.

837 Silver Spur Road
Rolling Hills, California

310-541-9157

New Addition...Host A Tea Party With Help From Bristol Farms. Teas, as we all know are fun & popular events for any or no occasion at all! I'm often asked at book signings about my own tea parties. Afternoon Teas at home are especially fun for me because I get a chance to be creative and bring out my pretty vintage plates, teacups, teapots, vases & Victorian lace. I keep my list of guests to eight friends for ease of conversation. Setting the table the day before really saves time. I also set a tea strainer for each guest.

Early in the day I pick dewy garden flowers, plunge them into squeaky clean vases of water and head to Bristol Farms in South Pasadena. I buy one large container each of tuna, chicken & seafood salads. Next, a stop at their bakery for 24 pre-ordered mini, or 8 large scones, 3 different loaves of bread for cookie-cutter shaped tea sandwiches and a dozen mini chocolate eclairs and cream puffs. I choose two 16 oz. jars of preserves & 3 small jars of lemon curd. I make my own cream, but they usually have clotted cream if you like. Edible blossoms, strawberries, grapes, kiwi, bananas & star fruit are a must. An extra bunch of flowers, and I'm off! To make your tea party more fun & "interactive" ask each of your guests to bring a different small package of tea. With individual teapots, it encourages tea-tasting & is a neat conversation facilitator. (But that's another book!) With 8 guests it's easier to have plates preset with 3 tea sandwiches, edible flowers, melange of fruit & a "teacup" of soup made from 4 packages of creamy asparagus soup, to which I add pre-cooked fresh asparagus bits. Scones are on individual plates. My bread pudding made from bread crusts is great! F.Y.I.If you prefer, pick-up a catered tea from Bristol Farms.

TEATIME SHOPPING: 8am-8pm, Mon-Sat. • 9am-8pm, Sunday
- May Accommodate Some Dietary Needs With Advance Request
- Non-Caffeine/Herbal Tea Available
- Wheelchair Accessible • Watercloset: Same Floor
- Large Free Parking Lot
- Credit Cards:V,MC,DIS&AE

Manager's
*Autograph*_____*Date*_____

ROSEVILLE ART CENTER

424 Oak Street
(Behind The Tower Theater)
Roseville, California

916-783-4117

ROSEVILLE ARTS CENTER

    Two Annual Benefit Teas, March & November At...Roseville Art Center's Haman House. The Roseville Art Center is located in the splendid Victorian Haman House. The house was built in 1909, the same year that Roseville became an incorporated city. It was built by the superintendent of the Roseville Ice & Beverage Company, William Haman. A visionary, Haman also became known as the "Father of Royer Park" when he created a lush green park from what was a sand dune, along Dry Creek.

    We are happy to announce that The Sugar Plum Fairy Tea is returning! This is great family entertainment, however seating is extremely limited. Please call for the November date, and to make your pre-paid reservations for this special holiday tea which feaures costumed Nutcracker characters. Also always a sellout, is the Annual English High Tea in March. Reserve your spot! This popular event benefits The Center's Restoration Project. Door prizes always; wear a fun hat! F.Y.I. Haman House is available for private parties & events for a minimum of 25 guests. Please call for details.

    $12.50 English High Tea... Glass of Sherry, finger sandwiches, famous Haman House scone, Devonshire cream & strawberry jam, assortment of sweets & lovely tea. March 14, 1998 and March 13, 1999. Please call to reserve & confirm dates & times.

    $10.00 Sugar Plum Fairy Tea.. Famous Haman House scone, tea sandwiches, assorted sweets, continuous cup of brewed tea. Children $8. Dates: 11/16/97, 11/15/98 & 11/14/99 Have fun!

NOVEMBER & MARCH BENEFIT TEAS: As Scheduled
- Seatings: 12:30pm & 2:30pm • Please Call To Verify Dates
- Watercloset: Same Floor
- **Advance Prepaid Reservations Required**
- Free Unlimited-Time Parking
- Credit Cards: MC&V

Director 's Or Volunteer's
*Autograph*_____*Date*_____

ABIGAIL'S B&B INN

2120 "G" Street
Sacramento, California

800-858-1568   **916-441-5007**

New Addition...It's Teatime On The Third Saturday Of The Month At...Abigail's B&B. Just when I was pondering, where are the tearooms in Sacramento? I had the good fortune to meet Susanne. She is the proprietor of Abigail's and very much enjoys serving Afternoon Tea. Her teas are often holiday inspired and of course, you don't need to be an overnight guest to enjoy them. During teatime she also gives a short history on tea.

Afternoon Tea is served in courses on two and three tiered caddies. Guests are seated in the living room at dining tables or on couches and arm chairs at low tables carefully draped in white or ivory linen as you might expect in Victorian times. Your tea is poured from silver or porcelain teapots with strainers. "We encourage folks to dress-up," says the proprietor who also makes little folded cards for each table announcing the day's bill-of-fare. This owner is into antiquing and these teas give her a great excuse to shop for collectible silver sugar tongs & unique sugar cube holders. Abigail's can accommodate up to 22 guests at each of two seatings.

$15.00 Traditional Afternoon Tea... The delectable bill-of-fare changes with each inspired tea, but always includes finger sandwiches, scones, cream & preserves, lovely sweet treats such as tarts, tea breads & cakes and a pot of brewed loose tea.

TEATIME: Usually On The Third Saturday Of The Month
• Two Seatings: 12:30pm & 2:30pm
• Non-Caffeine/Herbal Tea Available
• Watercloset: Second Floor, One Flight Up
• **Reservations Are Strongly Suggested**
• Free Off Street Parking & Limited Time Street Parking
• Credit Cards: V,MC,DIS,DC&AE Sorry, No Checks
Proprietor's
*Autograph*_____*Date*_____

MADAME FROGG'S
Gallery & Cafe

3440 "C" Street
(The Peter Cottontail Neighborhood)
Sacramento, California

916-447-3764

New Addition...It's Teatime At...Madame Frogg's. Warm childhood memories of Afternoon Teas led proprietors Hillary and Tanene to the fortuitous opening of Madame Frogg's, a holistic cafe and art gallery. Hillary is a chef by trade and is an expert in the preparation of English Afternoon & High Teas. Madame Frogg's offers High Tea classes periodically thru the year, but do stop by anytime to learn about brewing a proper pot of tea.

Afternoon Tea is informally served on "mellow" marble tables. Fabulous scones, bakery specialties and perfectly glazed confections are skillfully presented in this modern yet quaint & cozy spot of tea. Soft oak tones and mixed fabric patterns complement the casual dining atmosphere. Tanene's Grandma Fritz from Illinois and Hillary's friends in Victoria, B.C. must all be very proud. P.S. Ask about their High Tea Socials. Shop for tea & tea accoutrements too.

$12.50 Afternoon Tea... Quartet of finger sandwiches, scones & cinnamon twists served with creme fraiche & homemade jam, European dessert, and a pot of brewed loose tea.

TEATIME: Available 3:30 To 5:30 • By Advance Reservation
• May Accommodate Some Dietary Needs With Advance Request
• Non-Caffeine/Herbal Tea Available
• Children's Tea Parties Welcome
• Watercloset: Same Floor
• Wheelchair Accessible
• **Reservations Are Required**
• Unmetered, Limited Time Street Parking
• Credit Cards: V,MC,DIS&AE

Proprietor's
*Autograph*_____*Date*_____

MEADOWOOD
Napa Valley
900 Meadowood Lane
St. Helena, California

707-963-3646

New Addition...It's Teatime At...Meadowood.
Each time I walk through my grape arbor I think of our visit to the beautiful Napa Valley. One of the most beautiful resorts in Napa, or anywhere for that matter, is Meadowood. It is sequestered on 250 incomparable wooded acres and happens to be among other things, a splendid tea retreat. The veranda is quite a spot for Afternoon Tea!

English Country Teas are graciously presented under Terry's direction in The Meadowood Restaurant where tables are set with Rosenthal china, tapestry runners & fresh flowers. The decor features antique English pine furniture, leather sofas, a Persian carpet and magnificent stone fireplace. The twelve foot French doors lead outside to the beautiful terrace which overlooks the croquet lawns and golf course. Allow time to wander around, there are three small fine gift shops and a hiking trail. The Spa offers a "Day Sampler" if you need additional pampering. P.S. When you call to confirm teatime be sure they don't put you on the golf course!

$18.00 The Meadowood Tea... Finger sandwiches, smoked salmon & cream cheese on Foccacia, caramelized walnuts & Napa bleu cheese, fresh scones, Devon cream, lemon curd & Meadowood preserves, shortbread, fruit & nut bread, chocolate truffles, fresh berries, tea cookies, pot of brewed loose tea. Consider trying the Meadowood Blend Champagne Tea.

TEATIME: 3:00pm To 5:00pm • Seven Days A Week
- May Accommodate Some Dietary Needs With Advance Request
- Non-Caffeine/Herbal Tea Available
- Watercloset: Same Floor
- Wheelchair Accessible
- **Reservations Are Suggested**
- Free Parking Lot
- Credit Cards: V,MC,DC,CB&AE

L'autograph
*du Concierge*_____*Date*_____

THE ENGLISH ROSE
Tea Room

663 Laurel Street
San Carlos, California

650-595-5549

It's Teatime At...The English Rose Tea Room. How would you like to take tea at a rosy little spot in San Carlos? We have just the spot! It's The English Rose Tea Room.

Marilyn serves Afternoon Tea on "Garland" by Nikko bone china, with a pattern of miniature roses. The tables in this in rosy tearoom are also set with silk rose centerpieces, rosy tablecloths that match the rosy tea cozies and a lovely collection of fine china floral teapots. The decor includes English Memorabilia and forest green & pink cabbage rose wallpaper. Afternoon Tea plus a full menu of tempting homemade English specialties are featured including Rumpledethumps and Cornish Pasties. F.Y.I. Private tea parties are available for 20 to 38 guests. Marilyn is the friendly and gracious proprietor originally from Middlesex, England. She will be happy to help you plan a very special tea party. P.S. Take a peek around the shop to discover tea cozies and a few small specialty gifts.

$8.50 Afternoon Tea Plate... An assortment of English tea sandwiches, homebaked cakes, pastries and a pot brewed of tea.
$3.95 Devon Tea... Two fresh homemade warm scones served with Devonshire cream and a pot of brewed tea.

TEATIME: 9:00am To 3:30pm • Tuesday Thru Saturday
• May Accommodate Some Dietary Needs With Advance Request
• Non-Caffeine/Herbal Tea Available
• Watercloset: Same Floor
• **Reservations Are Suggested For Five Or More**
• Two Hour Street Parking On Weekdays
• Cash Or Check
Proprietor's
*Autograph*_____*Date*_____

BIT O'BRITAIN
3166 Midway Drive #108
San Diego, California

619-224-5541

It's Teatime At...Bit O'Britain. Stock up on your British gifts and groceries and enjoy Afternoon Tea at Bit O'Britain. On your way in the door you'll discover a "photo op," you may pose with fully-costumed mannequins! Say hello to Irene, she has lost most of her accent but guess where she's from. The shop is decorated with lots of English memorabilia.

Afternoon Tea is presented from an interesting three tiered caddie at tables set with creamy colored tablecloths and fine English china. Each table uses a different set of china. In addition to a traditional and reasonably priced Afternoon Tea, Bit O'Britain serves a wee bit of the flavor of the British Isles with tasty fresh baked house specialties such as bangers & mash, Scotch pie, Cornish pastie & steak pie. The food is interesting, especially if you are new to English cooking. Allow time to browse in the shop which is open 10:00am to 6:00pm.

$6.50 Afternoon Tea... Assorted finger sandwiches, sausage roll, scone served with jam, pastry and a pot of tea.

$2.50 Tea & Crumpets... Crumpet served with Butter & jam and a pot of tea.

$1.95 Tea & Scone... Scone served with Devon cream & jam and a pot of tea.

TEATIME: 2:00pm To 5:00pm • Seven Days A Week
• Non-Caffeine/Herbal Tea Available
• Watercloset: Same Floor
• Wheelchair Accessible
• **Reservations Are Not Necessary**
• Unlimited-Time Free Parking Lot
• Credit Cards: V&MC

Proprietor's
*Autograph*_____*Date*_____

FLEUR DE TEA
729 West Washington Street
San Diego, California

619-291-4TEA

New Addition...Teatime Shopping At...Fleur De Tea. Bonjour! Welcome to the little tea shop that was actually a service station many years ago. If you want friendly service, a new "caddie" or some "model Tea"...this is still the place! Today, there's a white picket fence, a trellis, flower boxes and a black & white striped awning beckoning you to Fleur de Tea. Carla has a knack for choosing neat tea gifts for her petite tea spot. She is very is customer oriented and tries to help you find whatever you may need. Bianca, in the black & purple teapot apron, is Carla's helpful assistant.

The arty decor features a black & white checkered floor, yellow walls with fruit border, and an abundance of decoratively displayed tea accessories, books, teapots, teacups, scone mixes & gifts everywhere! You'll have fun snooping about as you negotiate your way through this 600 square ft. shop.

A variety of over 80 bulk teas are available; by the tasting ounce too. Her tea gift baskets are great and may be shipped anywhere. Ask about their newsletter, tea tastings & special events which occur periodically. F.Y.I. On the third Wednesday of the month from 6:30-8:30pm you may join the teapot painting class! Own your own hand-painted and fired teapot for around $35.00. P.S. Fleur-de-tea can now cater an Afternoon Tea for you! Call for information.Don't miss Carla's collectible handmade teatime clocks.

$1.00oz.To $9.00oz Bulk Tea.. Ranging from English Breakfast tea to Pearl Jade Oolong, & a variety in-between!

TEATIME SHOPPING: 11am To 6:00pm • Tuesday Thru Friday
• 10:00am To 5:00pm Saturday • 12Noon To 5:00pm, Sunday
• Watercloset: Same Floor
• Credit Cards: V,MC&DIS
Proprietor's
*Autograph*_____*Date*_____

Did you forget your hat? No problem, borrow one of ours!

HORTON GRAND HOTEL

311 Island Avenue
(Historic Gaslamp District)
San Diego, California

619-544-1886

It's Teatime At...The Horton Grand. "A distinctive Victorian experience awaits the guests of The Horton Grand where service has been a cornerstone since 1886." The Horton Grand Hotel was actually two buildings, The Brooklyn Hotel and The Grand Hotel. They were purchased for $1.00 each, dismantled and moved to a new location to be rebuilt almost brick by brick. In 1986, this beautiful Victorian hotel re-opened as The Horton Grand Hotel. This is a wonderful spot with enchanting period artwork and grand hospitality. For added fun, you may take a horse-drawn carriage ride through the historic Gaslamp Quarter neighborhood.

Afternoon Tea is served in the lounge named after Madame Ida Bailey, San Diego's most famous madame and hostess. In fact, the site chosen for The Horton Grand was approximately the site of her famous and intimate "Canary Cottage." These days, Rebecca is your most gracious tea hostess. This is a perfect spot to wear your favorite hat, or you may borrow one from the hall tree. F.Y.I. Wyatt Earp once slept here, and you can too! P.S. Private tea parties are available, call for info. Don't miss the incredible carved staircase.

$13.50 Victorian Grand High Tea... Glass of Sherry, sausage roll, scotch eggs, finger sandwiches, scone with cream, butter & jam, chocolate truffle, petit fours & English Breakfast tea.
$9.95 Horton Grand Afternoon Tea. Tea sandwiches, scone with cream, butter & jam, petit fours & English Breakfast tea.

TEATIME: 2:30pm To 5:00pm • Tuesday Thru Saturday
- May Accommodate Some Dietary Needs With Advance Request
- Non-Caffeine/Herbal Tea Available
- Children's Tea Parties Welcome
- Watercloset: Same Floor
- Wheelchair Accessible
- **Advance Reservations Are A Must**
- Complimentary Park With Tea Validation
- Credit Cards: MC,V&AE

Hostess'
*Autograph*_____*Date*_____

Prune & Orange Scones

California Prune Board

3 Cups flour
1/2 Cups sugar
4 Teaspoons baking powder
1/2 Teaspoon salt
1/2 Cup margarine or butter
1 Egg
1 Cup buttermilk
1 Cup chopped pitted prunes
2 Teaspoons grated orange peel
Egg Wash: 1 egg beaten with 1 Tablespoon cream or milk

In large bowl mix flour, sugar, baking powder and salt. Using pastry blender or two knives, cut in margarine until mixture resembles coarse meal. In small bowl beat egg with buttermilk; add to flour mixture with prunes and orange peel. Mix well. Turn dough onto floured surface; lightly knead 5 or 6 times, adding more flour as needed to keep dough from sticking. Divide dough in 18 equal portions. Shape each portion into a ball; flatten into discs 1/2 inch thick. Place apart on ungreased baking sheet; brush lightly with egg wash. Bake in 375-degree oven 20 minutes or until golden brown. Serve warm or at room temperature. Scones can be tightly wrapped and frozen up to one month. Makes 18 scones.

Note: To make wedge-shaped scones, pat dough into three 6-inch circles; cut each circle into 6 wedges. Place apart on ungreased baking sheet. Brush lightly with egg wash and bake as above.

U.S. GRANT HOTEL
326 Broadway
San Diego, California

619-232-3121
800-237-5029 *Hotel Reservations*

It's Teatime At...The U.S. Grant Hotel. The U.S. Grant Hotel was built in 1910 by non other than Ulysses S. Grant Jr. Listed on The National Register of Historic Places, it has been a popular spot for visiting dignitaries from all over the world.

Afternoon Tea is served in the handsome chandelier-lit Lobby Lounge at tables set with tablecloths, fresh flowers and hand-painted Royal Albert English bone china. The setting is quite handsome with complementing groupings of rose pattern upholstered chairs and sofas, green floral carpet and marble-accented furnishings. A pianist or harpist usually plays in the background at teatime. Quite picturesque, it's not unusual to see brides posing for pictures in the lobby. P.S. Private tea parties are available, please call to plan your special event. F.Y.I. Allow time to browse, a gift shop is now open. Do look at the nice beaded pieces.

$12.00 Afternoon Tea... Assorted finger sandwiches, freshly baked scone and crumpet served with cream & fruit preserves, miniature pastries and a choice of brewed loose tea.

TEATIME: 3:00pm To 6:00pm • Tuesday Thru Saturday
• May Accommodate Some Dietary Needs, 1 Week Advance Request
• Non-Caffeine/Herbal Tea Available
• Children's Tea Parties Welcome
• Watercloset: Same Floor
• Wheelchair Accessible
• **Reservations Are Recommended**
• Three Hour Complimentary Valet & Self Parking
• Credit Cards: V,MC,DC,DIS&AE
Proprietor's
*Autograph*_____*Date*_____

 **WESTGATE HOTEL**
1055 Second Avenue
San Diego, California

Reservations **800-221-3802**   **619-238-1818**

New Addition...It's Teatime At...The Westgate Hotel. The magnificent European style Westgate Hotel was built in 1970 in the heart of downtown San Diego. In 1970, it was the most expensive hotel built in this country, designed along the lines of the classical European hotel palaces de grand deluxe. The splendid lobby of the Westgate is a re-creation of one of the anterooms at Versailles. French nobility used anterooms as waiting rooms, before being presented to His Majesty Louis XV. This is an elegant and luxurious hotel adorned with priceless antiques and paintings by the masters, breathtaking Baccarat crystal chandeliers, Aubusson and Beavais tapestries, and fine museum pieces.

Afternoon Tea is elegantly served in the grand lobby "anteroom" accompanied by the sweet refrains of one of the first five Steinway pianos ever manufactured. Tea tables are set with tablecloths, fresh flowers and "Depuis 1748" fine china by Villeroy & Boch. Truly Memorable.

$12.00 Afternoon Tea... Tea sandwiches, home baked scone served with preserves & honey, seasonal berries with Grand Marnier cream, medley of petit-fours, and a pot of brewed loose tea.

TEATIME: 2:30pm To 5:00pm • Monday Thru Saturday
• Non-Caffeine/Herbal Tea Available
• Watercloset: Same Floor
• Wheelchair Accessible
• **Reservations Are Required**
• Two Hour Validated Valet Parking
• Credit Cards: V,DIS,MC&AE

L'autograph
*du Concierge*_____*Date*_____

SAN DIMAS MANSION
121 San Dimas Avenue
San Dimas, California

909-394-6793

    Tea Parties For Groups...At The San Dimas Mansion... This wonderful mansion is rich in California history. It was originally built approximately 100 years ago as a hotel for weary train travelers to spend the night. Alas, it was never used for that purpose. The railroad stop was never built! So much for the best laid plans! The current owners have put a lot of care into the renovation of the mansion. It has real charm with artistic Victorian woodwork, a magnificent chandelier, fine artwork & more. Call for information and to plan your special event for 50 to 100 guests.

    Afternoon Teas are served at tables set with linens, cloth napkins, white china and candle centerpieces. The Main Dining Room & The Parlor are wonderful settings for private tea parties for your special events. Aloma & her staff will be happy to help you plan a very special tea party. Please call early to reserve your date.

    $35.00 A Victorian Tea... Sample Menu. Cream or oat-currant scone with Devonshire cream, lemon curd, jams & jellies, assorted tea sandwiches, hot selections such as shrimp puffs, seasonal fresh fruit, delectable dessert such as mini cream puffs or eclairs, petit fours, mini-fruit tarts, a pot of brewed loose tea. A special event cake may be substitued for desserts.

TEA PARTIES FOR GROUPS: As Scheduled
- Available Sunday Thru Friday (Excluding Saturdays)
- May Accommodate Some Dietary Needs With Advance Request
- Non-Caffeine/Herbal Tea Available
- Watercloset: Same Floor
- Wheelchair Accessible
- **Please Call To Plan Your Tea Party For 50 To 100 Guests**
- Free Off-Street Parking
- Credit Cards: V,DISMC&AE

Proprietor's
*Autograph*_____*Date*_____

THE CLIFT HOTEL

495 Geary Street
(Corner Geary & Taylor)
San Francisco, California

800-652-5438 *Hotel Reservations*   **415-775-4700**

December Holiday Teas At...The Clift Hotel. "A gracious environment for gatherings of distinction." Tea lovers who have enjoyed tea at The Clift will be happy to know that their holiday plans can still include the popular December Afternoon Tea.

Holiday Teas are expected to begin November 29th and continue through December 30th. "Yule" enjoy the beautifully decorated Christmas tree and the festive Victorian-Art Deco holiday ambiance of the elegant Lobby Lounge. "The room is filled with abundant cheerful sunlight by day....and glowing chandeliers at night." There are comfortable upholstered chairs, unique tea lamps, lovely silver service, fine linens, Royal Doulton or Mayer china and of course fine service. This is a beautiful hotel, try to allow a little extra time to stroll around. Merry Teatimes!

$18.00 December Holiday Teas...A selection of finger sandwiches, fresh baked scone served with Devonshire cream & strawberry or raspberry jam, pastries and petit fours made daily by the pastry chef, and a pot of Twinings brewed loose tea.

DECEMBER TEAS: 3:00pm To 5:00pm • Seven Days A Week
- May Accommodate Some Dietary Needs, Advance Request
- Non-Caffeine/Herbal Tea Also Available
- Watercloset: Same Floor
- Wheelchair Accessible
- **Reservations Are Advised**
- Nearby Structure Parking, No Validation
- Credit Cards: V,MC,CB,V&AE

L'autograph
*du Concierge*_____*Date*_____

THE FAIRMONT HOTEL

950 Mason Street
(Atop Nob Hill)
San Francisco, California

415-772-5000   *Tea Reservations* **415-772-5281**

It's Teatime At...The Fairmont Hotel. The Fairmont Hotel is a very well-known hotel located atop Nob Hill. Frequented by tourists and locals alike, the popular hotel has attracted many tea lovers over the years.

Afternoon Tea is served in the ornate Victorian Fairmont Lobby of the hotel. You'll find plush antique furnishings, black & red carpeting, attractive gold accents, fresh flowers, a harpist, and a delicious Afternoon Tea. By the way, the menu was notable as well. There are many a la carte choices. Ports and Sherries are offered by the glass. Please call for their extended December hours.

$18.00 English Afternoon Tea... Fresh homemade scone served with Devonshire cream & preserves, an array of finger sandwiches, a selection of pastries and a choice of teas.

TEATIME: 3:00pm To 6:00pm • Monday Thru Saturday
- 1:00pm To 6:00pm • Sunday
- May Accommodate Some Dietary Needs, 1 Week Advance Request
- Egyptian Camomile Non-Caffeine Available
- Watercloset: Same Floor
- Wheelchair Accessible
- **Reservations Are A Must**
- Two Hour Street Park, No Validation
- Credit Cards: MC,V,DC,DIS&AE

L'autograph
*du Concierge*_____*Date*_____

IMPERIAL TEA COURT

1411 Powell Street
San Francisco, California

800-567-5898   **415-788-6080**

It's Time To Taste Tea At...The Imperial Tea Court..."Experience the tradition. You may choose among rare and even legendary teas never before sold in the United States."

The Imperial Tea Court is a direct tea grower, they carries a wide variety of teas, many available in various grades. No complete listing of their inventory is available, so please call to inquire about your favorite tea, or to try a new variety of tea. Roy reminds tea lovers that the ideal water temperature & steeping time is not the same for all teas. The Imperial Tea Court prepares tea in the traditional ancient Chinese fashion.

This authentic Chinese tea establishment is handsomely decorated with imported Chinese silk fabrics, rosewood furniture, and a floor of imported Chinese marble. The shop sells many tea accouterments which include Yixing pots, Gaiwan teacups, electric automatic teakettles and tea storage containers. P.S. Ask about the Tea Brewing classes which take place periodically. Ask to receive the mail-order catalog.Look for The Imperial Tea Court on web too: www.imperialtea.com

$10.00 TO $380.00 Per Lb.

$3.00-$5.00 Gaiwan of Tea

$1.00 Tea Cookie   ™

TEA TASTING: 11:00am To 6:30pm • Seven Days A Week
• Chinese Snow Herbal Tea Available
• Watercloset: Same Floor
• Two Parking Garages Nearby, Sorry No Validation
• Credit Cards: V,MC&AE

Proprietor's
*Autograph*_____*Date*_____

JAPANESE TEA GARDEN

Golden Gate Park
San Francisco, California

415-668-0909
415-752-1171 *Gift Shop*

New Addition...It's Time For A Spot Of Tea At...The Japanese Tea Garden. Since 1893 people have been visiting the postcard perfect four acre Japanese Tea Garden. Allow time to appreciate the scenic garden paths, bridges, flowers and trees. Osaka, San Francisco's sister city has inspired much of the beauty in this park. Don't miss The Koi Fish Pond, The Zen Garden, The Drum Bridge, and Cherry Tree Blossom Lane with magnificent blooms on display in April & May.

Tea is presented by gracious Kimono costumed servers in the small Tea House, or in the beautiful gardens. A small selection of sweets is usually available. P.S. Don't miss the Japanese Tea Garden Gift Shop. You could spend days in Golden Gate Park's 1,017 acres which includes an amazing collection of museums, plus a herd of grazing Bison in their paddock.

$2.50 Pot Of Tea...Selection of tea & cookies.

TEATIME: 9:00am To 6:30pm • Seven Days A Week
• Possible Winter Hours: 8:30am To 5:00pm
• General Admission: $2.50, Seniors 55+ $1.00, Children 6-11 $1.00
• Watercloset: Common Area
• Wheelchair Accessible
• **Please Drop By**
• Park Free Monday Thru Friday At The Concourse
• Parking: $1. Saturday, Sunday & Holidays, Coin/Bill By Machine
• Cash
Proprietor's
*Autograph*_____*Date*_____

KING GEORGE HOTEL

334 Mason Street
(At Geary)
San Francisco, California

415-781-5050   **800-288-6005**

It's Teatime At...King George Hotel. The King George Hotel has long been known as a home away from home for its many visitors. The hotel opened its doors in 1914 and has maintained traditional old fashioned English style hospitality ever since. Considered one of Union Square's most charming hotels, the King George is well located near shopping and theaters.

English Afternoon Tea is a must at the King George. It is graciously served in the "Bread & Honey" Tearoom at tables set with cloth napkins, fresh flowers & fine china. The melodic strains of a classical pianist fill the air. A variety of tea selections including Hampshire, Kew Garden, Buckingham, Lady Biltmore & Surrey Tea are also offered & extremely reasonably priced at around $5.00.

$9.00 Afternoon Tea... Carousel of assorted finger sandwiches, tea biscuits, toasted crumpet served with jam, tipsy Trifle and a pot of King George special blend brewed loose tea.

$5.00 The Hampshire Tea... Six assorted traditional finger tip sandwiches and a pot of brewed loose tea.

$4.00 The Surrey Tea... Fresh baked raisin scone served with butter & whipped cream and a pot of brewed loose tea.

TEATIME: 3:00pm To 6:30pm • Tuesday Thru Sunday
• May Accommodate Some Dietary Needs With Advance Request
• Tea Room Is On The Mezzanine, Via Stairs Or Elevator
• Non-Caffeine/Herbal Tea Available
• Children's Tea Parties Welcome
• Watercloset: Same Floor
• **Reservations Are Suggested**
• Downtown Center Park $4.00 Each Hour Approximately
• Credit Cards: V,MC,DIS,AE&JCB

Proprietor's
*Autograph*_____*Date*_____

LOVEJOY'S
Antiques & Tearoom

1195 Church Street (At 24th.St. Near The "J "Church Muni Line)
San Francisco, California

415-648-5895

It's Teatime At...Lovejoy's Antiques & Tearoom.
"Something old, something new, a pot of tea and a scone too!" The
name Lovejoy was inspired by a series of mystery stories involving
a fictional antique dealer who became embroiled in mysteries.
Afternoon Tea is served at antique tables with tablecloths,
fresh flowers and English fine china. Most of the pretty cups and
saucers are for sale, for that matter so are the tables, chairs and
paintings. Many British specialties are on the menu and include
shepard's pie, smoked-kipper plate, pate with toast, English cheese
platter and Stilton-walnut salad. "Tea parties for the young and the
not so young are our specialty." Please call Clint to plan your special
event. P.S. An Evening Candlelight High Tea may be scheduled
from 7-9pm for up to 30 guests, with a $75.00 room fee.

$17.95 For Two ($9.95 For One) High Tea... Two
sandwiches, two salads & two scones with strawberry preserves &
double Devon cream, dessert, a pot of Lovejoy's blend of tea.
$7.75 Light Tea... Tea sandwich, scone, Devon cream &
strawberry preserves, dessert, and a pot of Lovejoy's blend of tea.
$5.95 Cream Tea... English fruit scone with double
Devon cream & strawberry preserves, and a pot of Lovejoy's tea.

TEATIME: 10:30am To 7:00pm • Tuesday Thru Sunday
• 10am-7pm •Saturday & Sunday (No Mondays, Except Holidays)
• May Accommodate Some Dietary Needs With Advance Request
• Non-Caffeine/Herbal Tea Available
• Children's Tea Parties Welcome
• Watercloset: Same Floor
• **Reservations Are Appreciated**
• Unmetered Street Parking
• Cash Or Check

Proprietor's
*Autograph*_____*Date*_____

MARK HOPKINS
Inter-Continental
999 California Street
(California & Mason-Nob Hill)
San Francisco, California

415-392-3434   **800-327-0200**

It's Teatime At...Mark Hopkins Inter-Continental.
Tea is served at the world famous "Top of the Mark," on the 19th floor of the Mark Hopkins Hotel. The hotel is situated atop prestigious Nob Hill which offers a spectacular view of the San Francisco Bay area and the Golden Gate Bridge.

Afternoon Tea is presented from three tiered cake stands at tables set with Rosenthal china & fresh flowers. A pianist plays from 4pm to 8pm adding to the ambiance. The delicacies at the Mark are prepared by the hotel's own European trained pastry chef. Eight varieties of tea including the Mark Hopkin's blend are featured. Consider trying the hand-rolled Jasmine Pearl tea. F.Y.I. I think you'll find the hotel's Ronnefeldt teapots from Germany, quite interesting. The teapots lay on their back while tea is steeping, then tilt to a 45 degree angle allowing the water to drip through. The leaves stay in the chamber but the tea ceases to steep.

$20.00 Afternoon Tea...(Selection changes daily) Assortment of crustless finger sandwiches, freshly baked variety of miniature scones with Devonshire cream & preserves, a selection of miniature French pastries, fresh fruit tartlets and brewed loose tea.

TEATIME: 3:00pm To 5:00pm • Monday Thru Friday
• May Accommodate Some Dietary Needs, 2 Day Advance Request.
• Non-Caffeine/Herbal Tea Available
• Watercloset: Same Floor
• Wheelchair Accessible
• **Reservations Are Recommended**
• $4.00 Parking With Validation
• Credit Cards: All Major

L'autograph
*du Concierge*_____*Date*_____

230

NEIMAN MARCUS
150 Stockton Street
San Francisco, California

415-362-4777 *The Rotunda Room*   **415-362-3900**

It's Teatime At...Neiman Marcus. Neiman Marcus has a reputation for carrying the finest of everything. One of the finest treasures not for sale here is the fabulous Rotunda glass dome considered part of the Neiman Marcus fine art collection." 'The Glass Ship' was built in 1909 as the official seal of the city of Paris store. The Latin inscription translates to read, 'It floats but does not sink.' In 1981 the dome's 2,600 pieces were sent to Massachusetts for restoration and in 1982 it was reinstalled by Neiman Marcus as the focal point of the rotunda. It is, to the best of accounts, the only stained glass dome to travel 6,000 miles to be positioned within 11 feet of its original location." Afternoon Tea is attentively served at Neiman Marcus in this grand room located on the fourth floor.

Afternoon Tea is presented from tiered caddies at tables set with linen napkins & tablecloths, petit plants and white teapots. Expect caring service, after all this is Neiman Marcus where the pleasure of classic tea and classic shopping come together!

$13.75 Full Afternoon Tea... Finger sandwiches, scone served with cream & preserves, assorted sweets and gorgeous brewed loose tea from The Tea Company from Larkspur. P.S. They have also blended the gourmet NM brand which you may purchase.

$7.25 Petite Cream Tea... Homemade scone served with cream & preserves, tartlet, cookie and brewed loose tea.

TEATIME: 2:30pm To 5:00pm • Seven Days A Week
- Hours May Vary Depending On The Tearoom Schedule, Please Call
- Non-Caffeine/Herbal Tea Available
- Watercloset: Same Floor
- Wheelchair Accessible
- **Reservations Are Advised, Especially During The Holidays**
- Nearby Union Square Parking Lot, Sorry No Validation
- Credit Cards: NM,AE&Bergdorf

Manager's
*Autograph*_____*Date*_____

PARK HYATT HOTEL

PARK HYATT

333 Battery Street
San Francisco, California

415-392-1234 **800-233-1234**

It's Teatime At...Park Hyatt Hotel. Understated elegance and quiet sophistication await you at the Park Hyatt Hotel located in San Francisco's Embarcadero Center business district. Afternoon Tea is served daily in the handsome Lobby with its rich Australian lacewood and neoclassical formality. Plush upholstered leather chairs seem to create the ambiance of an exclusive club.

Afternoon Tea is served at tables set with Wedgewood, Amherst china, linen place mats & fresh flowers, by servers in vests & bow ties. Allow time to explore the terrific Embarcadero Center. It is a five block area with cinemas, offices, bistros, shopping and now a 40 floor observation deck. "Here's lookin at you San Fran!"

$15.00 Tea Royale... Glass of Domaine Chandon Brut, assorted tea sandwiches, scone, Devonshire cream & preserves, pastry or fruit tartlet, a pot of Harney & Son's brewed loose tea.

$14.00 Teddy Bear Teas In December... Adorable finger sandwiches & treats especially for children. This wonderful tea usually takes place daily in December. Each child receives his or her very own precious stuffed bear as a gift! Price is approximate.

$11.00 The English Hotel Tea...A selection of tea sandwiches, fresh baked scone served with Devonshire cream & preserves, assorted pastry or fruit tartlet, a pot of brewed loose tea.

$7.50 Afternoon Tea Break... Homemade scone with Devonshire cream & strawberry preserves, pot of brewed loose tea.

TEATIME: 3:00pm To 4:30pm • Seven Days A Week
• May Accommodate Some Dietary Needs With Advance Request
• Non-Caffeine/Herbal Tea Available
• Children's Tea Parties Welcome
• Wheelchair Accessible • Watercloset: Same Floor
• **Reservations Are Requested**
• Valet & Reduced Rate Park W/ Validation At Embarcadero
• Credit Cards: Most Major
L'autograph
*du Concierge*_____*Date*_____

Photo of courtesy of Park Hyatt Hotel **An unforgettable tea party!**

RENAISSANCE STANFORD
Court Hotel

905 California Street
(Nob Hill)
San Francisco, California

415-989-3500

It's Teatime At...Renaissance Stanford Court Hotel. This grand historic hotel is the epitome of old world elegance. Guests enter the hotel through a carriage courtyard dramatically covered by a Tiffany style stained glass dome. There are fine antiques, Baccarat chandeliers, a beaux-arts fountain, Carrara marble floors and a grandfather clock which Napoleon Bonaparte actually presented to his minister of war in 1806.

A formal Afternoon Tea is presented on tiered caddies in the Lobby Lounge at tables set with tablecloths, cloth napkins, white Villeroy & Boch china & a bud vase. At 4:30, the pianist begins to play. F.Y.I. Breads, pastries and desserts are baked fresh daily on premises. A la carte selections are also available from the tea menu.

$16.00 Full Tea... Assorted tea sandwiches, mini scones served with cream & jam, petite pastry, fruit tartlet, assorted tea cookies and a pot of loose brewed tea.

$12.00 Light Tea... Mini scones with cream & jam, petite pastry, fruit tartlet, assorted tea cookies, a pot of loose brewed tea.

TEATIME: 2:30pm To 5:00pm • Seven Days A Week
- May Accommodate Some Dietary Needs With Advance Request
- Non-Caffeine/Herbal Tea Available
- Watercloset: Convenient
- Wheelchair Accessible
- **Reservations Are Advisable**
- Nearby Parking Structure Not Validated
- Credit Cards: V,MC,DIS,AE&JCB

L'autograph
*du Concierge*_____*Date*_____

THE RITZ CARLTON
San Francisco

600 Stockton Street
San Francisco, California

415-296-7465

THE RITZ-CARLTON®

It's Teatime At...The Ritz Carlton. The Ritz Carlton Hotels offer excellent Afternoon Teas in my experience. The San Francisco Ritz Carlton is an exceptional 88 year old neoclassical-style structure. After walking up the hill one day, I was thrilled to have a seat in the Lobby Lounge, have tea and just relax. Afternoon Tea is served in the comfortable and attractive Lobby Lounge with a view of the courtyard and financial district.

Afternoon Tea is graciously presented on tiered caddies at tables set with white cloths & white lace toppers, cloth napkins, Wedgewood, Kutani Crane china and fresh flowers. The lounge is elegant with beautiful crystal chandeliers and handsome furnishings. The Lobby Lounge has dining tables and groups of sofas and wingback chairs. A harpist plays gently in the background.

$18.00 Full Tea... Selection of tea sandwiches, freshly baked scone served with Devonshire cream, lemon curd & preserves, assorted English tea cakes such as fresh fruit tartlets, Madeleine, Florentine, shortbread and a pot of brewed loose tea.

$14.00 Light Tea... Fresh baked scone with Devonshire cream, lemon curd & preserves, assorted English tea cakes, mini fruit tartlet, Madeleine, Florentine and shortbread, a pot of loose tea.

TEATIME: Seven Days A Week
- 2:30pm To 4:30pm • Monday Thru Friday
- 1:00pm To 4:30pm • Saturday & Sunday
- May Accommodate Some Dietary Needs With Advance Request
- Non-Caffeine/Herbal Tea Available
- Children's Teddy Bear Teas in December
- Wheelchair Accessible • Watercloset: Same Floor
- **Reservations Are Recommended**
- Approximately $8.00 Valet Parking With Validation
- Credit Cards: V,MC,DC,DIS,AE&JCB

L'autograph
*du Concierge*_____*Date*_____

The day will be complete with Afternoon Tea!

SHERATON PALACE HOTEL
2 New Montgomery Street
San Francisco, California

415-392-8600

It's Teatime At...Sheraton Palace Hotel.
"Afternoon Tea reaches an exalted level in the historic setting of the Garden Court. It's not surprising why the Garden Court has captured the imagination of the world. In sheer size it's impressive. But that's just the beginning. The crowning glory of the Garden Court is its breathtaking domed ceiling of stained glass. When sunlight illuminates the dome, you feel as if you're sitting in a garden atrium with elegant chandeliers, towering marble columns and marble floors." The room is creamy off-white with comfy couches, upholstered chairs and iris blue carpet. Afternoon Tea is a treasured experience in this crystal atrium with the magnificent chandeliers glistening from the ceiling like priceless ornaments.

Afternoon Tea is presented on tiered caddies at comfy grouped couches and chairs. The tea tables are set with cream colored cloth napkins, place mats, Woodmere white china with gold trim and two pink roses in a cobalt blue vase. This is one of my very favorite spots. A memorable experience awaits you!

$19.00 The Garden Court Afternoon Tea... Assorted tea sandwiches, fresh baked scone with cream & preserves, assorted pastries & tarts, and a pot of brewed loose tea.

$16.00 Princess Tea...(Twelve years & under) Tea sandwiches, pastries, cookies, signature crown pastry & lemonade, apple juice or children's caffeine-free tea plus a Princess Crown and Scepter to commemorate her reign as "Princess of The Palace."

TEATIME: 2-4:30pm,Wednesday-Saturday • 2-3:30pm Sunday
• May Accommodate Some Dietary Needs With Advance Request
• Non-Caffeine/Herbal Tea Available
• Children's Tea Parties Welcome
• Watercloset: Same Floor • Wheelchair Accessible
• **Reservations Are Suggested, Required For Princess Teas**
• $5.00 Discount For Hotel Self-Parking
• Credit Cards: V,MC,DC,DIS,AE&JCB

L'autograph
*du Concierge*_____Date_____

Did you remember the Motorloaf?

TAL-Y-TARA
Tea & Polo Shoppe
6439 California Street (At 27th Avenue)
San Francisco, California

Tea and Polo Shoppe

888-TEA POLO   415-751-9275

New Addition...It's Teatime At...Tal-Y-Tara.
Here's something the "horsey-set" will really like. Tally-Ho! The marriage of tea & polo has arrived and you don't have to arrive side-saddle to appreciate the sweet treats at Tal-Y-Tara. One section of the shoppe carries a complete line of English riding apparel & polo equipment while the other carries a terrific assortment of bulk loose tea & tinned teas, teapots, cozies, books & gifts. "If you're not feeling well have a cup of tea; if you are feeling well, have a cup of tea anyhow," quips Hugh, who along with Melba owns Tal-Y-Tara.
　　Afternoon Tea is served at pub tables set with hunt scene tablecloths or "equestrian" place mats, J &G Meakin Pottery, The Classic Blue Nordic pattern and fresh flowers. P.S. You may take tea in the jasmine & wisteria flowering garden on the sunny south side. Ask Melba about the French tea. F.Y.I. There's a piano too.

　　$13.00 The "Motorloaf" & Tea For Two... The specialty of the house hails from an old New England recipe. A unique homemade tea sandwich of sorts described as "a special bread filled with sandwiches for two," and a pot of brewed loose tea. The "Motorloaf" was originally designed to fit comfortably on the front seat of a car or perhaps more appropriately here, a horse-drawn buggy, hence the name Motorloaf!
　　$6.00 English Trifle & Pot of Tea... Yummy a la carte sweet treat or scone with cream and a pot of brewed loose tea.

TEATIME: 10:00am To 6:00pm • Monday Thru Saturday
• May Accommodate Some Dietary Needs With Advance Request
• Non-Caffeine/Herbal Tea Available
• Watercloset: Same Floor
• **Reservations Appreciated For Larger Parties**
• Unmetered Limited Time Street Parking
• Credit Cards: V,MC,DIS&AE
Proprietor's
*Autograph*_____*Date*_____

TEA & COMPANY
2207 Fillmore Street
San Francisco, California

415-929-TEAS/8327

New Addition...It's Time For Tea At...Tea & Company. Jill and Gary of Tea & Company have incorporated the *essence* of tea into their lifestyle philosophy. This fine tea shop is 1600 square feet. Light, airy & inviting, the counters and tables are attractive in light woods, the chairs with comfortable wicker seats.

Drop in and enjoy a good cup of tea and sample a world wide variety of teas for your take home pleasure. There are Black Estate, Black Blends, Greens, Oolongs, Herb & Fruited and White Teas. All teas are blended by Tea & Company to "burst with flavor." Ask about "World Fruit Tea" considered a great children's tea. Gary says that approximately 200 cups can be made from one pound of tea verses 60 cups from a pound of coffee! P.S. Allow time to browse, in addition to tea accessories, strainers, infusers, teapots, mugs, books & gift box samplers, Tea & Company sells Mount Fuji Bath & Spa Salts based on their teas. F.Y.I. Donna Karan's new tea line features Tea & Company's teas!

$2.25, $3.75 Or $5.25 Pot Of Tea... Three sizes.
$4.25, $6.75 Or $10.50 Pot Of Rare Tea
$3.25 Fresh Baked Daily Pies
$1.85 Great Brownies, $1.75 Fig Rosemary Bars
$1.25 Fat Free Ginger Snaps...Soooo good!
$4.85 Chicken Tea Rolls.. Signature handmade dipping rolls poached in camomile tea for dipping into tea infused Lapsang Souchong or Shanghai Garden vinaigrette, served with a tall glass of iced tea. **$4.00 Tea Veggies Rolls.**

TEATIME: 8am-10:30pm • Seven Days • Till 11pm, Fri. & Sat.
• Non-Caffeine/Herbal Tea Available
• Watercloset: Same Floor Common Area • Wheelchair Accessible
• **Please Drop By**
• Metered Street Parking
• Credit Cards: V&MC
Proprietor's
*Autograph*_____*Date*_____

TEAZ ON THE SQUARE

900 Northpoint Street (Ghiradelli Square)
San Francisco, California

415-346-3488   **800-457-1904**

It's Teatime At...Teaz On The Square. Teaz, located in Ghiradelli Square, is a wonderful and whimsical spot for Afternoon Tea. Aside from carrying around 80 varieties of tea, tea-related gifts & accoutrements, Teaz is a fun spot for Afternoon Tea. The shop is decorated with antiques, teapot-pattern fabrics, teapot portraits, and clever tea phrases painted here and there on the floor. Afternoon Tea includes personalized menus & place cards, fabulous teatime menus, and a delightful visit with Vanessa, the manager.

Afternoon Tea is presented from tiered caddies at purple polka-dot painted tables with wire teapot centerpieces filled with fresh purple petaled plants. Positively perfect! Servers are attired in white jackets and black pants. Vanessa has creatively named the teas, look for "Tip Me Over & Pour Me Out," & "None Of Your Beeswax." Ask about fun Santa Claus Tea Parties at Christmas. P.S. Private tea parties are available for up to 35 guests. Please call for information and for possible extended seasonal hours.

$13.95 One Lump Or Two... Savories such as spinach-crab-citrus spirals, scone, jam, sweet surprises & brewed loose tea.
$8.95 Children's Teddy Bear Tea... Cut-out tea sandwiches, PB&J, cheddar & turkey, sweets, cocoa or "tea."
$7.95 Sweets... Array of sweets such as: a brownie, lemon square, Willie's kisses or French twist & brewed loose tea.

TEATIME: After 1:00pm • Seven Days A Week
• Shop Hours:10am To 6pm • Monday Thru Thursday & Sunday
• 10am To 9pm, Friday & Saturday • Call For Seasonal Hours
• Non-Caffeine/Herbal Tea Available
• Children's Tea Parties Welcome
• Wheelchair Accessible • Watercloset: Nearby
• **Reservations Are Recommended**
• One Hour Parking Validation With $5.00 Purchase
• Credit Cards: V&MC
Proprietor's
*Autograph*_____*Date*_____

Take a break, have fun...go for Afternoon Tea!

THE WESTIN
St. Francis Hotel

335 Powell Street
(Union Square)
San Francisco, California

415-397-7000   *The Compass Rose* **415-774-0167**

It's Teatime At...The Westin St. Francis. The Compass Rose in The Westin St. Francis Hotel, with its beautiful fluted columns and high ornate ceilings is a very aesthetically pleasing spot for Afternoon Tea. The room has rich wood paneling, exotic orchids, crystal lamps and museum quality objects brought in from all points on the compass. I was impressed with the very courteous and thoughtful staff particularly as I was taking tea alone.

The Compass Rose, close to Union Square has been a rendezvous destination since the hotel opened in 1904. At that time, the room was known as The Cafe. The hotel has a wonderful collection of art deco antiques and art which exhibit a blend of drama and humor. Give yourself a little time to appreciate these treasures.

$16.95 Compass Rose Tea... Fresh homemade scone served with Devonshire cream & preserves, selection of tea sandwiches, seasonal berries, Chef's selection of assorted petit fours, and a pot of brewed loose tea. Approximately $5.00 additional for a glass of Champagne.

TEATIME: 3:00pm To 5:00pm • Seven Days A Week
• May Accommodate Some Dietary Need With Advance Request
• Non-Caffeine/Herbal Tea Available
• Watercloset: Convenient
• Wheelchair Accessible
• **Reservations Are Advised**
• Non-Validated Parking, Nearby Lot
• Credit Cards: V,MC,DC,DIS,AE&JCB
L'autograph
*du Concierge*_____*Date*_____

FAIRMONT HOTEL
In San Jose/Silicon Valley

170 South Market Street
San Jose, California

408-998-1900

It's Teatime At...Fairmont Hotel. Whether you've been chatting about "chips" all day or doing your own thing, take a well-deserved break and enjoy Afternoon Tea with friends at the gracious Fairmont Hotel. The hotel's convenient business location combined with its comfortable easy atmosphere could make The Lobby Lounge in The Fairmont Hotel a fine spot to put together your next big "deal" or just to enjoy a relaxing tea. Besides, after sitting at the computer all day, you deserve Afternoon Tea.

Afternoon Tea is served with care, at tables set with linens, cloth napkins & fine Orchard Hill, English china in a delicate floral pattern with gold trim. Comfortable couches & over-stuffed chairs enhance the traditional Afternoon Tea experience.

$14.95 Fairmont Tea Ceremony... An assortment of finger sandwiches, fresh homemade scone served with Devonshire cream, lemon curd & fresh fruit preserves, French pastries and an individual pot of your choice of brewed loose tea.

TEATIME: 3:00pm To 5:00pm • Seven Days A Week
- May Accommodate Some Dietary Needs With Advance Request
- Non-Caffeine/Herbal Tea Available
- Wheelchair Accessible
- Watercloset: Same Floor
- **Reservations Are Required**
- Sorry No Parking Validation
- Credit Cards: V,MC,DIS,DC&AE

L'autograph
du Concierge _____*Date*_____

HENSLEY HOUSE B&B
456 North Third Street
San Jose, California

800-498-3537   **408-298-3537**

New Addition...Tea & Tour On Thursday And Saturday At...Hensley House B&B. Escape to the romance of Hensley House located within walking distance of downtown offices, the San Jose convention center, major hotels, restaurants, and Silicon Valley. Built in 1884, the historic Hensley House is a fine getaway at teatime.

Afternoon Tea is served amidst antiques, lace, crystal chandeliers, and stained-glass windows by Tony & Ron, your new hospitable proprietors. You may relax with tea in front of the fireplace in a cozy intimate setting, in a dormer window area, or in the dining room. Tea is served one course at a time at tables set with fresh flowers, pretty tablecloths and Royal Albert, Country Rose china. A tour of the Hensley House is included. Private tea parties are available for 6 to 40 guests with advance reservations. Gifts certificates are available.

$15.00 Hensley House High Tea... Three tea sandwiches such as, curried chicken with cream cheese & walnuts, and salmon & watercress, fresh baked scones & muffins, fresh fruit, dessert, and a pot of brewed loose tea.

TEATIME: 2:00pm To 5:00pm • Thursday & Saturday
• May Accommodate Some Dietary Needs With Advance Request
• Non-Caffeine/Herbal Tea Available
• Children's Tea Parties Welcome
• Watercloset: Same Floor
• **Reservations Are Required**
• Street Parking
• Credit Cards: V,MC,DIS,DC&AE
Proprietor's
*Autograph*_____*Date*_____

INTO THE LOOKING GLASS
Tea & Chocolate Shoppe

2202 Lincoln Avenue
San Jose, California

408-265-5665

New Addition...It's Teatime At...Into The Looking Glass. Tea & chocolate, hmmm sounds perfect to me! Tucked into a quiet corner, not far from the Silicon Valley and just south of Willow Glen, you'll discover "Into The Looking Glass." This spacious and airy shoppe has a wonderful Alice In Wonderland theme with high ceilings, a collection of mirrors of course, and soft classical background music.

Afternoon Tea is served at tables set with mix-n-match floral linens, fresh flowers, Woodsware "English Scenes" fine china & silver. Candied violet & rose petals are an extra special touch. The marvelous homemade specialties are prepared by Rebecca the proprietor who just happens to be a classically trained chef. A visit here is an epicurean treat. Many a la carte items are offered in addition to Afternoon Tea. You'll be mad as a hatter if you miss this spot, and don't be late! Private tea parties too for 30 to 50 guests.

$14.00 Tea Sampler For One... Assortment of tea sandwiches, Rebecca's signature homebaked scones served with curd & preserves, cakes & cookies & a pot of brewed loose tea.
$2.50-$10.00 Pot Of Tea For One... Over 50 Harney & Son's or Eastern Shore, Leaves, Royal Gardens fine teas.
$5.00-$10.00 Pot Of Tea For Two

TEATIME: 11:00am To 4:00pm • Wednesday Thru Sunday
- May Accommodate Some Dietary Needs With Advance Request
- Non-Caffeine/Herbal Tea Available
- Watercloset: Same Floor
- Wheelchair Accessible
- **Reservations Are Appreciated**
- Free Parking Lot
- Credit Cards: V,MC&AE

Proprietor's
*Autograph*_____*Date*_____

There may be a tea party in your future!

**Darling, I simply must have brewed loose tea!
And by the way, have you "got milk?"**

EAGEN HOUSE RESTAURANT

31892 Camino Capistrano
San Juan Capistrano, California

714-488-0409

New Addition...It's Teatime At...Eagen House.
This 1883 two-story Italianate Victorian is quite a romantic spot for Afternoon Tea. The house was built for its namesake Judge Richard Eagen. He lived alone here, as the presiding Judge and Justice of the Peace until his passing in 1923. Over the years this spot was home to offices and an art gallery until the current owner turned the house into a restaurant in April 1996. Gary the proprietor, received so many requests for Tea that he decided to add it to the lunch and dinner menu in early November of the same year.

Afternoon Tea is served at interesting theme tables that include The Celestial Table and The Madam Majeska Table. Madam Majeska was a local thespian and a very close friend of Eagen's. The decor of the house includes creamy white walls, beautiful paintings, antique wicker furniture, dark green window treatments, and wonderful hand painted murals of roses and grapevines. Private tea parties are available for 20 to 60 guests on the second floor via a flight of stairs, in The Harmony Hall. Tea-related gifts upstairs too.

$19.95 The Eagen House Tea... Finger sandwiches, scones with cream & preserves, dessert, a pot of brewed loose tea.
$9.95 Scones & Fruit... Scones, Devonshire cream & preserves, fresh seasonal fruit & a pot of brewed loose tea.

TEATIME: Seatings: 11:30am & 2:30pm • Saturday
• May Accommodate Some Dietary Needs With Advance Request
• Non-Caffeine/Herbal Tea Available
• Children's Tea Parties Welcome
• Watercloset: Wheelchair Accessible Unisex First Floor
• Wheelchair Accessible Downstairs • Watercloset: Second Floor
• **Reservations Are Required**
• Free Parking Lot
• Credit Cards: V,MC,DIS,DC&AE
Proprietor's
*Autograph*_____*Date*_____

THE TEA HOUSE
On Los Rios
31731 Los Rios Street
San Juan Capistrano, California

714-443-3914

*New Tea Room Brewing...***The Tea House On Los Rios.** Located in the heart of San Juan Capistrano within walking distance of the famous mission, you will discover The Tea House On Los Rios nestled on the oldest and perhaps most colorful historic residential street in California. The proprietors are busy renovating The Rodman House, a board & batten cottage built in the 1920's and still with its original wood floors and bead ceilings.

Afternoon Tea plans include tablecloths, unless the table is just too pretty, fresh flowers, an eclectic collection of fine china and glassware and artistically presented homemade specialties. Private tea parties will be available, in fact, they are already getting reservations. A unique gift boutique is beginning to take shape in the living room. After tea, plan to stroll the gardens and visit the shops in the little Los Rios Street community. Listen for the nostalgic mission bells and imagine yourself stepping off the train at the turn of the century. P.S. Keep an eye out for swallows!

$16.50 (Approximately) **The Los Rios Tea...**Assorted finger sandwiches, a selection of freshly homebaked scones served with California cream & preserves, dessert, and brewed loose tea.

$12.50 The Cottage Tea... Scone with California cream & preserves, sliced seasonal fruit with cream, and brewed loose tea.

ANTICIPATED **TEATIME:** 11am-4pm • Wednesday Thru Sunday
- May Accommodate Some Dietary Needs With Advance Request
- Non-Caffeine/Herbal Tea Available
- Watercloset: Same Level As One Of The Tearooms
- Wheelchair Accessible
- **Reservations Are Suggested**
- Free On-Site Parking/Structure Nearby
- Credit Cards: V,MC,DIS&AE

Proprietor's
*Autograph*_____*Date*_____

CUPS & COMPANY
at The Adobe Inn B&B

1473 Monterey Street
San Luis Obispo, California

805-549-0321

    New Addition...It's Teatime At...Cups & Company At...The Adobe Inn B&B. Jim and Shari are the new proprietors of The Adobe Inn. It is a 15 room refurbished motel turned European-style B&B situated just 6 blocks from downtown San Luis Obispo. With Olivia's help, they have designed a spot in the Inn called "Cups & Company," where Afternoon and Cream Teas are offered. The airy, well-lit English garden room is decorated with cream-colored walls, a tile floor, peachy curtains tied with mint bows, potted plants and shelves full of pretty teapots & teacups.
    Afternoon Tea tables are set with skirts, toppers, & flowers arranged in Twinning Tea canisters. Classical music fills the air while you enjoy tea treats on glass plates and white china. Please call for the schedule of theme teas which are held about six times a year. Private tea parties are welcome for up to 16 guests.

    $9.75 Afternoon Tea... Cucumber tea sandwiches, petit currant or melt-away strawberry scones with with fresh whipped cream & strawberry jam and a pot of brewed loose or bagged tea.
    $8.50 Cream Tea... Petit currant or melt-away strawberry scones served with fresh whipped cream & strawberry jam and a pot of brewed loose or bagged tea.

TEATIME: 3:00pm To 7:00pm • Seven Days A Week
• May Accommodate Some Dietary Needs With Advance Request
• Non-Caffeine/Herbal Tea Available
• Watercloset: Same Floor
• Children's Tea Parties Welcome
• **Reservations Are Appreciated, But Not Always Necessary**
• Free Parking Lot
• Credit Cards: V,MC&AE

Proprietor's
*Autograph*_____*Date*_____

RHYTHM CREEKSIDE CAFE

1040 Broad Street
San Luis Obispo, California

Rhythm
CREEKSIDE CAFE

805-541-4048

New Addition...It's Teatime Friday, Saturday & Sunday At...Rhythm Creekside Cafe. "Every little breeze seems to whisper tea...please," under the fragrant lemon trees in the Rhythm Courtyard at Rhythm Creekside Cafe. The cafe is located next to SLO's meandering creek, how's that for a touch of romance? Paul and Lucy have a neat little spot here, and they're fun to boot. They invite you to relax and enjoy being pampered beneath the sheltering arms of their lemon tree.

Afternoon Tea is served in courses at tables set with linens and fresh flowers. This "California casual" bistro is located only 1/2 block from the historic San Luis Obispo's Mission. This is a great spot for just walking around too. F.Y.I. Rhythm Creekside Cafe's menu features many locally grown & produced foods. P.S. Private tea parties are available on weekdays for parties of 12 to 40 guests.

$14.95 Full Tea... Finger sandwiches, fresh scones served creme fraiche, platter of pastries, pot of brewed loose tea.

$9.95 Light Tea... Fresh scones served with creme fraiche, platter of pastries and a pot of brewed loose tea.

TEATIME: 2:00pm To 4:00pm • Friday, Saturday & Sunday
• Outdoor Courtyard Seating Available Weather Permitting
• May Accommodate Some Dietary Needs With Advance Request
• Non-Caffeine/Herbal Tea Available
• Children's Tea Parties Welcome
• Watercloset: Up One Flight From The Courtyard
• **Reservations Are Required**
• Metered Street Parking & Non-Validated Nearby Lots
• Credit Cards: V,MC,DIS&AE

Proprietor's
*Autograph*_____*Date*_____

The very thought of tea...
makes me want to break into song!

OPUS 28 BAKERY & CAFE

2998 Huntington Drive
San Marino, California

626-286-3300

New Addition...It's Teatime At Opus 28 Bakery & Cafe. A classical music medley of creatively orchestrated teatime specialties awaits you at Opus 28! The proprietors, Wendy & May serve breakfast, lunch, & Afternoon Tea in casual upscale San Marino fashion. They totally renovated this corner spot, and decorated it in a most tuneful refrain, and the open, airy, full panoramic view of the distant San Gabriel Mountains is incomparable. All of the beautiful cakes & desserts are made here. They have splendid names such as, March of the Cocoa Bean, Waltz of the Flowers, and my favorite, Tira-Miss-You! The cakes are uniquely decorated with fine, edible gold music notes.

Afternoon Tea is presented from tiered caddies garnished with edible organic flowers at natural polished round wood tables which have been imprinted with the Opus 28 logo. The chairs are perforated pattern chrome-type high tech, and reflect the clean, light colored, contemporary design of the shop. Afternoon Tea "to go" is offered too, on classy "silver" trays. Plus gifts & neat "column tea!"

$14.00 High Tea Medley, Tea For Two. Four assorted finger sandwiches, two scones, fruit tarts, butterflies, Danishes, savory & cream puffs, small chocolate desserts & tea.

$7.95 Afternoon Tea Deluxe... Two assorted finger sandwiches, a scone, mini fruit tart, butterfly, Danish, savory puff, a cookie, chocolate dessert, and brewed loose "column" tea.

$5.95 Afternoon Tea Special...A finger sandwich, a scone, mini butterfly, Danish, savory puff, a cookie and brewed tea.

TEATIME: After 2:00pm • Seven Days A Week
- May Accommodate Some Dietary Needs With Advance Request
- Non-Caffeine/Herbal Tea Available
- Watercloset: "Sopranos & Tenors" Same Floor
- **Reservations Are Recommended** • Wheelchair Accessible
- Free Parking In Rear Lot
- Credit Cards: V&MC

Proprietor's
*Autograph*_____*Date*_____

A Spot of Tea   *San Marino, California*

TEA TIME

2060 Huntington Drive
San Marino, California   **Tea**  **Time**

626-576-4640

*New Tearoom Brewing...*It's **Teatime At Tea Time.** Four very talented ladies are about to declare that it's Teatime! Meet Cynthia, Brandie, Kristina and Aurora, all close friends or relations. Aurora is a wonderful baker, you're in for a real treat. The interior plans include a maroon & teal carpet, antique white, maroon & teal wallcoverings, and matching exterior awnings. A visiting harpist or violinist will be a very nice touch.

Afternoon Tea will be presented from two or three tiered caddies at tables set with tablecloths, seasonally inspired theme centerpieces, and an eclectic collection of china. Allow time to browse. The gift shop will feature all kinds of tea accoutrements, tea-theme accessories, books, & jewelry. Ask about the Candle Light Teas & the Kiddie Tea menu. If you're in the neighborhood stop by and tell them you're looking forward to "teatime!"

$10.99 Cynthia's Enchantment... Assorted finger sandwiches fruit, cookie, dessert & a pot of brewed loose tea.
$8.99 Aurora's Delight... Soup, salad, dessert & tea.
$8.99 Brandies Favorite... Assorted tea sandwiches, fruit, cookie, and a pot of brewed loose tea.
$7.99 Kristina's Confection... Choice of dessert, fruit, & a pot of brewed loose tea.

ANTICIPATED **TEATIME:** 7am To 7pm • Monday Thru Friday
• 9:00am To 7:00pm, Saturday • 10:00am To 5:00pm, Sunday
• May Accommodate Some Dietary Needs With Advance Request
• Non-Caffeine/Herbal Tea Available
• Children's Tea Parties Welcome
• Watercloset: Same Floor • Wheelchair Accessible
• **Reservations Are Required**
• Free Rear Parking Lot
• Credit Cards: V,MC,DIS,DC&AE
Proprietor's
*Autograph*_____*Date*_____

255

ROSE GARDEN. THE HUNTINGTON LIBRARY, ART COLLECTIONS, AND BOTANICAL GARDENS. SAN MARINO, CALIFORNIA

THE HUNTINGTON LIBRARY
Art Collections & Botanical Gardens
1151 Oxford Road
San Marino, California

Reservations **626-683-8131**   *Directions* **626-405-2141**

It's Teatime At...The Huntington Library, Art Collections & Botanical Gardens. It's a glorious hike along a blooming path from the parking lot to the wonderful Rose Garden Tea Room at The Huntington. There are so many special treasures to appreciate here. Allow time to self-tour the theme gardens, The Library and The Art Gallery. There are world renowned permanent and visiting exhibits here. "Pinkie" and "Blue Boy" are a must, but there are so many musts including the incredible double elephant folio book by Mr. Audobon entitled, *Birds Of America.*

Tasty Afternoon Tea specialties are generously presented buffet style. Tea is poured by your server at tables set with starched linens and beautiful fresh flowers. I think the scones here are absolutely delicious! P.S. Be sure to stop by the gift shop and take home memories of a delightful afternoon. There are many books, unique gifts, greeting cards & so much more! Inquire about membership benefits, lectures and plant sales while you're here. F.Y.I. Members enjoy free admission to The Huntington.

$11.00 English Afternoon Tea... An assortment of finger sandwiches, imported cheeses, fresh fruit, delicious assorted scones with cream & preserves, fruit tartlets, shortbread, freshly baked desserts and Prince of Wales or Jasmine brewed loose tea.

TEATIME: 12Noon To 4:30pm • Tuesday Thru Friday
• 10:45am To 4:30pm • Saturday & Sunday
• Closed Mondays & Holidays
• Non-Caffeine/Herbal Tea Available
• Watercloset: Same Floor • Wheelchair Accessible
• **Reservations Are A Must**
• Museum Admission: Approximately $7.50 Per Person
• Credit Cards: V,MC,DIS&AE
Manager's
*Autograph*_____*Date*_____

FALKIRK

1408 Mission Avenue
San Rafael, California

415-485-3328

New Addition...Quarterly Theme Teas At Falkirk. Built in 1888 for Ella Nichols Park, Falkirk is a California Queen Anne Victorian designed by architect Clinton Day and built at a cost of $30,000. After Ella's death in 1905, the estate was purchased by Captain Robert Dollar of Dollar Steamship fame; the same Captain Dollar credited with founding the Merchant Marine. Subsequent years of struggle over development of the property led to a grassroots citizens' effort to place the estate on the National Register Of Historic Places. Thankfully voters approved, and this estate named after a city in Scotland, became Falkirk Cultural Center. It is now maintained and run by the city of San Rafael.

Afternoon Theme Teas are planned as quarterly events and beautifully orchestrated by the volunteers. One can always find a pianist and violinist playing in the parlor and music rooms. These very popular events usually accommodate nearly 100 guests in an elegant, buffet style presentation. Allow time to visit The Living History Center, the Marin Poetry Center and The Green Man "growing" in the greenhouse. P.S. Tours may be available upon request or as scheduled. F.Y.I. In years past, admission to the Afternoon Tea was a cup & saucer, but now they have too many!

$8.50 Afternoon Tea... Tasty savories, assorted homemade sweets & cookies, a continuous cup of brewed loose tea.

QUARTERLY TEAS: As Scheduled, Please Call To Confirm Dates
• Valentine's Day Tea: Thursday Feb. 12, 1998 & Feb. 11, 1999
• Mother's Day Tea: Thursday May 7, 1998 & May 6, 1999
• Autumn Tea: Thursday Oct. 8, 1998 & Oct. 14, 1999
• Non-Caffeine/Herbal Tea Available
• Watercloset: Same Floor • Wheelchair Accessible
• **Reservations Are Requested**
• Nearby Parking Lot & Unmetered Street Parking
• Cash

Director's
*Autograph*_____*Date*_____

TEA-N-CRUMPETS

817 Fourth Street
San Rafael, California

415-457-2495

    It's Teatime At...Tea-N-Crumpets. This is one of my favorite spots for absolutely scrumptious crumpets. (Not easy to say!) Tea-N-Crumpets is Jena & Norman's very special bakery.

    Yummy crumpets are baked fresh daily, and a delicious variety is offered with freshly brewed tea. T-N-C is now directly importing green teas from China and offers about 20 new great greens & blacks. If you love the tea your sipping, it is now packaged for your take home pleasure. F.Y.I. These crumpets are fat free, without dairy, sugar or cholesterol and are approximately 75 calories each. Tea-N-Crumpets is the little cafe that's big on TLC! Crumpets are available for shipment anywhere in the USA. I know first hand that they are delivered fresh. We brewed tea and buttered our crumpets as soon as they arrived! Allow time to browse in the expanded gift area. There are sweet tea accent lamps, picture frames,books, tea accessories & more. Deeeelicious!

    $3.50 Pot Of Tea For Two... Excellent loose leaf tea.

    $1.75 Scone... Choice of blueberry, herb & cheddar, plain, or currant scone served with preserves or lemon curd.

    $.90 To 2.25 Crumpet... Select from a wonderful & creative variety of crumpets from plain to savory salmon.

    $1.00ish Cup Of Brewed Tea... Loose tea is freshly brewed throughout the day.

TEATIME: 7:30am To 6:00pm • Monday Thru Friday
- 9:00am To 5:30pm • Saturday
- Crumpets Are Available For Shipment Anywhere In The USA
- Non-Caffeine/Herbal Tea Available
- Watercloset: Same Floor
- Wheelchair Accessible
- **Please Drop By**
- Metered Street Parking, Pennies Too!
- Credit Cards: V&MC

Proprietor's
*Autograph*_____*Date*_____

DISCOVERY MUSEUM
Of Orange County

3101 West Harvard Street
Santa Ana, California

714-540-0404

Family Storybook Teas At...The Discovery Museum Of Orange County. The Discovery Museum presents their own series of fun Afternoon Storybook Teas for the enjoyment of parents and children ages 5 and up. They are scheduled throughout the year, so please call for dates and times. Some of these family teas include: The Three Bears Tea, Miss Arabela's Tea Party, 20,000 Leagues Under The Sea Tea, Peter Rabbit's Tea, Mad Hatter's Tea, Harvest Twilight Tea, Holly Berry Tea, Jingle Bell Storybook Tea, Valentine's Storybook Tea, Angel's Kite Tea and more. The lovely 11 acre site of the Discovery Museum with it's flower-filled grounds and gazebo is available for private parties too.

$12.50 Children's "Story Book Teas" (Members of The Discovery Museum pay $10.00.) Example of one of the favorite Storybook Teas is the "Miss Spider's Tea Party," a fanciful ghoulish tea, complete with witch's brew & spider cookies followed by the reading of the story. Children and parents have a hands-on activity, making skeleton puppets and haunted houses.

FAMILY STORYBOOK TEAS: Please Call For Schedule
- Non-Caffeine/Herbal Tea Available
- Wheelchair Accessible
- Watercloset: Separate Building
- **Reservations & Prepay Required**
- Free Off-Street Parking
- Credit Cards: MC&V

Director's
Autograph _____*Date*_____

Daddy & Me, and Mommy & Me Teas make cherished memories.

VICTORIAN TEA SOCIETY
an auxiliary of Discovery Museum Of Orange County

3101 West Harvard Street
Santa Ana, California

Reservations **714-540-0404**

The Victorian Tea Society Presents...Holiday Event Teas & Tours At...The Discovery Museum. These special event teas take place in the parlour and dining room of the Museum's historic Kellog House. Weather permitting, and for special events, Teas take place in the garden.This turn of the century museum invites you to relive the "good old days."

Event Teas are usually holiday inspired and include Valentine's Day, Mother's Day & Holly Berry Teas. These teas are eagerly anticipated about four times a year. Enjoy browsing around the gift shop which is open when teas are in progress. F.Y.I. Membership in The Victorian Tea Society includes membership to The Discovery Museum. When you call the museum for reservations, please tell them that you're reserving for the Holiday Event Teas presented by The Victorian Tea Society. (The Discovery Museum has their own series of teas, so this may avoid confusion.) Ask about the fall "1890's Market Day" which may become an annual event. Membership is encouraged, please call for info.

$16.50 Holiday Inspired Tea & Tours.. Assorted tea sandwiches, scone served with cream & preserves, sweet treats, and a continuous cup of brewed loose tea. Price is approximate.

HOLIDAY EVENT TEAS: Usually 4 Times A Year As Scheduled
- Non-Caffeine/Herbal Tea Available
- Watercloset: Nearby Building
- Wheelchair Accessible
- **Reservations Are A Must & Prepay Please**
- Free Off-Street Parking
- Credit Cards: MC&V

Victorian Tea Society President's
*Autograph*_____*Date*_____

BARCLIFF & BAIR
1112 State Street
Santa Barbara, California

805-965-5742

Afternoon Tea
O n   O u r   P a t i o

Friday Afternoon Teas At...Barcliff & Bair. Their location on State Street in "downtown" Santa Barbara doesn't get any better. This is a jewel of a spot with a casual yet rich decor, including a patterned clay tile floor, deep honey-colored polished wood, woven wood chairs, starched white tablecloths, fresh flowers on the tables and large outdoor planters filled with ivy and colorful geraniums. Outdoor patio dining under large market-style umbrellas with State Street ambiance is also available. An outdoor magazine rack full of recent magazines is a nice touch, so is the neat ceramic fishy. Breakfast, lunch and yummy fresh baked a la carte specialties are available with tea & scones Tuesday through Sunday.

Barcliff & Bair proudly offers a civilized addition to their delicious daily fare, a Friday Afternoon, High Tea. A touch of England right here on State Street! F.Y.I. I'm happy to say that expansion plans are on the drawing board. Barcliff & Bair is growing and so are their Afternoon Tea plans. They now offer private tea parties for up to 25 guests! What fun. Please call to plan.

$14.50 Friday Afternoon, High Tea... Fresh baked scone with cream, finger sandwiches, fresh fruit sorbet, cookies, inspirational surprise treat and a pot of brewed tea. Add $4.00 and B&B will add treats so you may share Afternoon Tea with a friend.

FRIDAY AFTERNOON TEA: 2:30pm To 4:30pm • Fridays
- May Accommodate Some Dietary Needs, 3 Day Advance Request
- Non-Caffeine/Herbal Tea Available
- Wheelchair Accessible • Watercloset: Same Floor
- **Reservations Are Advised**
- 90 Minute Free Parking In The Rear
- Credit Cards: V&MC

Proprietor's
*Autograph*_____*Date*_____

Four Seasons Resort's
SANTA BARBARA BILTMORE

1260 Channel Drive
Santa Barbara, California

FOUR SEASONS BILTMORE
Santa Barbara
A FOUR SEASONS · REGENT RESORT

805-969-2261

It's Teatime At...Four Seasons Resort's Santa Barbara Biltmore. The wonderful Four Seasons Biltmore is truly a landmark. The historic Spanish hotel was built in 1920, but the original charm remains today. Afternoon Tea takes place in The La Sala Lounge. La Sala means living room, which appropriately describes this comfy spot with couches and rich marble tables.

Afternoon Tea is presented on tiered caddies and served at tables set with crystal, fresh flowers, floral tablecloths, pink linen overlays & matching napkins which nicely complement the Royal Doulton china. A focal point of the room is the beautiful large fireplace with adjacent seating for Afternoon Tea. A large window in the lounge affords a fabulous view of the Pacific Ocean, worth the price alone! Outdoor seating is terrific on the "view" patio.

$16.75 Full Tea... Finger sandwiches, freshly baked currant scone with whipped Devonshire creme, pastries, a cookie and a pot of brewed loose tea. 20 canister tea selections, add a Champagne cocktail or glass of Sherry for approximately $8.00.

$12.75 Light Tea... Selection of tea pastries, a freshly baked scone with whipped Devonshire creme & preserves, a cookie, a pot of brewed loose tea with unique imported sugar cubes.

TEATIME: 3:00pm To 4:45pm, Monday Thru Friday • No Holidays
• Do Call To See If Saturday Teas Have Returned!
• May Accommodate Some Dietary Needs With Advance Request
• Non-Caffeine/Herbal Tea Also Available
• Children's Tea Parties Welcome
• Watercloset: Same Floor • Wheelchair Accessible
• **Reservations Are Advised**
• Free Self-Parking or Valet Park
• Credit Cards: V,DC,MC&AE
L'autograph
*du Concierge*_____*Date*_____

264

LITTLE WOMEN

1516 Chapala Street
Santa Barbara, California

805-965-4460

Little Girls' Tea Parties At...Little Women. Little girls ages 5 years old and up are invited to have fun and memorable dress-up tea parties at Little Women. The original proprietors of Little Women opened their doors in 1992 for what has become a very special way to celebrate a little girl's birthday or other special event in her young life. The children are treated to an afternoon of playing "grown-up." They are greeted in a darling "Victorian" parlor then escorted to the dressing area where they select feathery boas, hats, purses, gloves and sparkly costume jewelry for their day of "glamour". This includes make-up, nail polish and just the right hairdo. Miss Vickie seems to have as much fun as the girls do. The teatime meal is served from silver tiered trays, all rather elegant and lady like. Ask about theme teas which include a Teddy Bear Tea in December and a Dolly & Me Tea in May. F.Y.I. A tea party runs around 2 hours and accommodates 8 to 20 young ladies ages five years old and up. Host parents are welcome to stay. A keepsake photo of each child is a nice touch. P.S. Ask about etiquette classes and adult tea parties for 10 or more guests.

$295.00 Tea Party For 8 Girls...($22.00 for each additional child) Assorted tea sandwiches, Birthday Girl's take-home personal cake, fancy desserts and red raspberry "tea."

LITTLE GIRL'S TEA PARTIES: Minimum 8 Guests, Ages 5+
• May Accommodate Some Dietary Needs With Advance Request
• Red Raspberry Caffeine Free "Tea"
• Watercloset: Same Floor
• **Please Call To Reserve Your Party Date**
• Metered Street Parking
• Cash Or Check

Proprietor's
*Autograph*_____*Date*_____

CAFE NORDSTROM
(Paseo Nuevo) 17 West Canon Perido
Santa Barbara, California

805-564-8770

New Addition...It's Teatime At..Cafe Nordstrom.
In 1887, at the tender age of 16, John F. Nordstrom left his home in Sweden to come to the United States. He arrived in New York with five dollars in his pocket. A fortuitous meeting years later with Carl F. Wallin a Seattle shoemaker, resulted in the 1901 opening of the first "Wallin & Nordstrom" store on Fourth & Pike Streets in Seattle. Throughout the years, Nordstrom has been guided by its founder's philosophy. "Offer the customer the best possible service, selection, quality and value." I enjoy shopping at Nordstom, the idea of a pianist playing a baby grand piano while I browse for beautiful things suits me to a T. The comfy "oasis" which my spouse calls the "husband waiting area" is appreciated by both of us! When this customer friendly store began serving Afternoon Tea in many of the Cafes at Nordstrom, I wasn't at all surprised.

At teatime, Cafe Nordstrom tables are dressed-up with fresh flowers or plants, fine china, cloth napkins and special teatime silverware. You will be courteously greeted by an enthusiastic cafe manager or their friendly staff. F.Y.I. Outdoor patio dining is available at some of the Cafe Nordstrom locations.

$6.95 Afternoon Tea... Assorted finger sandwiches, scone served with berry-butter, a tasty dessert and a pot of tea.

TEATIME: 3:00pm To 5:00pm • Monday Thru Friday
• May Accommodate Some Dietary Needs With Advance Request
• Non-Caffeine/Herbal Tea Available
• Wheelchair Accessible • Watercloset: Same Floor
• **Reservations Are Required For Six Or More**
• Free Parking Lot
• Credit Cards: V,MC,AE&Nordstrom
Manager's
*Autograph*_____*Date*_____

266

Lemon Bread

Reprinted courtesy of VICTORIA Magazine

2 cups all-purpose flour	2 eggs
1 Tablespoon baking powder	Grated zest of 1 lemon
1/4 teaspoon salt	1 teaspoon lemon extract
1/2 cup (1 stick) butter, softened	3/4 cup lemonade
1 cup sugar	

1. Preheat the oven to 350 degrees F. Butter and flour a 9x5x3-inch loaf pan. Line the bottom of the pan with wax paper. Shake out excess flour.
2. In a medium bowl, thoroughly stir together the flour, baking powder and salt.
3. In the medium bowl of an electric mixer, beat the butter and sugar at medium speed until the mixture is light and fluffy, scraping the sides of the bowl often. Add the eggs, one at a time, beating well after each addition.
4. Add the lemon zest and lemon extract. With the mixer set at low speed, add the dry ingredients alternately with the lemonade, and mix just until blended. Spread the batter evenly in the prepared pan.
5. Bake for 60 to 65 minutes, or until a toothpick inserted in the center of the loaf comes out clean.
6. Cool the bread in the pan on a wire rack for 10 minutes. Then remove from the pan, peel off the wax paper, and let the bread cool completely on the rack.

"Because this bread is made with lemonade, lemon zest, and lemon extract, the flavor is wonderfully intense. We suggest making the lemonade for the bread from frozen concentrate rather than relying on pre-mixed lemonade or that from fresh lemons. The sweet loaf slices easily and requires no accompaniment other than a nice cup of tea." Yield: One 9-inch loaf

THE OLD SASH MILL CAFE

303 Potrero #1
Santa Cruz, California

408-426-7392

New Addition...Annual Teas, Private Tea Parties & *New Tearoom Brewing* At...The Old Sash Mill Cafe. The Annual Teas have been so popular at the lodge-chalet-style Old Sash Mill Cafe that proprietors Ann, Keith & son Seth are opening a new garden tearoom. Currently, you may enjoy The Teddy Bear Tea on the first Sunday after Thanksgiving and, A Colonial Tea usually on the third weekend in September. The cafe is situated in one of the town's unique business disticts designed with renovated barns, silos, shops, general rural charm & old-fashion hospitality.

Afternoon Teas are expected to be casually served at tables set with tablecloths, fresh flowers, Blue Betty English teapots & earthen stoneware. The interior of the tearoom features amber colored faux-painted walls, burgundy carpets, and Ann & Keith's personal collection of British memorabilia. P.S. Breakfast & lunch is also available. Private tea parties may be planned for 10-70 guests. There's a small gift area too with bulk teas, teapots & more.

$12.95 Midday High Tea For Two & Theme Teas... Hot entree or soup & roll, sweets, pot of loose brewed tea.
$10.95 Tea Lovers Selection For Two... Finger sandwiches, homebaked sweets and a pot of brewed loose tea.
$6.95 Tea For Two... Homebaked scones with cream & preserves and a pot brewed loose tea.

ANTICIPATED TEA TIME: 1pm To 4pm • Seven Days A Week
• May Accommodate Some Dietary Needs With Advance Request
• Non-Caffeine/Herbal Tea Available
• Children's Tea Parties Welcome
• Watercloset: Same Floor • Wheelchair Accessible
• **Reservations Are Appreciated**
• Free Parking Lots Nearby
• Credit Cards: V,MC&AE

Proprietor's
*Autograph*_____*Date*_____

Start an Afternoon Tea Club for cherished, and new friends.

Santa Monica, California · *A Spot of Tea*

ANGELS ATTIC
516 Colorado Avenue
Santa Monica, California

310-394-8331

Tea & Self-Tour And Christmas Fundraiser Tea At...Angels Attic. A unique museum with a heart, this volunteer staffed nonprofit corporation assists in the support of the Brentwood Center For Educational Therapy. Angels Attic is a museum of antique dolls, doll houses, miniatures & toys; a tour is a real treat. The site of the museum is an 1895 Queen Anne Victorian restored by the supporters of the Angels Attic Museum. You'll enjoy browsing in the gift shop where you can purchase furniture & accessories for your own doll house. Museum admission is $6.50 for adults, $4.00 for 65+ & $3.50 for children under 12. A "spot of tea" will enhance your self-tour. Tea is $7.50 per person, the prices below are for the Tea & Tour combination.

The Christmas Fundraiser Tea is accompanied by a Garden & Holiday Treasure Sale. The date changes so please call for the schedule. P.S. If antique doll houses are your thing, you may want to consider becoming a volunteer. F.Y.I. The gazebo and garden area are sometimes available for privately catered parties.

$20.00 Approx. **Christmas Fundraiser Tea...**Valet parking included for this special event. Assorted tea sandwiches, variety of finger foods, special cookies, and a continuous cup of tea poured from silver teapots. Hours: 1:00pm To 4:00pm.

$14.00 Tea & Self Tour... Bill-of-Fare includes adult self tour, homebaked cake & cookies and a selection of bagged teas. $11.50 for seniors age 65+, children under 12, $11.00.

TEA & SELF TOUR: 12:30pm To 3:30pm •Thursday Thru Sunday
• December Holiday Tea, Please Call For Date and Reservations
• Non-Caffeine/Herbal Tea Available
• Wheelchair Accessible • Watercloset: Convenient
• **Reservations For All Teas Are A Must**
• Pre-Paid Reservations Please For The Christmas Tea
• Metered Street Parking
• Credit Card: V&MC

Director's
*Autograph*_____*Date*_____

CAFE DANA
1211 Montana Avenue
Santa Monica, California

310-394-0815

It's Teatime At...Cafe Dana. Cafe Dana is a small cafe located in a quaint shopping village in Santa Monica. This a particularly good spot for strolling around after tea. Weather permitting, you may take tea in the pretty European style brick courtyard with a fountain and pots of colorful flowers and ivy.

Afternoon Tea is served by the friendly staff at tables are set with pink tablecloths, white china & fresh flowers. The cheerful cafe is decorated with flowers and "tea" prints. P.S. Be sure to say hello to the proprietors Donna and Bojan.

$9.95 Afternoon Tea... Assorted tea sandwiches, fresh homemade blueberry scone served with black currant or strawberry jam, mini quiche, strawberry and a pot of tea.

AFTERNOON TEA: 2:00pm To 5:00pm • Monday Thru Saturday
• May Accommodate Some Dietary Needs, 2 Day Advance Request
• Non-Caffeine/Herbal Tea Available
• Children's Tea Parties Welcome
• Watercloset: Same Floor
• **Reservations Are Not Necessary**
• Metered Street Parking
• Credit Cards: V,MC,DIS&AE
Proprietor's
*Autograph*_____*Date*_____

271

GILLILANDS
2424 Main Street
Santa Monica, California

310-392-3901

**New Addition...Tea Parties For Groups At...
Gillilands.** Gillilands is described as a California bistro with a touch of the Blarney. Traditional Irish Afternoon Tea parties are now offered for groups of 20 to 80 guests at Gillilands. Parties are held in the outdoor courtyard or in The Connemara Room.

Afternoon Tea is cheerfully served at tables set with fresh flowers & pretty chintz tablecloths with white toppers. Original works of art by an Irish watercolorist fill the walls. And of course, Irish music plays in the background. F.Y.I. Gerri is planning to serve Afternoon Tea on scheduled Saturdays throughout the year and more frequently during November and December for the holidays. Please call to check on the schedule.

$18.00 Traditional Irish Afternoon Tea... A glass of Sherry, assorted tea sandwiches, homemade scones with cream & Gilliland jam, four delectables from The Sweet Trolley such as fresh sour cream gingerbread, almond fingers with raspberry jam, traditional Gaelic shortbread cookies or Elizabethan pound cake with apricots & Madeira wine and a pot of brewed tea. There are special desserts during Christmas. (Price is per person plus tax & gratuity)

PRIVATE TEA PARTIES: 20 TO 80 Guests • Please Call To Plan
• May Accommodate Some Dietary Needs, 1 Week Advance Request
• Non-Caffeine/Herbal Tea Available
• Children's Tea Parties Welcome
• Watercloset: Same Floor
• Wheelchair Accessible
• **Reservations Are A Must**
• Metered Street & Nearby Metered Lot
• Credit Cards: MC,V,DIS,DC&AE

Proprietor's
*Autograph*_____*Date*_____

272

PACIFIC DINING CAR

2700 Wilshire Boulevard
Santa Monica, California

310-453-4000

It's Teatime At...Pacific Dining Car. This is a popular, elegant and intimate spot for Afternoon Tea in Santa Monica. Much like the Los Angeles Pacific Dining Car, it has a train motif and is decorated with memories of a bygone era. You'll have to bring your imagination along because they don't have a real train here. But you can CHOO CHOO-**OOLONG** anyway!

Afternoon Tea is served at tables set with peach tablecloths, a single rose and imported gold rimmed Woodmere china. Your very attentive and friendly server will presents each of your courses. P.S. Private tea parties are also available.

$10.00 Afternoon Tea... Assorted tea sandwiches, homebaked scone served with honey, strawberry jam & real whipped cream, slice of bread pudding , chocolate hazelnut cake with raspberry puree, fresh strawberries with whipped cream, a glass of Sherry, Bristol Cream, Dry Sack or Tio Pepe, and a pot of brewed loose tea.

TEATIME: 3:30pm To 5:30pm • Seven Days A Week
• May Accommodate Some Dietary Needs With A Few Days Notice
• Non-Caffeine/Herbal Tea Available
• Watercloset: Lift Available
• Wheelchair Accessible
• **Reserve For Larger Groups Please**
• Parking In Rear With Validation
• Credit Cards: MC,V,DC&AE
Proprietor's
*Autograph*_____*Date*_____

273

SCHATZI ON MAIN

3110 Main Street
Santa Monica, California

310-399-4800

New Addition...Monthly Saturday Afternoon Teas At...Schatzi On Main. A visit to Schatzi for the monthly Afternoon Tea event is a must. Deborah and Lynn coordinate the entertaining teas at this neat spot, owned by Arnold Schwarzenegger and Maria Shriver. Teas usually take place on the third Saturday of the month. Make reservations early as these tea are very popular.

Afternoon Teas are served on Schatzi's all-weather, lush garden courtyard patio at tables set with pastel linens, cloth napkins tied in ribbons, fresh flowers and Mikasa fine china. The music of a classical guitar fills the air. This lovely spot with hanging baskets of ivy & ferns is just a delicate breeze away from the ocean. These monthly events feature informal fashion shows or cosmetic/skin care presentations plus the chance to win door prizes donated by Schatzi or local merchants. Private tea parties are welcome for up to 150 guests. P.S. Be sure to stop by "Ynot," the gift shop in the courtyard. They carry Schatzi, Planet Hollywood and other unique gifts & accessories. F.Y.I. "Schatzi" is a term of endearment in Austria. You may also visit them at iMALL: www.schatzi.com

$25.00 Monthly Afternoon Tea... Assorted tea sandwiches, fresh fruit tarts, tea cakes, scones, chocolate dipped strawberries, champagne and tea. An 18% gratuity and sales tax will be added to each check total.

MONTHLY TEAS: On Scheduled Saturdays, Usually At 3:00pm
- May Accommodate Some Dietary Needs With Advance Request
- Non-Caffeine/Herbal Tea Available
- Children's Tea Parties Welcome
- Watercloset: Same Floor
- Wheelchair Accessible
- **Reservations Required, Walk-Ins May Be Accepted, If Space**
- $1.00 For The First 2 Hours W/Validation, Enter Marine Street
- Credit Cards: V,MC,DC&AE

Coordinator's
Autograph _____*Date*_____

SHUTTERS ON THE BEACH

One Pico Boulevard
Santa Monica, California

Ask For Catering **310-458-0030**

New Addition...Private Tea Parties At...Shutters On The Beach. Here's an escape your group will really enjoy. How about an Afternoon Tea at the only luxury hotel in Los Angeles that is nestled right on the sandy beaches of the Pacific Ocean? Afternoon Teas for groups of 25 to 50 guests are presented buffet style in the re-designed Handle Bar Room at Shutters. This private spot has a whitewashed rustic atmosphere and offers a fabulous unobstructed view of the white sand beaches and the bright blue shimmering ocean. Shutters has been open since 1993 and stands on the site of the old Edgewater Hotel, circa 1920. Shutters is expanding with the recent acquisition of the Casa del Mar next door. Please note, there is a room fee of $150.00 per event in addition to sales tax and gratuity, please call the catering department for details. F.Y.I. The hotel can accommodate up to 250 guests in the banquet rooms, and you are welcome to bring your own table centerpieces. P.S. This is a great spot for a romantic sunset or sunrise stroll.

$25.00 Afternoon Tea... A glass of champagne upon arrival, sliced fresh fruit with berries, assorted tea sandwiches, fresh baked mini scones with cream, lemon curd & preserves, French pastries and a continuous cup of tea. (Price is person plus applicable fees & taxes.)

TEATIME FOR 25+ GUESTS: Please Call Catering To Plan
• May Accommodate Some Dietary Needs With Advance Request
• Non-Caffeine/Herbal Tea Available
• Watercloset: Same Floor
• Wheelchair Accessible
• **Advance Reservations Are Required**
• Valet Parking W/ Validation, $3.00 First Three Hours
• Credit Cards: MC,V,DC,DIS&AE

Proprietor's
*Autograph*_____*Date*_____

TUDOR HOUSE
1403 Second Street
Santa Monica, California

310-451-4107

It's Teatime At...Tudor House. Established in 1962 this quaint English spot serves Afternoon Tea plus a full menu of English specialties. Harry also offers special Cream Tea Events such as the $15.95 Spiritual Cream Tea with British Psychic Anne Shaw. The antique furnishings and classical music are most inviting here.

Afternoon Tea is served in a cozy living room atmosphere at tables set with Willow pattern china. The Tudor House has their own bakery and prepares delicious scones and pies daily. F.Y.I. Private tea parties are available for up to 23 guests. P.S. Allow time to visit their British grocery and gift shop too.

$8.25 Tudor House Afternoon Tea...A homemade scone, sausage roll in puff pastry or vegetarian tea quiche, half-order of any of the sandwiches listed on their menu, pastry and tea. (Salmon and cucumber sandwich add .50)

$3.15 Tea & Tudor House Scone... Large homebaked scone served with jam & clotted cream and tea.

$5.95 Kiddies Afternoon Tea... Homebaked scone, two-egg mayonnaise finger sandwiches, jelly & ice cream, choice of tea, orange juice or cola.

TEATIME: 10:00am To 5:00pm • Monday Thru Saturday
- 11:00am To 5:30pm • Sunday
- Non-Caffeine/Herbal Tea Available
- Children's Tea Parties Welcome
- Watercloset: Same Floor
- Wheelchair Accessible
- **Reservations Are Required For Cream Tea Events**
- **Reservations Are Not Required For Afternoon Tea**
- Two Hour Free Public Parking
- Credit Cards: V,MC&AE

Proprietor's
*Autograph*_____*Date*_____

276

YE OLDE KING'S HEAD

116 Santa Monica Boulevard
Santa Monica, California

310-451-1402

New Addition...It's Teatime At...Ye Olde King's Head. It was so nice to get a call from Ruth announcing that Afternoon Tea had been added to the Ye Olde King's Head ever popular English menu. Customers will be happy to know that Theme Teas are also being planned. Call for upcoming schedule.

Afternoon Tea is served at old fashioned English dining tables with cane back chairs, in The Hunt Room. Tables are set with white tablecloths, cloth napkins, fresh flowers, English Dudson "Verna's Court" fine china, and matching three tiered caddies. The floral carpet from England in tones of grey, pink & burgundy is a nice backdrop along with the burgundy brocade fabric wall covering and the classical background music. The refined Hunt Room has original oils by Paul Roberts and a handsome antique buffet. Private tea parties are also available for up to 35 guests. F.Y.I. The Afternoon Teas in December include traditional treats from old family recipes. P.S. Allow time to browse in their lovely gift shop.

$11.95 Royal Afternoon Tea... Assorted finger sandwiches and savouries, homemade raisin scone served with Devonshire cream & English jam, tea cakes & assorted desserts such as: Victorian sponge cake, lemon bars or pecan bars and a pot of Taylors of Harrogate brewed loose tea.

TEATIME: 3:00pm To 5:00pm • Monday Thru Friday
• May Accommodate Some Dietary Needs With Advance Request
• Non-Caffeine/Herbal Tea Available
• Watercloset: Same Floor
• **Reservations Are Accepted**
• Non-Validated Parking Lot & Nearby Structure
• Credit Cards: V,MC&AE

Proprietor's
*Autograph*_____*Date*_____

Lisa Hemenway's
TOTE CUISINE

710 Village Court
Santa Rosa, California
(Montgomery Village)

707-578-0898

It's Teatime On Wednesdays & Fridays At Tote Cuisine. Afternoon Tea is served in Tote Cuisine's quaint tearoom that seems to magically appear when Lisa draws the curtain.

Tea is presented from a wooden tea cart and served at tables set with cream colored Damask linens trimmed in a floral grapevine pattern, fresh flowers & antique English bone china teacups.

Special Event Teas also take place at Tote Cuisine. Please call for information regarding events presented by Dana May. Reserve your spot early & join her for her stimulating Afternoon Teas which are great fun and always informative. It is Dana May's privledge to share her exper"TEAS" with you! Ask about Manners Teas, Etiquette Teas, Victorian Teas & Tea Tastings as well. P.S. Tea parties are available at Tote Cuisine for 10-40 guests.

$8.95 Afternoon Tea... Choice of three savories which may include a cucumber & basil-butter tea sandwich, seasonal mini-quiche, savory filled filo cups, and Lavosh sandwiches or other surprises, three sweets may include homemade currant or fruit scone with creme fraiche & homemade jams & lemon curd, cookies & petit fours, or chocolate dipped strawberries, and a pot of loose leaf tea.

TEATIME: 3:00pm To 5:00pm • Wednesdays & Fridays
• Private Tea Parties Available Any Day • Please Call
• May Accommodate Some Dietary Needs, 1 Week Advance Request
• Non-Caffeine/Herbal Tea Available
• Children's Tea Parties Welcome
• Watercloset: Same Floor • Wheelchair Accessible
• **Reservations Are Requested**
• Ample Free Parking Lot
• Credit Cards: MC,V,DC,DIS&AE

Proprietor's
*Autograph*_____*Date*_____

MAUDE'S TEA ROOM
at The Old Vic English Pub
731 Fourth Street
Santa Rosa, California

707-571-7555

It's Teatime For Groups On Fridays At...Maude's Tea Room. Maude prides herself on her attention to detail at Maude's Tea Room. Decorated in Victorian style, there are flower arrangements throughout the room, lovely etched glass, dark wood trim and deep burgundy accents. This is an interesting pub & restaurant that becomes a Dinner Theater on Saturdays Nights. In fact, it was named after Old Vic in London.

Afternoon Tea is presented on three tiered caddies at tables set with white linen tablecloths, fresh flowers and white china with matching teapots & milk jugs. Be sure to say hello to Christopher, Maude credits him with baking the delicious scones and Mrs. Pettigrew's lemon cake. Maude, makes very special Madeleines. P.S. Don't miss the antique bar!

$8.50 Afternoon Tea... Finger sandwiches such as salmon & cucumber, sardine on toast or sherried cheese on homemade French bread, scone with mock clotted cream, raspberry jam & lemon curd or toasted Yorkshire tea cakes, choice of chocolate cheese cake, lemon cake or trifle, pot of brewed loose tea.

TEATIME: 12:00Noon To 3:00pm • Friday 8-40 Guests
• May Accommodate Some Dietary Needs With Advance Request
• Non-Caffeine/Herbal Tea Available
• Children's Tea Parties Welcome
• Watercloset: Same Floor • Wheelchair Accessible
• **Reserve Are Required**
• Rear Parking Lot
• Credit Cards: MC&V
Proprietor's
*Autograph*_____*Date*_____

279

P.S. I LOVE YOU
Saratoga Tea Room

14443 Big Basin Way
Saratoga, California

408-867-1351

It's Teatime At...P.S. I Love You. This is a very active spot for Afternoon Tea. The decor is Victorian with faux fireplace mantels and furnishings in a palette of pinks, lavenders and creamy white. Guests may take tea in the upstairs tearoom with one large table accommodating up to 6 guests, or in the main tearoom.

Afternoon Tea is presented on two & three tiered caddies at tables set with cream colored china & fresh flowers by the friendly servers. Classical background music enhances your enjoyment. P.S. I Love You is available for lunch and brunch in addition to Afternoon Tea. P.S. Allow time to browse, gift items are displayed throughout the shop. Private tea parties for 8-35 guests may be arranged, ask Pat to cater an extravaganza of a tea party for you!

$9.00 Complete Afternoon Tea... Tea sandwiches, golden raisin scone served with Devon cream, lemon curd & preserves, tea cakes & cookies and pot of brewed loose tea.

$8.00 Devon Tea... Golden raisin scone served with Devon cream, lemon curd & preserves, fresh berries in season, tea cakes & cookies and pot of brewed loose tea.

TEATIME: 11:00pm To 5:00pm • Seven Days A Week
• May Accommodate Some Dietary Needs With Advance Request
• Children's Tea Parties Welcome
• Non-Caffeine/Herbal Tea Available
• Watercloset: Nearby, Same Floor
• Wheelchair Accessible
• **Reservations Are Requested**
• Rear Parking Lot, Street Park
• Credit Cards: V,MC&AE

Proprietor's
*Autograph*_____*Date*_____

THE GREEN DOOR
Tea Room

810 Electric Avenue
Seal Beach, California

562-431-3392

New Addition...It's Teatime At...The Green Door Tea Room. Walk through the green door in the hidden garden and meet the new proprietor of this familiar spot. The Green Door is a charming tearoom nestled in the heart of the quaint seaside village of Old Town, Seal Beach. The deep toned Victorian entry area has lots of gifts, books, teapots & collectibles plus tea tables. The main tearoom is bright & airy, and is my favorite spot. In fact, I celebrated my birthday here one year. Wear one of your favorite hats or borrow one of The Green Door's vintage chapeaus from the hat tree and get in the mood for Afternoon Tea. Tea is served with careful attention to detail. This is a popular spot for private tea parties for up to 20 guests, although Barbara can accommodate up to 50 guests between the two rooms. In the summer from May through October weather permitting, enjoy fruited iced tea in The Green Door Garden. P.S. You may want to order ahead to take home some yummy fresh berry scones. Ask about the custom made gift baskets.

$14.95 High Tea... Cornish pastie, beet salad, assorted vegetables, apple chutney, scone served with Devonshire cream & jam, fancy desserts and a pot of brewed loose tea.

$13.95 Complete Afternoon Tea.. Finger sandwiches, scone, Devonshire cream & jam, dessert, a pot of brewed loose tea.

$6.95 Cream Tea... Scone served with Devonshire cream & jam and a pot of brewed loose tea.

TEATIME: 11:30am, 1:30 & 3:30pm • Tuesday Thru Saturday
• Open Selected Sundays For Parties Up To 20 Guests
• May Accommodate Some Dietary Needs, 1 Week Advance Request
• Non-Caffeine/Herbal Tea Available
• Watercloset: Same Floor • Children's Tea Parties Welcome
• **Reservations Are Required For All Except For Cream Tea**
• Free Parking Lot In Front
• Credit Cards: MC&V

Proprietor's
*Autograph*_____  _Date_____

A Spot of Tea

MARMALADE

14910 Ventura Boulevard
Sherman Oaks, California

818-905-8872

Tea Parties For Groups At...Marmalade. You'll find an Old English atmosphere at Marmalade in Sherman Oaks. This spot is a welcome respite from busy & active Ventura Boulevard. Tea is served in the attractive semi-private dining room, quite a perfect spot for Afternoon Tea for your group.

Afternoon Tea is served from buffet platters at tables uniquely set with rich tapestries, cloth serviettes & imported Creamicor china. Tables can be arranged in small groups or one continuous table depending on your number of guests. Please call Lynne for information, she will be happy to help you plan a tea party for your special event. Tea parties may be scheduled for anyday between 3:30pm and 5:00pm. P.S. Lynne says you are welcome to bring in your own centerpieces.

$16.00 Afternoon Tea... Oat-currant scone served with double Devon cream & strawberry jam, a lovely assortment of tea sandwiches, zucchini bread, lemon bars & brownies miniature tarts, assorted cookies & Biscotti, and a pot of brewed tea. (Price is per person plus tax & gratuity.)

TEA PARTIES FOR GROUPS: As Scheduled, For 15-40 Guests
- May Accommodate Some Dietary Needs With Advance Request
- Non-Caffeine/Herbal Tea Available
- Watercloset: Same Floor
- Wheelchair Accessible
- **Reserve Your Tea Party Date Early**
- Valet Parking In The Rear Lot, Approx. $2.00
- Credit Cards: V,MC,DIS,DC&AE

Manager's
*Autograph*_____*Date*_____

BRITISH HOME
647 Manzanita Avenue
(Enter Ramona or Manzanita)
Sierra Madre, California

626-355-7240

It's Teatime At...The British Home's Annual June Fair. The British Home is a retirement home which was originally established in 1930 for retired English nannies. It occupies 4 1/2 acres in beautiful Sierra Madre and is now home to around 30 residents of various nationalities. This day long fair is a benefit for the home. The event is organized by the British Home and usually takes place the first Saturday in June, rain or shine. The various chapters of the D.B.E. create the festive booths and prepare wonderful homemade baked goods for sale.

The British Home is one spot that the Royals don't miss when visiting Southern California. The Queen visited in 1983, Margaret and Fergie soon after. If a member of The Royal Family can't make it to The British Home, then a British Home board member always goes as "Goodwill Ambassador" to greet them.

$6.00 British Afternoon Tea & June Fair. Homemade assorted tea sandwiches, plain scone served with butter & jam, English shortbread, jam tarts, and a pot of brewed tea.

ANNUAL JUNE FAIR: 10:30am-3:30pm • First Saturday In .June
• Please Call To Confirm The Date
• Tea Event Is From 12Noon Till The Food Runs Out
• Watercloset: Same Floor
• Wheelchair Accessible
• **Reservations Are Not Required**
• Street Parking Available
• Cash

Director's
*Autograph*_____*Date*_____

CLARISSA'S TEA PARTIES
& Fine Gifts

Clarissa's

90 North Baldwin Avenue Suite 3
Sierra Madre, California

626-836-0631

New Addition...Vintage Dress-Up Tea Parties At...Clarissa's. A colorful atmosphere awaits you at Clarissa's. The walls are rag textured & hand stenciled in a sunshine yellow garden theme. This is a cheery spot for both adults & children, with a wrought iron bistro set, fountain of a child and puppies, white picket fence and Waverly & Battenburg print fabric accents.

Children have great fun in the costume area where loads of dress-up clothing, hats, boas, gloves & jewelry await. Following play make-up, "hair-doings" & dress-up, there's a fashionable parade to the tearoom for Martha's delicious goodies. A gift awaits each child with an extra special gift for the honoree. F.Y.I. Host parents are encouraged to stay and enjoy the festivities.

$250.00 Children's Dress-Up Tea Parties...(For a group of 8 children. $13.00 for each additional child up to 20) Fun-shaped sandwiches, sugared scones with honey-butter, fruit, cookies & surprises, a mini take-home birthday cake for the honoree, lemonade or caffeine-free raspberry or fruit melange "tea."

$13.95 Adult Tea Parties...(Per person, 6-23 guests) Tea sandwiches, scones with cream & preserves, such as fresh homemade tarts or sweet surprise and a pot of brewed loose tea.

CHILDREN'S TEA PARTIES: 8 To 20 Guests • As Scheduled
• May Accommodate Some Dietary Needs With Advance Request
• Non-Caffeine/Herbal Teas Available
• Watercloset: Common Area, Tearoom Level
• Wheelchair Accessible By Ramp From Parking Lot To Tearoom
• **Advance Reservations Are A Must, Please Call To Plan**
• Two Hour Public Parking Lot on Baldwin
• Cash Or Check

Proprietor's
*Autograph*_____*Date*_____

Daughters Of
THE BRITISH EMPIRE

The British Home
647 Manzanita Avenue
Sierra Madre, California

909-698-2854 *Reservations For This*
D.B.E. Event

    It's Teatime At...The British Home. It's the Annual Afternoon Tea Benefit sponsored by the Daughters Of The British Empire known as the D.B.E. Mark your calendar for this outdoor event which takes place on the grand back lawn of the home. The event is quite festive and colorful thanks to the various chapters of the D.B.E. who are in competition with one another to decorate their tea tables. The members are very inventive, they create magnificent tables with imaginative themes.

    Afternoon Tea is served at tables set with fine English china and linens. Tea is graciously poured from lovely and unique teapots by very attentive volunteers. This is a wonderful opportunity to meet many lovely people who have spent their lives working as nannies for some very lucky people. This most genteel event is always the first Sunday in October regardless of the weather.

    $15.00 Afternoon Tea... Assorted tea sandwiches, fresh baked scone served with clotted cream & jam, sausage rolls, delicious pastries and a pot of brewed tea.

ANNUAL BENEFIT TEA: 3pm To 5pm • First Sunday In October
• Non-Caffeine Available By Request
• Watercloset: Same Floor
• Wheelchair Accessible
• **By Pre-Paid Reservation Only**
• Free Parking Available
• Cash Or Check In Advance

Director's
*Autograph*_____*Date*_____

FOUR SEASONS
Tea Room
75 North Baldwin Avenue
Sierra Madre, California

626-355-0045

New Addition...It's Teatime At...The Four Season's Tea Room. This is a wonderful new spot for Afternoon Tea. It is located in a charming business district in the delightful community of Sierra Madre. The proprietors of The Four Season's Tea Room are mother and daughter Ana and Kelly whose talents are well represented here. Both artistic, Ana designs and bakes very special wedding cakes and desserts. Kelly is a floral designer with a flair for presentation. They are very sweet and friendly, and will make you feel welcome at their new tearoom.

The tearoom was actually designed by this talented family. It is a converted two story tile roofed duplex. A wrought iron sign near the entrance reminds me of tearooms in Europe. The interior decor is pale sage with complementary moldings and trim. Tea is served at tables set with unique tablecloths, cloth serviettes & vases of fresh flowers. Vintage china, many sets with matching teapots, are used throughout the tearoom. Allow time to browse for gifts at Four Seasons, and on the second floor antique shops too.

$12.50 Afternoon Tea... Menu is seasonal. Assorted tea sandwiches, scone with cream & berry jam, surprise sweets, fresh seasonal fruit and a pot of brewed loose tea.

$6.50 Cream Tea... Scones served with cream & berry jam, and a pot of brewed loose tea.

TEATIME: 11:00 To 4:00 • Tuesday Thru Saturday
• May Accommodate Some Dietary Needs With Advance Request
• Non-Caffeine/Herbal Tea Available
• Children's Tea Parties Welcome
• Watercloset: Same Floor
• **Reservations Are Requested**
• Parking Lot Across The Street
• Credit Cards: V,MC,DIS&AE

Proprietor's
*Autograph*_____*Date*_____

A Spot of Tea   *Sierra Madre, California*

TWIGZ & TEAZ

24 West Sierra Madre Boulevard
Sierra Madre, California

626-355-1514

New Addition...It's Teatime At...Twigz & Teaz. The proprietors of Twigz & Tea, Becky and Tami are now busy arranging flowers in this sweet flower shop in addition to serving Afternoon Teas from their creative California Tea Menu. It seems like yesterday that they were waiting for the green light to open their new tearoom. In fact, one day when I talked to Becky, she and Tami were shopping for tea sets. Many of their regular flower customers stopped in to give them encouragement and a green thumbs up! And now here they are!

Afternoon Teas are presented in an informal garden setting, each tea selection named by floral inspiration. Plan to spend extra time for browsing around. Armoires are full of great gifts and tea accessories. Have fun dreaming up flowery names of teas to pass along to Twigz & Teaz. Maybe they will add it to their "bouquet."

$14.95 Wisteria Tea...A hearty meat pie, assorted finger sandwiches, fruit tart, sweets, fresh fruit, chocolate flower and a pot of brewed loose tea.

$10.75 Rose Tea... Assorted tea sandwiches, a warm scone served with Devonshire cream & Rose petal jelly, fresh fruit, assorted sweets, a chocolate flower and a pot of brewed loose tea.

$7.95 Sweet Pea Tea...(Children) PB&J sandwich, cookie, fresh fruit, lady bug chocolate, choice of beverage.

TEATIME: 2:00pm To 5pm • Seven Days A Week
• May Accommodate Some Dietary Needs With Advance Request
• Non-Caffeine/Herbal Tea Available
• Watercloset: Same Floor, Common Area
• Wheelchair Accessible
• **Reservations Please, For Six Or More Guests**
• Two Hour Limited Street Parking
• Credit Cards: V,MC,DC,CB,DIS&AE

Proprietor's
*Autograph*_____*Date*_____

STRATHEARN HISTORICAL
Park & Museum

137 Strathearn Place
Simi Valley, California

805-526-6453

New Addition...The Annual Benefit Tea & Tour At...Strathearn Historical Museum. This entertaining Tea is held each Fall just prior to the holiday season by the docents and board members of the Simi Valley Historical Society & Museum. The Strathearn House was built as an addition onto a two room old Simi Adobe house by Robert P.and Mary Strathearn in 1892. The house occupied the site of a Chumash Village named Shimiji, from which hailed the name "Simi." Other buildings were added to the grounds and in 1989 Rancho Simi was declared a California State Historic Landmark. The house and surrounding buildings were really shaken up in the Northridge Earthquake and retrofitting is still underway. As you might expect, many of the details of the Tea are sketchy but this delightful English Afternoon Tea is on schedule!

The Annual Benefit Tea is presented buffet style with tablecloths, disposable party sets & fresh flowers. The Tea program usually includes an amusing or educational speaker as well. Allow time to browse around, there's a gift shop, two houses furnished circa 1890, and two barns full of agriculture-related exhibits.

$10.00 Teatime In Rural Simi... Assorted finger sandwiches & finger foods, scones, an assortment of divine homemade surprise sweets and a continuous cup of brewed tea.

ANNUAL BENEFIT TEA: 1pm To 4:00pm • November 22, 1997
- Anticipated 1998 Date: November 21. Call To Verify 1998&1999
- Buffet Style May Accommodate Some Dietary Needs
- Non-Caffeine/Herbal Tea Available
- Watercloset: Same Floor
- Please Call Regarding Wheelchair Accessibility
- **Reservations Are Appreciated**
- Free Parking Lot A Short Hike Away
- Cash Or Check

Director Or Docent's
*Autograph*_____*Date*_____

THE VASQUEZ HOUSE
Tea Room
El Paseo Courtyard
(Off The Plaza At First St. East)
Sonoma, California

707-938-0510

New Addition...A Spot Of Tea At...The Vasquez House. Owned by The Sonoma League For Historic Preservation, this 1850's farmhouse is a most interesting spot for history buffs. Speculation continues to revolve around its original construction. It seems possible from all accounts that this house originally owned by Colonel Joseph Hooker was to some degree, an extremely early pre-fab home! Reports claim that C.W. Lubeck imported forty frame houses from his native Sweden and sold them to residents of Sonoma Valley. The houses were shipped in sections, numbered and easily assembled. They arrived on the brig Anna Maria in 1851!

A spot of tea is informally served at tables set with blue & white tablecloths, fresh flowers in unique containers, and a collection of mis-matched vintage china. The tea service is run by volunteers who truly enjoy their bright & airy little tearoom. The room is decorated with blue & white print curtains, a grapevine print wall border, and a teapot rail which holds new, nearly new and aniquey teapots. Outdoor seating is available as well. F.Y.I. If you plan on strolling a bit, you might be interested in the League's Sonoma Walking Tour guide. Ask about their $12.95 cookbook.

$1.00 Pot Of Tea
$1.00 Homemade Sweets... The variety of homemade sweets usually includes pie, cookies & cake or a surprise sweet.

A SPOT OF TEA: 1:30pm To 4:30pm • Wednesday Thru Sunday
• Non-Caffeine/Herbal Tea Available
• Children's Tea Parties Welcome
• Watercloset: Three Steps Up
• **Reservations: No**
• Two Hour Limited Time Street Parking
• Cash Only

Director's
*Autograph*_____*Date*_____

Sometimes the special people in our lives inspire us.

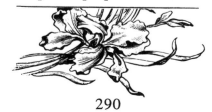

BABCIA'S TEAROOM
31 South Washington
Sonora, California

209-532-5656

New Addition...It's Teatime At...Babcia's Tearoom. Look for a burgundy awning welcoming you to Babcia's Tearoom. Diane it seems, is following in her grandmother's footsteps. Interestingly enough, her babcia Anna was the proprietor of a tearoom in Poland in the early 1900's. What wonderful inspiration! Diane's European style tearoom features many wonderful old family recipes. Breakfast and lunch is offered in addition to Afternoon Tea. Tea is served in the formal dining room decorated with comfortable burgundy & mauve velvet chairs, cream & green paisley pattern wallcoverings and beautiful floor lamps made by Diane's nephew Bill.

Afternoon Tea is presented on silver tiered caddies at tables set with tableskirts, raisin & white toppers, a collection of hand painted teacups, Mikasa gold rimmed white china, silver & gold flatware, tea lamps and fresh flowers in crystal vases. Servers are attired in cream & pink tea length pinafores. Ask for Babcia's schedule of quarterly High Teas, and about Children's Baking Teas. Plie, jete or tourne your way over to Diane's for tea tout de suite!

$12.50 Afternoon Tea... Assorted finger sandwiches, scone served with Devonshire cream & apricot honey preserves made from Patterson apricots, tart, cookies, petit four, cordial candy, and a pot of brewed loose tea which you sample first.

TEATIME: 2:00pm To 4:30pm • Seven Days A Week
• May Accommodate Some Dietary Needs With Advance Request
• Non-Caffeine/Herbal Tea Available
• Children's Tea Parties Welcome, Ages 6+
• Watercloset: Same Floor
• Wheelchair Accessible
• **Reservations Are Requested**
• Free Rear Parking Lot
• Credit Cards: V&MC
Proprietor's
Autograph _____*Date*_____

CANTERBURY'S
inside The Historic
Sonora Inn
160 South Washington Street
Sonora, California

209-532-6000

New Addition...It's Teatime At...Canterbury's. The historic Sonora Inn has been steeped in romance and history since its beginning in 1896 when it opened its doors as the Hotel Victoria. Interestingly, it was linked to Hollywood because of the many movies filmed in this area. Stars and film makers made the hotel their home away from home during production. In fact, years later during renovation, old darkrooms and tunnels were discovered!

A "Palace Guard" along with Vincent and Anita, welcome you to Canterbury's, now an English style restaurant & tearoom. Tables are set with doilies, fresh flowers, Royal Burlington teacups and Arthur Wood & Sons teapots by Staffordshire. Tea specialties are presented on two or three tiered caddies. The decor gets lots of oohs & aahs. The walls are covered with yellow English wallpaper & trimmed in white. Look up, the stained glass fan fixtures are real eye-catchers. P.S. Private tea parties, catered teas & a gift shop too!

$9.95 Canterbury Tea... Tea sandwiches, scone with butter, cream, lemon curd & jam, dessert, pot of brewed tea.

$7.95 Aristocrat Tea... Assortment of cheese, meats, crackers, fruit & jam tart, pot of brewed tea.

$5.95 Cream Tea... Two scones with butter, cream, lemon curd & jam, and a pot of brewed tea.

$3.95 Teddy Bear Tea... Tea sandwiches, scone, cocoa.

TEATIME: 11:30am To 8:30pm • Seven Days A Week
- May Accommodate Some Dietary Needs With Advance Request
- Non-Caffeine/Herbal Tea Available
- Watercloset:Same Floor • Children's Tea Parties Welcome
- **Reservations Are Not Required**
- Free Parking Lot Behind The Hotel
- Credit Cards: V,MC,DIS&AE

Proprietor's
*Autograph*_____*Date*_____

ARTISTS' INN B&B

1038 Magnolia Street
South Pasadena, California

888-799-5668 *Toll Free*
626-799-5668

Tea Parties For Groups At...The Artists' Inn B&B. The proprietor's artistic touches are everywhere in this 100 year old midwest Victorian style home. The Inn has been lovingly restored over the years, and nearly everything that was original was retained. The overall theme of The Artists' Inn, is art. Each room in the house expresses or represents a different period or different artist throughout history. You may choose to stay in The Van Gogh Room, The Impressionists' Room, Fauve Room, The Italian Suite or The Eighteenth Century English Room.

This is an especially charming spot for private tea parties of 20 to 25 guests. Both Janet and her Innkeeper Leah are very gracious and helpful. They, along with Ray, a chef from the California Culinary Academy, will help you create a memorable tea party event. P.S. Be sure to ask about their holiday open house.

$20.00 Afternoon Tea... Assorted finger sandwiches, fresh seasonal fruit, scone served with cream & preserves, lemon bars, cookies, chocolates and pot of loose or bagged tea. (Per person plus applicable sales tax, gratuity.)

GROUP TEA PARTIES: 20 To 25 Guests • Call To Plan
• May Accommodate Some Dietary Needs, 1 Week Advance Request
• Non-Caffeine/Herbal Tea Available
• Watercloset: Same Floor
• **Advance Reservations Are Required**
• Unmetered Street Parking
• Credit Cards: V,MC,DIS&AE

Inn keeper's
*Autograph*_____*Date*_____

BRISTOL FARMS

What The World Is Coming To.

606 Fair Oaks Avenue
South Pasadena, California

626-441-5450

New Addition...Host A Tea Party With Help From Bristol Farms. Teas, as we all know are fun & popular events for any or no occasion at all! I'm often asked at book signings about my own tea parties. Afternoon Teas at home are especially fun for me because I get a chance to be creative and bring out my pretty vintage plates, teacups, teapots, vases & Victorian lace. I keep my list of guests to eight friends for ease of conversation. Setting the table the day before really saves time. I also set a tea strainer for each guest.

Early in the day I pick dewy garden flowers, plunge them into squeaky clean vases of water and head to Bristol Farms in South Pasadena. I buy one large container each of tuna, chicken & seafood salads. Next, a stop at their bakery for 24 pre-ordered mini, or 8 large scones, 3 different loaves of bread for cookie-cutter shaped tea sandwiches and a dozen mini chocolate eclairs and cream puffs. I choose two 16 oz. jars of preserves & 3 small jars of lemon curd. I make my own cream, but they usually have clotted cream if you like. Edible blossoms, strawberries, grapes, kiwi, bananas & star fruit are a must. An extra bunch of flowers, and I'm off! To make your tea party more fun & "interactive" ask each of your guests to bring a different small package of tea. With individual teapots, it encourages tea-tasting & is a neat conversation facilitator. (But that's another book!) With 8 guests it's easier to have plates preset with 3 tea sandwiches, edible flowers, melange of fruit, and a "teacup" of soup, made from 4 packages of creamy asparagus soup to which I add pre-cooked fresh asparagus bits. Scones are on individual plates. My bread pudding made from bread crusts is great!F.Y.I. If you prefer, pick-up a catered tea from Bristol Farms!

TEATIME SHOPPING: 8:00am To 9:00pm • Seven Days A Week
• May Accommodate Some Dietary Needs With Advance Request
• Tins Of Non-Caffeine/Herbal Tea Available
• Wheelchair Accessible • Watercloset: Same Floor
• Large Free Parking Lot
• Credit Cards:V,MC,DIS&AE
Manager's
*Autograph*_____*Date*_____

SOMEWHERE IN TIME
34 Main Street
Sutter Creek, California

209-267-5789

New Addition...It's Teatime At...Somewhere In Time. I've met numerous tea lovers at booksignings who tell me how much they enjoy their visits to Somewhere In Time in Sutter Creek. Beverly the proprietor is certainly doing something worth talking about! A saloon in 1860, this spot was also an antique store before becoming the romantic and enchanting tearoom it is today.

Afternoon Tea is served at tables set with floral table skirts, mauve toppers & serviettes, depression glass plates with doilies, and English bone china. The timeless beauty of roses is everywhere. The romantic decor includes vintage brick walls, dark green carpet, several overstuffed chairs, tall twinkle lit trees and the original stained glass windows. Don't miss the portrait of Beverly's family attired in Victorian clothing above the fireplace. Look for vintage cabinets full of magnificent gifts, teas, books & treasures. P.S. Private tea parties are welcome for up to 35 guests.

$13.50 English Traditional Tea... Finger sandwiches, quiche, fresh fruit, special veggies, banana nut bread, scone served with Devonshire cream & preserves, brewed loose tea of the day.
$6.50 Cream Tea.. Sweet buttery raisin-filled scones with Devonshire cream & preserves, pot of loose brewed tea du jour.

TEATIME: 11:00am To 2:30pm • Seven Days A Week
• May Accommodate Some Dietary Needs With Advance Request
• Non-Caffeine/Herbal Tea Available
• Children's Tea Parties Welcome, Ages 9+
• Watercloset: Same Floor, With A Muraled Door
• Wheelchair Accessible
• **Reservations Are Required**
• Free Parking Lot
• Credit Cards: V,MC&DIS
Proprietor's
*Autograph*_____*Date*_____

THE CHEZ CAFFE

9071 East Las Tunas Boulevard
Temple City, California

626-286-0173

New Addition...Theme Teas For Groups At...The Chez Caffe. The Chez Caffe started out as an ambitious small neighborhood Victorian style tearoom. But catering to Afternoon Tea lovers became only part of the picture for Shari who found that her tea-business was tea-tering. To keep her dream out of hot water, and feeling the pulse of the area, she added the bean. She is now known as the coffee cafe that has tea parties for 10-20 guests. Her long time tea customers enjoy planning fun & casual tea parties, and Shari couldn't be happier. Presto...out come the lacey Victorian accessories, and it's teatime at this homey coffee stop. Easy job for this former set designer accustomed to quick scene changes!

Teddy Bear Teas are complete with bear centerpieces and there's a separate table set just for the kids' own, brought along dressed-up teddy bears! The bears sit quietly and grin with miniature tea sets. The children's server dressed in a handmade nanny outfit, reads stories aloud to her young charges. P.S. Angel Teas, Victorian Serenade & other theme tea parties are available for the older set. They usually include lace tablecloths, and Duchess fine china. Prices are per person plus tax & gratuity, and no room fee.

$5.95 Teddy Bear T.PB&J sandwiches, cookie & "tea."
$8.00 Victorian Tea... Finger sandwiches, scone with cream & preserves, fruit, dessert, a pot of loose French pressed tea.

THEME TEAS FOR GROUPS: 10 To 20 Guests, Call To Schedule
• May Accommodate Some Dietary Needs With Advance Request
• Non-Caffeine/Herbal Tea Available
• Children's Tea Parties Welcome
• Watercloset: Same Floor
• **48 Hour Advance Reservations Required**
• Limited Street Parking, Rear Entrance Parking Lot
• Credit Cards: V&MC
Proprietor's
*Autograph*_____*Date*_____

OLIVIA'S DOLL HOUSE
Tea Room

1321 East Thousand Oaks Boulevard
Thousand Oaks, California

805-381-1553

New Addition...Children's Dress Up Tea Parties At...Olivia's Doll House Tea Room. Catered dress-up tea parties for 6 to 20 children are a delight for so many little girls. They are invited to have their hair styled, have makeup and nail polish applied, and play dress-up. They may borrow gowns, hats, boas and costume jewelry and participate in a fashion show. Little boys are not excluded, with costumes for them as well, and young guests receive a photo button of themselves in their attire.

Birthday attendees sit at a big heart shaped table with the honoree sitting at the "royal" throne. He or she as host, gets to ring the bell for service. To the delight of parents and guardians, the favors, food and birthday or special occasion cake is included. Children attending receive a favor, while the honoree receives a handmade doll as gifts from Olivia's. Olivia's also prepares a record of all gifts received. Hosting and guest parents or guardians are welcome to stay and enjoy the festivities. Parties are two hours and one party is scheduled per time period. Please call for further details.

$225.00 Children's Dress Up Party For 6 Children... Each additional child $25.00. Fruit & dip platters, tiny pizzas, cocktail wieners, sandwiches, candy, heart-shaped brownies, cake, lemonade or iced tea.

TEATIME: As Scheduled
• May Accommodate Some Dietary Needs With Advance Request
• Non-Caffeine Beverages
• Watercloset: Same Floor
• Wheelchair Accessible
• **Reservations & Deposit At Least Two Weeks In Advance**
• Free Parking Lot
• Cash Or Check

Proprietor's
*Autograph*_____*Date*_____

297

THOUSAND OAKS
Antique Center & Tea Room
3727 East Thousand Oaks Boulevard
Thousand Oaks, California

805-494-1450

*New Location...*It's Teatime At...Thousand Oaks **Antique Center & Tea Room.** This new spot looks very similar to John and Ann's original English cottage, but the Antique Center & Tea Room has moved a few doors down. This inviting tearoom with a living room atmosphere is decorated in deep floral tones. I especially like the beautiful, appropriately worn vintage black floral carpet. You'll enjoy visiting with these friendly proprietors who attentively hurry about with pots of fresh hot tea.

Afternoon Tea is served at antique barley twist oak tables set with pretty vintage lace cloths, English china & fresh flowers. This new location is complete with an outdoor tea garden for your dining pleasure. Also, you may now purchase many of the tasty items to take home. Allow time to browse through the antique center, I always find something tea-riffic! P.S. This is a wonderful spot for private tea parties too, for up to 40 guests.

$14.50 High Tea.. Assorted tea sandwiches, scone with butter, apple scone with Devon cream, lemon curd, preserves, pastries, brewed loose Yorkshire Gold Tea.

$10.50 Afternoon Tea... Fresh baked scone served with Devon cream, lemon curd & preserves, hot Cornish Pastie or hot spinach puff, pot of brewed loose Yorkshire Gold Tea.

$6.50 Morning Tea... Fresh baked breakfast scone with Devon cream, lemon curd, preserves and a pot of brewed loose tea.

TEATIME: 11:00am To 4:00pm • Wednesday Thru Friday
- 11:00am To 7:00pm, Saturday • 12Noon To 4:00pm, Sunday
- Non-Caffeine/Herbal Tea Available
- Watercloset: Same Floor • Wheelchair Accessible
- **Reservations Are Required**
- Free Parking Lot
- Credit Cards: MC,V,DIS&AE

Proprietor's
*Autograph*_____*Date*_____

Orange-Ginger Scones

Compliments of **TEA A MAGAZINE**, *Scotland, Connecticut*

2 cups King Arthur (unbleached) flour

4 Tablespoons baking powder	2 teaspoons sugar (optional)
1/2 teaspoon salt	4 ounces butter
1 teaspoon ground ginger	1/3 cup orange juice
1 teaspoon grated orange rind	2 eggs (well-beaten)

Preheat oven. Mix dry ingredients together; cut butter into dry ingredients; add grated orange rind and mix in eggs and orange juice. Roll out on a floured surface; let stand for ten minutes, then fold and roll once again. Cut into shapes about one inch high. Place on an ungreased baking pan. Bake at 425 degrees F. for 8-10 minutes. Yields 12-18 scones.

Invigorating Bath Sachet

Compliments of **Harney & Sons Fine Teas**

"This blend of herbs, oils and teas, can be used for an invigorating soak in the tub or brewed for a refreshing cup. Take a square of cheesecloth and fill the center with a teaspoon each of the following herbs and tea, and a sprinkle of lemon oil. Tie it with a bit of string and hang it with a bit of string and hang it from your faucet in the stream of hot water filing your tub. For a further lift, you can also brew up a cup of this blend to enjoy while you soak.

Peppermint...for increased concentration
Lemon Verbena...for dispelling depression
Japanese Sencha...green tea for longevity
Cornflower and Marigold petals...for astringency and beauty
Lemon Oil...for uplifting scent."

ANTIQUE COUNTRY TEA ROOM
at Days Inn, Torrance

4111 Pacific Coast Highway
Torrance, California

Ask For The Tearoom **310-378-8511**

New Addition...It's Teatime At...Antique Country Tea Room. Tearooms pop up in the most unique spots. The Antique Country Tea Room is located at the Days Inn. Loretta, the upbeat proprietor prepares her award-winning Mennonite family recipes to the delight of tea lovers who have just discovered her.

International Theme Teas are served at tables set with linens & fresh flowers or centerpieces by the cheerful staff. Private tea parties are welcome for 10 to 100 guests. Loretta will help you plan a special event with novel add-on attractions if you like, such as a Fairy Godmother Story-Teller, Tea-Leaf Reader, Puppeteer, Face Painter or Belly-Dancer. Lots of antiques & collectibles here too. P.S. Loretta can bring a tea party to you too, for 10 or more guests.

$12.95 English Tradition... Barley soup, cucumber & salmon sandwiches, salad, scones, fruit, dessert, pot of English tea.

$12.95 Exotic India... Dall soup, watercress salad, curry chicken croissant, pilau rice, fruit, India dessert, India tea.

$7.95 Little Princess Tea & Children's Dress-Up Tea Parties... Chicken noodle soup, Vienna sausage crescents, sandwich, fries, dessert, hot cocoa or hot cider. (Parties are for a minimum of 10 children, $7.95 per child. Add $25.00 to the total price for dress-up, make-up, & nails! Or, add $100.00 for a storyteller/magician/balloon artist! What fun!

TEATIME: 11:00am To 4:00pm • Seven Days A Week
- May Accommodate Some Dietary Needs With Advance Request
- Non-Caffeine/Herbal Tea Available
- Children's Tea Parties Welcome
- Watercloset: Same Floor • Wheelchair Accessible
- **Reservations Are Required**
- Free Parking Lot
- Credit Cards: V,MC,DIS&AE

Proprietor's
*Autograph*_____*Date*_____

300

CRICKETT'S TEA ROOM

2651-A Pacific Coast Highway
(Rolling Hills Plaza)
Torrance, California

310-517-8777

It's Teatime At...Crickett's Tea Room. Elizabeth and Gus along with their friendly staff, have created a cheerful & fanciful atmosphere at Crickett's. There are exceptionally wonderful fresh flower bouquets on each table which contribute to the multicolored palette. The menu is creative, my cress and cream cheese tea sandwiches were quite wonderful with avocado and Mandarin oranges, very "California."

Gus is a catering specialist so it's no surprise that everything here is homemade & artistically presented. Allow time to peruse the gift shop for tea-related gifts, greeting cards, books & Crickett's own packaged scone mix. P.S. Crickett's is available for private tea parties & lunch. F.Y.I. Crickett's Plaza Catering will be happy to bring Afternoon Tea to your group, even on Sundays.

$10.95 Crickett's High Tea... Cup of soup, salad of the day, choice of two mini croissant sandwiches, warm scone served with Devonshire cream & imported English strawberry jam & lemon curd, dessert & English tea. (Monday-Saturday, 11- 2pm)

$8.95 Classic Afternoon Tea... Tea sandwiches, warm scone served with Devonshire cream & imported English strawberry jam & lemon curd, assorted mini desserts and imported English tea.

TEATIME: Open 7 Days, 11am To 3pm • Sunday Thru Thursday
• 11:00am To 6:00pm • Friday & Saturday
• May Accommodate Some Dietary Needs With Advance Request
• Non-Caffeine/Herbal Tea Available
• Watercloset: Same Floor
• Wheelchair Accessible
• **Reservations Are Recommended**
• Free Parking Lot
• Credit Cards: V,MC&DIS

Proprietor's
*Autograph*_____*Date*_____

301

THE BLACK ROSE

721 West First Street
Tustin, California

Message **714-835-0992**   **714-573-7567**

New Addition...It's Teatime At...The Black Rose.
Look for a unique awning atrium complete with fish & turtles, on your way into this new tearoom. The architecture may seem familiar to you, but this spot of tea has its own unexpected ambiance.

The hues of the exotic black rose are reflected in the mauve & black decor of both The Windsor Room & The Rose Garden Room at The Black Rose. Doreen carries a select variety of gifts, tea accoutrements, books, antiques and silk flowers arrangements in their new tearoom & gift shop. Continental breakfast & lunch are served addition to Afternoon Tea.

Afternoon Tea is served at tables set with mauve and black coordinating table linens, fresh flowers and an eclectic collection of fine china by servers in black & white outfits and dusty rose aprons. Banquette seating is available as well. The Windsor Room & The Ivy Room have wonderful floor to ceiling decorative fireplaces. P.S.Private tea parties are available for up to 100 guests seven days a week, please call to plan. Weather permitting, dine al fresco.

$18.95 Old English Teas... Complimentary glass of champagne, scone served with Devonshire cream, jam & lemon curd, assorted tea sandwiches, choice of four desserts, fresh seasonal fruit, and a pot of brewed loose tea.

TEATIMES: 11:00am & 4:00pm • Tuesday Thru Saturday
• May Accommodate Some Dietary Needs, 1 Week Advance Request
• Non-Caffeine/Herbal Tea Available
• Children's Tea Parties Welcome
• Watercloset: Same Floor • Wheelchair Accessible
• **Reservations Are A Must**
• Free Parking Lot
• Credit Cards: MC&V

Proprietor's
*Autograph*_____*Date*_____

JUSTIN PORTERFIELD, LTD.
Mrs. McKee & Me Tea Room

17350 East 17th Street
(The Enderle Center)
Tustin, California

714-544-5223

New Addition...Private Tea Parties For Groups At...Justin Porterfield, Ltd. Many of you have been waiting for Justin Porterfield to start Afternoon Teas once again. Well I have good news...they're back! Private Afternoon Teas & High Teas are served once again, in the intimate tearoom just one flight up. This sweet tearoom is cheerfully decorated, and accented with paintings, tea accessories and twinkle-lit floral grapevines.

Teas are served at tables set with linens, English bone china, fresh flowers, and lit teapot warmers by servers attired in white Battenburg pinnies. Allow time to browse, there's lots to see. Justin Porterfield, Ltd. specializes in elegant and unique Victorian gifts, home decor, collectibles, and once again Victorian Teas. F.Y.I. They will be happy to bring a tea party to you through their catering department. Prices here are per person, plus tax & gratuity. Call to plan your special event. Ask about holiday inspired theme teas too.

$25.00 High Tea... Seasonal, apple sausage roll, assorted tea sandwiches, tea scones served with butter, double cream & preserves, assorted mini pastries, pot of brewed loose tea.
$25.00 Afternoon Tea... Watercress soup, scone with creme fraiche, ginger chicken salad on fresh pineapple garnished with fresh fruit, rosemary raisin roll, elegant dessert, brewed tea.

PRIVATE TEA PARTIES: As Scheduled
• May Accommodate Some Dietary Needs With Advance Request
• Non-Caffeine/Herbal Tea Available
• Watercloset: Nearby Common Area
• **Advance Reservation & Prepay Only**
• Free Parking Lot
• Credit Cards: V,MC,DIS&AE
Proprietor's
*Autograph*_____*Date*_____

303

McCHARLES HOUSE
Tea Room
335 South "C" Street
Old Town Tustin, California

714-731-4063
888-MY CUP OF TEA

It's Teatime At...McCharles House Tea Room.
This lovingly restored 1885 California Victorian Cottage is a very popular spot for Afternoon Tea. McCharles House has been around since 1985 when many other tearooms were just a twinkle in a tea lover's eye! Enjoy Afternoon Tea, served throughout this adorable shop. Bring in your June 1997 issue of Victoria for an autograph!

Afternoon Tea is served at tables set with linens, fresh garden flowers & an eclectic collection of mis-matched English china. Antiques, and vintage fabric window treatments are part of the pretty picture. Allow time to browse in the gift shop called, My Cup Of Tea. Look for Audrey & Vivian's family collection of over 100 teacups! F.Y.I. Candlelight Teas are served Thursday, Friday & Saturday evenings from 5:30-8:00pm. Ask about Victoria Magazine Theme Teas usually on the first Sunday of the month. P.S. Private tea parties may be arranged for 10 guests, or 16 in the glorious garden, weather permitting. Lunch & dinner are also available. Ask about "McCharles by Mail," and share "Teatime all the day!" P.S. Don't miss Audrey's signed & numbered lithograph!

$1600 Victorian Afternoon Tea... Tea sandwiches, scone served with cream & preserves, dessert and brewed loose tea.

$15.00 Chocolate Tea... Chocolate chunk scone, cream & preserves, chocolate fruit & nuts, dessert, and brewed loose tea.

TEATIME: 11:30am To 4:00pm • Tuesday Thru Saturday
• Sunday Reserved For Special Tea Celebrations
• May Accommodate Some Dietary Needs, 1 Week Advance Request
• Non-Caffeine/Herbal Tea Available
• Children's Tea Parties Welcome
• Wheelchair Accessible • Watercloset: Same Floor
• **Reserve For Six Or More, & Evening Teas**
• Limited-Time Street Parking
• Credit Cards: MC&V

Proprietor's
*Autograph*_____*Date*_____

THE 1913 BEVERAGE COMPANY
Restaurant & Tea House

180 El Camino Real
Tustin, California

714-832-8941

New Addition...It's Teatime At...The 1913 Beverage Company. Welcome to this cozy, two-story Craftsman bungalow built in 1913 by architect William Bowman. The 1913 Beverage Co.serves breakfast & lunch in addition to Afternoon Tea.

Afternoon Tea features Arthur Wood & Son fine English, Staffordshire bone china. Tea specialties are presented either on individual plates, or from tiered caddies...your choice. You may take tea service in the bungalow's airconditioned first or second floor tearoom, or outside on the patio. The tearooms have soothing background music and are decorated in rose, lavender and mauve tones with antique or traditional bistro-style furniture. Evening Candlelight Teas and private tea parties are also available. Please call Kay the proprietor to reserve your date & to plan your special event.

$16.95 "1913" High Tea... Two heart-shaped fruit, almond, or plain scones with clotted cream & preserves, homemade soup, assorted tea sandwiches, fruit, surprise dessert, chocolate dipped strawberry, and a pot of darjeeling or brewed loose tea.

$6.95 Tea & Dessert... Pot of tea & dessert du jour.

TEATIME: 1:00pm To 5:00pm • Monday Thru Thursday
• Friday &Saturday, Till 8:30pm
• Private Tea Parties For 20-40 Guests On Sundays
• May Accommodate Some Dietary Needs With Advance Request
• Non-Caffeine/Herbal Tea Available
• Children's Tea Parties Welcome
• Watercloset: First Floor • Wheelchair Accessible
• **Reservations Are Required**
• Free Parking Behind The House
• Cash Or Check

Proprietor's
*Autograph*_____*Date*_____

BRITISH EMPORIUM
& Tea Room
908 -910 North Central Avenue
Upland, California

909-920-9110

It's Teatime At...British Emporium & Tea Room. Afternoon Tea & Cream Tea are served all day at The British Emporium. Many authentic British dishes are featured here. Treat yourself to spotted dick with custard, English plum pudding or bangers among other specialties. The atmosphere is much like an English cottage with dark green carpet, coach lights and a fireplace.

Afternoon Tea is served at tables set with rose colored tablecloths & toppers, Royal Albert Country Rose china, silver & fresh flowers. F.Y.I. The shop carries a unique collection of gifts and antiques. Almost everything you see is for sale..just ask! P.S. Jane, the proprietor is a frequent speaker on the subject of a proper Afternoon Tea. Private tea parties are available.

$12.50 Authentic Victorian Cream Tea... Assorted tea sandwiches, scone served with Devon cream & jam or lemon curd, Sherry trifle, cheese & crackers, and a pot of brewed tea.

$9.50 Authentic Afternoon Tea... Assorted tea sandwiches, scone served with Devon cream & jam or lemon curd, assortment of English biscuits and a pot of brewed tea.

TEATIME: 10am-5pm, Monday To Saturday • 10am-4pm, Sunday
- May Accommodate Some Dietary Needs, 2 Day Advance Request
- Non-Caffeine/Herbal Tea Available
- Children's Tea Parties Welcome, Ages 7+
- Wheelchair Accessible • Watercloset: Same Floor .
- **Reservations Are Appreciated**
- Shopping Center Parking Lot
- Credit Cards: V&MC

Proprietor's
*Autograph*_____*Date*_____

FAMILY TIES TEA ROOM
160 East "C" Street
(Between 2nd & Euclid)
Upland, California

909-982-8685

    It's Teatime At...Family Ties Tea Room. If you see a burgundy colored awning, two topiary trees and a late 1800's historic building in Upland, you must be at the entrance to Family Ties. Ribbons and bows are everywhere as it's Jenny's way of celebrating her own family "ties."

    Afternoon Tea is served at tables set with forest green or burgundy cloths & white lace toppers. Tea courses are served via tea cart, and attentive servers scurry about to pour your tea before you do, even though you have your individual pot. Family Ties is referred to as an American tearoom, by its proprietor. Browse around, the gift shop carries teacups, teapots & handmade items by local artisans. P.S. If you only have time for Afternoon Tea to go...no problem, Family Ties can pack-up a tea party for you. Private tea parties are welcome for 15 to 21 guests. Theme teas are being planned, please call for information.

    $10.75 Full Tea... Petite sandwiches buttermilk scone with creme & jam, cookie, dessert such as: cheesecake with pureed raspberry sauce, berry tart, chocolate or lemon mousse, a pot of tea.

    $9.50 Savory Tea... Petite tea sandwiches, garnish, fresh baked buttermilk scone with creme & jam, cookie, pot of tea.

    $9.50 Sweet Tea... Fresh baked buttermilk scone with creme & jam, garnish, cookie, choice of dessert and a pot of tea.

    $7.25 Petite Tea... Daily fresh baked buttermilk scone served with creme & jam, garnish, cookie and a pot of tea.

TEATIME: 11:00am To 1:30pm • Wednesday Thru Saturday
• May Accommodate Some Dietary Needs, 2 Day Advance Request
• Non-Caffeine/Herbal Tea Available
• Wheelchair Accessible • Watercloset: Same Floor
• **Reservations Are Highly Recommended**
• Street Parking & Rear Public Lot
• Credit Cards: MC&V

Proprietor's
*Autograph*_____*Date*_____

A TOUCH OF CLASS
25914 McBean Parkway
(Granary Square)
Valencia, California

805-259-1625

It's Teatime At...A Touch Of Class. "A step back in time," that's the feeling described upon entering A Touch Of Class tearoom & gift shop which specializes in feminine apparel and gifts.

Afternoon Tea is served at tables set with fresh flowers, fine china & unique tea lamps. You'll find artwork, antiques and beautiful silver everywhere and many of these special items are for sale. Decor is seasonal, Christmas, Valentine's Day, and Mother's Day have lovely decorations. F.Y.I. Tea parties may be arranged for groups of 15 to 25 guests, call for information. P.S. Be sure to ask Gail, Sandy & Sherry about their upcoming theme teas.

$15.50 Full English Tea... Tea sandwiches, freshly baked warm scone served with mock Devonshire cream & jam, an assortment of petite desserts and a pot of brewed loose tea.
$15.50 French Tea... Tea sandwiches, warm fresh baked scone with mock Devonshire cream & jam, seasonal fresh fruit and a pot of brewed loose tea.
$8.50 Cream Tea... Warm freshly baked scone served with mock Devonshire cream & jam, an assortment of lovely petite desserts and a pot of brewed loose tea.

TEATIMES: 11:30am, 1:00 & 2:30pm • Wednesday Thru Sunday
• May Accommodate Some Dietary Needs With Advance Request
• Non-Caffeine/Herbal Tea Available
• Children's Holiday Teas
• Watercloset: Convenient • Wheelchair Accessible
• **Reservations Are Advised**
• Free Parking Lot
• Credit Cards: V,MC,DIS&AE
Proprietor's
*Autograph*_____*Date*_____

ROBIN HOOD BRITISH
Pub & Restaurant

13640 Burbank Boulevard
Van Nuys, California

818-994-6045

It's Teatime At...Robin Hood British Pub & Restaurant. The Robin Hood Pub could be the perfect spot if one of you is in the mood for kidney pie, and the other for Afternoon Tea. This tearoom is also an authentic English pub that specializes in homemade dishes such as steak & kidney pie, Rock Cakes, Eccles Cakes, vanilla slices and tasty scones. Your proprietors Lorraine & Michael welcome you to their little British empire.

Afternoon Tea is served in the newly expanded smoke-free dining room at tables set with blue & white Willow pattern china, pink tablecloths & fresh flowers. The dining room features used brick and is decorated with burgundy Regency stripe wallpaper, oak paneling, a decorative fireplace, burgundy flowers & Royal memorabilia with brass accents here and there. Allow time to visit The Friar Tuck Shop, well-known in the area for imported British tin foods & gifts. F.Y.I. Private tea parties are now available for your special events. Please call for details.

$9.95 Afternoon Tea... Petite sandwiches such as salmon, cucumber, egg-cress, home baked pink and yellow Battenburg cake with Marzipan coating, scone served with Devon cream & strawberry jam and a "cozy" pot of tea.

TEATIME: 3:00pm To 5:00pm • Seven Days A Week
• Non-Caffeine/Herbal Tea Available
• Watercloset: Convenient
• **Reservations Are Suggested**
• Parking Behind The Pub & Street Park
• Credit Cards: V,MC,DIS&AE

Proprietor's
*Autograph*_____*Date*_____

**cat in the garden
TEA and coffee HOUSE**

CAT IN THE GARDEN

451 East Main Street, Suite 8
Ventura, California

805-641-9477

New Addition...It's Teatime At...Cat In The Garden. This is a perfect spot to stop for casual Afternoon Tea after strenuous antiqueing along Main Street in the heart of Ventura's neat "antique/collectible/retail/thriftstore/vintage" boutique district. You'll need your eagle eye to spot this little gem too, as Cat In The Garden is tucked away behind some shops. Your short path from Main Street will take you up a few steps past vine-covered shops, and along a stone walkway to almost the end of an historic shopping arcade. Voila! The Cat In The Garden.

Afternoon Tea is served at tables set with garden green tablecloths, fine china & English place mats. Weather permitting, dining al fresco on the European-style walkway is nice. Tasty tea sandwiches and friendly service are Jean and Katherine's specialty. Where is the cat you might ask? Look around for the white ceramic cat sleeping in a corner. The cat theme continues with wire cat tiered caddies, books, and a basket of stuffed kittens. P.S. Private tea parties and children's tea parties are also available.

$4.50 Morning Tea...(Served All Day) Fresh baked scone with cream, lemon curd & preserves, pot of brewed loose tea.

$8.50 Afternoon Tea... Assorted finger sandwiches, fresh baked scone served with cream, lemon curd & preserves, a trio of sweets and a pot of brewed loose tea.

TEATIME:11am-6pm, Monday Thru Saturday • Noon-6pm, Sunday
• May Accommodate Some Veggie Needs With Advance Request
• Non-Caffeine/Herbal Tea Available
• Children's Tea Parties Welcome
• Tiny Watercloset: Same Floor
• Unmetered, Limited Time Street Parking
• **Reservations Are Welcomed**
• Credit Cards: V,MC&DIS

Proprietor's
*Autograph*_____*Date*_____

Tea & Honey Cake

One of the author's favorites

1 Cup Honey
2 Eggs
1 Cup Brown Sugar
1 Cup Brewed Strong Black Tea
1 1/2 Teaspoons Baking Powder
3 Tablespoons Oil
1/2 Teaspoon + 1 Pinch Baking Soda
3 Cups Flour
1 Teaspoon Cinnamon

Preheat oven to 325 degrees F. Grease and flour a 9x13-inch pan. **Beat** honey and eggs together. **Add** sugar, and mix again.
Mix tea with baking powder and oil, and add to egg mixture.
Add baking soda, flour and cinnamon & beat together well **Bake** for 55 minutes to one hour, or until toothpick inserted in the center comes out clean. Yumm!

Visitors may be waiting for the cake to cool on the window sill!

NONA'S COURTYARD CAFE
at The Bella Maggiore

67 South California Street
Ventura, California

Nona **805-641-2783**   *Bella* **805-652-0277**

**Tea Parties For Groups Of 25 To 60 Guests At...
Nona's Courtyard Cafe.** This European-style, artistically covered outdoor garden courtyard is a charming spot for a tea party for your special event. This uniquely designed dining spot is spacious, airy, green & lush. I'm partial to Nona's Renaissance-like decorative lion wall fountain. Nona's was co-created by Jonathan, the general manager. I'd say they did an outstanding job!

Afternoon Tea is graciously served at tables set with tablecloths, cloth serviettes, French Acroc fine china & fresh flowers. P.S. If your guests wish to spend the night in Ventura, The Bella is a charming B&B. We've stayed here a number of times usually on a Friday night or for a weekend get-away. F.Y.I. Across the street there's often a terrific Farmer's Market on most Saturday mornings. To my delight, my husband always buy me a dozen long-stem roses for about $6.00! Also, there's a very nice Victoriana gift shop and garden shop attached to The Bella.

$15.00 Afternoon Tea... Assorted finger sandwiches, fresh baked scone with Devonshire cream & preserves, seasonal fresh fruit and a variety of sweets such as cream puffs & chocolates, and a continuous cup of tea. (Per person plus tax & gratuity.)

TEA PARTIES FOR GROUPS: Reserve Your Party Date Early
- Non-Caffeine/Herbal Tea Available
- Watercloset: Same Floor
- Wheelchair Accessible
- Rear & Street Parking
- **Advance Reservations Are An Absolute Must**
- Credit Cards: V,DIS,MC&AE

*Manager's
Autograph*_____*Date*_____

312

SHELLY'S PLACE
14366 Atstar Drive
Victorville, California

760-245-5506

It's Teatime On The First Wednesday & Saturday Of The Month At...Shelly's. The charm begins as soon as you open the door to Shelly's. A garden effect has been created with a fountain, a park bench, and a mural of a landscape which covers an entire wall. The tearoom is furnished with antiques and is decorated in tones of dusty rose & burgundy. Florals accents are picked up in the chintz & green ivy wallpaper and the carpeting. Shelly describes her place as a spot which elicits memories of grandma's house or a favorite aunt's. Henrietta's Afternoon Tea is a lovingly named after Shelly's mom. P.S. Ask her about theme teas.

Afternoon Tea is served at tables set with linens, cloth napkins, fresh flowers & fine china. Homemade "almost everything" is part of Shelly's signature teas, Henrietta would have been proud I'm sure. Shelly's has a full dining room and an espresso bar as well. Enjoy the gift items tucked in nooks & crannies on the way to the tearoom. P.S. Tea parties are available for 25-40 guests any afternoon by advance reservation.

$15.50   Henrietta's Tea...(Includes Tax & Gratuity) Tea sandwiches, warm savory such as a wild mushroom tart, heart shaped scone, Devonshire cream & raspberry preserves, tea treats such as cream puff or chocolate cake, Harney brewed loose tea.
$5.00 Scone & A Pot of Tea

TEATIME: First Wednesday & Saturday Of The Month, 2-4:00pm
• Scone & Tea During Shop Hours: 7am-3pm • Seven Days A Week
• May Accommodate Some Dietary Needs With Advance Request
• Non-Caffeine/Herbal Tea Available
• Children's Tea Parties Welcome
• Wheelchair Accessible • Watercloset: Same Floor
• **Reservations Are Strongly Suggested**
• Unlimited Free Parking Lot
• Credit Cards: MC,V,DIS&AE
Proprietor's
*Autograph*_____*Date*_____

BEN MADDOX HOUSE

601 North Encina Street
Visalia, California

209-739-0721

It's Teatime On Sundays In December At...Ben Maddox House. Built in 1876, this interesting redwood home is listed on the National Register of Historic Homes. Ben Maddox was the president of the Mount Whitney Power Company and owner of the Visalia Daily Times. A proponent of new forms of energy, Mr. Maddox's home was the first home in Visalia to have an electric stove. The manicured grounds are lit by four 1927 antique post lights acquired from the city of Pasadena.

Christmas Teas are served in the parlor and dining room of the Ben Maddox House which Diane has beautifully decorated for Christmas. Tables are set with white linens, fresh flowers, a collection of fine china, and gold flatware. There is always a musician or carolers who entertain during the Christmas Teas. P.S. Private tea parties are available for up to 12 guests.

$14.95 Christmas Tea... Assorted tea sandwiches such as salmon & cream cheese, egg & watercress, Braunschweiger pate, scone with Devon cream & orange marmalade & lemon curd, cheesecake, cookies, chocolate truffles, a pot of brewed loose tea.

DECEMBER CHRISTMAS TEAS: 1:00pm & 4:00pm • Sundays
• Every Sunday In December, Please Call To Confirm Dates
• May Accommodate Some Dietary Needs With Advance Request
• Non-Caffeine/Herbal Tea Available
• Watercloset: Same Floor
• **Reservations Are Required**
• Off Street &Street Parking
• Credit Cards: V,MC,DIS&AE

Proprietor's
*Autograph*_____*Date*_____

THE SECRET
Garden Mansion B&B

1056 Hacienda Drive
Walnut Creek, California

510-945-3600

New Name...Holiday Inspired Teas As Scheduled At...The Secret Garden Mansion B&B. Originally built in 1860, this historic mansion formerly known as The Mansion At Lakewood was carefully renovated by the Inn's current owner, Sharyn. The proprietor is most proud of the ambiance of the Secret Garden Room. In the early 1900's, the room was a ballroom with five floor-to-ceiling French windows which remain today. The Secret Garden has a wall mural and a working wall fountain.

English Holiday Tea Luncheons are presented on tiered caddies at tables set with pastel tablecloths, fresh flowers and pink glassware. Servers wear English caps and vests or coordinating tea-length dresses and bonnets on occasion. Please call for the schedule of Holiday Teas which take place around Christmas, Easter and Mother's Day. Teas range in price from around $18.50 to $32.00. Private tea parties are available for 10-30 guests. P.S. Look for the cabinet full of Sharyn's personal treasures, tea gifts & accessories.

$18.50 English Holiday Tea Luncheon...(Includes a Mansion & Garden Tour.) Assortment of tea sandwiches, scone served with jam & cream, cheese sticks, cookies, chocolates, French pastries and a continuous cup of brewed loose tea.

HOLIDAY TEAS: Please Call For Schedule
• May Accommodate Some Dietary Needs, 1 Week Advance Request
• Non-Caffeine/Herbal Tea Available
• Children's Tea Parties Welcome
• Watercloset: Same Floor
• **Reservations Are A Must**
• Free Off-Street Parking
• Credit Cards: V,MC&DIS

Proprietor's
*Autograph*_____*Date*_____

ELIXIR TONICS & TEAS

8612 Melrose Avenue
West Hollywood, California

1-888-4TONICS   310-657-9300

New Addition...A Tea Education & More At...Elixir Tonics & Teas. I just had the nicest chat with John, the tea guru at one of L.A.'s newest tea spots. The shop is owned by Edgar and Jeff, whose main focus is tea education. Learn proper brewing techniques for their own fine quality "Te Chine" teas.

The shop was originally a small bungalow that was completely gutted and re-worked to create this hip tea spot. The shop is decorated in shades of green tea & creamy yellow tones. Take a peek at the wonderful copper-topped tea bar which has earned a great patina over the years. Somewhat minimalist in design, there are double French doors, beechwood shelves, framed antique Chinese poster prints and dark rich wood beamed ceilings. F.Y.I. Many of the teas are available to touch, feel and smell in little tasting bowls set-up for your tactile appreciation.

Take a pot of terrific tea into the garden courtyard and relax by the meditation fountain. You can think about how taking time for tea may improve your life. Worth mentioning is Elixir's micro-water processing system; which really good tea deserves! P.S. Tea accessories and accoutrements from all over the world and a mail-order catalog are available here too. Web Site: www.elixirnet.com

$6.50-$7.50 Dim Sum...A variety of specialties
$2.00-$8.00 Pot Of Tea...10-12 oz. pot of fine tea.
$.50-$2.00... Fresh scone or muffin.

TEA & MORE: 10:00am To 6:30pm • Monday Thru Saturday
• 12Noon To 6:00pm, Sunday
• Non-Caffeine/Herbal Tea Available
• Watercloset: Rear Building, Same Floor
• Wheelchair Accessible
• **Please Drop In**
• Metered Street Parking
• Credit Cards: V,MC&AE

Proprietor's
*Autograph*_____*Date*_____

OLIVIA'S DOLL HOUSE
Tea Room

8804 Rosewood Avenue
West Hollywood, California

310-273-6631

New Addition...Children's Dress Up Tea Parties At...Olivia's Doll House Tea Room. Catered dress-up tea parties for 6 to 20 children are a delight for so many little girls. They are invited to have their hair styled, have makeup and nail polish applied, and play dress-up. They may borrow gowns, hats, boas and costume jewelry and participate in a fashion show. Little boys are not excluded, with costumes for them as well, and young guests receive a photo button of themselves in their attire.

Birthday attendees sit at a big heart shaped table with the honoree sitting at the "royal" throne. He or she as host, gets to ring the bell for service. To the delight of parents and guardians, the favors, food and birthday or special occasion cake is included. Children attending receive a favor, while the honoree receives a handmade doll as gifts from Olivia's. Olivia's also prepares a record of all gifts received. Hosting and guest parents or guardians are welcome to stay and enjoy the festivities. Parties are two hours and one party is scheduled per time period. Please call for further details.

$225.00 Children's Dress Up Party For 6 Children... Each additional child $25.00...Fruit & dip platters, tiny pizzas, cocktail wieners, sandwiches, candy, heart -shaped brownies, cake, lemonade or iced tea.

TEA PARTY TIME: As Scheduled, Please Call To Plan
• May Accommodate Some Dietary Needs With Advance Request
• Non-Caffeine Beverages
• Watercloset: Same Floor
• Wheelchair Accessible
• **Reservations & Deposit Required Min. Two Weeks In Advance**
• Free Parking Lot
• Cash Or Check

Proprietor's
*Autograph*_____*Date*_____

ARGYLE LOS ANGELES

8358 Sunset Boulevard
West Hollywood, California

Please Call Catering   **213-848-6612**

Private Tea Parties For Groups Of 10 To 100 Guests At...The Argyle Los Angeles. The Argyle is a most historically interesting place to visit. It recently underwent a $40 million reconstruction and restoration program and quite by surprise, some interesting artifacts were uncovered. Subsequently, the hotel and one of its rare palm trees were placed on the National Registry of Historic Places. The architecture of The Argyle Hotel includes some magnificent art deco features, and many of the hotel's furnishings are revival art deco museum pieces obtained from the Beaux Arts Museum in Paris and the Metropolitan in New York.

Afternoon Tea is served through the catering department at tables set with linens and Mikasa china. Once upon a time, The Argyle was home to such stars as Marilyn Monroe, Errol Flynn, Jean Harlow and Clark Gable to name a few. Consider having your party in The Library Room, it's quite a popular spot. The friendly catering department will be happy to help you plan your event.

$30.00 Afternoon Tea... Crudites with fresh cucumber dip, assorted finger sandwiches, dipped strawberries, scone served with whipped cream & strawberry preserves, an array of desserts, you may select three including chocolate truffles, a continuous cup of brewed tea. Price is per guest; service fee & tax will be added.

PRIVATE TEA PARTIES: Call Catering Department To Plan A Tea
- May Accommodate Some Dietary Needs With Advance Request
- Non-Caffeine/Herbal Tea Available
- Watercloset: Same Floor
- Wheelchair Accessible, Lift available
- **Please Call Early To Reserve Your Date**
- Parking Approximately $5.50 With Tea Validation
- Credit Cards:V,MC&AE

L'autograph
*du Concierge*_____*Date*_____

BRISTOL FARMS

140 Promenade Way
Westlake Village, California

805-370-9197

What The World Is Coming To.

   New Addition...Host A Tea Party With Help From Bristol Farms. Teas, as we all know are fun & popular events for any or no occasion at all! I'm often asked at book signings about my own tea parties. Afternoon Teas at home are especially fun for me because I get a chance to be creative and bring out my pretty vintage plates, teacups, teapots, vases & Victorian lace. I keep my list of guests to eight friends for ease of conversation. Setting the table the day before really saves time. I also set a tea strainer for each guest.

   Early in the day I pick dewy garden flowers, plunge them into squeaky clean vases of water and head to Bristol Farms in South Pasadena. I buy one large container each of tuna, chicken & seafood salads. Next, a stop at their bakery for 24 pre-ordered mini, or 8 large scones, 3 different loaves of bread for cookie-cutter shaped tea sandwiches and a dozen mini chocolate eclairs and cream puffs. I choose two 16 oz. jars of preserves & 3 small jars of lemon curd. I make my own cream, but they usually have clotted cream if you like. Edible blossoms, strawberries, grapes, kiwi, bananas & star fruit are a must. An extra bunch of flowers, and I'm off! To make your tea party more fun & "interactive" ask each of your guests to bring a different small package of tea. With individual teapots, it encourages tea-tasting & is a neat conversation facilitator. (But that's another book!) With 8 guests it's easier to have plates preset with 3 tea sandwiches, edible flowers, melange of fruit & a "teacup" of soup made from 4 packages of creamy asparagus soup to which I add pre-cooked fresh asparagus bits. Scones are on individual plates. My bread pudding made from the bread crusts is great! F.Y.I.If you prefer, pick-up a catered tea from Bristol Farms!

TEATIME SHOPPING: 8:00am To 9:00pm • Seven Days A Week
• May Accommodate Some Dietary Needs With Advance Request
• Tins Of Non-Caffeine/Herbal Tea Available
• Wheelchair Accessible • Watercloset: Same Floor
• Large Free Parking Lot
• Credit Cards:V,MC,DIS&AE

*Manager's
Autograph*_____*Date*_____

GREEN ARBOR
inside Village Green
8109 South Greenleaf Avenue
Whittier, California

562-698-9461

New Addition...It's Teatime At...Green Arbor Luncheon & Tearoom. Stroll through the green arbor and discover a little gift shop and the Green Arbor Luncheon & Tearoom. Tea is served in either The Arbor Room or The Garden Room. Both spots offer an attractive, welcome retreat for business teas or "linger-awhile-with-friends" teas.

 Afternoon Tea is served on Johnson Bros. "Castle Across The Lake," octagon-shaped English bone china. The Arbor Room features jewel tone linens and seasonal fresh flowers. The walls, covered in linen textured deep gray granite tones which nicely accent the black-marbled tile floor. Colorful Chinese vases and an antique Scottish sideboard from the late 1800's are nice designer touches. The Garden Room in contrast, is quite airy. Sunlight filters through the green lattice-work from a south facing window. Walls are covered in blue, green, ivory and black tones. Both rooms highlight paintings by local artists. Be sure to ask Beryl about tea parties for up to 100 guests, tea classes, catering & book events.

 $12.95 Afternoon Tea... Finger sandwiches, scones, Devonshire cream & preserves, sweets, pot of brewed loose tea.
 $6.95 Cream Tea... Scones served with Devonshire cream & preserves and a pot of brewed loose tea.

TEATIME: 11:30am To 3:30pm • Monday Thru Friday
- Saturdays, Sundays & Evenings By Appointment Only
- May Accommodate Some Dietary Needs With Advance Request
- Non-Caffeine/Herbal Tea Available
- Children's Tea Parties Welcome
- Wheelchair Accessible • Watercloset: Same Floor
- **Reservations Are Encouraged For Six Or More Guests**
- Free Parking Lot North Of The Building
- Credit Cards: V,MC,DIS&AE

Proprietor's
*Autograph*_____*Date*_____

GREENLEAF COTTAGE
Antique Center & Tea Room

6512 Greenleaf Avenue
Whittier, California

562-696-3600

New Addition...It's Teatime At...Greenleaf Cottage Antique Center & Tea Room. The charming Greenleaf Cottage in Old Town Whittier is a wonderful spot for Afternoon Tea. Intimate Afternoon Teas are Greenleaf Cottage's specialty. They are served throughout Wendy's cottage in the petite Ivy Room, The Brick Yard, or in front of the fireplace. On a beautiful Southern California day you might want to take tea on the outdoor Tea Terrace facing quaint Greenleaf Avenue or under market umbrellas in the sunny Secret Garden with a fountain.

Afternoon Tea is served in three courses at tables set with colorful tablecloths & napkins, mis-matched antique china & flatware and fresh flowers. Allow time to browse, there are neat antiques and collectibles for sale throughout this adorable Tudor-style cottage. F.Y.I. If you love your teacup, it's probably for sale! It seems that I always find something I can't seem to live without!

$13.95 Tea Of Perfection.. Finger sandwiches, scones served with cream & jam, fresh fruit, array of desserts, pot of brewed tea. (Quiche available for $2.50 additional.)

$8.95 Tea Of Indulgence... Scone served with cream & jam, assorted desserts, fruit garnish and a pot of brewed tea.

$6.95 Tea Of Tranquility... Scones served with cream & jam, fruit garnish and a pot of brewed tea.

TEATIME: 11am To 3pm • Sundays From Noon • Closed Tuesday
• Non-Caffeine/Herbal Tea Available
• Watercloset: Same Floor
• **Reservations Are Required**
• Level Street Parking Available In Rear Lot
• Credit Cards: V,MC,DIS&AE
Proprietor's
*Autograph*_____*Date*_____

321

PAST TYME TEA PARLOUR
& Gift Shop

6550 Greenleaf Avenue
Historic Uptown Whittier, California

562-945-9462

New Proprietors...It's Teatime At...Past Tyme Tea Parlour. Pleasant fragrances, unique gifts and soft music seem to greet you as you open the door to Past Tyme. The gracious new proprietors of this Victorian theme tea parlour are Chris and her daughter Noelle. We really enjoyed our chat on a recent visit to Historic Uptown Whittier. A section of the parlour is dedicated to gifts and tea accessories including an extensive and unique collection of tea-related jewelry, paintings and floral pieces.

Afternoon Tea is served at tables set with hand-pressed vintage linens, flowers & fine china. The tearoom area with a cheery wall mural is located through the "Wisteria" arbor. Drop by for an impromptu pot of tea & cookies almost anytime but be sure to make reservations for Afternoon, Cream, Dessert & Queen's Tea. Dining is away from the gift area, quite perfect for private tea parties.

$12.95 Afternoon Tea... Assorted tea sandwiches, homemade scone served with cream & jam, seasonal fresh fruit, various sweets & chocolates & pots of brewed loose tea on request.
$10.95 Dessert Tea... Homemade scone served with cream & jam, fresh seasonal fruit, various sweets and pots of tea.
$7.95 Cream Tea... Homemade scone served with cream & jam, seasonal fresh fruit & pots of brewed loose tea on request.

TEATIME: 11:30am To 4:00pm • Tuesday Thru Sunday
- May Accommodate Some Dietary Needs, 3 Day Advance Request
- Non-Caffeine/Herbal Tea Available
- Children's Tea Parties Welcome
- Watercloset: Same Floor • Wheelchair Accessible
- **24 Hour Advance Reservation Requested**
- Three Hour Free, Parking Lot
- Credit Cards: V,MC&DIS

Proprietor's
*Autograph*_____*Date*_____

BRISTOL FARMS

6227 Topanga Canyon Boulevard
Woodland Hills, California

What The World Is Coming To.

818-227-8400

New Addition...Host A Tea Party With Help From Bristol Farms. Teas, as we all know are fun & popular events for any or no occasion at all! I'm often asked at book signings about my own tea parties. Afternoon Teas at home are especially fun for me because I get a chance to be creative and bring out my pretty vintage plates, teacups, teapots, vases & Victorian lace. I keep my list of guests to eight friends for ease of conversation. Setting the table the day before really saves time. I also set a tea strainer for each guest.

Early in the day I pick dewy garden flowers, plunge them into squeaky clean vases of water and head to Bristol Farms in South Pasadena. I buy one large container each of tuna, chicken & seafood salads. Next, a stop at their bakery for 24 pre-ordered mini, or 8 large scones, 3 different loaves of bread for cookie-cutter shaped tea sandwiches and a dozen mini chocolate eclairs and cream puffs. I choose two 16 oz. jars of preserves & 3 small jars of lemon curd. I make my own cream, but they usually have clotted cream if you like. Edible blossoms, strawberries, grapes, kiwi, bananas & star fruit are a must. An extra bunch of flowers, and I'm off! To make your tea party more fun & "interactive" ask each of your guests to bring a different small package of tea. With individual teapots, it encourages tea-tasting & is a neat conversation facilitator. (But that's another book!) With 8 guests it's easier to have plates preset with 3 tea sandwiches, edible flowers, melange of fruit & a "teacup" of soup made from 4 packages of creamy asparagus soup to which I add pre-cooked fresh asparagus bits. Scones are on individual plates. My bread pudding made from the bread crusts is great! F.Y.I.If you prefer, pick-up a catered tea from Bristol Farms!

TEATIME SHOPPING: 8:00am To 9:00pm • Seven Days A Week
• May Accommodate Some Dietary Needs With Advance Request
• Tins Of Non-Caffeine/Herbal Tea Available
• Wheelchair Accessible • Watercloset: Same Floor
• Large Free Parking Lot
• Credit Cards:V,MC,DIS&AE
Manager's
*Autograph*_____*Date*_____

CAMBRIDGE CUPBOARD

22456 Ventura Boulevard
Woodland Hills, California

818-225-7316

It's Teatime At...The Cambridge Cupboard. This quaint English shop opened nearly 20 years ago exclusively as an English grocery store. Anne's customers were anxious for the Afternoon Tea experience and encouraged her to start serving tea.

Afternoon Tea is served in a relaxed and informal setting at The Cambridge Cupboard. Tables are set with with imported English china and sandwiches are presented in a silver-toned wedding basket. You may dine inside seated at English Oak tables with benchwood chairs & rose floral cushions or outside on the patio. The interior is cozy and intimate with green moire & rosebud wall covering and wainscotting. A full menu of English specialties is available. Browse around, you'll find a selection of British groceries & gifts. Private tea parties may be arranged for up to 30 guests. Parties of at least twenty guests will have the room to themselves. Anne says, "We get quite a bit more gussie for private tea parties."

$11.50 Full Set Tea... Assorted finger sandwiches, (vegetarian friendly), two fresh baked scones served with jam & Double Devon cream, or two crumpets with lemon curd & butter or your choice from the dessert cart and a pot of brewed tea.

$5.00 Cream Tea... Two scones served with double Devon cream & preserves, or special English desserts, or two crumpets and lemon curd, and a pot of brewed tea.

TEATIME: 2:00pm To 3:30pm • Tuesday Thru Friday
- 1:15pm To 3:00pm • Saturday & Sunday
- May Accommodate Some Dietary Needs, 1 Week Advance Request
- Non-Caffeine/Herbal Tea Available
- Children's Tea Parties Welcome
- Watercloset: Same Floor • Wheelchair Accessible
- **Reservations Are A Must**
- Free Parking Lot
- Credit Cards: V&MC

Proprietor's
*Autograph*_____*Date*_____

LITTLE WOMEN
21938 Costanso Street
Woodland Hills, California

818-348-3320

Little Girls Tea Parties At...Little Women. Little girls 5 years old and up, have fun and memorable dress-up tea parties at Little Women. Tea parties have become quite the fashion, these proprietors opened their doors in 1992 for what has become a very special way to celebrate your little girl's birthday or that special event in her young life. The children are treated to an afternoon of playing "grown-up". Miss Beth and Miss Sarah have found what brings glee to these little women's hearts!

Upon arrival, the children are greeted in a darling Victorian style parlor and escorted to the dressing room where they select feather boas, hats, purses, gloves and sparkly costume jewelry for their day of "glamour". This includes of course, make-up, nail polish and just the right hairdo. Miss Sarah and Miss Beth seem to have as much fun as the girls do. The teatime meal is served from silver tiered trays, all rather elegant and lady like.

Little Women also has theme teas including a Teddy Bear Tea in December and a Dolly and Me Tea in May. A tea party runs about 2 hours and can accommodate 8 to 20 young ladies ages five years old and up. Host parents are welcome to stay. A keepsake photo of each child is a nice touch. P.S.Ask about etiquette classes.

$325.00 Tea Party For 8 Girls...($22.00 each additional child) Tea sandwiches, Birthday Girl's personal take home cake, assorted fancy desserts and red raspberry "tea."

LITTLE GIRL'S TEA PARTIES: Minimum 8 Guests
• May Accommodate Some Dietary Needs With Advance Request
• Red Raspberry Caffeine Free "Tea"
• Watercloset: Same Floor
• **Please Call Early To Reserve Your Party Date**
• Metered Street Parking
• Cash Or Check

Proprietor's
*Autograph*_____*Date*_____

THE IVY COTTAGE
Tea Room
4973 Yorba Ranch Road
Yorba Linda, California

714-693-0531

It's Teatime At...The Ivy Cottage Tea Room. Well-named, The Ivy Cottage Tea Room has a beautifully trellised romantic Victorian garden atmosphere with ivy accents everywhere. Colorful and artistic signs at the doorway beckon you to enter.

Afternoon Tea is served at vintage tables set with fine china, fresh flowers and Battenburg lace or Waverly table coverings. The proprietors have created a warm tea-friendly atmosphere here. Linger a while after tea and browse through the darling Ivy Cottage Shop with its 6 or 7 cabinets brimming with great gift items. The shop has attractive seasonal decorations but Fall and Christmas are extra special. Please call for seasonal shop hours. P.S. Private tea parties for 15-32 guests are Ivy Cottage's specialty, call for details.

$19.95 Special Event Theme Teas... The Ivy Cottage features special event theme teas which include, Hats Off To You, Queen For A Day, Daddy And Me, Victorian White Linen, Best Of Friends and Teddy Bear Picnic, call for a schedule of these events.

$17.95 "The Ivy Cottage" Special Tea... Fruit scone served with jam & Devonshire cream, petite quiche, English tea sandwiches, fresh salad, sweet surprise, a pot of brewed loose tea.

$12.95 Sweet Surprise Tea.. Scone, Devonshire cream & preserves, dessert & brewed loose tea. Tuesday thru Friday only.

TEATIME: 11:30am & 1:00pm • Tuesday Thru Friday
- 11:30am & 3:30pm, Saturday • 1:00pm, Sunday
- May Accommodate Some Dietary Needs, 1 Week Advance Request
- Non-Caffeine/Herbal Tea Available
- Children's Tea Parties Welcome
- Watercloset: Same Floor
- **Reservations Are A Must**
- Free Off-Street Parking
- Credit Cards: DIS,MC,V&AE

Proprietor's
*Autograph*_____*Date*_____

TEA & TEACUPS
adjoining Traditional Elegance

18160 Imperial Highway
(Yorba Linda Station Plaza)
Yorba Linda, California

714-572-9825

New Addition...It's Teatime At...Tea & Teacups. This delightful English Tea Room adjoins Traditional Elegance which is Mike & Sarah's well-appointed gift shop & design studio. Sarah is an Interior Designer and her artistic talents are exhibited everywhere. The tearoom is decorated in burgundy and green with delicate ivy stenciling, Wainscoting, teacup border prints, lace curtains & framed prints. The deep tone pattern carpet and Windsor-style chairs with tapestry seats nicely complement the decor. In addition, there is a decorative fireplace and trickling wall fountain.

Afternoon Teas are artistically prepared on premises by Mary Lou and her friendly staff. Tables are set with English bone china, pretty teapots, sugar cubes in porcelain baskets, unique tablecloths with toppers, and petite vases of fresh flowers. Ask about the special event & theme teas which take place throughout the year. P.S. Private tea parties may be arranged for 22 to 28 guests. F.Y.I. The room fee is waived for parties up to two hours in length.

$10.95 Elegant Tea... Assorted tea sandwiches, English scone served with imported Devonshire cream & strawberry jam, a unique dessert, and a pot of brewed loose tea.

TEATIME: 10:30am To 5:30pm • Monday Thru Friday
• 10:30am To 5:00pm, Saturday • 11:00am To 4:00pm, Sunday
• May Accommodate Some Dietary Needs With Advance Request
• Non-Caffeine/Herbal Tea Available
• Children's Tea Parties Welcome
• Watercloset: Same Floor
• **Reservations Are Recommended**
• Free Parking Lot
• Credit Cards: V&MC

Proprietor's
*Autograph*_____*Date*_____

Photo courtesy of Carole Weingarten

I think what you need my dear is a nice cup of tea.

328

Nevada

PABLO'S PERKASSO
inside The Sampler Shoppes
6115 West Tropicana
Las Vegas, Nevada

702-362-0499 *Reservations*   **702-368-1170** *The Sampler*

New Addition...It's Teatime At...Pablo's Perkasso. An "antique nut" as she calls herself, Lita a former antique dealer turned proprietor of Perkasso's has filled her tearoom with loads of antiques. Her tearoom has a trickling fountain and she did have a fireplace, but someone bought it! Originally from Louisiana, Lita serves up Southern hospitality & homemade specialties that she bakes herself. P.S. You may want to order ahead so you can take home Lita's fresh baked Rum Cake, Cream Cheese Pound Cake, her famous Quiche or Southern Style Pecan Pie.

Afternoon Tea is served at antiquey tables set with tablecloths, vintage china, and vintage teacup & teapot centerpieces with gently dried flowers. F.Y.I. If you prefer al fresco dining, please note that the new spray misting devices make outdoor patio dining comfortable, even in the hot summer months. Private tea parties available for 6-25 guests. Allow time for treasure hunting.

$14.95 High Tea... Fruit compote, three tea sandwiches, scones, lemon curd & jam, sweets, and a pot of brewed loose tea.
$10.95 Teatime... Cream cheese & cucumber demi-sandwich, cream cheese on sweet bread, fresh fruit served with cream, and a large pot of brewed loose gourmet tea.
$7.95 Children's Tea Parties...(Per Child) Fruit, mini scones, three tea sandwiches, goodies & sweets and tea or cocoa.

TEATIME: 2:00pm To 4:00pm • Seven Days A Week
• May Accommodate Some Dietary Needs With Advance Request
• Non-Caffeine/Herbal Tea Available
• Children's Tea Parties Welcome
• **Reservations Required Only For High Tea**
• Free Parking Lot
• Credit Cards: V&MC
Proprietor's
*Autograph*_____*Date*_____

TRICIA'S TEAS
inside Red Rooster
Antique Mall

1109 Western Avenue
Las Vegas, Nevada

702-876-0682

It's Teatime At...Tricia's Teas. (By Reservation)"Las Vegas' best kept secret!"A very special and whimsical Afternoon Tea for tea lovers from 5 to 95! The fun begins when you're greeted at "grandmother's parlor" by one of Tricia's etiquette-perfect, tea-lady personas. Remember the fun of playing dress-up? If you have a favorite vintage outfit, this is the place to wear it! Guests may borrow hats (gents included), boas, gloves, and period costume jewelry to complete your "dress for tea" ensemble! Guests have 30 minutes to adorn themselves before Patricia "rings."

Aside from the delectable treats there's lots of lace, antiques, a collection of fine china & silver, over 300 vintage hats & amusing parlor games to entertain you. My father actually balanced a spoon on his nose! Patricia is a hoot, and this is a neat spot for a tea party. You can be sure she'll dream up something special. The $20.00 room rental fee per party is well spent. P.S. Book early, especially for large parties. F.Y.I. Tea for Two, by special request is $65.00. Private tea parties are available for 5 to 20 guests. Have fun!

$20.00 Angel Tea... These heavenly events take place in November & December. No hats for this tea, you'll don angel wings & halos, the menu is simply *divine*. Please call for schedule.
$15.00 Afternoon Tea... Finger sandwiches, scone with Devonshire cream & jam, pastries may include rock cakes, lemon bars or Madelines, fresh fruit, and a pot of properly prepared tea.

TEA PARTIES FOR GROUPS: Minimum Five Guests
- May Accommodate Some Dietary Needs, 7 Day Advance Request
- Non-Caffeine/Herbal Tea Available By Advance Request
- Children's Tea Parties Welcome, Ages 5+
- Watercloset: A Jaunt Away
- **Reservations Are A Must! At Least One Week In Advance**
- Off-Street Parking
- Cash Or Check

Proprietor's
*Autograph*_____Date_____

The Junior League's
COUNTRY GARDEN RESTAURANT
inside Arlington Garden Mall

606 West Plumb Lane
Reno, Nevada

702-825-0213

Tea Parties For Groups At...Country Garden Restaurant. (For 20 To 100 Guests) The Junior League of Reno is the proud proprietor of Country Garden Restaurant. This quaint European style tearoom is a registered historical landmark. At one time however, it was a garden nursery and then a teahouse. Country Country is open for lunch and private tea parties.Please call for the Holiday Etiquette Theme Tea schedule.

Afternoon Tea is served in the lovely dining room decorated in tones of sage and burgundy. Two sets of French doors lead out onto the cobblestone courtyard which is a fine spot for tea during the summer months, weather permitting. Dine at umbrella tables surrounded by lattice, plants and garden greenery. P.S. Country Garden offers catering and will be happy to bring a tea party to you.

$10.00ish Afternoon Tea... Tea sandwiches, scone served with butter & preserves, tea breads such as cranberry, banana-nut, and cinnamon-apple, desserts such as mini-tarts or "Kahlua" fudge squares, a continuous cup of the famous spiced tea. (Per person, plus tax, gratuity and room fee.)

$25.00 Holiday Inspired Afternoon Etiquette Teas. Please call for details & dates of these teas.

TEA PARTIES FOR GROUPS: By Reservation For 20-100 Guests
- May Accommodate Some Dietary Needs With Advance Request
- Non-Caffeine/Herbal Tea • Children's Tea Parties Welcome
- Watercloset: Same Floor • Wheelchair Accessible
- **Please Reserve Your Party Date Early**
- Mall Parking Lot
- Credit Cards: MC,V&AE

Manager's
Autograph _____*Date*_____

Oregon

You'll take home beautiful memories of the Pacific Northwest.

FLINN'S TEA PARLOUR
222 First Avenue West
Albany, Oregon

541-928-5008   800-636-5008

New Addition...Historic Saturday Theme Teas & Tea Parties For Groups At...Flinn's Tea Parlour. Tea is served in fashionable Victorian style at Flinn's, literally! The proprietors Ellen and Bill are dressed in Victorian garb when they greet & serve their guests. Flinn's Living History Institute, Theater & Tea Parlour are major tourist attractions. Ellen told me that Bill is an awesome baker and that his breads are absolutely marvelous. (I'm thinking of having a loaf overnighted!) Flinn's Tea Time always features interesting historic recipes which are colorfully described by your tea hostess. The menu varies weekly.

Afternoon Tea is served in three courses at tables set with lacey tablecloths, centerpieces, and mis-matched china. The teas are "theme-creative" and include "Father's Chocolate Galaxy Tea," a Halloween Tea with ghost puffs & candied bat guava, Martha Washington Tea, etc, etc, etc. Theme Teas take place every Saturday and are all different! F.Y.I. Groups who meet the minimum number may enjoy Tea Time anytime during the week. You may opt for a Tour of Historic Homes, theater or a Covered Bridge Tour with tea.

$13.25 Flinn's Tea Time... "The Tea Breads" include scones and scrumptious homebaked bread served with butter & jams, there is also "The Tea Sandwiches & Delicacies," "The Tea Sweet Things," and The Pot of Tea," brewed loose.

TEATIME: 12Noon To 4:00pm, Saturday
- May Accommodate Some Dietary Needs With Advance Request
- Non-Caffeine/Herbal Tea Available
- Children's Tea Parties Welcome, Ages 5+
- Watercloset: Same Floor
- Wheelchair Accessible
- **Reservations Are Required For All Teas**
- Free Parking Lot Across The Street
- Cash Or Check

Proprietor's
*Autograph*_____*Date*_____

335

For many of us, our love of roses begins early.

ANGELINA'S
French Country Tea Parlor

21317 Highway 99 East
Aurora, Oregon

503-678-3303

New Addition...It's Teatime At...Angelina's French Country Tea Parlor. Just 20 minutes from downtown Portland in historic Aurora you'll be delighted to discover Angelina's, named after the oldest tea parlour in Paris. Marilyn, the ebullient proprietor has perfected the fine art of elegant tearoom hostessing. She does it all, every detail! She even fills the water glasses by wearing white gloves to carry a chilled decanter of water surrounded by roses in ice! A pampered experience awaits you at her adorable tea parlor in a restored 1875 cottage, on 2.5 acres.

Afternoon Tea is served at tables set with lace tablecloths, fresh flowers and an eclectic collection of new & vintage china. If you simply must have that teacup, chances are it's for sale. By the way, this is a fine spot to don a favorite chapeau or borrow one from Marilyn's vintage collection. There is a lace museum on the second floor too, be sure to stop by. Allow time to browse, there are well-chosen gift and clothing accessories throughout the parlor. Ask about Children's Dress-Up Teas and Etiquette Classes. This is a perfect spot for your special event tea parties for up to 25 guests.

$22.50 Royal Tea... Assorted tea sandwiches tied in ribbons, strawberries in cream, fresh baked scone served with Devonshire cream & homemade Champagne jelly, French brie, apple & pear slices, shortbread, English trifle or "hat"petit four and Angelina's special blend teas or imported French tea.

TEATIME: 4:00pm • Wednesday, Friday, Saturday & Sunday
• Non-Caffeine/Herbal Tea Available
• Children's Tea Parties Welcome, Ages 4+
• Watercloset: First Floor • Wheelchair Accessible On First Floor
• **Reservations Are A Must** • Free Parking Lot
• Cash Or Check

Proprietor's
*Autograph*_____ *Date*_____

BARBARA ANN'S
Tea Room & Gift Parlour
116 West Main Street
Carlton, Oregon

503-852-4440

New Addition...It's Teatime At...Barbara Ann's Tea Room & Gift Parlour. Move over popcorn, hello tea, it's show time! You can't miss the marquee announcing Barbara Ann's Tea Room & Gift Parlour. Why it's the old Carlton Theater built around in 1920's when Carlton was a thriving logging town. I have to say, this is a rather unique spot for a tearoom.

Afternoon Tea is served at tables set with ecru lace tablecloths, teacup centerpieces, tea strainers and mis-matched china, by servers in tea length skirts. Barbara Ann describes her pink tearoom as having a cozy "village tea shop" atmosphere complete with lace curtains and teapot & teacup framed prints. Allow time in the gift parlour. Barbara Ann's carries collectible little tea sets, fine china, linens, cozies, silver-plated accouterments, packaged scone mix, Walker shortbread, packaged teas & more. Many of the products & teas are packaged under the Barbara Ann label. P.S. You may want to inquire about mail-order products too.

$12.50 Afternoon Tea.. Tea sandwiches, scone, savory, fresh fruit, cookie, and a choice of brewed loose teas.

$6.50 Garden Tea... Scone, tart, cheese, choice of tea.

$5.50 Nursery Tea... Scone or cinnamon toast, fruit filled tart, banana & jam sandwich and fruit, hot chocolate or tea.

TEATIME: 11:00am To 5:00pm • Tuesday Thru Saturday
• Please Call For Possible Extended Summer Hours
• Sunday For Groups, By Advance Reservation
• May Accommodate Some Dietary Needs With Advance Request
• Non-Caffeine/Herbal Tea Available
• Watercloset: Same Floor • Children's Menu Available
• **Reservations Are Appreciated For Parties Of 4 Or More**
• Limited Time Street Parking
• Credit Cards: V&MC

Proprietor's
*Autograph*_____*Date*_____

THE CAMPBELL HOUSE
A City Inn
252 Pearl Street
Eugene, Oregon

541-343-1119

New Addition...Theme Teas In May & December, And Private Tea Parties At...The Campbell House. The Campbell House was built in 1892 for Idaho Cogswell Frazer, a gift from her father John Cogswell. The house was vacant for nearly 20 years when Myra bought and refurbished this vine covered house...talk about a secret garden! Myra does has a passion for gardens and saw the potential here.

These very popular Afternoon Teas are served in the library, dining room or parlor at tables set with white Damask linens, fresh flowers, and matching fine china place settings. Tea specialties are presented on tiered caddies by Judith, Lydia, and the gracious staff clad in dresses with handmade white aprons. Ask to tour the Inn which is beautifully decorated in Victorian tones of hunter green, cranberry & rose. Don't miss the tiny gift shop near the front foyer. Tea parties are available for up to 50 guests. A room fee is required for fewer guests. Please visit at: http//www.campbellhouse.com

$16.00-$18.00 Mother's Day High Tea & Victorian Christmas & Holiday Teas... Fruit mousse or fruit cup, assorted finger sandwiches, homemade scones with preserves, crumpets, mini desserts, a continuous cup of brewed Tetley's tea.

$8.00 Mini Mother's Day Tea... Tea in the gazebo or gardens, tea sandwiches, scone, dessert, a continuous cup of tea.

HOLIDAY TEAS: Call For Mother's Day & Christmas Tea Dates
• Non-Caffeine/Herbal Tea Available
• Children's Tea Parties Welcome
• Watercloset: Same Floor
• **Reservations Required For All Except Mini Mother's Day Tea**
• Free Parking Lot
• Credit Cards: V,MC,DIS&AE

Proprietor's
*Autograph*_____*Date*_____

Shelton-
McMurphey-
Johnson
House

SHELTON-McMURPHEY-JOHNSON House

303 Willamette Street
Eugene, Oregon

541-484-0808

New Addition...Teatime Sunday & High Tea In April & November As Scheduled At...Shelton-McMurphey-Johnson House. If only there were a "month of Sundays!" You see, on the first Sunday of the month the Victorian Queen Anne Revival, Shelton-McMurphey-Johnson House sponsors their sociable "Tea Time." This fabulous 1888 Victorian home is now owned & managed by the city of Eugene and staffed by dedicated volunteers & Jan, the director & events coordinator.

High Teas are very special and popular events so do reserve your spot early. Tables are set with tablecloths, fresh flowers, bone china teacups & mis-matched vintage accessories. Tea is graciously served by the costumed Junior Docents. Live music wafts throughout the house while a story teller visits each table of guests to tell a special story for them only. P.S. Tea admission also includes a tour of the house & shopping in the Victorian Gift Shop.

$12.50 High Teas... First Sunday in November & third Sunday in April. Tea sandwiches, mini scones, fresh seasonal fruit, homemade desserts including lemon tarts, tea breads, cakes & cookies, steaming pots of English Breakfast & Rose Mint Tea.

$4.00 Tea Time Sunday... Mini scones, dessert, pot of brewed loose tea. Drop in without reservations.

TEATIME SUNDAY: 1:00pm To 4:00pm
- May Accommodate Some Dietary Needs With Advance Request
- Non-Caffeine/Herbal Tea Available
- Children's Tea Parties Welcome
- Watercloset: Same Floor
- **Reservations & Prepay Are Required For High Teas Only**
- Free Parking Lot, Then A Short Walk Up The Hill
- Cash Or Check

Proprietor's
*Autograph*_____*Date*_____

LOVEJOY'S
Restaurant & Tearoom

195 Nopal Street
Old Town Florence, Oregon

541-902-0502

New Addition...It's Teatime At...Lovejoy's. Marianne and Martin started the Lovejoy's Restaurant & Tearoom tradition in the San Francisco Bay area. Their recent move to Oregon has resulted in another Lovejoy's, plus a British Grocery & Deli. The shop was named after the famous British detective & antique dealer Lovejoy, a character on British TV, by author Jonathan Gash.

Afternoon Tea, plus British lunch & dinner specials are available in addition to Afternoon Tea. Tea is served in a living room atmosphere at tables set with tablecloths, fresh flowers and a collection of English bone china. Almost everything here is for sale. The tearoom features plaid lacey curtains, seven chandeliers & antique furnishings. The proprietors are quite knowledgeable about antiques, you're bound to find that something special. Tea parties are available for up to 40 guests. Bulk teas & British gifts too.

$9.95 High Tea... Tea sandwiches, two salads, two scones with Devon cream & preserves, dessert, pot of brewed tea.
$7.75 Light Tea... Sandwich, scones with Devon cream & luxury strawberry preserves, a petite dessert, and a pot of brewed loose Taylor of Harrogate Tea or non-caffeine Yorkshire Gold.
$5.95 Cream Tea... Fruit scone, Devon cream & luxury strawberry preserves, brewed loose pot of the tearoom blend.

TEATIME: 2:00pm To 5:00pm • Tuesday Thru Sunday
• Hours Are Seasonal • Closed Monday Off-Season
• May Accommodate Some Dietary Needs With Advance Request
• Non-Caffeine/Herbal Tea Available
• Children's Tea Parties Welcome
• Watercloset: Same Floor • Wheelchair Accessible
• **Reservations Are Requested For Your Comfort**
• Free Parking Lot
• Credit Cards: V,MC&DIS

Proprietor's
*Autograph*_____*Date*_____

ANNIE FENWICK'S
Restaurant & Tea Room

336 North Main Street, Suite B
Gresham, Oregon

503-667-3768

New Addition...It's Teatime At...Annie Fenwick's Restaurant & Tea Room. What a pleasure talking to Jan the gifted proprietor of this fun tea spot. Jan has created a delightful indoor garden at Annie's complete with a hand-painted sky, watering-can fountain, lacey curtains and sponge painted walls.

High Tea is served along with a full menu of homemade specialties. You'll find unique scones too, thanks to the in-house scone bakery. Tables are set with colorful black floral tablecloths & white toppers, flowers & antique china. Sometimes this classically trained proprietor takes over the piano for a surprise tune! She is truly a one-woman band, ask her what she does in her spare time. Browse around, the shop has tea-related books, accoutrements & gifts. Ask Jan about Holiday Theme Teas, especially the 5 course Nutcracker Tea, Victorian Tea & Dickens' Tea in December with the unforgettable flaming plum pudding. Tea parties & evening teas too.

$14.95 "High Tea"...8-10 Tea sandwiches, 5-6 hot & cold savories, scone, (white chocolate, apricot, carmel-apple, lemon creme, triple chocolate, fresh raspberry, coconut Bavarian or oatmeal-honey, etc.) with Devonshire cream & raspberry jam, fruit with heart shaped watermelon slice, 7-12 desserts, & brewed loose Xanadu tea poured from silver teapots. Tea selection may change.
$7.95 Tea Sandwiches...16! Two of each & fresh fruit.

TEATIME: 11:30am-5pm, Tuesday-Friday •11:30am-4pm, Saturday
- May Accommodate Some Dietary Needs With Advance Request
- Non-Caffeine/Herbal Tea Available
- Children's Tea Parties Welcome
- Watercloset: Same Floor • Wheelchair Accessible
- **Reservations Are Advised**
- Free Street Parking & Nearby Lots
- Cash Or Personal Checks

Proprietor's
*Autograph*_____*Date*_____

STRATFORD HOUSE
207 East Main Street
Hillsboro, Oregon

503-648-7139

New Addition...It's Teatime At...Stratford House. This historic 100 year old two-story building is home to a sweet gift shop and a little tearoom hidden in back. Welcome to Steve and Alice's Stratford House Gift Shop & Tearoom. Alice loves the fancy, detailed, artistic aspect of Afternoon Tea and it shows! There seems to be no limit to her patience as demonstrated when she sugar frosts fresh grapes or "dresses" her lemon baskets. She even skillfully carves flowers out of oranges during the winter, when flowers are out of season in Oregon.

Afternoon Tea is presented on a three tiered stand at tables at with antique china & silver. Each course is served at the sound of a bell! Special Event Teas are scheduled throughout the year, about 14 of them! The novel "Guilt Free" low fat Tea is in January. (Perfect for that holiday indulging!) The decor is Victorian with jewel tone linens, fresh flowers, decorative mantels and vintage cupboards. A unique chandelier & silver slop bowl are at each table. Steve and Alice dress in period garb to add to the fun. You may borrow hats & boas. Ask about private tea parties & Mommy & Me Tea too.

$19.95 Special Event "High Tea"... Six courses. Finger sandwiches & warm savories, scones with Devonshire cream & lemon curd, soup, fresh fruit, dessert, pot of brewed loose tea.
$14.95 Traditional Afternoon Tea... Tea sandwiches, scone, Devonshire cream, fruit, decadent dessert, a pot of loose tea.

TEATIME: 3:00pm • Tuesday, Wednesday & Thursday
• Please Call For Schedule Of Saturday Special Event Teas
• May Accommodate Some Dietary Needs With Advance Request
• Non-Caffeine/Herbal Tea Available
• Children's Tea Parties Welcome
• Watercloset: Same Floor • Wheelchair Accessible
• **24 Hour Advance Reservations A Must & Guarantee Required**
• Two Hour Unmetered Street Parking
• Credit Cards: V&MC
Proprietor's
*Autograph*_____*Date*_____

343

THE TEA COTTAGE

235 East California Street
Jacksonville, Oregon

541-899-7777

New Name...New Proprietor...It's Teatime At...The Tea Cottage. Meet Susan & Lisa, the new proprietors of The Tea Cottage formerly known as Brit-ish Fare. This building was once the property of local dentist Dr. Will Jackson and his wife Hattie Thompson Jackson. Hattie bought the property sometime around the late 1860's for $600.00 in gold coin. Ask Susan about the narrow escapes experienced by Will and Hattie. Their history is very interesting and she will be happy to fill you in.

Tea For Two Deluxe is presented from tiered caddies at tables set with tablecloths, fresh flowers, cloth napkins, and Churchill England Blue & White Willow or English Royal Wessex, fine china. Soft background music and prompt friendly service is part of the picture at The Tea Cottage. Through the years the building was used as a residence, dental office, telephone exchange office, antique shop & tearoom before becoming The Tea Cottage. Enjoy authentic British teatime specialties in the Victorian, Welsh or English theme tearooms. Allow time to browse, there are Victorian treasures in the gift shop which is situated at the rear of the building.

$17.50 Tea For Two Deluxe... Assorted finger sandwiches, scone, cream & jam, dessert du jour & brewed house tea. Add $1.00 for flavored teas, $.25 for homemade lemon curd.

$6.95 Sherlock Holmes... Daily special, soup or garden salad & a pot of brewed house tea.

$3.95 CottageTea... Scone, cream & jam & brewed tea.

TEATIME: 11:00pm To 4:00pm • Tuesday Thru Saturday
- Non-Caffeine/Herbal Tea Available
- Watercloset: Same Floor
- **Reservations Are Encouraged For More Than 2 Guests**
- Unmetered Limited Time Street Parking
- Credit Cards: V&MC

Proprietor's
*Autograph*_____*Date*_____

LADY DI'S
420 Second Street
Lake Oswego, Oregon

503-635-7298

It's Time For Tea & A Scone At...Lady Di's. This is a sweet Tudor-style shop complete with an English garden walkway. This shop located in lovely Lake Oswego is well known by locals for its variety of imported British foods and gifts. Diane, the proprietor calls it, "Your British Connection."

You may request your Cream Tea to be served in the very popular tiny Tea Cozy Room which looks very much like a miniature living room with a fireplace & a little dresser. It seats 7 guests. Fresh flowers, English Royal Vale fine china, and pink or green tablecloths adorn the tea tables. The interior of the shop has cream colored walls, lacey curtains, and features British memorabilia.Shop hours are 10:00am to 5pm, Monday thru Saturday. If you would like to take tea in the Tea Cozy Room, please call and reserve the spot. F.Y.I. Lady Di's also carries specialties from South Africa such as Rooibos Tea, Five Roses Tea, Peck's Anchovette & Mrs. Ball's Chutney.

$4.50 Cream Tea...A sultana raisin scone served with Devonshire cream & strawberry jam and a pot of brewed tea.

TEA & SCONES: 10:30am To 3:30pm • Monday Thru Saturday
• Non-Caffeine/Herbal Teas Available
• Watercloset: Same Floor
• **Reserve Only For The Tea Cozy Room**
• Unmetered Street Parking
• Credit Cards: V,MC&AE
Proprietor's
*Autograph*_____*Date*_____

YOUR HOUSE OR MINE

117 South College Street
Newberg, Oregon

503-538-7155   503-281-0001

New Addition...Private Tea Parties At...Your House Or Mine. Suzanne and Cathie are the two ambitious proprietors of this tea spot. Their collaboration began a number of years ago when they realized their knack for simple creative solutions to home organization and seasonal interior decoration. Their love of artistry in the home, as well as of cooking & baking, prompted them to host English Teas. Soon they started "Your House or Mine." Although teas are usually presented in the dining room of Cathie's 1896 Queen Anne Victorian home, they may also take place at Suzanne's, or at your own home.

Afternoon Tea at Cathie's can accommodate 6 to 16 guests at one or two tables set with linens, fresh flowers & fine china. The interior is eclectic with quilts, wicker furnishings, gorgeous original crown molding, taupe walls, plate & picture rails, a tea cart and artistic seasonal accessories highlighted by the pretty yellow & white pinstripe window treatment. Guests gather in the living room while waiting for their party, then proceed down the entry hall to pick out a vintage hat, gloves and boa which they may borrow for tea. P.S. Ask about High Teas and tea parties at "Your House."

$15.00 Afternoon Tea...(Per Person) Fresh baked cream & currant scones served with homemade blackberry & raspberry preserves, assorted finger sandwiches, compote of fresh fruit, shortbread, something chocolate & surprise sweets, and a continuous cup of loose tea.

PRIVATE TEA PARTIES: By Appointment Only For 6-16 Guests
- May Accommodate Some Dietary Needs With Advance Request
- Non-Caffeine/Herbal Tea Available
- Children's Tea Paries Welcome, Ages 8+
- **Advance Prepaid Reservations Required**
- Unlimited, Unmetered Street Parking
- Cash Or Check

Proprietor's
*Autograph*_____*Date*_____

A Spot of Tea   *Newport, Oregon*

TEA & TOMES
716 N.W. Beach Drive
Newport, Oregon

541-265-2867

*New Tearoom Brewing...*It's Teatime At...Tea & Tomes. Be sure to mention to "Tuppence" and Bert that you found their interesting new tearoom in this tome! They have been arduously working on Tea & Tomes, their Victorian style tearoom which is planned to open soon in the heart of downtown Nye Beach. Built in 1910, this three-story building was once home to live theater and probably vaudeville too. Sometime in the 1920's or 30's it became Newport's first movie house, in use until the late 1950's when it became a clothing store. Little remains of the old theater, only fir hardwood floors & bearded board wainscotting.

The new proprietors have a great vision for Tea & Tomes. Afternoon Tea will be served at overstuffed couches or traditional tables with lace tablecloths, fresh flowers, and a collection of mismatched china. Light specialties and bakery treats will also be offered. English cast iron old coal burning fireplaces are part of the decor, but they will be used to keep guests warm on chilly overcast beach days. The gift side of the shoppe will feature unique books, specialty foods, gifts and tea accouterments. Private tea parties are available. Ask about the original sloped theater floor.

$6.95 To $9.95 Afternoon Tea... Expected to include tea sandwiches, scone, sweets and brewed loose Twinning teas.

ANTICIPATED **TEATIME:** 11am To 5:00pm • Closed Wednesday
• May Accommodate Some Dietary Needs With Advance Request
• Non-Caffeine/Herbal Tea Available
• Children's Tea Parties Welcome, Ages 3+
• Watercloset: First Floor
• Wheelchair Accessible
• **Reservation Appreciated For Parties Of Six Or More**
• Free Parking Lot
• Credit Cards: Please Call
Proprietor's
*Autograph*_____*Date*_____

BRITISH TEA GARDEN
725 S.W. Tenth Avenue
Portland, Oregon

503-221-7817

It's Teatime At...British Tea Garden. Here's a delightful spot for Afternoon Tea & British specialties. Partake of Afternoon Tea, Cornish Pasty, Ploughman's Lunch, Banger's & Mash or naughty but nice sweets, and so much more. Judith is the proprietor who started the whole thing, you'll get a kick out of her!

Afternoon Tea is served at tables set with colorful cloths and English Royal Doulton china. A variety of special tea events are held throughout the year including tea-leaf readings, children's tea parties, Sherlock Holmes Teas and a variety of musical events as well. One of the favorite musicians is the Celtic Harpist. (Pronounced Keltic) There's a British Tea Garden Gift Shop too.

$8.25 Garden Set Tea... Choice of finger sandwich (four triangles), scone served with Devonshire clotted cream & jam, fresh baked tart and a pot of house brewed loose tea if you choose.

$5.25 "Time For Tea" Scone... Served a la carte, with Devonshire clotted cream & jam and a pot of "specialty tea for one."

TEATIME: 10:00am To 6:00pm • Tuesday Thru Friday
- 10am To 5pm, Monday & Saturday • 12Noon To 4:00pm, Sunday
- May Accommodate Some Needs With Advance Request
- Non-Caffeine/Herbal Tea Available
- Children's Tea Parties Welcome
- Watercloset: Same Floor
- Wheelchair Accessible
- **Reservations Are Advised**
- Parking Structure Nearby
- Credit Cards:V,MC,DIS&AE

Proprietor's
*Autograph*_____*Date*_____

THE GATE LODGE
at Pittock Mansion
presents Yours Truly

3229 N.W. Pittock Drive
Portland, Oregon

503-823-3627 *Reservations*

New Addition...It's Teatime At...The Gate Lodge Tea Room...Presented By Yours Truly. Thanks to the Junior League of Portland and the City of Portland's Bureau of Parks, the renovated 1914 Italianate Pittock Mansion Gate Lodge opened its doors to the public in June 1984. The four-story lodge was strategically located on a steep hill that led to the mansion. The Gate Lodge was the residence of the gatekeeper, whose job was to open and close the gate to the mansion. Tour price is around $4.50.

A Teaplate and delectables are served by the tuxedo clad, Yours Truly staff. You may dine in the living room which features a fireplace & old framed prints, the master bedroom "Tearoom" with old family photos and French doors, or a converted upstairs bedroom with charming classic dormer windows. Tables are set with blue floral tablecloths and ivory floral Homer-Laughlin china. F.Y.I. The sweet Gift Shop is located in the carriage house. P.S. Wear comfortable walking shoes, or ask to be dropped off at The Gate Lodge. Private tea parties are available.Be sure to say hi to Gloria, the longtime hostess & manager of the tearoom.

$8.75 Tea Plate... Finger sandwiches, finger sweets, fruit, scones, mini-muffins and a pot of tea.

TEATIME: 11, 11:30, 1, 1:30, 3, 3:30 & 4pm • Daily In December
• Closed Christmas Day & Closed January 1, To January 23, Yearly
• February-November: Monday-Saturday, 11-2pm • No Sundays
• May Accommodate Some Dietary Needs With Advance Request
• Non-Caffeine/Herbal Tea Available
• **Reservations Appreciated, But During December, A Must**
• **Reservations & Prepay Deposit For 8+Guests Required**
• Free Parking Up The Hill At The Pittock
• Credit Cards: V,MC,DC&AE

Proprietor's
*Autograph*_____*Date*_____

THE HEATHMAN HOTEL

1001 S W Broadway (At Salmon)
Portland, Oregon

503-241-4100

It's Teatime At...The Heathman Hotel. Experience a very nice Afternoon Tea in this downtown Portland hotel. The historic Tea Court with its deep wood tones and late 18th century canvases by French landscape artist Claude Gellee is quite a handsome spot for Afternoon Tea. A beautiful chandelier which originally hung in a foreign embassy now graces the Tea Court, as does a vintage Eucalyptus tree circa 1926.

Afternoon Tea is served on "Lugano" Dudson fine English china. Susan Boulot the pastry chef, carefully designs the menu to enhance this age old observance which..."will transport you elegantly, to another place in time, and deliver you back refreshed." Tea plates are beautifully arranged and presented individually by lace-aproned tea servers at tables set with perfectly starched white linens. Non smoking. P.S. A great spot for business teas too.

$15.95 Heathman Afternoon Tea... Layered sandwich, crostini with tapenade & roasted pepper, scone, Mascarpone cream, butter cookie, tea tartlet,Tazo brewed loose tea.

$15.95 Holiday Teas... Always a sellout event, teas take place next to the Victorian two-story Christmas tree! Entertainment includes Dickens-like carolers and a harpist or harpsichordist regaling patrons with traditional Christmas music.

$7.95 Peter Rabbit Tea For Little Sippers... For guests 12 and under. Peanut butter & jam sandwich, tuna, carrot & raisin sandwich, cheddar blocks, fresh fruit, cookie and hot cocoa.

TEATIME: 2:00pm To 4:00pm • Seven Days A Week
- May Accommodate Dietary Needs, 1 Week Advance Request
- Non-Caffeine/Herbal Tea Available
- Children's Tea Parties Welcome
- Watercloset: Same Floor • Wheelchair Accessible
- **Reservations Are Appreciated**
- $2.00 Per Hour Valet Hotel Parking Before 5pm
- Credit Cards: V,MC,DC&AE

Proprietor's
*Autograph*_____*Date*_____

WILD ROSE TEA ROOM
adjacent to The Memory Shop

422 S.W .Sixth Street
Redmond, Oregon

541-923-3385

New Addition...It's Teatime At...Wild Rose Tea Room. I originally spoke with Bessie when she was open only a week, and my how things have progressed! We are very pleased to include her in our second edition. The "garden cottage" tearoom is neatly finger-sandwiched between two antique stores. Good friends, loyal family members and inspiration from great tea books made Bessie's dream of The Wild Rose a reality.

Afternoon Tea is served in an English garden setting filled with music, antiques, and the fragrant aromas of Miss Bessie's kitchen. Something good is always baking! Browse around, there are gifts and antiques to check out. Private tea parties, theme teas & children's dress-up tea parties are available for 15 to 40 guests.

$14.95 High Tea... Presented by reservation only, on Fridays & Saturdays. Seating At 11am, 1pm & 3pm. Please Call.
$7.95 Luncheon Plate... Assorted tea sandwiches, scone served with preserves, fruit, and a pot of brewed loose tea.
$6.95 Fruit Plate With Scone & Tea... Daily selection of scone with cream & lemon curd, fruit, a pot of brewed loose tea.
$2.25 Scone... Scone served with cream or lemon curd.

TEATIME: 10:00am To 4:30pm • Tuesday Thru Saturday
• May Accommodate Some Dietary Needs With Advance Request
• Non-Caffeine/Herbal Tea Available
• Children's Tea Parties Welcome
• Watercloset: Same Floor • Wheelchair Accessible
• **Reservations Are Suggested For Groups Of Six Or More**
• Limited Time Street Parking
• Credit Cards: V,MC,DIS,DC,AE&JCB
Proprietor's
*Autograph*_____*Date*_____

TUDOR ROSE
Tearoom & Gift Shoppe
480 Liberty Street S.E.
Salem, Oregon

503-588-2345

New Addition...It's Teatime On Wednesdays & Saturdays At...Tudor Rose Tearoom & Gift Shop. For more than a decade Tudor Rose Tearoom has been serving Afternoon Teas of distinction. New proprietors Bob & Terry are proud of their tearoom and look forward to meeting you.

Afternoon Tea is presented from two tiered caddies at tables set with pink tablecloths, lace toppers, cloth napkins & Johnson Bros."Friendly Village," ironstone. This cheery tearoom is decorated with floral wallpaper and floral prints. Relax with tea at a table that overlooks peaceful Pringle Creek. Browse around, Tudor Rose has a large gift shop. They stock British groceries & specialties as well as collectible artwork. P.S. Their English trifle is said to be quite wonderful, if you have room! F.Y.I. Many British luncheon specialties are offered in addition to Afternoon Tea.

$5.85 Teaplate...A sandwich or meat pie, two biscuits, jam tart & tea cake plus a pot of brewed tea.
$7.95 Afternoon Tea... Changes monthly but includes a selection of two savories & four sweets, and a pot of brewed P.G. Tipps. Available Wednesday & Saturdays only 12Noon To 5:00pm.

TEATIME: 12Noon To 5:00pm • Wednesday & Saturday
• May Accommodate Some Dietary Needs With Advance Request
• Non-Caffeine/Herbal Tea Available
• Children's Tea Parties Welcome
• Watercloset: Same Floor
• **Reservations Are Appreciated**
• Free Parking Lot In Front
• Credit Cards: V,MC&DIS
Proprietor's
*Autograph*_____*Date*_____

SWEET PEA
Victorian Tea Room
340 N.W. First Street
Old Town Sherwood, Oregon

503-625-4479

New Addition...It's Teatime At...Sweet Pea Victorian Tea Room. Don't you just love sweet peas? Just the mention of their name evokes thoughts of colorful blooms reaching up a fence to meet the sunshine; unless you happen to be a fan of Olive Oyl that is! Meet Shelly, the proprietor of this cozy new tearoom. Sweet Pea is in a circa 1892 Queen Ann Victorian, located in quaint Old Town Sherwood. I met Shelly through her cousin Jo who resides in Southern California. Jo's visit to "la-Tea-da," in Arcadia, California helped inspire Shelly to open Sweet Pea. Jo was as thrilled to tell me about Sweet Pea, as I was to hear about it.

The tearoom is decorated with pale pink walls and rose wallpaper and accented with white lace curtains & lace tablecloths. Weather permitting, take tea on the wrap-around front porch. Allow time to browse in their sweet petite gift shop with tea accessories, dolls, jewelry and books. Tea parties for up 100 guests.

$8.95 Luncheon Tea... Assorted tea sandwiches, fresh fruit, choice of dessert and a pot of brewed loose tea.
$6.95 Sandwich Tea... Assorted tea sandwiches, fresh fruit, cookie and a pot of brewed loose tea.
$5.75 Dessert Tea... Dessert, fresh fruit, brewed tea.
$4.50 Desset Tea Sans Fruit

TEATIME: 11:00am To 4:00pm • Wednesday Thru Saturday
• And By Special Arrangement, Sunday Thru Tuesday
• May Accommodate Some Dietary Needs With Advance Request
• Non-Caffeine/Herbal Tea Available
•Children's Tea Parties Welcome
• Watercloset: Same Floor
• **Reservations Are Recommended, Especially On Saturdays**
• Unmetered Street Parking
• Credit Cards: V,MC&DIS
Proprietor's
*Autograph*_____*Date*_____

I can't wait to turn this place into a tearoom!

Washington

By Michael Upton
HM Consul
Seattle, Washington USA

CHEERS!

"It may sound like heresy, coming from the land of coffee drinkers...the marketing efforts of Starbucks, Seattle's Best Coffee, Tully's and others have rightly conferred the title of 'latte-land' on the Seattle Metropolitan area, but I prefer tea! And lots of it. Made correctly, with hot water and a little milk. (How I despair when so many of the finest hotels in the area get it all wrong, with lukewarm water, once I was even served a tea-bag and cold water! And a stingy slice of lemon.)

So all power to those who pop in for a "cuppa," rather than a double shot of almond-flavoured skimmed milk-hold the cinnamon- or whatever the coffee of the day is! Cheers!

COPPER KETTLE
Tea Room
26 "B" Street North East
Auburn, Washington

253-833-2404

New Addition...It's Teatime At...Copper Kettle.
If you see a huge copper kettle on a window sill you're probably at the right place. Welcome to Margery and Clive's Copper Kettle, which is fondly reminiscent of the alliterative Johnny Carson clip on the "Clive Copper Clapper Caper!" Once the home of an eccentric attorney, this spot now serves up tasty homemade British dishes and tea in a charming and delightful light hearted atmosphere.

Afternoon Tea is presented on a three tiered caddie at tables set with pink tablecloths, embroidered toppers, fresh flowers or potted plants, and a collection of English bone china teacups. The terrifically tudor decor is "somewhat pub-ish and includes antique furnishings, greenish gray carpet and uncomfortable chairs," Clive added. P.S. Allow time to snoop around, the Copper Kettle carries imported foods & gifts including English chocolates. Ask Clive about English cockney rhyming slang!

$9.95 Castle Tea... Assorted finger sandwiches, scone served with Devonshire cream & jam, small crumpet, fancy cake, Trifle or Paulova and a pot of brewed loose or Yorkshire Gold Tea.
$8.50 Cottage Tea... Assorted finger sandwiches, scone, Devonshire cream & jam, fancy cakes, a pot of brewed loose tea.
$3.50 Morning Tea...(Served From 10:30am-11:30am) Scone with Devon cream & jam, or a crumpet with house tea.

TEATIME: 2:00pm To 4:30pm • Tuesday Thru Saturday
• May Accommodate Some Dietary Needs With Advance Request
• Non-Caffeine/Herbal Tea Available
• Watercloset: Same Floor
• Wheelchair Accessible
• **Reservations: No**
• Free Parking Lot
• Cash Or Check
Proprietor's
*Autograph*_____*Date*_____

LISA'S TEA TREASURES
10687 N.E. Second Street
Bellevue, Washington
425-453-4832

It's Teatime At...Lisa's Tea Treasures. Enjoy tea and treats from around the world in an atmosphere of Old World elegance in the heart of downtown. A wide selection of teas accompany the afternoon and evening teas featuring savories, finger sandwiches, delicate tea cakes and scones, and delicious pastries.

Karen's gift parlour has fine china, tea ware & gourmet specialties, many exclusively imported by Lisa's Tea Treasures. Teapots, teacups, jams, fruit curds, and of course tea, make elegant yet practical gifts that are certain to please. You may take tea in the Garden Room, King's Parlour, Morris Room, Teddy Bear Room or Library for up to 40 guests. Lovely Victorian touches include deep burgundy patterned wallpaper and chandeliers. Extensive a la carte selections from around $5.50 to $13.00, and a multicourse Sunday brunch for around $10.95. Great spot for business teas too.

$12.00-$13.95 Traditional & Contempory Tea. Tea sandwiches, scone, savory & sweets, pot of Connoisseur full-leaf tea. A range of seven fabulous selections.
$10.95-$13.95 Light Dinner Tea... Soup or salad & choice of entree & a pot of loose brewed tea.Friday & Sat Evening
$23.95 Traditional Victorian Evening Tea...Friday & Saturday...Soups, salad, and three entrees along with savory pudding, dessert, fresh fruit & tea sorbet, and a pot of loose leaf tea.

TEATIME: 11:00am To 5:00pm • Sunday Thru Thursday
- 11:00am To 8:00pm • Friday & Saturday
- May Accommodate Some Dietary Needs With Advance Request
- 99.6 % Caffeine-Free Tea Available
- Children's Tea Parties Welcome
- Watercloset: Same Floor • Wheelchair Accessible
- **Reservations Are Suggested**
- Validated Underground Parking
- Credit Cards: V,MC,DIS&AE

Proprietor's
*Autograph*_____*Date*_____

358

NORDSTROM
The Garden Terrace
100 Bellevue Square
Bellevue, Washington

425-455-5800

New Addition...It's Teatime At...Nordstrom. In 1887, at the tender age of 16, John F. Nordstrom left his home in Sweden to come to the United States. He arrived in New York with five dollars in his pocket. A fortuitous meeting years later with Carl F. Wallin a Seattle shoemaker, resulted in the 1901 opening of the first "Wallin & Nordstrom" store on Fourth & Pike Streets in Seattle. Throughout the years, Nordstrom has been guided by its founder's philosophy. "Offer the customer the best possible service, selection, quality and value." I enjoy shopping at Nordstom, the idea of a pianist playing a baby grand piano while I browse for beautiful things suits me to a T. The comfy "oasis" which my spouse calls the "husband waiting area" is appreciated by both of us! When this customer friendly store began serving Afternoon Tea in many of the Cafes at Nordstrom, I wasn't at all surprised.

At teatime, The Garden Terrace tables are dressed-up with fresh flowers or plants, fine china & cloth napkins. You will be courteously greeted by the friendly Nordstrom staff.

$7.95 Afternoon Tea... Assorted finger sandwiches, petit fours, and a pot of brewed loose tea.

TEATIME: 3:00pm To 5:00pm • Seven Days A Week
• May Accommodate Some Dietary Needs With Advance Request
• Non-Caffeine/Herbal Tea Available
• Wheelchair Accessible • Watercloset: Same Floor
• **Reservations Are Advised For Six Or More Guests**
• Free Parking Lot
• Credit Cards: V, MC,AE&Nordstrom
Manager's
*Autograph*_____*Date*_____

359

THE PEWTER POT
Restaurant

THE Pewter Pot RESTAURANT

124 1/2 Cottage Avenue
Cashmere, Washington

509-782-2036

New Addition...It's Teatime At...The Pewter Pot. "Come away to yesterday," beckons Kristi the proprietor of this perfectly delightful spot of tea. The flowers & lace have prompted folks to refer to it as "the sissy restaurant." That's ok with Kristi who asks gents in her brochure, "Are you man enough to eat here?" And, from the looks of things most are!

Afternoon Tea is served on pedestal plates at tables set with chintz & burgundy linens and fresh flowers. Theme teas are presented throughout the year and include an annual March High Tea, Mad Hatter's Tea Party, Children's Christmas Tea, Holiday Quilt Show & Afternoon Tea and many others. Most events cost around $5.95 for adults and $3.95 for children. Rabbits, Bears & Dolls are free. Private tea parties available for up to 40 guests. Call for schedule of these entertaining events. Call ahead for Marionberry pie or "The Chocolate Affair" to take home.F.Y.I. If you're low on your supply of "Applets & Cotlets" this town is where they're from.

$9.95 Authentic English High Tea... Sausage rolls, steak and kidney pie, ham with piccalilli, chicken salad, game pie, scones, lemon curd, Scottish shortbread, trifle, fruit tarts, pot of tea.

$5.95 Afternoon Tea... Tea sandwiches, homemade scone served with butter & jam & lemon curd, shortbread cookie, fruit tart or cake and a pot of tea.

TEATIME: 2:00pm To 3:00pm • Tuesday Thru Saturday
• Closed December 22-January 13 For Pewter Pot Family Time
• Non-Caffeine/Herbal Tea Available
• Children's Tea Parties Welcome
• Watercloset: Same Floor
• **Reservations Required For Theme Teas &**
  Highly Recommended For Afternoon Tea
• Unmetered Street Parking
• Credit Cards: V&MC

Proprietor's
*Autograph*_____*Date*_____

IVY TEA ROOM
at BJ'S Corner Cottage
30 SouthWest 12th Street
College Place, Washington

509-525-4752

New Addition...It's Teatime At...Ivy Tea Room At BJ'S Corner Cottage. This is a unique spot with all occasion gifts, flowers, antiques, UPS Service, photocopying...and now a tearoom! Pat's mission at the Ivy Tea Room is to provide her guests with tasty low fat meals, specializing in vegetarian dishes. A full menu of homemade dishes are offered in addition to High Tea.

High Teas are served in courses at tables set with crocheted lace tablecloths under glass, cloth napkins, gold flatware, antique English teacups, heart-shaped dishes, white Maryland china & centerpieces. The tearoom ambiance is quite Victorian, and features black, mauve & burgundy patterned wallpaper, ornate mirrors, a rose-pattern carpet, chandeliers with soft pink glow lights, a fireplace, and a fountain. The High Teas often reflect the holiday spirit. For example, on Valentine's Day heart confetti is sprinkled under the table glass. Private tea parties may be planned for 2 to 30 guests. Please call to plan your special event. Allow time to browse. Pat carries bulk teas and American herbal infusions for your take home pleasure in addition to a variety of tea accoutrements.

$12.50 High Tea... Four course menu: fruit plate, salad, open-face tea sandwiches, dessert finale & brewed loose tea.

HIGH TEAS: By Reservation
• Drop In...For Sweets & Tea
• May Accommodate Some Dietary Needs With Advance Request
• Non-Caffeine/Herbal Tea Available • Very Veggie Friendly
• Children's Tea Parties Welcome, Ages 5+
• Watercloset; Same Floor
• **24 Hour Advance Reservations Are Required For High Tea**
• Free Parking Lot On The North & East Side
• Credit Cards: V&MC

Proprietor's
*Autograph*_____*Date*_____

THE VILLAGE TEA ROOM
inside Village Crafts & Collectables
(Perrinville Village) 7526 Olympic View Drive, Suite A
Edmonds, Washington

425-670-2898　　　**425-778-8872** *Reservations*

New Addition...It's Teatime At...The Village Tea Room & Gift Shop. "When you think of Washington, do you think of tea?" asks Terry. She is sure you will after a visit to her little tearoom located in the back of Village Crafts & Collectables. This is a fun spot complete with a red velvet fainting couch. The shop has loads of hats, and is decorated with an austrian crystal chandelier, crackling faux fireplace, gilded mirror, arm chairs, vintage tables, teal green floral carpet, wall sconces, and lamps with old-fashioned fringed shades. The walls are peachy tone with floral wallpaper that Terry put up herself. Her 7' tall "Teacup" Tree is up all year round. Private tea parties may be arranged for 1-30 guests.

Afternoon Tea is served in traditional Victorian style with white or ecru lace tablecloths and doilies, some which have been stained with a spot of tea! There are personally-pressed cloth napkins, fresh flowers & mis-matched china. Small tole painted clocks sit on each table telling you when your tea has steeped to perfection. Almost everything here is homemade. Allow time to browse, there are handmade gifts and a variety of pre-packaged teas.

$15.00 Monthly Fashion Show Tea... Usually the second Saturday of the month, 12-2pm. Ask about other theme teas.

$13.00 Afternoon Tea... Assorted tea sandwiches, sweet cream scones served with clotted cream & lemon curd, assorted sweets such as Scottish shortbread, tea breads, muffins, and cookies and a pot of brewed loose tea. (Includes tax & tip.)

TEATIME: As Scheduled
• May Be Planned For 11am-4pm • Tuesday Thru Saturday
• May Accommodate Some Dietary Needs By Advance Request
• Non-Caffeine/Herbal Tea Available
• Children's Tea Parties Welcome
• Watercloset: Same Floor
• **24 Hour Advance Reservations Required**
• Free Parking Lot
• Credit Cards: V,MC,DIS&AE

Proprietor's
*Autograph*_____*Date*_____

362

WINDSOR GARDEN
Tea Room
110 4th. Avenue North
Edmonds, Washington

425-712-1387

New Proprietor...It's Teatime At...Windsor Garden Tea Room. "Elegance and charm have come to Edmonds." This charming 1936 brick residence was once home to a doctor's office as noted by the original mosaic MD tile logo.Joy is the new proprietor of Windsor Garden Tea Room. The entrance of the tearoom features an interesting, gathered fabric effect in lavender, pink, green & burgundy and, the chair cushions just happen to match. A sliding glass door leads outside onto the garden where you may enjoy a cool summer iced tea. One of the most popular rooms at the Windsor Garden is the watercloset! For artistic reasons it is extra special. There is a beautiful floral pedestal sink which is practically on the tearoom tour!

Tea is served a la carte in the Garden Room at tables set with off-white & rose tablecloths, linen napkins, fresh flowers and an eclectic collection of European fine china. Soft classical baroque background music is a nice addition. The wall coverings are pale teal & pink floral, a lacey window curtain is a nice accent. P.S. Visit the Cherub Room for bulk & packaged teas, antique teacups and special gifts. Private tea parties for up 30 guests. Call for summer hours.

$5.25-$5.95 Tea Sandwich Platter...A seasonal selection of finger sandwiches.
$2.75-$4.50 Cucumber Sandwiches
$2.50-$4.00 Pot of Brewed loose Tea
$2.00...Scone

TEATIME: 10:30am To 5:00pm • Monday Thru Friday
• 10:00am To 5:00pm, Saturday • 11:00am To 5:00pm, Sunday
• May Accommodate Some Dietary Needs With Advance Request
• Non-Caffeine/Herbal Tea Available
• Watercloset: Same Floor
• **Reservations Are Appreciated**
• Limited Time Street Parking
• Credit Cards: V&MC

Proprietor's
*Autograph*_____*Date*_____

363

THE COUNTRY REGISTER
Cafe & Tea Room

8310 Gage Boulevard
Kennewick, Washington

509-783-7553

It's Teatime At...The Country Register Cafe & Tea Room. Good things come from Afternoon Tea! Did you know that you can enjoy Afternoon Tea and get married here? This spot could meet many of your romantic needs. Be sure to ask Bobbi Jo about tying the knot at The Country Register Ivy Chapel.

Afternoon Tea is served at tables set with Victorian floral print tablecloths, cloth napkins, Seville china with pink flowers and sweet teapot centerpieces. It was a creative touch to have the server's vests match the floral print tablecloths. The archways in the tearoom are neat spots for tea when not being used by wedding couples repeating vows. P.S. Be sure to try the homemade bread pudding made from the proprietor's own secret recipe. Browse around for gifts, cozies, teapots, tea sets & more. F.Y.I. Private tea parties available for your many special events. Please call to plan.

$10.00 Buffet Theme Teas... Call for schedule of theme teas such as: Mother & Daughter Tea and Garden Tea.
$7.25 High Tea By Reservation... Cucumber tea sandwiches, scone served with Devonshire cream & preserves, lemon curd, sweet treats and a pot of brewed loose tea.

TEATIME: 2:00pm To 4:00pm • Monday Thru Saturday
• May Accommodate Some Dietary Needs, 1 Week Advance Request
• Non-Caffeine/Herbal Tea Available
• Children's Tea Parties Welcome
• Watercloset: Same Floor
• Wheelchair Accessible
• **Teas Are By 24 Hour Advance Reservation Only**
• Free Unlimited-Time Parking Lot
• Credit Cards: V,MC&AE

Proprietor's
*Autograph*_____*Date*_____

THE WOODMARK HOTEL

1200 Carillon Point (On Lake Washington)
Kirkland, Washington

800-822-3700 *Hotel*   **425-803-5595** *Tea Reservations*

It's Teatime At...The Woodmark Hotel. This is a most distinctive hotel, situated on the shores of Lake Washington. It is located 7 miles east of Seattle and three miles north of Bellevue. Carillon Point is a waterfront community fashioned after a European piazza with shops, restaurants, a 205 slip marina and more. In the central plaza there are six carillon bells that chime every half hour.

Afternoon Tea is served in the hotel's comfortable and inviting Library Bar Lounge. Take a seat by the fireplace on a cool late afternoon and enjoy the chef's lovely Afternoon Tea presentation. Tables are set with Lenox china and white tablecloths, draped with colorful sashes. Investigate the interesting collection of books on The Library Bar shelves.

$14.00 Full Tea... Finger sandwiches, fruit scone with butter, cream & jam, raspberry mousse in a chocolate tulip cup, petit fours, lemon bar, brewed loose Barnes & Watson tea.
$8.00 Savories & Tea... Finger sandwiches, fruit scone with creamed butter, cream & jam, brewed loose B&W tea.
$8.00 Sweets & Tea... Fruit scone with creamed butter, cream & jam, raspberry mouse in a chocolate tulip cup, petit fours, lemon bar, pot of brewed loose Barnes & Watson tea.
$6.00 Children's Tea... Little finger sandwiches, fruit scone with creamed butter, cream & jam, lemon bar, tea or milk.

TEATIME: 2:00pm To 4:00pm • Monday Thru Friday
• Saturday & Sunday Hours Are Seasonal, Please Call
• May Accommodate Some Dietary Needs With Advance Request
• Non-Caffeine/Herbal Tea Available
• Watercloset: Same Floor • Wheelchair Accessible
• **Reservations Are Required**
• Valet Or Two Hour Self-Park With Validation
• Credit Cards: MC,V,DC&AE
Proprietor's
*Autograph*_____*Date*_____

THE ROSE & THISTLE
Tea Room & Antiques

ROSE and THISTLE
Tea Room and Antiques

606 East Morris Street
LaConner, Washington

360-466-3313

New Addition...It's Teatime At...The Rose & Thistle. All of Anella's new desserts must pass the "husband" test before she serves her guests. So, it's understandable that David keeps volunteering his services! The Rose & Thistle is located in a small, charming Victorian home built in the late 1800's.

Afternoon Tea is served in either of the two dining rooms or weather permitting, outside on the porch near the swing. Tables are set with tablecloths & lace toppers, vintage china and silk teacup centerpieces. Anella has flower arrangements everywhere; that must be the rose part but I'm still not sure about the thistle! The decor includes dark green carpet with pink accents, slate floors, stained glass windows & lace curtains. Allow time to browse, there are enticing antiques, gifts, books, teacup wreaths, miniature tea sets and tussie mussies. Private parties are available for up to 20 guests.

$9.95 Queen Tea... Five tea sandwiches, currant or cinnamon scone with heather-honey-cream & jam, delectable such as: Italian rum cake, German chocolate or coconut lemon cream cake, plus sherry trifle, and a pot of brewed loose tea.
$7.95 Victorian Tea... Three tea sandwiches, scone with heather-honey-cream & jam, sherry trifle, a pot of brewed loose tea.
$5.95 School House Tea... Two tea sandwiches, scone served with heather-honey-cream & jam, a pot of brewed loose tea.

TEATIME: 11:00am To 5:00pm • Seven Days A Week
• May Accommodate Some Dietary Needs With Advance Request
• Non-Caffeine/Herbal Tea Available
• Children's Tea Parties Welcome
• Watercloset: Same Floor • Wheelchair Accessible
• **Reservations Requested For Four Or More Guests**
• Free Parking Lot
• Credit Cards: V,MC,DIS&AE
Proprietor's
*Autograph*_____*Date*_____

LANGLEY TEA ROOM
221 Second Street #15 B
(Langley Village)
Langley, Washington

888/360-221-6292

It's Teatime At...Langley Tea Room. Enter through the purple Wisteria arbor to find this pretty English Country style tearoom. A muraled wall nicely picks up the country cottage theme.

Pat serves Afternoon Tea at tables layered with peony chintz & Battenburg lace tablecloths and always, fresh flowers. Langley's tea service is Blue Willow imported English china. You may also take tea outdoors weather permitting, in the beautiful brick courtyard garden. There's even a fountain for that extra soothing touch. Allow time to browse through the gift shop. There are tea accoutrements, books & original art. Tea parties are available for up to 15 guests. Ask about the new mail-order catalog.

$7.25 Afternoon Tea... Tea sandwiches, salad, a pot of fresh whole leaf tea "swirling merrily about in bonny boiled water."

$5.25 Cream Tea... Scones served with imported clotted cream & preserves and a small pot of whole leaf tea.

$3.95 Tea Break... Delicate fruited tea bread served with cream cheese and a small pot of whole leaf tea.

TEATIME: 11:00am To 5:00pm • Closed On Wednesday
• Non-Caffeine/Herbal Tea Available
• Children's Tea Parties Welcome
• Watercloset: Same Floor
• Wheelchair Accessible
• **Reservations: No**
• Unlimited Time Free Parking Lot
• Credit Cards: V&MC
Propriutor's
*Autograph*_____*Date*_____

ATTIC SECRETS
4229 76th Street N.E. Suite 101
Marysville, Washington

360-659-7305

New Addition...It's Teatime At...Attic Secrets.
Oh, the treasures and secrets one's attic reveals! Welcome to Jeni and Chris's wonderful Victorian tearoom, full of treasures and much more. Attic Secrets originally opened its doors as a gift shop. Their loyal customers are credited with encouraging this mother and daughter to open a tearoom.

Afternoon Tea is served in either the Waverly-printed, floral & frilly, Out Front Tea Room as it is popularly called, or the Garden Room with its hand painted Victorian garden mural, and wicker or wrought iron furniture. Tables are set with Battenburg tablecloths, fresh flowers, silver dome-covered butter dishes, matching imported white china and English tea strainers. Nearly everything here is homemade by Jeni and presented on individual three tiered caddies. Great shopping opportunities with antiques, home decor, "Bunnies By The Bay," jewelry, teapots, teacups, pictures, swags, books, tea party invitations and on. Private tea parties too, for up to 20 guests.

$12.95 Queen's Tea... Four finger sandwiches, scone, lemon curd & jam, fancy dessert, brewed loose Republic of Tea.
$9.95 Victorian Tea... Three finger sandwiches, scone, lemon curd & jam, cookies, tea bread, a pot of brewed loose tea.
$7.95 Garden Tea... Veggie finger sandwiches, fresh fruit, scone with lemon curd & jam, a pot of brewed loose tea.

TEATIME: High Tea: 11:00am To 3:00pm •Monday Thru Saturday
- Afternoon Tea: 3:00pm To 4:00pm • Monday Thru Saturday
- May Accommodate Some Dietary Needs With Advance Request
- Non-Caffeine/Herbal Tea Available
- Children's Tea Parties Welcome
- Watercloset: Common Area Same Floor • Wheelchair Accessible
- **Reservations Are Requested**
- Free Parking Area
- Credit Card V,MC&DIS

Proprietor's
*Autograph*_____*Date*_____

368

KATE'S TEA ROOM
& Curios

121 North Lewis Street
Monroe, Washington

425-794-5199

It's Teatime At...Kate's Tea Room & Curios. Welcome to Kathy's cheerful new tearoom. The tearoom has an inviting white picket fence and umbrella tables in the front yard for al fresco garden teas. The interior decor is pretty peachy with peachy floral prints, wallcovering, lace curtains and accent pieces.

Afternoon Tea is served in the dining room at tables set with vintage linens, assorted linen napkins, teapot centerpieces, and an eclectic collection of mis-matched china. Allow time to browse, a book room is planned for those who want a "spot of tea" and a good read. Look for vintage clothing, feathers for hats, collectibles, garlic products from Gilroy, local artwork, crafts, books, tea-related accessories and even outdoor & indoor natural log products made by her brother in law. P.S. You may want to reserve a spot by the fireplace. Tea parties may be planned for up to 25 guests.

$9.95 Garden Tea... Three tea sandwiches, scone served with Devonshire cream, pastries & sweets, pot of brewed loose tea.
$6.95 Teddy Bear Tea... Tea sandwiches, scone & jam, cookies, chocolate surprise and children's Storytime tea.
$5.95 Afternoon Delight... Scone, cream & jam, tea.

TEATIME: 10:00am To 5:00pm • Monday Thru Saturday
• May Accommodate Some Dietary Needs With Advance Request
• Non-Caffeine/Herbal Tea Available
• Children's Tea Parties Welcome
• Watercloset: Same Floor
• **Reservations Appreciated For Parties Of 10+ Guests**
• Free Parking Lot Rear & Side
• Cash Or Check
Proprietor's
*Autograph*_____*Date*_____

THE GARDENS CAFE
& Tea Room
1598 Best Road
Mount Vernon, Washington

360-466-1325

New Name...It's Teatime At...The Gardens Cafe & Tea Room. The Gardens Cafe & Tea Room is the new name for The Granary. The establishment is actually a converted granary built in 1913. The interior of the shop is rustic barnwood, and just like a picture out of a magazine, flowers are drying from the ceiling.

The Gardens Cafe is situated on an 11 acre English-style garden that is in bloom from March through October. The timeless feel of yesterday is present today. Stroll through the beautiful gardens with over 200 varieties of roses, an apple orchard, a pond, and cut-flower farm. It will surely put you in the mood for Afternoon Tea. "You just have to give us a day's notice and your Afternoon Tea will be served in the tearoom or out under the trees." Terry really enjoys visiting with her customers, so don't be shy. Afternoon Tea is served by advance reservation only. Allow time to browse through the rustic gift shop. F.Y.I. The Gardens Cafe & Tea Room is available for weddings during the summer months and private tea parties for 1 to 25 guests.

$11.50 Afternoon Tea. Savory tea sandwiches, seasonal fruit, homemade scone with cream, and a pot of brewed loose tea.

TEATIME: As Scheduled
- Available:11am-4pm, Monday-Saturday •11am-2pm, Sunday
- By Advance Reservation, Small Groups One Day In Advance, Please
- May Accommodate Some Dietary Needs With Advance Request
- Non-Caffeine/Herbal Tea Available
- Watercloset: Same Floor
- Wheelchair Accessible
- **Advance Reservations Are Required**
- Off-Street Parking
- Cash Or Check Please

Proprietor's
*Autograph*_____*Date*_____

Fat-Free, Low Sugar Pumpkin Bread

"Diabetes is not a piece of cake" The Cookbook

*1 cup prune puree
1/2 cup sugar
1/2 teaspoon salt
2 2/3 cup all-purpose flour
2 teaspoons baking powder
1 teaspoon ground cinnamon
1 cup egg substitute (equal to 4 eggs)
1 cup Sugar Twin brown sugar substitute
6 envelopes Sweet One artificial sweetener

1/2 teaspoon ground cloves
1/4 teaspoon ground ginger
1/4 teaspoon ground nutmeg
1 cup canned pumpkin
1 teaspoon baking soda

Preheat oven to 350 degrees F.   Makes 32 servings.

Combine flour, sugar, artificial sweeteners, baking powder, baking soda, salt and spices. In a separate bowl blend prune puree, egg substitute, and pumpkin.

Add prune mixture to flour mixture and blend thoroughly. Spoon batter into a 9-inch loaf pan sprayed with cooking spray. Bake 60-70 minutes or until toothpick inserted in center comes out clean. Cool 10 minutes in pan on rack, remove from pan and finish cooling on rack.

*Note: To make prune puree, combine 1 1/3 cups (8 oz.) pitted prunes and 6 tablespoons water in a food processor. Pulse process until prunes are finely chopped. Makes 1 cup.

May be foil wrapped and frozen up to one month.

70 calories
15 g carbohydrate
1 bread exchange

2 g protein
0 fat

Bring your favorite dolly to tea!

VICTORIAN ROSE TEA ROOM
& Springhouse Dolls

1130 Bethel Avenue
Port Orchard, Washington

Tea Room **360-876-5695**
360-876-0529

New Addition...It's Teatime At...Victorian Rose Tea Room. This tearoom is one big adorable two-story pink, mauve & gold doll house complete with a turret, dormers, and lampposts. It is a grown-up version of what many little girls dream, as it must have been for Sandy, the proprietor. This spot is home to Victorian Rose Tea Room & Springhouse Dolls, Sandy's creations.

Afternoon Cream Teas are presented by servers in traditional black & white Victorian dress. Tables are set with linens, cloth napkins and white embossed fine china. The tearoom is decorated in dark green & mauve cabbage-rose wallpaper with carpet to match. The unique window seating for all guests is quite wonderful. On occasion, deer actually come up & feed on the planters! Ask for the schedule of holiday inspired theme teas including "Santa Teas" and Mother's Day Teas. Private tea parties available for 10 to 75 guests. Breakfast & lunch served daily. Be sure to visit the village shops.

$12.95 High Tea...4th Saturday of the month. Veggies & dip, hot scones, whipped butter & jams, assorted tea sandwiches, mini quiche, desserts, pot of brewed tea. $19.95 with a teacup gift.
$6.95 Afternoon Cream Tea... Fresh scones with flavored whipped butters & jam, desserts, and a pot of brewed tea.

TEATIME: Afternoon Cream Tea: 2:30 To 4:30pm • Daily
• May Accommodate Some Dietary Needs With Advance Request
• Non-Caffeine/Herbal Tea Available
• Children's Tea Parties Welcome
• Watercloset: Same Floor • Wheelchair Accessible, First Floor
• Stairway To Additional 2nd. Floor Dining Room & Gift Shop
• **Reservations Are Required For High Teas Only**
• Free Parking Lot
• Credit Cards: V,MC&DIS

Proprietor's
*Autograph*_____*Date*_____

JUDITH'S TEAROOMS
& Rose Cafe

18820 Front Street
(Across From The Marina)
Poulsbo, Washington

360-697-3449

Judith's Tearooms
and Rose Café

Lunch • Tea
Banquet Facilities Available
Charles & Judith Goodrich
(360) 697-3449
Front Street, Poulsbo, Washington

New Addition...It's Teatime At...Judith's Tearooms & Rose Cafe. Judith describes her tearoom as casual, romantic and "a little tiny bit elegant." Judith and Charles love their customers and welcome you to take tea outside on their lovely patio weather permitting, or up a few steps in either the Cafe, the "Middle Tearoom," or the "Back Tearoom." Everything at Judith's is freshly homemade without preservatives, she's famous for her bread pudding with the bourbon sauce & fresh whipped cream. Ask Judith about her popular cookbook which is also available in the shop.

Afternoon Tea is served at tables set with handmade tablecloths, seasonal centerpieces and an eclectic mix of imported fine china, with English teapots & teacups. A full menu of sandwiches & specialties are available in addition to Afternoon Tea. F.Y.I. Judith's sells bulk tea along with the "Judith's Blend." Private tea parties are available for 20 to 110 guests. Please call for information & to reserve your date.

$10.95 Full Lunch Tea... Small salad or cup of soup, tiny tea sandwiches, fruit, cheese, dessert, pot of brewed loose tea.
$8.50 Sandwich Tea Lunch... Assortment of small tea sandwiches, cheese, fruit, and a pot of brewed loose tea.

TEATIME: 2pm-5pm, Daily • Cafe Hours: 11am-5pm, Sun.Till 4pm
• May Accommodate Some Dietary Needs With Advance Request
• Non-Caffeine/Herbal Tea Available
• Watercloset: Same Floor
• Free Parking Lots & Street Park
• **Reservations Are Gladly Accepted**
• Credit Cards:V,MC&DIS
Proprietor's
*Autograph*_____*Date*_____

YE OLDE COPPER KETTLE

18881 "B1" Front Street
Poulsbo, Washington

360-697-2999

New Addition...It's Teatime At...Ye Olde Copper Kettle. Welcome to Ye Olde Copper Kettle. Please drop by and meet Tina and John the charming proprietors of this English tearoom. Originally from England, they moved to the historic Scandinavian town of Poulsbo and opened their tearoom in 1992.

Afternoon Tea is served at pink linen clad tables with pink & violet pattered china and silk rosebud centerpieces. The walls are soothing pink with framed prints & posters of English scenes and landmarks. Copper Kettles, new and olde adorn the shelves. In fact, if you have one you don't want, do bring it along. A wide variety of homemade traditional English specialties such as Shepherd's Pies, Ploughman's Lunch, Cornish Pastie and Scotch Pie are served in addition to Afternoon Tea. Private tea parties are available for up to 30 guests. P.S. Ye Olde Copper Kettle can bring a tea party to you!

$7.95 "High Tea"... Cucumber & smoked salmon finger sandwiches, scones with cream & strawberry preserves, (Double Devon cream add $.85), and a pot of P.G. Tips tea.

$5.95 Dessert Sampler... For those who can't decide and want it all! The sampler includes: Scone, Bakewell tart, Victoria sandwich cake, chocolate log royale and chocolate almond pate.

$1.25 Pot of English Tea.

TEATIME: 10:30am To 3:30pm • Tuesday Thru Thursday
• 10:30am To 4pm, Friday & Saturday • 11am To 3:00pm, Sunday
• May Accommodate Some Dietary Needs With Advance Request
• Non-Caffeine/Herbal Tea Available
• Watercloset: One Step Down
• Children's Tea Parties Welcome
• **Reservations Appreciated For Four+ Guests**
• Free Street Parking & Nearby Lot
• Credit Cards: V,MC&DIS

Proprietor's
*Autograph*_____*Date*_____

BRITISH PANTRY, LTD.

8125 161 Avenue N.E.
Redmond, Washington

425-883-7511

It's Teatime At...The British Pantry Ltd. British Flags wave proudly outside The British Pantry in Redmond. Make a point of meeting Mavis the proprietor, she's lots of fun.

Afternoon Tea is served on blue and white "Willow" pattern English Ironstone, each person is presented their own plate. This quite authentic English tearoom is decorated in tones of burgundy and green with copper teapots all about. The tables are covered in cream-colored tablecloths with tapestry toppers & tea lamps. Also, don't miss the gift shop featuring a colorful variety of English teapots, teacups and mugs. The proprietor takes a great deal of pride in the holiday gifts she selects for the shop which include wonderful miniature English fine china tea sets. Ask about the very special Mother's Day Tea. F.Y.I. Fish & Chips been added to the menu.

$11.00 Mother's Day Special "Silver" Buffet Tea.
$7.95 A Full Afternoon Tea... Four cucumber & cream cheese sandwiches, home baked raisin scone with jam & whipped cream (parties of 6 or more can order real Devonshire cream for an additional $1.00 per person), small Bakewell-tart iced with a cherry on top, fruit garnish and a pot of house or brewed loose tea.
$4.50 Crumpets & Tea... Two Crumpets served with fruit, butter & strawberry jam and a pot of house or tea.

TEATIME: 2:30pm To 4:30pm • Seven Days A Week
- May Accommodate Some Dietary Needs With Advance Request
- Non-Caffeine/Herbal Tea Available
- Children's Tea Parties Welcome
- Watercloset: Same Floor
- **Reservations: No**
- Rear Parking Lot & Private Street Park
- Credit Cards: V&MC

Proprietor's
*Autograph*_____*Date*_____

CHEZ NOUS
723 Broadway East
Seattle, Washington

206-324-3711

New Addition...It's Teatime At Chez Nous.
Jennifer & Charles are the gracious hosts of this elegant new private dining spot. Their lovely and contemporary 1903 home reveals the style and elegance of an English Manor with interesting antiques & art objects which are sure to enhance an Afternoon Tea experience.

Afternoon Tea is presented from beautifully decorated tiered caddies at tables set with floral tablecloths, yellow overlays & Italian white china. Jennifer is actually a chef by trade, and many of her menus feature wonderful old family recipes. The interior of Chez Nous is bright and cheery with Jennifer's designer touches everywhere. The handsome peach & yellow fabrics have been dyed to match the peachy carpet. You'll also enjoy the piano music from the seven foot concert grand piano, the fireplace, and various pieces of artwork & memorabilia from Jennifer & Charles' travels. Private tea parties may be planned for up to 40 guests. Weather permitting, courtyard dining too. Ask about the Chez Nous signature teas & the beautiful designer garden Chez Nous B&B.

$18.75 "Traditional English Tea"... Assorted finger sandwiches with edible flowers, hot buttered cheese scones, fruit scones with double cream & strawberry jam, sweets such as: petite chocolate eclairs & fresh seasonal fruit tarts, traditional English Sherry trifle, Chez Nous specially blended English Breakfast tea.

TEATIME: Seating At 2:30pm • Tuesday Thru Saturday
• Or By Special Arrangement
• May Accommodate Some Dietary Needs With Advance Request
• Non-Caffeine/Herbal Tea Available
• Watercloset: Same Floor
• **Reservations Are Requested**
• Pay Parking Lot Across The Street
• Credit Cards: V&MC

Proprietor's
*Autograph*_____*Date*_____

377

FOUR SEASONS
Olympic Hotel
411 University Street
Seattle, Washington

206-621-1700

It's Teatime At...Four Seasons Olympic Hotel.
The picturesque Garden Court is the spot for Afternoon Tea at the lovely Four Season's Hotel in Seattle. Count on elegant, impeccable service & grand style at the Four Seasons Hotels. The hotel is well-located within walking distance of The Pike Place Market, Seattle's Art Museum and the waterfront. Give yourself a lot of time because you can easily loose track of time in this "happening" location.

Afternoon Tea is served at tables set with Royal Doulton fine china, fine linens & fresh flowers. Don't miss the hotel's festive December Holiday Teas which often take place in the Georgian Court and are priced around $18.00. Please call for date & times.

$15.75 Afternoon Tea... Two sweet currant scones with Devonshire cream & strawberry preserves, tea sandwiches, a selection of petit fours, sweet breads and a pot of brewed loose tea.

$9.50 Light Tea...A selection of Petit fours and sweet breads and a pot of brewed loose tea.

$8.00 Scones & Tea... Two currant scones with Devonshire cream & strawberry preserves and a pot of brewed tea.

TEATIME: 3:00 To 5:00pm • Monday Thru Saturday
• 3:30pm To 5:00pm, Sunday
• May Accommodate Some Dietary Needs, 1 Week Advance Request
• Non-Caffeine/Herbal Tea Available
• Watercloset: Same Floor
• Wheelchair Accessible
• **Reservations Are Appreciated**
• Nearby Parking Garage
• Credit Cards: All Majors

L'autograph
*du Concierge*_____*Date*_____

KADO TEA GARDEN
Seattle Asian Art Museum
(Volunteer Park)
Seattle, Washington

206-344-5265

TEA & FLOWERS

   It's Time For Tea, Scones & Sweets At....Kado Tea Garden. "Tea is the International beverage. The nuances of each country and each culture are unveiled in a cup of tea. Savor each sip as an adventure of discovery; your passport to the world of tea." A relaxing Zen-like quality pervails, with Asian music in the background and water trickling from a soothing rock fountain.

   "Tea service includes your choice of tea properly brewed in your individual teapot and presented on a tea tray with a tea cozy, tea strainer and a cup & saucer traditionally suited to the tea you have chosen. And of course, a delectable selection of scones, light lunch cookies and treats to accompany your tea. A stop at Kado Tea Garden is a must for any tea lover." On Saturdays watch a demonstration of Ikebana, the Japanese art of arranging fresh cut flowers in rhythmic and decorative designs. P.S. Museum admission is not required. Ask about poetry readings and seasonal hours. Catering and mail-order available too.

   $2.50-$3.50 Tea Service...A selection of specialty teas & tisanes, blacks, oolongs & greens. Also, Kado Koko with cocoa.
   $3.50-$7.00 Sandwiches & Specialties... Including quiche, fresh garden salads & humbao.
   $2.00 To $5.00 American Or Asian Sweets

A LA CARTE TEATIME: 11:00am To 5:30pm, Thursday
- 11:00am To 4:30pm, Friday, Saturday & Sunday
- Non-Caffeine/Herbal Tea Available
- Watercloset: Same Floor
- Wheelchair Accessible Via Elevator
- **Please Drop By**
- Free Parking Strip
- Credit Card: V

Proprietor's
*Autograph*_____*Date*_____

Photo courtesy of McCormick & Company, Inc.   **Spice up your life with tea!**

PEKOE, A GLOBAL TEAHOUSE
inside World Spice Merchants

1509 Western Avenue
(Below Pike Place Market)
Seattle, Washington

206-682-7274

New Addition... "Sugar & Spice & Tea...How Nice!" At...Pekoe, A Global Teahouse. If you love tea and adventure, you'll be most attracted to World Spice Merchants, the new tea and spice spot located in the historic 1910 Fix Building. Tony is the lively and charming proprietor who has traveled the globe bringing back colorful accessories for the shop's world-eclectic decor. There are old safari trunks and tapestries, and swords and I'm quite sure there's a lost ark somewhere!

Tea and spices are sold bulk for your take home pleasure. The proprietor is expecting soon to offer a tea service at comfortable couches and casual tables in an at home setting. Plans include a new interesting level-price structure. P.S. This is a great spot to stop and pause along the incline, after visiting the bustling Pike Place Market. E-Mail: wsm@worldspice.com   http:www.worldspice.com

$2.25 Tea Sampling...A unique three cup tea-tasting experience so that you can have a basis for comparison.

TEA & SPICE TIME: 10:00am To 7:00pm •Monday Thru Saturday
- 12Noon To 6:00pm, Sunday
- Please Call For Extended Summer Hours
- Non-Caffeine/Herbal Tea Available
- Watercloset: Common Area
- Wheelchair Accessible
- **Reservations: Please Drop By**
- Parking: Next Door, Non-Validated At Market Parking Deck
- Cash Or Check

Proprietor's
*Autograph*_____Date_____

PERENNIAL TEA ROOM

1910 Post Alley
Seattle, Washington

206-448-4054

It's Time For A Spot Of Tea At...The Perennial Tea Room. "We've personally chosen rare and unique loose teas for our tea salon." Teas are hand-packed and "how to brew the perfect cup" instructions accompany each package of your tea. Put the kettle on and enjoy.

There are a wide variety of bulk teas, choose from blacks, blends, greens, oolongs, special flavors and decaf wild cherry. In addition, there are all kinds of tea accouterments, everything you need for Afternoon Tea according to the proprietors Julee and Sue who enjoy informing customers about their new products and teas. You'll love the Teapot Gallery which features favorite teapots ranging from the from basic Brown Betty to fabulous limited edition collectibles. But the most important teapot is the one at Perennial Tea Room's entrance, letting you know you're at the right place!

$2.25 A Spot of Tea... Share a two cup pot of the loose brewed, "Tea of The Day" hot or iced in season, includes a package of shortbread cookies or biscuits from England. The Passion fruit iced tea is quite wonderful!

SPOT OF TEA: 10:00am To 5:30pm • Monday Thru Saturday
• 10:00am To 5:00pm • Sunday
• Non-Caffeine/Herbal Tea Available
• Watercloset: No
• **Please Drop In**
• Validated Park With $20.00 Purchase At Easy St. Or Market Garage
• Credit Cards:,V,MC,DIS&AE

Proprietor's
Autograph _____*Date*_____

QUEEN MARY
2912 N. E. 55th Street
(University of Washington Area)
Seattle, Washington

206-527-2770

It's Teatime At...Queen Mary In Seattle. You will be transported to a quaint world of gracious dining surrounded by fresh flowers and rich Victorian texture at Queen Mary. For nearly 11 years, Mary the ebullient proprietor, has entertained your Afternoon Tea dreams with fastidious attention to detail. Mary prepares everything fresh, from scratch here.Queen Mary enjoys the culinary talents of this proprietor's very creative mom too. Delicious baked goods and traditional tea specialties are her forte.

Honey colored wicker chairs, beautiful fabrics, and an eclectic collection of elegant, antique fine china teacups and teapots are just a hint of the charm that awaits you at Queen Mary. Full menu available in addition to a formal Afternoon Tea. The gift shop carries a splendid selection of teapots and tea accoutrements as well as other unique gifts. Private Afternoon Tea parties may be arranged for up to 40 guests. There is a Children's Tea menu & gift certificates too.

$14.95   Afternoon Tea... Fresh fruit sorbet trio, assorted tea sandwiches such as chicken-almond, and tomato-basil, miniature currant scones with homemade whipped cream & whipped butter and preserves, crumpets and English muffins, fresh seasonal fruit, thumbprint cookie, sugar cookie, lemon curd tarts, chocolate raspberry cake, seasonal fresh fruit & pots of brewed loose tea.

TEATIME: 2:00pm To 5:00pm • Seven Days A Week
• May Accommodate Some Dietary Needs With Advance Request
• Non-Caffeine/Herbal Tea Available
• Watercloset: Same Floor
• Wheelchair Accessible
• **Reservations: For Parties Of Six Or More**
• Street Parking
• Credit Cards: V&MC
Proprietor's
*Autograph*_____*Date*_____

383

SHERATON SEATTLE
Hotel & Towers
1400 Sixth Avenue
Seattle, Washington

206-621-9000

New Addition...It's Teatime At...Sheraton Seattle Hotel & Towers. Talk about a room with a view! The Club Lounge is located on the 32nd floor of this exceptional hotel. A lovely Afternoon Tea is featured along with a terrific view of downtown Seattle and Puget Sound. I guess you could say they really rise above the rest! Originally designed as a feature just for hotel guests, Afternoon Tea has recently been expanded to include all tea lovers, so be sure to include them in your tea-travels.

Afternoon Tea is presented on a tiered plate at tables set with cream & floral linens, a rose bud vase, and Villeroy & Boch "Palermo" china. The room was recently renovated in dramatic gold and black with comfy leather high back chairs, a television, even a computer. Say hello to Rob, the F&B manager who oversees The Club Lounge. By the way, The Club Lounge has a nice display of Chihuly glass and artwork from the Northwest.

$8.95 Afternoon Tea... Assorted small finger sandwiches, fresh baked daily mini scones filled with berries and nuts, served with whipped cream & preserves, tea cookies and brewed loose tea served fresh from a French press placed on the table. Steep to your preference.

TEATIME: 2:00pm To 4:00pm • Seven Days A Week
• Non-Caffeine/Herbal Tea Available
• Watercloset: Same Floor
• Wheelchair Accessible
• **Reservations Are Not Required**
• Non-Validated, Underground Parking
• Credit Cards: V,MC,DIS,DC,AE&JCB

L'autograph
*du Concierge*_____*Date*_____

SORRENTO HOTEL

900 Madison Street
Seattle, Washington

206-622-6400
800-426-1265 *Hotel Reservations*

New Addition...It's Teatime At...Sorrento Hotel.
Inspired by my favorite period in art history, the Italian Renaissance, the Sorrento Hotel is reminiscent of a fine European residence. Nearly 100 years old, this beautiful hotel has maintained its original grand facade designed by noted Pacific Northwest architect Harlan Thomas in 1908.

　　Afternoon Tea is served in the wonderful Fireside Lounge. This elegant living room has marble and mahogany tables, an historic fireplace, handsome fixtures, and most gracious Four Star, Four Diamond service. Tea is presented on a three tiered caddie at tables set with Eschenbach fine china, linen serviettes & crystal. P.S. This is a lovely spot for your special event tea parties. Please call catering to make arrangements. F.Y.I. Delectable personalized cakes made by the hotel's pastry chef may also be ordered.

　　$15.00　Afternoon　Tea...(Seasonal Menu) Selection of savories, canopies and tea sandwiches may include: ham salad, egg salad and smoked salmon. Selection of sweets: seasonal fruit, white chocolate truffle, pecan honey diamond, lemon bar, Milano cookie, almond macaroon, chocolate mousse cup, and sour cherry & dried apricot scone, creme fraiche, Barnes & Watson brewed loose tea.

TEATIME: 3:00pm To 5:00pm • Seven Days A Week
• May Accommodate Some Dietary Needs With Advance Request
• Non-Caffeine/Herbal Tea Available
• Watercloset: One Flight Down With Elevator
• Wheelchair Accessible
• **Reservations Appreciated For Five Or More Guests**
• Non-Validated, Valet Parking For $7.00
• Credit Cards: V,MC,DC,DIS&AE
Proprietor's
*Autograph*_____*Date*_____

SURROGATE HOSTESS
Tearoom
(The Capitol Hill Area) 1907 East Aloha
Seattle, Washington

Please Ask For Catering **206-324-1945 Or 206-328-0908**

New Addition...Tea Parties For Groups At...The Surrogate Hostess Tearoom. Look for the prolific grapevine and kiwi arbor on your way from the parking lot into The Surrogate Hostess Tearoom. This French Provencial tearoom was added to The Surrogate Hostess in 1994. Over the years, this 1906 building was a library and a barber shop before becoming a dining spot.

Afternoon Tea is presented on tiered caddies and served at tables set with tablecloths, herb centerpieces or fresh flowers and mis-matched collectible china. The bright & airy tearoom has ivory stucco walls and is decorated in warm earth tones with baskets & copperware hanging from the ceiling, handsome black & white floors. A local gallery provides a visiting exibit. Allow time to browse, the gift shop carries bulk & packaged teas, cozies, teapots & kitchen accessories. The bakery specialty is Black Bottom Cake, yum! Private tea parties may be arranged for 6-40 guests. Did I mention they cater Afternoon Teas too? As your Surrogate Hostess!

$14.00 High Tea... Finger sandwiches such as: Mushroom-walnut pate and cucumber with mint butter, smoked salmon mousse, orange blossom muffins, scones with cream & preserves, mini brie en brioche, fruit trifle, pot of brewed loose tea.
$7.50 Low Tea... Finger sandwiches, scones & muffins, fresh fruit with Devon cream, lemon & ginger cookies, a pot of tea.

PRIVATE TEA PARTIES: As Scheduled
• May Accommodate Some Dietary Needs With Advance Request
• Non-Caffeine/Herbal Tea Available
• Children's Tea Parties Welcome, Ages 3+
• Watercloset: Same Floor
• **Advance Reservations Are Required**
• Free Parking Lot
• Cash Or Check
Proprietor's
Autograph _____*Date*_____

TEACUP

2207 Queen Anne Avenue North
Seattle, Washington

206-283-5931

New Addition...Tea & Scones At...Teacup. Lots of tea cups and teapots as you might expect, and a truly amazing number of teas. They sell "tons" of fine quality bulk tea in the store and through mail order. In fact, they carry a combination of over 125 greens, blacks, oolongs and herbals as well as ginsengs, chai, and organic tea. Enjoy a pot of brewed tea in their expanded seating area while checking out many of the tea-related gift items. The basic wooden tables each have colorful teapots filled with plants, although counter service is also available. P.S. Try their Morning Teacup Tea and black scented teas from Paris which are available in 2, 4 & 8ounce, as well as one pound packages.

The north wall of the shop is nearly filled to the ceiling with shelves full of teapots including authentic Yixing pottery from China and packaged goods. The shop also creates tea gift baskets and kits mailed worldwide. Tea demonstrations are usually held during the Queen Anne Christmas Walk and during the merchant Halloween event when many shops hand out goodies to the children. Call Brian or Karen for the schedule of new classes & events brewing. Ask to be on the mailing list for the newsletter and mail-order catalog too.

$4.00ish Tea & Scone... Four cup pot of brewed tea & fresh baked plain or black currant scone with butter & preserves.

TONS OF TEAS & SCONES TOO: Hours Are Seasonal
- 9:00am To 6:00pm • Monday Thru Saturday
- 10:00am To 5:00pm • Sunday
- Non-Caffeine/Herbal Tea Available
- Watercloset: Same Floor
- Wheelchair Accessible
- **Reservations: No**
- Limited-Time Street Parking
- Credit Cards: MC&V

Proprietor's
*Autograph*_____*Date*_____

TEAHOUSE KUAN YIN

1911 North 45th Street
Seattle, Washington

206-632-2055

Tea Etc. At....Teahouse Kuan Yin. If you appreciate the International experience of Afternoon Tea, you won't want to miss Teahouse Kuan Yin. A visit here is relaxing yet invigorating, as you are "transported" to other parts of the world. Kuan Yin offers about 12 Black Teas, 5 Oolongs, 11 Greens and 8 Herbal Tisanes.

There are wonderful tea related items too like, "half-round" cozies custom made from beautiful batik and ikat fabrics brought from the Orient by the proprietor; plus cups and Yixing pots. (Pronounced "yee-shing".) Kuan Yin's decor is as colorful as their variety of teas. Wall hangings from the Orient, upholstered Italian-brocade steel chairs, a collection of handmade teapots, even an aquarium of colorful designer fish are part of a very nice picture at Teahouse Kuan Yin in this upscale, quaint neighborhood. Terrific teas are sold in bulk by the friendly and knowledgeable staff.

$1.88 Per Person..A Pot Of Tea.
$1.35 Scone.. Choice of apricot, hazelnut, orange/currant, raspberry, blueberry or cranberry scone.

$1.50 Green Tea Ice Cream
$3.50 South Indian Curried Vegetables

TEA, ETC: 10:00am To 11:00pm • Sunday Thru Thursday
- 10:00am Until Midnight • Friday & Saturday
- Non-Caffeine/Herbal Tea Available
- Watercloset: Same Floor
- **Just Drop By**
- Street Parking Is Plentiful
- Credit Cards: V&MC

Proprietor's
Autograph _____*Date*_____

VILLAGE TEA ROOM & BISTRO

17651 First Avenue South
(Normandy Park)
Seattle, Washington

Village Tea Room
& Bistro

206-439-8842

It's Teatime At...Village Tea Room & Bistro. Welcome to this cozy and intimate European-style tearoom located just five minutes from SEATAC.

Almost everything for the Afternoon Tea is homemade from scratch! The pastry chef Amy, makes a wonderful Bailey's white chocolate cheesecake, and then there's the ever popular Key Lime pie! Sally, the proprietor takes great pride in her presentation of Afternoon Teas. Delicately presented, there are always fresh flowers, floral linens, classical music and thoughtful, attentive service. Tea is served on a unique collection of all white mismatched china. Allow plenty of time also to peruse the gift shop and antique mall. Private tea parties for your special events are available for 15 to 35 guests. The tearoom is also open for lunch. P.S. The Village Tea Room has been featured in Mademoiselle Magazine.

$9.95 High Tea... Fresh homemade cream-currant scone served with "Village" Devonshire Cream & raspberry jam, four assorted finger sandwiches, four assorted homemade pastries, such as lemon curd tart or chocolate petit four, cookie, teabread, and a proper pot of brewed loose tea presented with a tea strainer.

TEATIME: 2:00pm To 5:00pm • Tuesday Thru Saturday
• Sundays May Be Reserved For Private Teas
• May Accommodate Some Dietary Needs With Advance Request
• Non-Caffeine/Herbal Tea Available
• Children's Tea Parties Welcome
• Watercloset: Same Floor
• Wheelchair Accessible
• **Reservations Are Appreciated**
• Free Parking Lot
• Credit Cards: V,MC&DIS

Proprietor's
Autograph _____Date_____

THE WELLINGTON
A Victorian Tea Room

4869 Rainier Avenue South
(Historic Columbia City Area)
Seattle, Washington

206-722-8571

It's Teatime At...The Wellington, A Victorian Tea Room. The Wellington is located in a 1910 brick establishment which was originally a pharmacy & soda fountain. Today, it is The Wellington, A Victorian Tea Room. Gwyn, the proprietor says she specializes in true southern hospitality. This charming tearoom is decorated predominantly in deep green tones with pretty flowers and topiary tree accents around the room. Each of the tables has a unique theme, so you'll enjoy making the rounds with each visit. To complete this picture, you have servers in full Victorian dress.

Be sure to visit the gift shop and take home the Wellington LTD. house blend tea. Our congratulations to The Wellington! They are a recipient of The National Mayors' Small Business Of The Year Award. Lunch and dinner have been added to Afternoon Tea. There is now a Wine Bar, & Jazz on the first Friday of the month. Enjoy!

$11.95 Wellington High Tea... Tea sandwiches, fresh scone, fine pastries, tea breads and a proper pot of brewed tea.

$6.95 Dessert Tea... Fine pastries, tea breads & tea.

$5.95 Children's Tea... Tea sandwiches & treats.

$5.95 Cream Tea... Scone, cream & jam, pot of tea.

TEATIME: 12:00Noon To 9:00pm • Monday Thru Friday
• 9:00am To 5:00pm, Saturday • Sunday By Reservation Only
• Hours Are Seasonal, Please Call To Confirm
• May Accommodate Some Dietary Needs With Advance Request
• Non-Caffeine/Herbal Tea Available
• Watercloset: Same Floor • Wheelchair Accessible
• **Reservations Are Appreciated**
• Two Hour Street Parking
• Credit Cards: MC&V

Proprietor's
Autograph _____*Date*_____

COUNTRY TEA GARDEN

220 Johnson Road
Selah, Washington

509-697-7944

New Addition...It's Teatime At...The Country Tea Garden. Tea lovers patiently wait each year for the first Tuesday in June when Bev opens her magical tearoom. It seems, as the story goes...that Bev had been asking her husband for a gazebo for about 35 years until one day she got her wish. Soon, she wished for a pond...presto! several ponds. Before long her "park" started to look like a tea garden according to her husband who suggested she start serving Afternoon Teas. "I don't know about tea, I'm a coffee person," she said. "I know you could learn," He replied. Bev liked the idea of having a few ladies over now and again for tea but she would need four more gazebos. "If I don't have to wait 35 more years, I'll do it!" And she did. Not long after, an article broke in a local paper and Bev was in the tea business big time. "It's the only place of its kind anywhere around these parts." And that's the story of how Bev's tearoom began.

Afternoon Tea is served outside, guess where? Or, inside the tearoom & gift shop by Bev and her daughter Renelle her partner, and granddaughters Cotton, Echo, Tiffini, Lindsay, Leah and Leslie. Tables are dressed in pastel cloths, lace toppers, cloth napkins, fresh flowers, vintage china and antique creamers & sugar bowls. Private parties are available for 20-60 guests. P.S. A neat gift shop too, with a great selection of Santa & Angels at Christmas.

$5.50 Afternoon Tea... Tea sandwiches or fresh baked scone, lemon curd & cream, tea bread or dessert, and pot of tea.

TEATIME: 10am-4pm, Tuesday-Friday • From The 1st Tuesday In June Thru The Last Friday In September
• 3rd Tuesday In November Thru December 21, Tues.-Sat. 4pm-8pm
• May Accommodate Some Dietary Needs With Advance Request
• Non-Caffeine/Herbal Tea • Watercloset: Outside, Same Floor
• **Reservations Appreciated For Parties Of Six+ Guests**
• Free Parking Lot • Credit Cards: V&MC

Proprietor's
Autograph _____*Date*_____

CHEZ CONSTANCE
at Tea & Crumpets

203 West Railroad Avenue
Shelton, Washington

360-427-1681

New Addition...Teatime At...Chez Constance *At* **Tea & Crumpets.** She bought the bank, literally! The proprietor of Tea & Crumpets has just bought a wonderful turn of the century bank with high ceilings & handsome wainscotting. Enjoy Afternoon Teas and Constance's other popular Theme Teas in The Fireplace Room or a number of other wonderful spots throughout this interesting spot. Connie is well-known for Christmas & Mother's Day Teas and cute quotes such as, "Sit down and feed, & welcome to our table," by William Shakespeare sprinkled on her menu.

Afternoon Tea will be served at tables set with tablecloths, an eclectic collection of fine china, & fresh flowers. The Children's Tea menu is inspired by childhood stories and include "Beatrix Potter Tea" and a full menu of luncheon specialties such as Mrs. Tiggy Winkle's Favorite Salad, and Peter Rabbit's Garden. F.Y.I. Dinner & lunch are available in addition to Afternoon Tea. The homemade pastries & desserts are baked fresh daily. Private tea parties for may be arranged for 6-24 guests. *"Take some more tea, the March Hare said to Alice, very earnestly." Lewis Carroll*

$9.95 Afternoon Tea... Tea sandwiches, fruit cup, fancy pastries, scone with cream & jam, and a pot of loose brewed tea.
$5.95 Peter Pan & Wendy Tea... Shaped sandwiches, pastries, and tea, milk or hot chocolate.
$5.95 Cream Tea... Pastries, scone, jam & cream & tea.

TEATIME: 1:00pm To 4:00pm • Monday Thru Saturday
• May Accommodate Some Dietary Needs With Advance Request
• Non-Caffeine/Herbal Tea Available
• Watercloset: Same floor • Children's Tea Parties Welcome
• **Reservations Are Advised**
• Free Parking Lot & Unmetered Two Hour Street Parking
• Credit Cards:V,MC,DIS&AE
Proprietor's
Autograph _____Date_____

PICCADILLY CIRCUS

1104 First Street
Snohomish, Washington
(About 40 miles N. of Seattle)

360-568-8212

New Addition...It's Teatime At...Piccadilly Circus. Thanks to proprietors Geoff & Marion, you no longer have to cross the pond to get to Piccadilly Circus. Yes, it's right here in scenic downtown Snohomish, known by some as the antique capitol of the Northwest. Situated in an early 1900's building, Geoff & Marion have created quite an interesting garden setting. Inspired by the domed "sky" ceiling at Caesar's shopping mall in Las Vegas, they decided to duplicate this experience in miniature inside their beautiful new Tea Garden.

Afternoon Tea is presented from tiered caddies at tables set with linens, fresh flowers, and Royal Albert or Bluewater china. Almost everything is homemade, even a bakery is on premises. You can buy a dozen scones to go too. P.S. They serve English breakfast, and lunch in addition to Afternoon Tea. Allow time to browse, Picadilly Circus specializes in fine British imports, gifts & collectibles. They have one of the largest collections of teapots in the Northwest. Ask Geoff about his beloved Manchester United team.

$13.95 Afternoon Tea In The Garden... Picadilly Circus scones served with Devon cream & preserves, trio of finger sandwiches, cakes, pastries & confections, seasonal fruit, sorbet & a pot of brewed loose tea.

TEATIME: 11:30am To 5:00pm • Seven Days A Week
• May Accommodate Some Dietary Needs With Advance Request
• Non-Caffeine/Herbal Tea Available
• Children's Tea Parties Welcome
• Watercloset: same Floor
• Wheelchair Accessible
• **Reservations Are Requested**
• Unmetered Street Parking
• Credit Cards: V&MC
Proprietor's
Autograph _____*Date*_____

BRAMBLEBERY COTTAGE
Tea Shoppe
North 122 Argonne Road, Suite C
Spokane, Washington
(Inside The Francisco Building)

509-926-3293

*New Tea Spot Brewing...*It's Teatime At **Bramblebery Cottage.** Melanie and her daughter Dawn are busy selling gifts and working diligently on their new tearoom. The tearoom will offer a welcome little respite from the joy of shopping.

The parlor-style tearoom is planned to have comfortable couches & chairs with low tables, soothing background music and yummy "pick-me-up" sweets to go with freshly brewed tea. But, you don't have to wait to visit Bramblebery Cottage...stop by for craft supplies, and to learn about interesting & instructive classes which include those in tatting and beading. The shop specializes in handcrafted gifts and always serves up friendly conversation along with tea! F.Y.I. The shop carries lots of tea accoutrements, lemon birds and collectible teapots too. P.S. Melanie is looking for "tea birds" if you happen to know where she can find them. Stop by and let the ladies know you too, are anxiously waiting for their tearoom.

$4.00 Spot of Tea Special... Sweet of the day & a cup of loose brewed Metropolitan, Market Spice, or Kinnell teas.

ANTICIPATED **TEATIME:** 1pm To 4pm • Tuesday Thru Saturday
• Closed Christmas Week Thru The First Week In January
• Non-Caffeine/Herbal Tea Available
• Watercloset: Same Floor
• **Reservations Are Always Appreciated**
• Free Parking Lot
• Credit Cards: V&MC
Proprietor's
Autograph _____*Date*_____

FOTHERINGHAM HOUSE

2128 West Second Avenue
Spokane, Washington

509-838-1891

New Addition...Tea Parties From October Through April For Groups Of 16 To 28 Guests At...The Fotheringham House. Congratulations to Jackie and Graham whose restoration efforts on behalf of this 1891 Queen Anne Victorian earned them The Inland Northwest Home Award. They received awards as well, from The Spokesman Review and The Eastern Washington Historical Society. The house was built by David B. Fotheringham, Spokane's first mayor. Did you notice that the phone number just happens to be end in 1891!

Gather your group and enjoy Afternoon Tea presented by Penny of P.J.'s Parties, at tables are set with lace tablecloths, fresh flowers and Spode, Lenox or Beleek china. Tea is elegantly served from an antique samovar. Fotheringham House with its wonderful architectural features, curved glass, carved fireplace, intricate ball and spindle fretwork and antique furnishings most definitely puts you in the Victorian mood. During tea, Susan the proprietor of Virtuous Endeavors presents a trunk show of clothing made from new and antique fabrics & laces, from turn of the century patterns. A tour here is a treat, don't miss the stone path Victorian garden.

$15.00 Afternoon Tea & Tour... Three kinds of tea sandwiches, hot mushroom tarts, fruit or nut breads, scones served with fresh lemon curd & Devonshire cream, three desserts of which one is always chocolate and Kinnell's loose tea. Price includes tax.

TEA & TOUR FOR GROUPS: May Be Scheduled On Tuesdays & Wednesdays From October Thru April
- For Groups Of 16 To 28 Guests Only
- Non-Caffeine/Herbal Tea Available
- Watercloset: Same Floor
- **Please Reserve Your Date Early**
- Unmetered Street Parking
- Credit Cards: V,MC&DIS

Proprietor's
Autograph _____*Date*_____

TEA AN' TIQUES
North 618 Monroe
Spokane, Washington

509-324-8472

It's Teatime At...Tea An' Tiques. Nestled in an interesting antique shop amongst the old an' new an' nearly new collectibles, you'll discover an unexpected treasure... a spot for tea. Tables, chairs, linens and china keep changing as customers buy them out from under, but you can count on delightful tea served on a fun collection of mis-matched china and funky dishes.

The proprietor Jackie, is a "one woman show". She bakes, cooks, serves, does dishes and sells her lovely collections. Tea An' Tiques is located in one of Spokane's earliest turn of the century commercial districts. Today, the area is fast becoming a destination for "treasure" seekers as more and more antique, collectible and vintage shops crop up. Private tea parties are available on Sundays and Mondays for parties of 8 or more guests with advance deposit. Tea and antiquing, does it get any better? Happy hunting!

$10.50 Afternoon Tea... Tea sandwiches, scone with butter, jam & whipped cream, dessert, a pot of brewed loose tea.
$4.75 A Sip & A Scone... Bowl of soup of the day, scone with jam, butter & whipped cream, a pot of brewed loose tea.
$2.50 Tea & Scone... Scone with jam, whipped cream & butter, or banana bread with cream cheese, chutney, curry and almonds, and a pot of brewed loose tea.

TEA & SCONES PLUS: 11:00am-4:00pm • Tuesday Thru Saturday
• May Accommodate Some Dietary Needs With Advance Request
• Non-Caffeine/Herbal Teas Available
• Children's Tea Parties Welcome
• Wheelchair Accessible
• Watercloset: Same Floor
• **Afternoon Tea Is By 24 Hour Advance Reservation Only**
• Parking In Rear
• Cash Or Check

Proprietor's
Autograph _____Date_____

TEA & OTHER COMFORTS
9730 SR 532 Suite F
Stanwood, Washington

360-629-2668

New Addition...It's Teatime At...Tea & Other Comforts. Lace, flowers and Victorian charm will surround you when you visit Tea & Other Comforts. Your comfort is Kerri's concern. She and her mother Dawn are the proud proprietors of this adorable tearoom. Talk about comfort food, a variety of tasty specialties are featured including waffles, soups & sandwiches.

Afternoon Tea is presented on a three tiered silver caddie at tables set with tablecloths and mis-matched vintage china. There are a number of nice touches here including sugar bowls filled with colorful crystals & fresh flower garnishes on the tables. The lace curtains, floral wall coverings, long draperies, floral swags, overstuffed chairs, and watercolor paintings are evident of the artistic attention paid to details. F.Y.I. All produce here is purchased fresh from local growers. Browse about for tea accoutrements, great gifts & crafts by talented local artisans. If your child has asked for a tea party, the Teddy Bear Room here is just the spot!

$12.95 Victorian Tea... Four tea sandwiches, scones with Devonshire cream & lemon curd, crumpet with honey, cheese wafer & artichoke spread, pastries & sweets, and brewed loose tea.
$8.95 Cream Tea... Three tea sandwiches, scone with Devonshire cream, pastries & sweets, pot of brewed loose tea.
$5.95 Teddy Bear Tea... Tea sandwiches, scone & jam, cookies, chocolate banana and children's tea.
$3.25 Elevenses... Scone with cream & jam, pot of tea.

TEATIME: 10am To 6pm, Monday Thru Friday, Till 5pm, Saturday
• May Accommodate Some Dietary Needs With Advance Request
• Non-Caffeine/Herbal Tea Available
• Children's Tea Parties Welcome
• Watercloset: Same Floor • Wheelchair Accessible
• **Reservations: No**
• Free Parking Lot
• Credit Cards: V,MC,DIS,DC&AE
Proprietor's
Autograph _____Date_____

VICTORIAN TEA POTTS CAFE
inside Pacific Run Antique Mall

10228 Pacific Avenue
Tacoma, Washington

253-537-5371 *Reservations*   *Mall* **253-539-0117**

New Addition...It's Teatime At...The Victorian Tea Potts Cafe. Did you know that there is another Mrs. Potts? In fact, there are two, right here at The Victorian Tea Potts Cafe located in the back of the Pacific Run Antique Mall. Drop-in and meet Virginia Potts & Val Potts, the mother-in-law and daughter-in-law proprietors of this new tea spot. Their goal is simply to offer a variety of palate pleasers in an atmosphere of comfort and fun, "with a whole lot of friendliness on the side!" Virginia and Val both enjoy baking breads & tasty pastries, so opening a cafe was a natural.

Afternoon Tea is presented on a two tiered caddie at tables set with linens, fresh flowers and clear glass Canterbury plates, cups & saucers with an etched flower. A varied lunch menu is available in addition to Tea. Ask about the framed prints & teapots which the cafe sells. Antique lovers, allow time for shopping!

$14.95 "Tea For Two"...Assorted mini open-face tea sandwiches, fresh fruit, crumpets or mini scones served with cream & preserves, dessert of the day such as petit fours & petite pastries, and individual pots of brewed loose tea.

$7.95 Afternoon Tea...As Above, For One.

TEATIME: 10:00am To 6:00pm • Seven Days A Week
• Non-Caffeine/Herbal Tea Available
• Children's Tea Parties Welcome
• Watercloset: Same Floor
• **Reservations Are Appreciated**
• Credit Cards: V,MC&DIS

Proprietor's
Autograph _____*Date*_____

398

JEAN-PIERRE'S
Garden Room

316 Schmidt Place
Tumwater, Washington

360-754-3702

New Addition...It's Teatime At...Jean-Pierre's Garden Room. Plan ahead and reserve your spot for tea with Kerri and Jean-Pierre at their elegant tearoom formerly known as Sister's. The beautifully renovated historic Victorian home which belonged to Tumwater's founder, Michael T. Simmons is the spot for Jean-Pierre's Garden Tea Room. Born and raised in Southern France, Chef Jean-Pierre adds a French flair to all of his culinary creations.

High Tea is served on Mikasa Crystal and fine china, from Kerri's personal collection. These fine china pieces date back to her great grandmother and have been collected from all corners of the world. Kerri and Jean-Pierre invite you to sit back in an easy chair, or in front of the fireplace and enjoy a fine, relaxing tea with lots of pampering and a little history too. The proprietor shares amusing and interesting stories with you about High Tea. Private tea parties are available for 1 to 75 guests. Children's Tea Parties too. $8.50 per guest includes a bit of tea etiquette with Kerri.

$10.50 Jean-Pierre's High Tea... Traditional delicate finger sandwiches, homemade pastie, scones with fruited butters, assorted seasonal fruits, homemade pasties and brewed loose tea.

TEATIME: 11:30am To 2:30pm • Monday Thru Saturday
• May Accommodate Some Dietary Needs With Advance Request
• Non-Caffeine/Herbal Tea Available
• Children's Tea Parties Welcome
• Watercloset: Same Floor
• Wheelchair Accessible
• **24 Hour Advance Reservations Are Required**
• Free Parking Lot
• Credit Cards: V,MC,DIS&AE

Proprietor's
Autograph _____*Date*_____

CHESHIRE CAT
2801 Fort Vancouver Way
Vancouver, Washington

360-735-1141

New Addition...It's Teatime At...Cheshire Cat. It was a real pleasure to meet Avril the proprietor of Cheshire Cat. Born in India, Avril whose father was with the RAF, has traveled extensively. In fact, she served in the British Navy herself, primarily in Gibralter. Whether you hail from across the pond or not, you will find Cheshire Cat to be a warm, friendly and fun spot.

High Tea and a la carte Afternoon Teas are served at ceramic tile tables set with pretty English mis-matched bone china teacups. The tearoom is decorated in mauve tones and features a fountain, oil paintings by local artists, floral garlands and relaxing background music. P.S. Allow time to browse, Avril carries lots of British foods & gifts. If she doesn't have what you're looking for, she'll try her darndest to get it for you. She is very customer service oriented and thoroughly enjoys spending time with her visitors. F.Y.I. The dapper young gent at the shop is Avril's grandson Wes.

$8.95 High Tea... Tea sandwiches, scone, cream & jam, trifle & biscuits, Yorkshire Red, Taylor's of Harrogate English Tea.
$5.50 Tea Sandwiches... Dainty tea sandwiches include corned beef, smoked turkey breast & cream cheese with cucumber.
$4.00 Tea & Scone... Scone served with cream & jam.

TEATIME: 10:00am To 6:00pm • Wednesday Thru Sunday
• May Accommodate Some Dietary Needs With Advance Request
• Non-Caffeine/Herbal Tea Available
• Children's Tea Parties Welcome
• Watercloset: Same Floor
• Wheelchair Accessible
• **Reservations Are Appreciated, But Required For High Tea**
• Free Parking Lot
• Credit Cards: V&MC
Proprietor's
Autograph _____*Date*_____

400

POMEROY CARRIAGE HOUSE
Tea Room

20902 N.E. Lucia Falls Road
Yacolt, Washington

360-686-3537

It's Teatime At...Pomeroy Carriage House Tea Room. The Pomeroy House was built in 1920 by E. C. Pomeroy on a farm in the picturesque Lucia Valley. Logs used for the first story of the house were felled right on the site. It is the oldest house in the Lucia Valley. If you get a chance, say hello to Lil, the proprietor. Her grandparents were the Pomeroys! Now an educational museum, the Pomeroy estate depicts farm life in the 1920's before electricity. The farm provides a sensory experience to guests who participate in various activities. Assisted by costumed interpreters, you may grind coffee, wash clothes on a scrub board, feed the animals, pump water or visit a blacksmith shop. The Pomeroy Living History Museum is open to the public on first full weekends of the month from June thru October, with admission fee.

Located in the renovated carriage house, you'll discover the British Gift Shop & Carriage House Tea Room. Gift Shop hours: Monday thru Saturday 10-5, Sunday 1-5, closed Thanksgiving, Christmas, New Years & Easter. E-Mail: Pomeroy@Pacifier.com

$10.00 Once-A-Month Theme Teas.. Held in the historic log Pomeroy House. Themes have included: Flower Fairies, Winnie The Pooh, and Anne of Green Gables. Call for schedule of these theme events. Reservations are required for theme teas.

$6.50 Tea Plate... Tea sandwiches, scone, soup or fruit, sweets & tea. (Wednesday-Saturday 11:30am to 3pm, no reservations.)

TEATIME: 11:30am To 3:00pm • Wednesday Thru Saturday
• Tearoom Is One Flight Up On The Second Floor
• Non-Caffeine/Herbal Tea Available
• Watercloset: Same Floor
• **Reservations Are Required Only For Once-A-Month Theme Teas**
• Free Parking Lot Available
• Credit Cards: V&MC

Proprietor's
Autograph _____Date_____

CHAI WALLAH
30 South Colville
Walla Walla, Washington

509-525-2807

New Addition...It's Time For Tea At...Chai Wallah. Don & Kate describe Chai Wallah as an Asian tea house. It is situated in an old Masonic Temple located in a college town area of Walla Walla, Washington. Chai Wallah actually means a seller of tea; Wallah being a Hindi word for a seller or merchant. In what better town to open a shop named Chai Wallah? Don told me that he and his wife hoped to fill a tea void in the area with the opening of Chai Wallah. This is a fine opportunity to discover new teas & accessories for your at home brewing pleasure.

This colorful & casual tea house has several small tables at which to enjoy a pot of tea and repast. The shop features relaxed low lighting and primary colors. The walls are yellow, the ceiling dark red, and the floors & shelves are royal blue.Drop by and meet Don & Kate, you're in for an International tea adventure!

$2.85-$12.00 Per 4 Oz. Of Bulk Tea.. Ranging from Ceylon to Chinese Dragonwell, with emphasis on Asian teas.
$1.75 Samosa... An Indian specialty with potato & peas.
$2.50 Mochi... An Japanese treat made with sweet rice.
$2.00 Pot Of Tea... Pot of brewed loose tea.
$1.20 Scone... Your selection of the scones of the day.

POT OF TEA TIME: 10:00am To 6:00pm • Seven Days A Week,
• Till 9:00pm On Thursday & Friday Evenings
• Non-Caffeine/Herbal Tea Available
• Watercloset: Nearby Common Area, Same Floor
• Wheelchair Accessible
• **Please Drop By**
• Free Parking Lot Behind The Shop
• Credit Cards: V&MC

Proprietor's
Autograph _____*Date*_____

British Columbia

By Brian Austin
British Consul-General
Vancouver, British Columbia Canada

Sharing A Tradition

"'Tea began as a medicine and grew into a beverage,' thus states The Book of Tea by Okara Kakuzo the classic account to which I am greatly indebted. According to his work, the custom of offering a guest a cup of tea began five centuries before the Christian era when Kwauyin, a disciple, offered a cup to the philospher Laotse, the founder of Taoism at the gate of the Han Pass. Ever since, tea has been as much a ritual as a beverage. In the eighth century the poet Liwah formulated the Code of Tea, therby becoming the patron of all Chinese tea mercahnts. Tea had spread from China to Japan as early as 729 and seeds were planted there in 801. The enjoyment of tea in Japan grew into the art of the tea ceremony, reaching its height in the sixteenth century in its formal simplicity.

It was also at this time that tea first came to Europe, brought by the DutchEast India Company in 1610. It reached England in 1650, described as 'That excellent and by all physicians approved China drink, called by the Chineans Tcha, and by other nations Tay, alias Tea.' A luxury, tea became one of the bonds between east and West, stimulating trade and bringing with it porcelain, art and fashion. It civilized English social life, with the teahouse and coffee shop replacing the tavern as the meeting place for those who wished to keep their minds clear and their wits stimulated. Soon it became a necessity of life, something the tax man could rely on for revenue.

Its popularity grew and its price fell as tea plantations spread to India and Ceylon (as it was then). Tea became an essential part of the social life of Britain and the British Empire, an oasis in the daily round where friends and family could meet and enjoy a quiet ritual, boiling the water, heating the pot, opening the tea caddie, measuring spoonfuls and savouring the aroma as freshly boiling water was poured on the dried, crinkled leaves. 'A cup of tea' became the instant response in crisis and stress, a drink to calm the nerves, refresh the spirits and speak of silent sympathy.

Tea offers something to everyone, bringing East and West together in its enjoyment. From the full spread of the English high tea to the delicate accompaniment to a Chinese meal, tea can be savoured by all. Enjoy this book, the teas and the tea houses, remembering as you do so, that you are sharing and continuing a centuries old tradition."

Brian Austin, British Consul-General

BRITANNIA HOUSE
Restaurant & Tea Room
Highway 99 (Between Vancouver & Whistler)
Britannia Beach, British Columbia
"You can't miss it!"

604-896-2335

New Addition...It's Teatime At...Britannia House. Built in 1905, the inviting Britannia House is owned by Howard and his wife Eileen known as "The Queen of Scones," a moniker which has stuck since she started baking scones in their new restaurant & tearoom in 1995. Britannia House is 45 km north of Vancouver (27 miles). Take a comfortable seat in the front room with a spectacular view of the ocean, mountains and the Murchison Glacier or, on the forest-side patio in season, with visiting squirrels. Britannia House offers a full menu in addition to the Afternoon Tea.

Afternoon Tea is presented on a three tiered caddie at tables set with floral linens, Belgian lace toppers, silk centerpieces and an eclectic collection of English china. Decor includes soft yellow walls, photographs, ornate green chairs with white seats, hand-painted vases and antiques. Classical background music and a wood-burning fireplace for chilly winter afternoons, nicely completes the picture. Tea parties are available for up to 30 guests.

$19.95 Classic Afternoon Tea For Two...A selection of petit sandwiches, rich scones served with a Devon cream mixture, tea treats & desserts, and a pretty pot of brewed tea.
$5.75 Cream Tea... Rich scones served with a Devon cream mixture, butter & jam, and a pretty pot of brewed tea.

TEATIME: 2:00pm To 5:00pm • Thursday Thru Monday
• May Accommodate Some Dietary Needs With Advance Request
• Non-Caffeine/Herbal Tea Available
• Free Parking Lot
• **Reservations Advised For Weekend Afternoon Teas**
• **No Reservations For Cream Tea**
• Credit Cards: V&MC
Proprietor's
Autograph _____*Date*_____

HARP AND HEATHER

9749 Willow Street
Chemainus On Vancouver Island
British Columbia

250-246-2434

It's Teatime At...Harp & Heather. What's happening today in Chemanius? Once a thriving sawmill town, Chemainus quickly became a very quiet community after the sawmill closed. Most of the establishments fell into classic disrepair; only a few businesses remained. Thanks to the dream of Karl Schultz and a few supporters, Chemainus again became a hot spot. Artists began painting murals in the village, and businesses again started to grow. Now, the town gets worldwide attention and thousands of visitors.

One of the spots they're heading to is Harp & Heather for Afternoon Tea with proprietors Janet and John. Surprisingly enough, there are locals who don't yet know about Harp & Heather. The concierge at a BIG hotel in Vancouver called and thanked me for telling him about them. Harp & Heather is situated in a turn-of-the-century library, which later became a bank, and still later, a land management office. Harp & Heather is full of old world charm.

$9.75 Celtic Afternoon Cream Tea... Assorted sandwiches, sweets, scone, cream, strawberry preserves, pot of tea.

$7.75 Harp & Heather Low Tea... Tea sandwiches, sponge cake with cream, scone with cream & preserves, pot of tea.

$6.35 Welsh Cream Tea... Two Scones served with cream & preserves, butter and a pot of brewed tea.

TEATIME: 10:00am To 5:30pm • Seven Days A Week
- May Accommodate Some Dietary Needs With Advance Request
- Non-Caffeine/Herbal Tea Available
- Watercloset: Same Floor
- Wheelchair Accessible
- **Reservations Are Appreciated**
- Unmetered Street Parking
- Credit Cards: V,MC&AE

Proprietor's
Autograph _____*Date*_____

THE CANADIAN MUSEUM
of Rail Travel Tearoom

One Van Horne Street
Cranbrook, British Columbia

250-489-3918

New Addition...Tea & Scones, A Tradition On Saturdays...At The Canadian Museum Of Rail Travel Tearoom. (Daily in July and August from 10:00am to 6:00pm.) A spot of tea & the museum's famous scones are served in the "Argyle" dining car tearoom. The Argyle is a restored 1929 first class deluxe sleeper. Tables are arranged to accommodate two and four persons and are set with tablecloths and fresh flowers.

Also on display in this room is the largest public collection of Canadian Pacific Railway china, silverware, and glassware in the country. Several china patterns from different eras are portrayed here, including the plain crest, the Alexandra band, the blue maple leaf pattern, and perhaps the most valuable-the brown maple leaf pattern, made by English "Minton" and French "Limoges." Canadian Pacific always tried to supply the best available, including the monogrammed quadruple "Elkington plate" silverware. Catalogs on this collection are on view when the tearoom is open. F.Y.I. This neat spot is available for private parties for your train lover.

$3.95 Scone Or $2.50 Half Scone... These large raisin scones are made from the Fort Steele recipe, they are served with butter, whipped cream & strawberry jam or marmalade.

$1.50 Large Pot of Murchie's Tea (6-7 cups) "All teas are made by pouring boiling water over loose tea leaves, in pre-heated pots. The tradition of good tea-making for fuller flavour."

TEATIME: 12Noon To 5:00pm • Saturday
• Expanded Summer Season Hours: 10am To 6pm In July & August
• Non-Caffeine/Herbal Tea Available
• Watercloset: A Few Stairs Away
• **Please Drop By For A Visit**
• Free Parking Lot
• Credit Cards: V&MC

Director's
Autograph _____*Date*_____

PANDORA'S TEA GALLERY
& Collectibles

682 Second Avenue
Fernie, British Columbia

250-423-7818

New Addition...A Spot Of Tea & Tea Leaf Readings At...Pandora's Tea Gallery. They say you can't believe everything you read, but I don't know if they had tea leaves in mind! Charlene, the proprietor of this popular little spot is brewing a lot of loose tea and serving light fare as well.

Tea is served at tables set with pastel teal green tablecloths which match the walls and tile floors, and the "Cafe Royal" Syracuse china. Look for the little "sniffle" tea jars as Charlene calls them, to help you make your tea selection. Allow time for your visit to Fernie, it's a neat little tourist town popular for biking, skiing, boating and...shopping! Lots of unique little shops dot this quaint area. F.Y.I. Pandora's carries everything from candles to bone china teapots and gourmet Canadian foods such as Saskatoon Rhubarb Jam and chocolate covered ginger. Gift baskets too. P.S. If you need an ice cream chaser, there's an ice cream parlour here. F.Y.I. Saskatoons are native berries.

$15.00 Tea Leaf Reading
$2.00 Pot of Tea
$3.95 Gourmet Cake
$1.25 Scone... Fresh baked Fernie scones served with Saskatoons & heavy cream.

TEATIME: 9:30am-5:30pm, Mon.-Thurs.,Saturday, Till 9pm Friday
• Low Caffeine Tea Available
• Watercloset: Same Floor
• **Reservations Are Requested For Tea Readings Only**
• Unmetered Street Parking
• Credit Cards: V&MC

Proprietor's
Autograph _____*Date*_____

THE GRASSROOTS
Tea House
262 Lorne Street (Riverside Park)
Kamloops, British Columbia

250-374-9890

New Addition...New Proprietor...It's Teatime From May 1, To September 30, At...The Grassroots Tea House. This neat little teahouse is located on the grounds of Riverside Park, known for its many summer attractions. The stone front cottage known as the Grass Roots Teahouse was built in the 1950's, and was run for years by Louise Grass. Louise is still at the teahouse assisting Thom the new proprietor. Thom, formerly with The Royal Canadian Mounted Police, has recently modified the name ever so slightly, welcome to The Grassroots Tea House.

English Afternoon Tea is served a la carte at teatime. All baking is done on premises. Tables are set with linens, fresh flowers and a nice collection of mis-matched china. This quaint teahouse has hardwood floors, "grassroots" green carpet, lace curtains, wall-sconces, and framed prints in a hunt theme motif. Weather permitting, enjoy tea on the garden patio overlooking the park, hanging baskets of flowers, chirping birds...it's summertime! Call about lunch & dinner too. P.S. Patio view of the Thompson River, Mt. Peter & Mt. Paul. F.Y.I. He didn't get to keep his horse.

$7.00 Afternoon Tea...A La Carte. Two finger sandwiches, two tea biscuits with butter, jam & honey, a muffin, cheese portion, and a pot of brewed loose tea.

TEATIME: May 1-Sept. 30, 2pm To 4pm • Tuesday Thru Saturday
• Call To Confirm Hours & Specialties, Under New Proprietorship
• May Accommodate Some Dietary Needs With Advance Request
• Non-Caffeine/Herbal Tea Available
• Watercloset: Same Floor • Wheelchair Accessible
• **Reservations Are Requested**
• Free Parking Lot
• Credit Cards: V&MC
Proprietor's
Autograph _____*Date*_____

CALICO CAT
Tea House
1081 Haliburton Street
Nanaimo, British Columbia

250-754-3865

New Addition...It's Teatime At...Calico Cat Tea House. This Heritage 1910 cottage is a purrrrfectly delightful spot for Afternoon Tea and a variety of other tempting house specialties. You may also be happy to know that the tea leaves have predicted a B&B in Heather and Doug's future; Calico Cat will expand to become a B&B soon, if all goes as planned.

Afternoon Tea is presented on two or three tiered caddies at tables set with burgundy linens and floral toppers. This cozy spot is decorated in greens, aqua and burgundy tones and nicely accented with turn of the century prints. The original fireplace and stained glass windows are lovely architectural features. Patio seating too.

Curious about your future? Heather can schedule a fun tea-leaf reading for you too. Be sure to choose loose tea! P.S. Consider planning a visit to Calico Cat when you ferry between Nanaimo and Victoria. Ask about "Dinner & Teacup Reading Evenings."

$14.95 Two For Tea... Dessert tray of homemade scones, a selection of sweet treats and a pot of brewed tea.

$12.95 Afternoon Tea... Finger sandwiches, scone with cream & lemon curd or strawberry jam, sweet treat, pot of tea.

$10.50 Tea Cup Reading.. Advance reservations please.

TEATIME: 2:00pm To 4:00pm • Monday Thru Saturday
• Please Call For Sundays Hours
• May Accommodate Some Dietary Needs With Advance Request
• Non-Caffeine/Herbal Tea Available
• Children's Tea Parties Welcome
• Watercloset: Same Floor • Wheelchair Accessible
• **Reservation Are Required For Tea-Leaf Readings**
• Free Parking Area
• Credit Cards: V&MC

Proprietor's
Autograph _____Date_____

JARDIN ANTIQUES
& Tea Garden
5225 9th Avenue At Highway 97
Okanagan Falls, British Columbia

250-497-6733

New Addition...A Spot Of Tea At...Jardin Antiques & Tea Garden. If you enjoy estate jewelry as much as I do, you'll especially enjoy a trip to Jardin Antiques & Tea Garden. Theresa is actually a gemologist and fine baubles are her specialty. The shop has a large collection of antiques & collectibles as well.

A "spotta" and a sweet are served at cozy tables in this quaint Victorian farm house. Lace tablecloths, old-fashioned china, hardwood floors, an antique wood-burning stove, pale pink walls with raspberry trim, and artistic seasonal decor are all part of the atmosphere at Theresa and Gerald's shop. Weather permitting, consider taking tea on the flowering patio "jardin" with the delicate iridescent humming birds. P.S. It can get pretty warm up this way, so you'll be happy to know that Jardin is airconditioned.

$1.25-$1.65 Pot Of Tea

$.95-$2.50 Sweets... Ranging from the ever popular Nanaimo Bars to "squares" to fresh homemade pie.

TEATIME: 10:00am To 5:00pm • Monday Thru Saturday
- 10:00am To 4:00pm, Sunday
- Non-Caffeine/Herbal Tea Available
- Watercloset: Same Floor
- Wheelchair Accessible
- **Please Drop In**
- Free Parking Area
- Credit Cards:V&MC

Proprietor's
Autograph _____Date_____

411

VILLAGE COUNTRY INN
& Tea Room
7557 Canyon Avenue
Radium Hot Springs, British Columbia

250-347-9392

New Addition...It's Teatime At...Village Country Inn & Tea Room. Sasha and Gorm just want you to be happy and content after visiting their tearoom. Everything is freshly homemade here, nothing frozen. The grand tearoom features European elegance and country charm blended together by a floor to ceiling stone fireplace in the centre of the tearoom.

Afternoon Tea is served a la carte in the dining room or on the veranda weather permitting. Tables are set with floral place mats, fresh flowers, candles, doilies and Dudson fine china. I have selected my favorite chocolate items to feature here, but there a number of other selections available. Enjoy the state of the art sound system which fills the room with classical music. Enjoy the award-winning photographs, a bird house collection and country crafts. Glance out the window for a beautiful view of the Village Park and mountains surrounding Radium Hot Springs. viconinn@rockies.net See: www.radiumhotsprings.com/villagecountryinn

$5.50 Open Face Sandwiches... By Reservation Only
$4.00 Chocolate Torte Or Chocolate Eclairs
$2.50 Black Currant Scones... Served with fresh yogurt and fresh fruit.
$2.50 Pot Of Tea... Large pot of brewed loose tea.

TEATIME: 2:00pm To 5:00pm • Seven Days A Week
• May Accommodate Some Dietary Needs With Advance Request
• Non-Caffeine/Herbal Tea Available
• Watercloset: Same Floor
• Wheelchair Accessible
• **Reservations Are Highly Recommended**
• Credit Cards: V&MC

Proprietor's
Autograph _____*Date*_____

412

BRITISH HOME
3986 Moncton Street
(In Steveston Village)
Richmond, British Columbia

604-274-2261

New Addition...Cream Teas At...British Home.
"We're not fancy, just down home folks," say Ray and Mary the darling proprietors of the British Home who originally hail from Birmingham, England. "It's like being at home here, our British Home." Practically everything here is homemade and served in a casual setting at old oak tables and chairs. Even the blue cross-stitched gingham tablecloths were homemade by one of Mary's friends. This couple's social life truly revolves around their little shop in this fishing village. Friends like you just like to stop by!

Cream Teas are most informal at this spot where old friends from across the pond gather and meet new friends. The shop is decorated with British memorabilia and pictures of the "Royals." The British Home is also a fine spot for British groceries & gifts. P.S. Traditional English fare is available in addition to Cream Tea.

$3.25 Cream Teas...A fresh baked currant scone served with Devon cream & homemade strawberry or raspberry jam and a pot of brewed English Typhoo tea.

TEATIME: Winter: 11:00am To 6:00pm • Seven Days A Week
• Summer: Till 8:00pm • Thursday, Friday & Saturday
• Non-Caffeine/Herbal Tea Available
• Watercloset: Same Floor
• **Reservations: No**
• Free Parking Lot In The Rear Thru The Alley
Proprietor's
Autograph _____*Date*_____

413

COTTAGE TEA ROOM

12220 Second Avenue Unit 100
(Stevenson Village)
Richmond, British Columbia

604-241-1853

New Addition...It's Teatime At...Cottage Tea Room. This charming seaside community is home to Margaret's Cottage Tea Room. Her friendly "hello" is very familiar to her regular customers, and cheerfully welcomes new visitors. She brings fond memories of time spent in England to her tearoom.

Afternoon Tea is usually presented on three tiered caddies at tables set with linens & seasonal centerpieces. The walls are painted white and accented with colorful Royal memorabilia. Margaret's specialties include wonderful homemade soups, fresh-baked scones and pies from old family recipes. These tasty dishes are freshly prepared throughout the day. You may take tea outside in season, weather permitting at umbrella tables. Browse around, the Cottage Tea Room carries British groceries, teapots, tea ware, English aprons and imported tea towels. Ask Margaret about her personal collection of unique tea towels.

$6.50 English High Tea... Finger sandwiches, scones served with Devon cream & jam, chocolate, cookies, and a selection of brewed tea.

TEATIME: 10:00am To 5:00pm • Seven Days A Week
• Please Call For Seasonal Hours, Longer During The Summer
• May Accommodate Some Dietary Needs With Advance Request
• Non-Caffeine/Herbal Tea Available
• Children's Tea Parties Welcome
• Watercloset: Same Floor
• **Reservations Are Usually Required**
• Unmetered Street Parking
• Cash Or Check

Proprietor's
Autograph _____*Date*_____

414

SIDNEY TEAROOM
9732 First Street
Sidney, British Columbia

250-656-0490

New Addition...It's Teatime At...Sidney Tearoom. Sidney Tearoom recently opened its doors in this retired metal-sided granary, built from all accounts in the late 1800's. Years ago it was a tearoom known as The Harrington Wyatt Tearoom and in recent years it has been a number of different restaurants. Murray, the new proprietor offers a full menu of lunch entrees in addition to a Tea Service selection. The spirit of Afternoon Tea lives on!

Tea is served in the dining room at tables set with tablecloths and fresh flowers. In season, the plates are garnished with fresh flowers as well. The decor includes gray carpet and soft tan walls accented by framed prints. Non-smoking.Sidney is approximately 30-35 k from Victoria.

$8.50 Tea Service... Assorted tea sandwiches, fresh baked raisin scones served with Jersey cream & strawberry jam, fruit tarts and a pot of tea.

$3.50 Scones... Fresh baked daily raisin scones served with Devonshire cream & strawberry jam.

TEATIME: 11:30 To 4:00pm • Monday Thru Saturday
• May Accommodate Some Dietary Needs With Advance Request
• Non-Caffeine/Herbal Tea Available
• Watercloset: Same Floor
• Wheelchair Accessible
• **Reservations Are Recommended**
• Unmetered Street Parking
• Credit Cards; V,MC&DIS

Proprietor's
Autograph _____Date_____

415

POINT NO POINT
1505 West Coast Road
Sooke, British Columbia

250-646-2020

New Addition...It's Teatime At...Point No Point.
Described as a small tearoom with an immense view, Point No Point
is not exaggerating. The view from this tearoom is hard to beat with
two walls of windows overlooking the Strait of Juan de Fuca, the
Pacific Ocean and the snow capped Olympic Mountains. A scenic 40
mile (64 km) drive west of Victoria along Hwy 14, Point No Point
Resort is located about 25 km past the town of Sooke.
    Afternoon Tea is served at white tables set with blue place
mats, fresh flowers & white china, by friendly servers in long
flowery dresses. Nearly everything at Stuart and Sharon's tearoom
is homemade from scratch. P.S. Consider spending the night here.
How about a log cabin complete with a fireplace, kitchen, private
bath & a view of the ocean? You might even get lucky and see killer
and grey whales, seals & otters! F.Y.I. "Point No Point" is a
surveying term: "a geographical spot can be seen from only one
location." Stuart and Sharon are looking forward to your visit.

$7.95 Afternoon Tea... Raisin scone served with
whipped cream & strawberry jam, finger sandwiches such as
Alaskan smoked salmon & cream cheese, and cucumber & sprouts,
carrot cake with cream cheese topping, fresh fruit crumble, fresh
fruit, and a brewed pot of famous Point No Point tea.

TEATIME: 2:30pm To 4:30pm • Seven Days A Week
• Closed Some Holidays, Please Call
• Non-Caffeine/Herbal Tea Available
• Watercloset: Same Floor
• **Reservations Are Not Required**
• Free Parking Lot
• Credit Cards: V,MC&AE
Proprietor's
Autograph _____*Date*_____

THE TRICKLE INN
5290 Trans Canada Highway
Tappen, British Columbia

250-835-8835

New Addition...It's Teatime At...The Trickle Inn.
The Trickle Inn graces a hillside overlooking the beautiful Shuswap Lake, midway between Calgary and Vancouver. This spot originally known as The Carlin House, has been considered the centre of hospitality for the community since the turn of the century. Carol became the new proprietor and substantially renovated the Inn in 1995 turning it into a Victorian style B&B. "Enjoy our natural setting...the forest is our backyard. Listen to the trickling mountain brook after which The Trickle Inn was named. Smell the stately cedars and relax beneath the fruit trees in our yard."

High Tea and Tea & Scones are served in the dining room at a magnificent 10 foot long, elaborately carved oak dining table set with linens and fine china. Ask to tour the Inn, there's a long history of warmth and friendship here, and don't miss the gazebo constructed in the Shuswaps. F.Y.I. An antique shop is expected to open shortly. The Gift Shop run by Eve & Paul features collectibles, estate jewelry, glassware, silver, linens, crystal, china and more.
E-Mail:trickle@jetstream.net   See: www.shuswap.bc.ca./sunny/tricklin.htm

$20.00 High Tea... Three finger sandwiches such as: salmon with dill, cucumber with cream cheese, shredded carrots with cottage cheese & hazelnuts, etc. mini quiche, fresh scones, cream & jam, shortbread cookies, fruit, wee bit of chocolate and a pot of brewed loose tea.

$8.00 Scones & Tea... Fresh baked scone served with cream & jam, and a pot of brewed loose tea.

TEATIME: 1:00pm To 4:00pm • Seven Days A Week
• May Accommodate Some Dietary Needs With Advance Request
• Non-Caffeine/Herbal Tea Available
• Watercloset: One Flight Up
• **Advance Reservations Are Required**
• Free Parking Lot
• Credit Cards: V,MC&AE

Proprietor's
Autograph _____*Date*_____

HOTEL VANCOUVER

900 West Georgia Street
Vancouver, British Columbia

604-684-3131

It's Teatime At...Hotel Vancouver. The custom of tea-drinking is one of the great traditions of mankind. The Hotel Vancouver is tipping their cup in a new direction now that Afternoon Tea is served in the renovated bright and vibrant colored Griffins Restaurant. The designers of this yellow, California-inspired bistro commissioned the talents of local artists for the restaurant's interesting paintings. Near the top of the walls, stenciled griffins remind you where you are.

Afternoon Tea is served in a somewhat unusual three tiered presentation. The caddie is black iron, with vibrant colored tea plates in keeping with the theme of the room, and the teacups are checkerboard-like. The Griffins Restaurant offers about 20 different teas, some bagged, some loose served in individual white porcelain teapots. Enjoy this lively fun atmosphere, where conversation flows and spirits lift. P.S. Just in case you still have room after tea, there's a dessert buffet priced around $8.50.

$13.95 Griffins Tea...A selection of tea sandwiches, pastry table with scones, Devonshire cream & fresh preserves, French pastries, fresh fruit in season and a pot of your choice of classic or fruit infusion bagged or loose tea.

$6.95 Scones & Tea... Scones served with Devonshire cream & preserves and a pot of your choice of bagged or loose tea.

TEATIME: 2:30pm To 4:30pm • Seven Days A Week
- May Accommodate Some Dietary Needs With Advance Request
- Non-Caffeine/Herbal Tea Available
- Watercloset: Same Floor
- Wheelchair Accessible
- **Please Walk In, No Reservations**
- Valet Parking, Sorry No Validation
- Credit Cards: DC,DIS,MC,V,AE&JCB

L'autograph
du Concierge _____*Date*_____

Bath Buns

Daughters of the British Empire   Sierra Madre, CA.

"Traditional recipe from the city of Bath, Somerset, England."

4 cups sifted warm flour
1 teaspoon salt
1 cup warm milk
1 ounce yeast creamed with 1 teaspoon sugar
1 stick margarine
3/4 cup of sugar
3 eggs
3/4 cup of raisins
2 Tablespoons candied lemon peel
2 Tablespoons coarsely crushed cube sugar
Egg or sweetened milk for glaze

Add creamed yeast to tepid milk. Pour into a well in the warmed sieved flour and salt, knead lightly. Cream the fat and sugar and beat in the eggs. Work this mixture into the dough with the raisins and peel. Put to rise for 40 minutes. Shape into buns and put on greased cookie sheet. Leave to rise for 15 to 20 minutes. Brush with beaten egg or sweetened milk and sprinkle with the crushed cube sugar. Bake at 375 degrees for 20 to 30 minutes.

Can be served warm from the oven or cooled. Delicious with coffee in the morning or afternoon tea.

*"A tearoom is a spot where old friends gather
and new friends meet."*

Photo courtesy of Jane Warren Antiques   Pasadena, California

A "Mote" spoon from the 1600's. "The Mote spoon was used to remove particles or mote from the surface of the tea when in the cup or in the spout of the pot. They were often included in sets of teaspoons or caddies." Notice the pointy end too. The spoon is from the collection of Jane Warren Antiques.

MURCHIE'S

Many Locations In The Lower Mainland & Victoria

Mail Order **800-663-0400**

It's Teatime At...Murchie's In British Columbia.
103 years ago, John Murchie began importing tea. A passionate and knowledgeable tea blender, John created wonderful blends which he delivered by horse-drawn carriage to his discriminating customers. Today, Murchie's is one of the foremost tea merchants. Their signature teas, and custom blends are proudly served to a discriminating International clientele of fine hotels & establishments. Murchie's packaged teas are available along with a nice assortment of tea accoutrements, at the following locations. Be sure to ask about Murchie's Earl Grey Tea Jelly and their mail-order catalog.

Locations In British Columbia With Tea & Coffee Bars

- **Burnaby**...5000 Kingsway Street...604-432-6800
- **Richmond**...(Centre)...6551 #3 Road...604-278-6024
- **Vancouver**...970 Robson Street...604-669-0783
- **Vancouver**...850 Park Royal N. (Shopping Centre) 604-922-3136
- **Vancouver**...City Square Centre...555 W.12th Ave....604-872-6930
- **W.Vancouver**...Memorial Library 1950 Marine Dr...604-925-4551
- **Victoria**...1110 Government Street...250-383-3112
- **White Rock** (S.Surrey) Windsor Sq. Ctr.1959 152 St. 604-531-7275

$2.00-$3.00 Tea & Scone... Cup of brewed tea, many blends from which to choose, and a tasty fresh baked scone.

TEA & SCONES: Store Hours Vary • Seven Days A Week
- Peppermint Herbal Tea Available
- Wheelchair Accessible
- **Just Pop In**
- Street Park Or Parking Lot
- Credit Cards: MC&V

Manager's
Autograph _____*Date*_____

ROEDDE HOUSE MUSEUM

1415 Barclay Street (West End)
Vancouver, British Columbia

604-684-7040

New Addition...It's Tour & Teatime At...The Roedde House Museum On The Second, Third & Fourth Sundays Of The Month. Built in 1893 for Mathilda and G.A. Roedde, Vancouver's first bookbinder, the Roedde House has been painstakingly restored & authentically decorated in Victorian-Edwardian style within a beautiful parkside setting. It is owned by the city of Vancouver and operated by their non-profit volunteer group, Roedde House Preservation Society. The architectural design of this Queen Anne house is attributed to the notable Francis M. Rattenbury. He also designed The Parliament Buildings, The Empress Hotel in Victoria, and The Vancouver Court House which is now The Art Gallery.

Tea is served by volunteers at tables set with fine bone china and a handsome silver service. F.Y.I. You may join "Friends of Roedde House" and for $10.00, receive the quarterly newsletter with advance notice of the lecture series, and their musical evenings and special events. If you live in the area you may want to consider the volunteer opportunities. Ask about holding a privately catered tea party. P.S. Allow a little time to glance about at cards & gifts, etc. Be sure to visit their picturesque Edwardian Gazebo Garden.

$5.00 "Afternoon Tea" & Tour...A downstairs tour of this fascinating house plus tea and a biscuit. Seniors $3.00

TEA & TOUR: 2:00pm To 4:00pm, 2nd., 3rd. & 4th. Sundays
- Tea & Tour Is Every Sunday From July 1, To Labor Day Weekend
- Non-Caffeine/Herbal Tea Available
- Watercloset: Same Floor
- Wheelchair Accessible
- **Reservations Are Appreciated For Larger Groups**
- Limited Parking Available
- Cash

Curator's
*Autograph*_____*Date*_____

SECRET GARDEN
Tea Company
5559 West Boulevard (Kerrisdale Area)
Vancouver, British Columbia

604-261-3070

New Addition...It's Teatime At...Secret Garden Tea Company. One of Kathy and Andrea's customers told me about The Secret Garden. What a delight! These proprietor's along with their friendly staff bake everything daily on premises, serve tea, cater tea parties and enjoy their visits with customers.

High Teas are presented on three tiered caddies and served at antiquey tables set with linens, flowers in pots & evening candles. The building outside is green. The interior is creamy yellow with dark forest green accents.Something of a gallery, local artists display their work at Secret Garden in a rotating exhibit. P.S. Secret Garden packages tea under their own label. Don't miss the cabinets full of tea accoutrements, gifts & books. Private tea parties may be arranged for 20-50 guests. F.Y.I. The lemon curd tarts are a must!

$14.95 High Tea... Smoked salmon on pumpernickel, cucumber on savory heart biscuit, ginger cream cheese pinwheels, famous fab lemon curd tarts, raspberry cake, petite chocolate eclairs, mini scones with Devon cream & jam, a pot of brewed loose tea.

$6.00 Mini High Tea... Two mini pastries, fresh baked sweet scone with Devonshire cream, small pot of brewed loose tea.

$8.95 Children's Tea... Teddy Bear sandwiches, PB & Banana pinwheels, lemon tarts, Rice Krispy squares & jelly, tea.

TEATIME: 1:30pm To 5:30pm • Seven Days A Week
• May Accommodate Some Dietary Needs With Advance Request
• Non-Caffeine/Herbal Tea Available
• Children's Tea Parties Welcome
• Watercloset: Same Floor
• **24 Hour Advance Reservations For High Tea**
• Credit Cards: V&MC

Proprietor's
Autograph _____Date_____

SUTTON PLACE HOTEL

845 Burrard Street
Vancouver, British Columbia

604-682-5511

The Sutton Place Hotel

It's Teatime At...The Sutton Place Hotel. The Sutton Place Hotel is an elegant residential style hotel with a distinct European flair. It is located in the heart of Vancouver's business district at the corner of the famous Robson-Strasse. This area is well known for boutiques & specialty shops. The following is a quote from the hotel, "To celebrate the city's International community, the Five Diamond, AAA-rated Sutton Place Hotel presents Tea Time featuring European, Chinese and Japanese Afternoon Teas."

Afternoon Tea is served up a few steps in the newly renovated Cafe Fleuri, a lovely open airy spot. It is decorated in deep floral tones with a beige floral carpet and dark floral table skirts with fresh cut flowers on each table. F.Y.I. For those of you who love chocolate as I do, inquire about The Sutton Place's delicious evening Chocolate Buffet!

$15.00 Afternoon Tea... Traditional English finger sandwiches, French pastries, a hot scone with jams & Devonshire cream & choice of loose tea, including signature "Sutton Blend".

$7.50 Tea & Scones... Two Scones served with Devonshire cream & preserves, and your choice of loose tea, including their signature "Sutton Blend."

TEATIME: 2:30pm To 5:00pm • Monday Thru Saturday
- May Accommodate Some Dietary Needs With Advance Request
- Non-Caffeine/Herbal Tea Available
- Watercloset: Same Floor
- Wheelchair Accessible
- **Reservations Are Requested**
- Non-Validated, Approx. $3.00 Per Hour Self-Parking
- Credit Cards: V,MC,DIS,CB,JCB,DC&AE

Proprietor's
Autograph _____*Date*_____

TEAROOM T

2460 Heather Street
Vancouver, British Columbia

604-874-8320

New Addition...It's Teatime At...Tearoom T.
"Too many cooks spoil the brew," not so however here at Tearoom T, where seven active proprietors and nearly an equal number of silent ones keep this tearoom hoppin! Christine, Petra and Garret are just a few who you are most likely to meet when you drop in for over 160 fine teas and all kinds of tea accoutrements.

That's not all. Tearoom T offers tea education, enlightenment, and tea symposiums to their customers. They seek to become an oasis of Serenity, Purity, Harmony & Tranquility in the midst of a frantic world. Learn a bit about Japanese and Chinese tea ceremonies with experts from the Urasenke Foundation who present complimentary tea classes periodically. Interesting and multi-cultural tea adventures are usually offered for your T-edification, monthly. The proprietors are very community oriented. You will often see them sampling tea at various town events. Please call for a schedule of upcoming Theme Teas and remember to reserve your spot early.

$5.00 Saturday & Sunday...Afternoon Cream Tea.
Scone with Devonshire cream & jam, pastry, and brewed loose tea.
$4.00 A La Carte Cream Tea... Available most anytime, scone with Devonshire cream & jam, brewed loose tea.

TEATIME: 9:30am To 7:00pm, Monday Thru Friday
- 10:00am To 7:00pm, Saturday • 11:00am To 6:00pm, Sunday
- Non-Caffeine/Herbal Tea Available
- Watercloset: Same Floor
- **Reservations Are Required For Quarterly Theme Teas**
- Metered Street Parking & Metered Underground
- Credit Cards: V&MC

Proprietor's
Autograph _____*Date*_____

WEDGEWOOD HOTEL

845 Hornby Street
Vancouver, British Columbia

604-689-7777   800-663-0666

New Addition...It's Teatime At...The Wedgewood Hotel. Named after Lord Wedgwood of Wedgwood china fame, the Wedgewood Hotel in the heart of Vancouver also enjoys an impeccably fine reputation. Sisters Joanna and Eleni are the artistic proprietors who in tandem, run this small luxury European-style hotel. With meticulous attention to detail, the sisters have filled their hotel with fine furnishings, English antiques and original art.

Afternoon Tea is served in the fabulously renovated 1.5 million dollar Bacchus Lounge and presented on three tiered caddies at tables set with linens, fresh flowers and Royal Albert china. The new Bacchus Lounge is decorated in "mission romance" style. With its imported treasures, it is most definitely a "must see." You'll enjoy gracious service at this quaint and charming hotel which overlooks Hornby Street and Robson Square. Bacchus really has something to smile about now! F.Y.I. The wonderful Afternoon Tea baked goods are all made in the hotel's own kitchen.

$12.95 Afternoon Tea... Fresh fruit cocktail, assorted finger sandwiches, homemade scone served with Devon cream & preserves, homemade fruit cake, chocolate square, tea pastries and a pot of the Wedgewood blend or a variety of other brewed teas.

TEATIME: 2:00pm To 4:00pm • Seven Days A Week
• May Accommodate Some Dietary Needs With Advance Request
• Non-Caffeine/Herbal Tea Available
• Watercloset: One Flight Down Or Elevator To Second Floor
• **Reservations Are Appreciated**
• Non-Validated Parking Beneath The Hotel Or Valet Park
• Credit Cards: V,MC,DIS&JCB&AE
Proprietor's
Autograph _____Date_____

THE "STOREHOUSE"
Victorian Gift Shop & Tea Room
3001 25th Street
Vernon, British Columbia

250-549-4540

New Addition...It's Time For Tea & Scones At...The StoreHouse. Nestled in the back of this adorable 1904 heritage Victorian cottage amongst patio & pond, gifts & treasures you will find The StoreHouse Tea Room. This spot of tea was created by proprietors Janis and Doug with a little help from Janis' daughter April. The shop specializes in home decor, garden accessories, antique reproductions, collectibles and Victorian charm.

Tea tables are set with linens and small flower arrangements or petite tea lamps. Tea is presented in individual teapots and placed on lit tea-warmers on your table. F.Y.I. The lunch menu is quite varied at this cozy spot where everything is homemade. The StoreHouse is artistically decorated in burgundy and green tones. The hardwood floors are original, from 1904! P.S. Tea parties are available for up to 15 guests. Weather permitting, outdoor seating accommodates up to 20 guests.

$6.45 Scones & Strawberries & Tea... Light & fluffy scones with strawberry compote, Devon cream, pot of featured tea.

TEATIME: 11:00am To 4:00pm • Monday Thru Saturday
• May Accommodate Some Dietary Needs With Advance Request
• Non-Caffeine/Herbal Tea Available
• Children's Tea Parties Welcome, Ages 10+
• Watercloset: First Floor
• Free Off Street Parking
• **Reservations Are Appreciated**
• Credit Cards: V&MC
Proprietor's
Autograph _____*Date*_____

ADRIENNE'S TEA GARDEN
at Mattick's Farm

5325 Cordova Bay Road
Victoria, British Columbia

250-658-1535

New Addition...It's Teatime At...Adrienne's Tea Garden. Mattick's Farm is reminiscent of an old country market. The "market" features the talents of local artists and crafts people, as well as housing a garden center, an apparel shop, tack shop and a Scandinavian weaver. And, this is where you'll find Adrienne's Tea Garden. Fay offers breakfast, lunch and totally enticing sweets such as Belgian Chocolate Mouse and her famous Apple Crisp in addition to "High Tea." There are lots of shopping opportunities from Fay's homemade scones & jams to cozies & Adrienne's music cassettes.

Afternoon Tea is served outdoors weather permitting, or in the popular Sun Room at antique tables set with blue place mats and fresh flowers. Servers are attired in navy & white "ticking" aprons with "jam jar" trim. Paintings by local artists are on loan in the shop and may be purchased. Ask about the "deli" and Grandma Fay's Ice Cream Parlour with homemade confetti-colored waffle cones and fresh locally made ice cream. Enjoy!

$10.95 "High Tea"...Tea sandwiches, dainties, raisin scone with cream & jam, ice cream or fruit cup, a pot of brewed tea.
$3.95 Scone...Choice of scone served hot with butter, homemade jam & Devonshire style cream.

TEATIME: 12Noon To 4:30pm • Seven Days A Week
• May Accommodate Some Dietary Needs With Advance Request
• Non-Caffeine/Herbal Tea Available
• Watercloset: Common Area, Same Floor
• Wheelchair Watercloset: Nearby Common Area
• **Reservations Please, On Weekends & For Parties Of 6+**
• Free Parking Lot
• Credit Cards V, Interact&MC
Proprietor's
Autograph _____*Date*_____

428

BLETHERING PLACE
Tea Room
2250 Oak Bay Avenue
Victoria, British Columbia

250-598-1413

New Addition...It's Teatime At...Blethering Place. Ken, the proprietor hails from New Zealand. He is warm and friendly and enjoys blethering away with his customers! According to Mr. Webster of dictionary fame, blethering or blathering is defined as, "foolish talk; loquacious nonsense."

This tearoom is quite large with 35 tables. The Blethering Place offers a full menu in addition to Afternoon Tea. The decor of this local hang-out has been described as "classy casual", with flowers and lace, floral carpeting and interesting bric-a-brac on the walls. The servers scurry about in white floral eyelet pinnies. High Tea, at 6:00pm is especially nice as live piano music accompanies your delicious meal. Take note of the large blackboard which informs patrons of future guest musicians. Browse around, The Blethering Place has a gift shop and carries many British and tea-related items from candies to handcrafted cozies.

$10.95 High Tea... Petit sandwiches, sausage roll, warm tea biscuits with Devonshire cream & strawberry jam, English Trifle, sweets, fruit, a pot of brewed tea. Loose tea on request.

$7.95 Light Tea...A smaller portion of the High Tea, without the English Trifle.

TEATIME: 11:00am To 8:00pm • Seven Days A Week
• May Accommodate Some Dietary Needs With Advance Request
• Children's Tea Parties Welcome And Quite Popular Here
• Non-Caffeine/Herbal/Organic Tea Available
• Up Three Stairs To The Watercloset
• **Reservations Are Suggested**
• Free Two Hour Street Parking
• Credit Cards: JCB,V,MC,DIS&DC&AE

Proprietor's
Autograph _____*Date*_____

429

Enjoy the romance of beautiful gardens and Afternoon Tea.

THE BUTCHART GARDENS

800 Benvenuto Avenue
Victoria, British Columbia
(Brentwood Bay)

The Dining Room
RESTAURANT

250-652-8222

It's Teatime At...The Butchart Gardens. "Serving tea at The Butchart Gardens is a time honoured event. Join us in Mrs. Butchart's home, please sit down and enjoy our own traditional Afternoon Tea." Years of nature, loving nurture and gracious generosity have produced one of the country's most splendid gardens. After a grand walk about, relax at Mr. and Mrs. Butchart's fabulous well-appointed former home for Afternoon Tea.

Afternoon Tea is graciously presented by attentive servers on tiered caddies at tables set with white linens and red serviettes. No surprise, there are beautiful fresh flower arrangements everywhere. P.S. Allow time to browse in the gift shop. I purchased a Butchart Garden T-shirt as a memento of a delightful day. F.Y.I. Admission fee to the grounds is required for restaurant & Afternoon Tea service. Call for the current rate, as well as extended seasonal hours. P.S. Consider a twelve month ticket if you expect to get back this way soon. It offers discount benefits for Afternoon Tea, and is well worth the conservative investment.

$17.95 The Butchart Gardens Afternoon Tea. Seasonal fruit cup with citrus yogurt cream, assorted tea sandwiches, candied ginger scone with whipped vanilla Devon cream & homemade jam, an assortment of homemade sweets such as: apple strudel, banana date loaf, chocolate brandy Napoleon slice, raspberry thumbprint cookie, dipped strawberry, pot of brewed tea.

TEATIME: 12:00pm To 4:00pm • Seven Days A Week
- Watercloset: Same Floor
- Non-Caffeine/Herbal Tea Available
- Wheelchair Accessible
- **Reservations Are Suggested**
- **Seasonal Admission Fees Range From $8.-$14.50**
- Free Parking Lot
- Credit Cards: V,MC&AE

Hostess'
Autograph _____*Date*_____

EMPRESS HOTEL
THE EMPRESS   *721 Government Street*
                                          Victoria, British Columbia
800-441-1414 *Hotel Reservations*   **250-384-8111**

It's Teatime At...The Empress Hotel... Afternoon Tea has been a beloved pastime at The Empress Hotel since 1908. Time honored traditions and attentive guest service abounds. Known as the "Grand Dame of Afternoon Tea", The Empress' Afternoon Tea is a <u>must</u> experience if you are fortunate enough to find yourself in beautiful Victoria. Afternoon Tea accompanied by a pianist, is beautifully presented in The Tea Lobby. During peak season, Tea may be also be served in The Empress Room and the splendid glass-domed Palm Court.

Afternoon Tea is presented on tiered caddies at tables set with fine silver and "Empress" china. The food is exquisite with service to match. Please note, proper dress is required.Smart casual. Walking shorts (bermudas), and dress jeans are permitted, walking shoes ok. Non-smoking. P.S. Allow time to wander through The Empress. It's rich history and architectural features are impressive.

$29.00 Afternoon Tea... Goblet of fresh strawberries or seasonal fruit, toasted honey crumpets, a three tiered china rack offers plump homemade raisin scones served with thick whipped Jersey cream & strawberry preserves, assorted tea sandwiches: smoked salmon, deviled egg, cucumber, variety of Empress Pastries, and brewed Empress blend tea.

TEATIME: 12:30, 2:00pm, 3:30pm & 5:00pm • Seven Days A Week
• May Accommodate Some Dietary Needs With Advance Request
• Non-Caffeine/Herbal Tea Also Available
• Children's Tea Parties Welcome
• **Reservations Are Strongly Recommended**
• Wheelchair Accessible • Watercloset: Same Floor
• Non-Validated Subterranean Parking
• Credit Cards: V,MC,DIS,DC&AE

L'autograph
du Concierge _____Date_____

Our fun & memorable Afternoon Tea at The Empress Hotel!

Orange-Scented Madeleines

Maureen O. Wilson

"Orange -Scented Madeleines are one of my tea favorites."

1/2 cup butter
2 large eggs, room temperature, lightly beaten
2/3 cup white sugar or 3/4 cup (6oz.) powdered sugar
Pinch of salt
1/2 teaspoon baking powder or baking soda
2 teaspoons orange liqueur or 1/2 teaspoon orange extract
Finely grated rind of 1 well-washed orange (about 2 teaspoons)
1 cup all-purpose flour

Preheat oven to 375 degrees F. With additional softened butter, lightly butter with an even coating and lightly flour the scallop-shaped Madeleine molds. Shake out the excess flour. Melt 1/2 cup butter in saucepan; cool to room temperature. With mixer at medium speed, beat eggs; gradually beat in sugar. Reduce mixer speed to low; blend in salt, liqueur or extract, and finely grated orange rind. In a separate bowl, mix flour with salt and baking powder or baking soda. Blend in flour mixture. Stop beating as soon as flour is incorporated. Fold in the cooled butter until just blended. Do not overbeat. Drop by tablespoonfuls into Madeleine molds, filling about two-thirds to three-fourths full. (This must be done quickly before the butter begins to separate from batter.) Bake in preheated 375 degree F. oven for 10 to 14 minutes or until the Madeleines are golden and lightly browned around the edges and beginning to shrink slightly from the molds. Unmold cookies from shells after cooling for a minute or two; place them on wire racks to finish cooling. The cookies will keep about 2 days. To finish, sift powdered sugar lightly over the curved, decorative tops of the Madeleines. This recipe makes about 40 small or 20 large Madeleines. Enjoy!

FOUR MILE HOUSE
Tearoom & Restaurant
199 Old Island Highway
Victoria, British Columbia

250-479-2514

New Addition...It's Teatime At...Four Mile House. Welcome to this renovated 1858 historical spot. Afternoon Teas have been served here for more than 15 years and the tradition continues even though Four Mile House has expanded to include a full restaurant, beer & wine store, neighborhood pub and catering.

Afternoon Tea is presented on three tiered caddies and served at tables set with linens and fresh flowers. The dining room has beamed ceilings and is decorated in shades of rose, burgundy and green. The stained glass windows bring in a beautiful spectrum of sunshine. Be sure to say hello to Cheryl, she is the sister of one of the owners and is usually hard at work at Four Mile House. P.S. They can also cater an Afternoon Tea for you.

$16.95 Set Tea For Two...A selection of tea sandwiches, cream & raisin scones served with whipped cream, butter & jam, fresh lemon tart, pound cake, fruit and a pot of tea.
$8.95 Set Tea For One... As above tailored for one.
$6.95 Devon Splits For Two...A covered basket of freshly baked scones, whipped cream, butter & jam. $4.95 for one.

TEATIME: 2:00pm To 5:00pm • Seven Days A Week
• Year Round Except Christmas Day
• May Accommodate Some Dietary Needs With Advance Request
• Non-Caffeine/Herbal Tea Available
• Watercloset: Same Floor
• Wheelchair Accessible
• **Reservations Are Required**
• Free Parking Lot
• Credit Cards: V,MC,DC&AE
Proprietor's
Autograph _____Date_____

THE GAZEBO

5460 Old West Saanich Road
Victoria, British Columbia

250-479-7787

New Addition...New Proprietors...It's Teatime At...The Gazebo. Situated on a sublime one acre country setting in Victoria, discover a 1971 Tudor house known as, The Gazebo. Recently, long time restauranteurs and hospitality specialists Michael and Treva became the proprietors of The Gazebo. For approximately 17 years it was known as a teahouse and tea garden, so in keeping with tradition, Afternoon Tea will continue to be served. They have however, expanded their focus with a mouth-watering new menu.

Afternoon Tea is presented on a three tiered caddie at tables set with Royal Doulton china, fresh flowers & cloth napkins. You may want to reserve the spot by the fireplace. Private tea parties are available for up to up to 40 guests. Weather permitting, 110 guests may be accommodated outdoors in a lovely fountain-gazebo setting.

$14.95 Gazebo Tea... Canapes such as: smoked duck, creamed cheese & cilantro, seasonal fresh fruit, homemade blackberry scone served with strawberry preserves and "Gazebo" cream, pastries may include tarts filled with white chocolate mousse, and carrot cake, and a pot of Tazo tea.
$3.25 Fruit Scone... Served with "Gazebo" cream.

TEATIME: May 15 -Sept 31: 11:00am To 4:00pm • Seven Days
• October 1-May 14: 11:00am To 4:00pm • Wednesday-Sunday
• May Accommodate Some Dietary Needs With Advance Request
• Non-Caffeine/Herbal Tea Available
• Children's Tea Parties Welcome
• Watercloset: Same Floor
• Wheelchair Accessible
• **Reservations Are Appreciated**
• Free Park Lot
• Credit Cards: V&MC
Proprietor's
Autograph _____*Date*_____

JAMES BAY
Tea Room

332 Menzies Street
Victoria, British Columbia

250-382-8282

New Addition....It's Teatime At...James Bay Tea Room. A friendly and inviting staff welcomes you to the James Bay Tea Room located in what once was the corner store back in 1910. Today, you'll find quite a different picture; Tiffany chandeliers, walls full of interesting Royal memorabilia, dining tables covered in navy pinstripes, lace curtains and red carpets. Today... it's the corner "Victorian" James Bay Tea Room!

    The James Bay Tea Room features a full menu in addition to Afternoon Tea. Private tea parties are available for up to 50 guests. F.Y.I. The tearoom is 100% non-smoking. By the way, the tea cozies were made by a local crafts person. These recycled tea cozies are for sale. They're gently worn, and come pre-stained!

    $9.60 James Bay Sunday High Tea... Egg and tuna tea sandwiches, small sweet scones served with cream & jam, a lovely English trifle, and a pot of brewed tea by request.

    $6.60 Afternoon Tea... Egg and tuna, tea sandwiches, small sweet scones served with cream & jam a pot of brewed tea.

TEATIME: 7:00am To 9:00pm • Monday Thru Saturday
- 8:00am To 9:00pm, Sunday
- May Accommodate Some Dietary Needs With Advance Request
- Children's Tea Parties Welcome
- Watercloset: Same Floor
- Wheelchair Accessible
- **Reservations Are Appreciated**
- One Hour Free Street Park &Pay Lot
- Credit Cards: V,MC&AE

Proprietor's
Autograph _____*Date*_____

OAK BAY BEACH HOTEL
1175 Beach Drive
Victoria, British Columbia

250-598-4556

New Addition...It's Teatime At...Oak Bay Beach Hotel. This is a charming and quaint European style hotel that among other things, offers a great view of Chatham Island, San Juan Island and Mt. Baker from the patio. We spent a few warm late afternoons sitting outside on the rear deck watching flocks of commerants migrate for the evening to Chatham Island. After a relaxing Afternoon Tea, it just seemed like the thing to do!

Afternoon Tea is served in the dining room, one flight down from the lobby. Tea tables are set in green linens with white toppers, matching cloth serviettes, and fresh flowers. The decor includes floral print wall-covering, emerald carpet and chairs upholstered in lipstick red. For a romantic "tea for two" ask for the spot by the fireplace. This is a Four Diamond hotel with very attentive and thoughtful service. The lobby with vintage comfy couches is a perfect place to enjoy the day's first spot of tea! Private tea parties are welcome, please call to plan.

$16.50 Afternoon Tea... Assorted petit finger sandwiches, scone served with cream & preserves, crumpet, homemade fruit trifle or pastry, and a pot of brewed tea.

TEATIME "SEASON": April 15 thru October 15
- 2:30pm To 5:00pm • Seven Days A Week In Season
- May Accommodate Some Dietary Needs With Advance Request
- Watercloset: Up Two Flights Of Stairs, From Dining Room
- **Reservations Are Highly Recommended**
- Free Parking Lot
- Credit Cards: V,MC,DC&AE

Proprietor's
Autograph _____*Date*_____

438

Children's Etiquette Teas foster poise and good manners in young ladies and gentlemen.

OAK BAY TEA ROOM
2241 Oak Bay Avenue
Victoria, British Columbia

250-370-1005

New Addition...It's Teatime At...The Oak Bay Tea Room. If you're in the quaint Oak Bay area of Victoria, you'll be very happy to know that there is an Oak Bay Tea Room. The tearoom is describes as an English and French in style.

Afternoon Tea is served at tables set with matching linens, fresh flowers and tapestry upholstered chairs by servers in traditional black and white uniforms. The room is decorated in soft green and rose tones with gold mirrors and wall sconces which compliment the paintings. Soft classical background music contributes to the lovely European atmosphere. P.S. Private tea parties are available for up to 60 guests.

$8.95 Oak Bay "High Tea"...(Two Guests...$13.95). Finger sandwiches such as: tomato-cream cheese, and egg, raisin scone served with Devonshire cream, chocolate dipped seasonal fruit treat, and a pot of brewed tea.
$7.25 Oak Bay Afternoon Tea...Tea sandwiches, fruit cup, and a pot of brewed tea.
$6.75 Afternoon Tea...English Trifle or crumpet or muffin or scone with Devonshire cream & preserves, and pot of tea.

TEATIME: 8:00am To 8:00pm • Seven Days A Week
• May Accommodate Some Dietary Needs With Advance Request
• Non-Caffeine/Herbal Tea Available
• Children's Tea Parties Welcome
• Watercloset: Same Floor
• Wheelchair Accessible
• **Reservations Are Recommended**
• Free Two Hour Parking At Monterey Center
• Credit Cards: MC,V&AE
Proprietor's
Autograph _____Date_____

OLDE ENGLAND INN

429 Lampson Street
Victoria, British Columbia

Reservations **250-388-4353**

New Addition...It's Teatime At...Olde England Tea Room. Known as the cottage home of Anne Hathaway the wife of William Shakespeare, this wonderful Tudor Inn built in 1909 is also famous for its treasure trove of antiques.

Afternoon Tea is served in the original drawing room of what once was Hathaway's private home. The decor includes velvet burgundy drapery, antique paintings and needlepoint wall-hangings. The room's crowning glory is the ceiling with three angelic hand-painted murals. The tea service includes blue floral fine Dudson china from Trent, England and lovely crotched lace tablecloths. Servers are formally attired in blue and burgundy period costumes. The ladies in bonnets, and the gents in lace jabots, tunics and knickers-style britches. What a darling spot! Don't miss the Olde Curiosity Shop, great English gifts. Tea parties for up to 60 guests.

$9.95 Full English Tea... Hot buttered English crumpet, black currant scone with fresh cream & homemade jam, a portion of Melton Mowbray Tye, (spicy pork and aspic), teabread and cheese, black currant tart, English Sherry Trifle as prepared by Escoffier for Queen Victoria, and a pot of fragrant custom blended bagged Darjeeling and Orange Pekoe teas by Murchie's.

$3.95 Light Afternoon Tea... Hot buttered English crumpets or black currant scones with homemade jam, a pot of tea.

TEATIME: 12Noon To 4:30pm • Monday Thru Saturday
- 2:00pm To 4:30pm, Sunday
- The Inn And Dining Room Are 3 Steps Up From The Entrance.
- Non-Caffeine/Herbal Tea Available
- Children's Tea Parties Welcome
- Watercloset: Same Level As The Dining Room
- **Reservations Are Requested For Parties Of Six+ Guests**
- Free Parking Lot
- Credit Cards: MC,DC/En Route,DIS,AE&JCB

Proprietor's
Autograph _____*Date*_____

POINT ELLICE HOUSE
2616 Pleasant Street
Victoria, British Columbia

250-380-6506

New Addition...It's Teatime In Season At...Point Ellice House. This captivating house is a perfect spot for Afternoon Tea and other heart-warming social pleasantries. Access to Point Ellice House is convenient by car or by boat. If you'd like to go by boat, Victoria Harbour Ferry Company is the only inner harbour ferry. They can be reached at 250-480-0971 and Elinor will be happy to book your 15 minute, $7.00 ride.

Afternoon Tea at Point Ellice is served under a pavilion on the serene rose-garden lawn by a gracious, period-garbed staff. A tour of Point Ellice is a must. It will give you a fascinating peek into the lives of the family who occupied this home continuously for 108 years. Almost everything they owned is still in the house. It's almost as if they turned the key and left with everything in its place. A virtual museum of its time!

$14.95 Afternoon Tea & Tour... Finger sandwiches, fresh fruit, scone with cream & jam, fruit tart, shortbread, famous lemon-poppy seed cake, and lovely brewed tea. Seniors $13.95

TEATIME: 12Noon To 4:00pm • Seven Days A Week In Season
• May 10, Thru Around Mid-September, Please Call
• May Accommodate Some Dietary Needs With Advance Request
• Non-Caffeine/Herbal Tea Available
• Children's Tea Parties Welcome
• Watercloset: First Floor
• Wheelchair Accessible
• **Reservations Are Recommended**
• Free Parking Lot
• Credit Cards: V&MC
Server's
Autograph _____*Date*_____

442

SILK ROAD TEA COMPANY

1624 Government Street
(China Town)
Victoria, British Columbia

250-382-0006

    New Addition...Taste Exotic Teas At...Silk Road Tea Company. Enjoy tea and history at Silk Road Tea Company. The "Silk Road" refers to the historic route traveled by caravans in ancient times, along which spices, rich silks and tea were traded.
    It's much easier to get tea now; just visit Silk Road Tea Co. in Victoria. This is a great spot to taste tea and learn a bit about the world of exotic blends and ancient blending techniques from the knowledgeable and friendly proprietors Daniela and Nancy. The Silk Road Tea Company is located in an historic or "character," building in Victoria's China Town. This interesting spot is earning rave reviews. It is decorated in "Chinese" red, black and gold. A red cabinet is full of treasures, and a little oasis with a big tea-cupboard is quite special. Guests are seated at cute little Silk Road-style round tables trimmed in gold braid. Creatively packaged, decorative tins of wonderful green, semi-green and black teas, plus herbal infusions and rare limited-edition teas are available. Browse around too for teapots and tea ware that are sure to be great gifts. Inquire about their Tea of the Month Club and mail-order purchasing as well. Web site or E-Mail: Silkroad@silkroadtea.com

    $1.50 Pot of Tea... Three cup pot of exquisite loose brewed tea. Try the exotic iced teas too, Moonlight On The Grove.

TEATIME: 11:00am To 5:30pm • Tuesday Thru Saturday
- 12:00Noon To 5:00pm • Sunday & Monday
- Non-Caffeine/Herbal Tea Available
- Watercloset: Same Floor
- **Please Drop By**
- Metered Street Parking, Nearby "Parkade"
- Credit Cards: Interact, V&MC

Proprietor's
Autograph _____*Date*_____

VICTORIA HARBOUR
House Restaurant
607 Oswego Street
Victoria, British Columbia

250-386-1244

New Addition...It's Teatime In June, July & August At...Victoria Harbour House Restaurant. "The summer months are lovely for Afternoon Tea, wouldn't you agree my dear?" Across from the Hidden Harbour near the Parliament Building & Quadra Park, you will find Victoria Harbour Restaurant for a charming summer's Afternoon Tea. This a terrific location for a walk-about in downtown Victoria with its great shops and sights. You're also just a stone's skip to a ferry ride or catamaran.

Afternoon Tea is served with linens and fresh flowers in this popular restaurant where nearly everything is homemade. The staff is very friendly here and will make you feel most welcome. This cozy spot is decorated in light oak with English and hunt theme accent prints on the walls. A full menu including dinner, is available in addition to Afternoon Tea. P.S. Private tea parties are also available. There is outdoor seating on the terrace overlooking Quadra Park weather permitting, but on a cool afternoon you'll appreciate a seat indors by the cracking fireplace.

$8.50 Afternoon Tea... Traditional tea sandwiches, scone with cream & preserves, a square, fruit tart, and a pot of tea.

TEATIME: 11:30am To 4:00pm • Seven Days A Week
- Summer Hours Are 11:30am To 11:30pm
- Non-Caffeine/Herbal Tea Available
- Watercloset: Same Floor
- **Reservations Are Not Necessary**
- Public Parking Lot Nearby
- Credit Cards: MC,V&AE

Proprietor's
Autograph _____*Date*_____

WINDSOR HOUSE
Tearoom & Restaurant
2540 Windsor Road
Victoria, British Columbia
(Oak Bay Area)

250-595-3135

New Addition...It's Teatime At...The Windsor House Tea Room. The charming 1930's leaded glass, Tudor-style Windsor House Tea Room is situated right across from the Windsor Park. The house was originally built as the residence for the B.C. Supreme Court Judge. Today, it is a quaint Victorian style tearoom serving delectable English lunches such as Ploughman's Lunch and The Londoner and of course, Afternoon Tea. Drop by and meet the hospitable proprietors Hank and Anne.

Afternoon Tea is presented from three tiered caddies at tables set with off-white tablecloths and sweet centerpieces. The shop is decorated with Royal memorabilia, photos, prints and colorful posters. You may be seated in either of two dining rooms upstairs or the main floor dining room. Private tea parties are available for up to 12 guests. P.S. Don't miss their little gift shop.

$22.95 Traditional High Tea For Two... Hot buttered crumpets, cream scones, finger sandwiches, butter tart, almond shortbread, Sherry Trifle, a Brown Betty of Murchie's tea.

$6.95 Tea & Scone... Classic cream scone served with jam & clotted cream and a "Brown Betty" of Murchie's tea.

TEATIME: 12:00Noon To 5:30pm • Tuesday Thru Saturday
• May Accommodate Some Dietary Needs With Advance Request
• Non-Caffeine/Herbal Tea Available
• Child's Menu Available
• Watercloset: Same Floor
• **Reservations Appreciated For Groups Of 6+ Guests**
• Unmetered Street Parking
• Credit Cards: V&MC

Proprietor's
Autograph _____*Date*_____

CHATEAU WHISTLER RESORT

4599 Chateau Boulevard
Whistler, British Columbia

Tea **604-938-2033**
Hotel **604-938-8000**

New Addition...It's Teatime At...Chateau Whistler Resort... This is just a beautiful part of the world. The air is clear and the scenery is breathtaking. We're not skiers, but we truly enjoyed our summer, "off-season" trip to Whistler. This Four Diamond chateau style resort is most exceptional, and will afford you an experience you won't soon forget.

Afternoon Tea is served daily in either The Wildflower or The Mallard Lounge. The Mallard is quite inviting with comfy couches, a fireplace and an interesting ceiling. Enjoy the full bay-window view of the mountains from The Mallard. The Wild Flower by contrast has country elegance and charm. The burgundy and mustard tones complement the "Canadiana," decor. The room features French country antiques and a real birdhouse. F.Y.I. This resort is located at the bottom of the tallest vertical drop in North America ! This resort was rated #2 in the world by Conde Nast. P.S. Be sure to inquire about the Tea Dances.

$14.95 Afternoon Tea... Fresh seasonal berries, finger sandwiches, treacle tart, scones served with clotted cream, pot of bagged Lipton, or brewed loose "T," tea during the winter season.

TEATIME: 2:00pm To 4:30pm • Seven Days A Week
- May Accommodate Some Dietary Needs With Advance Request
- Non-Caffeine/Herbal Tea Available
- Watercloset: Same Floor
- Wheelchair Accessible
- **Reservations Are Recommended**
- Free Hotel Parking With Validation
- Credit Cards: MC,V,DIS,DC&AE

L'autograph
du Concierge _____*Date*_____

DURLACHER HOF
7055 Nesters Road
Whistler, British Columbia

604-932-1924

New Addition...It's Teatime From Mid June Thru September At...Durlacher Hof. There may be no greater ambassador of goodwill & hospitality in the resort town of Whistler, than Erika the proprietor of Durlacher Hof. Whatever the language, she and Peter say "Wilkommen" with their hearts. Afternoon Tea was traditionally offered only to overnight guests until recently. Now, visiting tea lovers can enjoy Afternoon Teas at this neat spot during the summer months from mid-June thru September. Be sure to call ahead for reservations when you make your travel plans.

Afternoon Tea is served in the outdoor courtyard weather permitting, or in the lounge at tables set with Damask tablecloths, Villeroy & Boch Petite Fleur fine china & fresh flowers or plants. The proprietors say it's easy to get to Durlacher Hof but difficult to leave. This is a beautiful and scenic spot with breathtaking views of Whistler, Blackcomb & Wedge Mountains. Allow time to just "hang-out" in Whistler, we enjoyed our trip here during the summer immensely. Ask Erika to lead you to my favorite dessert, "Death by Chocolate!" P.S. Tea parties for groups here too.

$12.00 Afternoon Tea... Fresh berries & cream in chocolate cups, assorted open face finger sandwiches, warm scones served with sweet butter & homemade preserves, puff cheese sticks, savory biscuits, sweet surprises such as flan or plum kuchen or rhubarb & hazelnut meringue pizelles, and a pot of brewed tea.

SUMMER TEAS: 2pm To 5pm • Seven Days A Week In Season
• May Accommodate Some Dietary Needs With Advance Request
• Non-Caffeine/Herbal Tea Available
• Watercloset: Same Floor • Wheelchair Accessible
• **Reservations Are Required**
• Free Parking Lot
• Credit Cards: V&MC
Proprietor's
Autograph _____*Date*_____

DELPHINE LODGE
Country Inn, B&B
Main Avenue At Wells
Wilmer, British Columbia

250-342-6851

New Addition...It's Teatime In June, July & August At...Delphine Lodge Country Inn. "This place is the biggest thing in Wilmer, you can't miss us," that's how Anne and David describe their 100 year old western-style historic Inn. The townsite was actually laid out in 1899. That same year, the town's first hotel was built by George Stark and named after his wife Delphine. When I asked Anne about the parking here, she told me they were lucky to have a street! Seasonal Cream & Formal Afternoon Teas are a summer highlight at Delphine Lodge. The lodge is located in the heart of the Columbia Valley, 5 km from both Lake Windermere and the town of Invermere. This is a superb spot for hiking, biking, skiing & bird watching, or relaxing with tea!

Afternoon Tea is often presented on tiered caddies at tables set with tablecloths, fresh flowers and "Botanic Garden" fine china, by Port Meirion. Anne has many sets of china and quite a collection of serving pieces. Sometimes she uses her Spode for small groups or the set of Royal Doulton depending on the group. F.Y.I. Anne is a self-declared "techno-peasant" so don't look for an E-Mail address here, just a neat spot to stay the night & enjoy tea with new friends.

$10.00 Formal Afternoon Tea. (4-12 Guests) Assorted finger sandwiches, fresh baked scones with cream & jam, and tea.

$7.00 Cream Tea... A great homemade scone served with cream & jam, dessert, and a pot of fresh brewed Murchie's tea.

SUMMER TEAS: June, July & August • 2pm To 4pm, As Scheduled
- May Accommodate Some Dietary Needs With Advance Request
- Watercloset: One Flight Up • Non-Caffeine/Herbal Tea Available
- **Reservations Are Required For Both Cream & Formal Teas**
- Unmetered Street Parking
- Credit Card: V

Proprietor's
Autograph _____*Date*_____

448

CREEKSIDE GARDEN
Tours & Tea Room
4795 Dell Road
Windermere, British Columbia

250-342-6354

New Addition...It's Tea & Tour At...Creekside Garden. Put on your walking shoes, it's time to commune with nature. A visit here will really inspire you to go home & pull weeds! There are 21 interesting theme gardens in 2 acres ranging from Butterfly Island to Wildflower Hill. But before the adventure begins, stop for tea and delectable, many were homegrown. If you love roses, you'll be happy to know that there are over 300 species.

Tea is served at tables set with...you guessed it, fresh flowers, by friendly servers in flowery aprons. The covered pine sunroom with green shutters is a nice spot for tea. It's near the creekside, and has a unique lacey curtain effect created by ivy. Be sure to say hello to Linda, the proprietor. She no doubt has some great gardening tips for you. Allow time to browse in the gift shop, there are lots of tea and gardening accessories. Creekside Gardens are award-winning gardens for Stokes Seeds & Gardens West.

$20.00 Guided Tour & Tea... Garden salad, fresh seasonal berries, scone, homemade cream & preserves, brewed tea.

$16.00 Guided Tour & Tea... Seasonal fruit & berries, scone with cream & preserves and brewed tea.

$12.00 Guided Tour & Tea... Cookie & brewed tea.

SEASONAL TEAS & TOUR: May Thru October 1.
- Seven Days A Week In Season • 10:00am To 6:00pm
- May Accommodate Some Dietary Needs With Advance Request
- Non-Caffeine/Herbal Tea Available
- Children's Tea Parties Welcome, Ages 8+
- Watercloset: Same Floor • Wheelchair Accessible
- **Reservations Preferred**
- Free Parking Lot
- Credit Card: V

Proprietor's
Autograph _____*Date*_____

449

Please join us for a casual Afternoon Tea.

Alaska

A nice hot cup of tea would really hit the spot!

AnchorAge Senior Center & KOBUK COFFEE CO.

504 West 5th Avenue
Anchorage, Alaska

907-272-3626 *Kobuk*

Kimball Building, 1915

New Addition...It's Teatime Quarterly At...AnchorAge Senior Center. I had the nicest chat with Deborah who, along with siblings Mike and Nina own the Kobuk Coffee Company situated in the historic 1915 Kimball Building. They carry the largest selection of bulk tea in Anchorage, maybe all of Alaska, with nearly 50 varieties. In addition, they sell fine china, teapots, infusers, cards & books. They say, "Kobuk Coffee Co. brings a bit of culture to the last frontier!"

Afternoon Teas are presented quarterly by Kobuk Coffee Co. at the AnchorAge Senior Center, 1300 E. 19th Street. Three courses of teas are attentively poured by the proprietors thru bone china strainers at tables set with fresh shipped-in flowers, linens, gold rose teaspoons and fine antique china. Fresh teacups and a "teatorial" are offered for each new tea introduced.

Teas are planned for May, August, November & February, please call Kobuk Coffee Co. for dates and times. Tea-lovers can now join the new Kobuk Tea Club with a newsletter and 3 monthly tea plans from which to choose. E-Mail: sourmerk@alaska.net

$15.00 A Proper English Tea... Assorted tea sandwiches such as Alaskan smoked salmon, scones with cream & Alaskan wild berry preserves, desserts, and three brewed loose teas.

QUARTERLY TEAS: At The AnchorAge Senior Center
- May Accommodate Some Dietary Needs With Advance Request
- Non-Caffeine/Herbal Tea Available
- Wheelchair Accessible • Watercloset: Same Floor
- **Reservations Are Required, Call Kobuk Coffee Co.**
- Parking Lot At The Senior Center
- Credit Cards: V,MC, DIS&AE

Director's
Autograph _____*Date*_____

HOTEL CAPTAIN COOK

5th & "K" Streets
Anchorage, Alaska

800-843-1950   **907-276-6000**

New Addition...Holiday Teas In December At...The Hotel Captain Cook. When you hear those sleigh bells ringing, and it's Christmas time in the city, dash through the snow to The Hotel Captain Cook for their fabulous Dickens' Tea. The Captain Cook is an outstanding luxury hotel built in 1965 by Alaska's legendary entrepreneur Walter J. Hickle. Hickle became governor after statehood, and later served as U.S. Secretary of the Interior during the 1960's. He saw the Pacific Rim as a gateway to the world, and Alaska...the key to this global perspective.

Spirited Dickens Teas are served in The Pantry Shop from December 1 thru Christmas Day. These very popular teas are eagerly anticipated by hotel guests and residents as well. The hotel takes on the look of Charles Dickens with the "Cratchit" family decorating the Christmas tree in the lobby and "Scrooge" peering over the top of his glasses from his desk in his usual "humbug" fashion. Tea is served along with a special menu of English treats such as: Bath Buns, Bangers and Bubbles & Squeak, by attendants clad in period garb. A dessert cart with tempting homemade sweets is wheeled about the room. Carolers can be heard thru the noon hour. P.S. Be sure to look for whales, they've been spotted in the inlet waters below the Crow's Nest Restaurant high atop the hotel's Tower III.

$17.95 Dickens Afternoon Tea... Assorted tea sandwiches, scones served with lemon curd & preserves, delectable dessert, and a pot of brewed loose tea served with tea strainers.

DECEMBER HOLIDAY TEAS: 12Noon-5pm •Seven Days A Week
- May Accommodate Some Dietary Needs With Advance Request
- Non-Caffeine/Herbal Tea Available
- Watercloset: Same Floor
- Wheelchair Accessible
- **Reservations Are Required**
- Metered Street Parking & Pay Lot
- Credit Cards: V,MC,DIS,AE&JCB

L'autograph
du Concierge _____Date_____

THE FIDDLEHEAD
Restaurant & Bakery
429 West Willoughby Avenue
Juneau, Alaska

907-586-3150

New Addition...Holiday High Teas At...The Fiddlehead Restaurant & Bakery. "Sleigh bells ring...are you listening?" Victorian costumed Christmas Carolers add to the festive Holiday Teas at The Fiddlehead. F.Y.I. Fiddleheads grow in abundance on the mountainsides of Southeast Alaska. In early spring, the fern's tightly coiled shoot grows close to the earth. At this stage, it is delicious to eat sauteed in butter and prized as a salad ingredient. It's Deborah's goal to produce food that is both delicious and close to the earth! These Holiday High Teas are a Juneau favorite and have been a Juneau Christmas tradition since 1978.

High Teas are served in The Fireweed Room at tables set with fresh flowers, runners and cloth napkins. The room has an open & airy atmosphere, and a scenic mountain view. Christmas Carolers and the beautifully decorated christmas tree add to the festivities. Be sure to make your reservations early. P.S. Ask about The Fiddlehead Restaurant cookbook, a great holiday gift!

$12.95 Holiday High Tea...(Price is Approximate) Assorted finger sandwiches such as shrimp, smoker turkey, and cucumber, scones & preserves, fresh fruit, carrot cake, select teas.

DECEMBER HIGH TEA: 4pm-6pm, Mid December, As Scheduled
• Usually Two Days In December, Please Call For Dates
• May Accommodate Some Dietary Needs With Advance Request
• Non-Caffeine/Herbal Tea Available
• Children Welcome ($6.95 Approximately)
• Watercloset: Same Floor
• Wheelchair Accessible
• **Reservations Are A Must**
• Parking: Free Lot
• Credit Cards: V,MC,DC,DIS&AE

Proprietor's
Autograph _____*Date*_____

THE SILVERBOW INN
Bagel Bakery

120 Second Street
Juneau, Alaska

907-586-YUMM

New Addition...It's Teatime At...The Silverbow Inn. This newly restored historic 1914 Inn is located in downtown Juneau. Over the years, it has very much been a part of Alaska's history. If Afternoon Teas were to catch-on in the area, the dining room at this terrific historic Inn would be the first place people would look for a traditional tea in Juneau. The Mid-Afternoon Tea is served in the Bagel Bakery rather than the fine dining room. Be sure to find Jill and say hello. She's the new proprietor, originally from New York City. Mid-Afternoon Teas are somewhat non-traditional. They're served on the 1914 side of the Inn with it's high ceilings, antique furnishings, flowery wallpaper and hardwood floors.

Tea is served at tables set with unique fresh flower arrangements. F.Y.I. The Silverbow bakery established in 1890 is actually the oldest bakery in Alaska! They bake a yummy selection of breads, muffins & cookies. Ask to tour the "touch of home" Inn. Make plans to dine at their award winning Silverbow Restaurant.

$5.00 "Silverbow Inn Mid-Afternoon Tea" Fresh bagel cucumber & cream cheese quarters, seasonal fresh fruit, cookie, a Hershey kiss, and a pot of brewed loose Blue Willow tea.

TEATIME: 3:00pm To 5:00pm • Monday Thru Friday
• May Accommodate Some Dietary Needs With Advance Request
• Non-Caffeine/Caffeine/Herbal Tea Available
• Watercloset: Same Floor
• Wheelchair Accessible
• **Please Drop By**
• Free Parking Lot
• Credit Cards: MC&V
Proprietor's
Autograph _____*Date*_____

Aloha!

Double Pineapple Cheesecake Bars

Courtesy of Dole Food Company

Makes 24 servings

1 can (20 oz.) DOLE® Crushed Pineapple
2 teaspoons cornstarch
2 cups all-purpose flour
1 1/2 cups packed brown sugar
1/2 cup margarine
1 cup chopped walnuts
1 package (8 oz.) sweetened condensed milk
1 egg

• **Drain** pineapple well, reserve juice. Measure 1/2 cup
• **Measure** 1/2 cup pineapple for filling, set aside. Combine reserved juice, remaining pineapple and cornstarch in saucepan. Cook, stirring until topping boils and thickens.
• **Combine** flour, sugar and margarine. Beat until finely crumbled. Stir in walnuts. Press firmly and evenly on bottom of 13x9-inch pan. Bake at 350 degrees F. 15 minutes.
• **Beat** cheese until fluffy; gradually add milk, beat until smooth. Add egg and reserved 1/2 cup pineapple; mix well. Pour over baked crust. Bake 20 to 25 minutes longer or until lightly browned around edges. Cut into bars. Spoon pineapple topping over bars and serve.

CHALET KILAUEA
The Inn At Volcano

Corner Of Wright Road & Lauka Road
Volcano Village, Hawaii (3,800 Ft. Elevation)

808-967-7786

New Addition...Tea & Tour At...Chalet Kilauea. There's nothing like a relaxing Afternoon Tea when your chalet is nestled in a cool Hawaiian fern forest. Chalet Kilauea is a mere mile from the powerful beauty of Volcanoes National Park!

Everything here is made on premises. Afternoon Tea is served at tables set with Wedgewood fine china, cloth napkins & Dutch-lace doilies. Have a comfy seat in front of the fireplace or at various tables throughout the guest living room and enjoy the soft background music. You'll enjoy your visit with Lisha and Brian, the warm and friendly proprietors of this exciting spot. Ask them about their various travels as evidenced by the exotic collection of "souvenirs" on display throughout the Chalet.

F.Y.I. Complimentary Cream Teas are available daily for overnight guests of the Chalet. Please note, readers should plan ahead and make reservations for the very special Afternoon Tea designed especially for "A Spot of Tea" lovers. Aloha aikane!

$15.95 "A Spot of Tea"...Afternoon Tea & Tour... Assorted tea sandwiches, fresh island fruit, delicious homemade macadamia nut pastry, and a pot of brewed loose tea.

TEA & TOUR: Please Call To Schedule
• May Accommodate Some Dietary Needs With Advance Request
• Non-Caffeine/Herbal Tea Available
• Watercloset: Same Floor
• **Reservations Are Required**
• Free Parking Lot
• Credit Cards: V,MC&AE

Proprietor's
Autograph _____Date_____

PRINCEVILLE HOTEL

Ka Haku Road
Princeville, Kauai, Hawaii

808-826-9644   **800-826-4400**

New Addition...It's Teatime At...Princeville Hotel. "Gaze across this ever scenic and historic stretch of ocean and lose yourself in its eons of lore." One of the great resort hotels of the world and jewel of Kauai's North Shore, the Princeville Hotel offers an absolutely extraordinary, panoramic view of Hanalei Bay and famous Bali Hai. Hollywood has fallen in love with her mystical shores as well. South Pacific and Raiders Of The Lost Ark among others were filmed here.

Afternoon Tea is beautifully served in the breathtaking Living Room at black granite tables set with fresh flowers and Lenox "Autumn" fine china. There are comfortable couches and cushioned chairs, so relax and enjoy! You will be nearly surrounded by windows in The Living Room, affording an unforgettable view. P.S. Private tea parties are welcome for 1 to 20 guests. F.Y.I. This resort has one of Hawaii's highest ranking golf courses, if tea and tee is your thing, this is the place!

$12.00 Afternoon Tea...A selection of traditional tea sandwiches, scones with Devonshire cream, macadamia honey & strawberry preserves, slice of English tea bread, miniature French pastries, fresh fruit tarts, and a pot of brewed loose tea. Add $6.50 for strawberries with Grand Marnier & whipped cream.

TEATIME: 3:00pm To 5:00pm • Seven Days A Week
• May Accommodate Some Dietary Needs With Advance Request
• Non-Caffeine/Herbal Tea Available
• Children's Tea Parties Welcome
• Watercloset: Same Floor
• Wheelchair Accessible
• **Reservations Are Required**
• Free Parking Lot
• Credit Cards: V,MC,DIS,AE&JCB

L'autograph
du Concierge _____*Date*_____

LODGE AT KOELE

Kaemoku Highway
(Ask Directions At Car Rental Office)
Lanai City, Lanai, Hawaii

808-565-7300

New Addition...It's Teatime At...Lodge At Koele.
The Hawaiian Island of Lanai was at one time known for its glorious pineapple plantations, in fact it was called "The Pineapple Island." Today, the beauty of the island is appreciated by golfers and resort lovers seeking what could be, the perfect secluded island hideaway. The lodge and its sister resort were developed by Castle & Cooke Inc., the corporate successors to the Dole Corporation.

The Lodge At Koele is reminiscent of a fine country estate situated in a tropical Hawaiian setting complete with a Japanese hillside, and fruit garden. Secluded among decades-old towering Norfolk pines at an elevation of 1,600 feet, the Lodge has heavy timbers, beamed ceilings and natural stone fireplaces.

Afternoon Tea is casually served buffet style usually in the Tea Room, the adjoining porch, or the lovely Music Room; all featuring classical background music. Everything at the Lodge is homemade and embraces the essence of Hawaii. Aloha malihini!

$12.00 Afternoon Tea Repast... Assorted finger sandwiches, the famous Koele scones served with lemon curd, tasty coconut macaroon cookies, and brewed tea.

TEATIME: 3:00pm • Seven Days A Week
• Non-Caffeine/Herbal Tea Available
• Watercloset: Same Floor
• Wheelchair Accessible
• **Reservations Are Not Usually Required**
• Free Parking Lot
• Credit Cards: V,MC,JCB,DC,CB&AE
L'autograph
du Concierge _____Date_____

RITZ CARLTON HOTEL
Kapalua

THE RITZ-CARLTON®

1 Ritz Carlton Drive
Kapalua, Maui, Hawaii

808-669-6200

New Addition...It's Teatime At...The Ritz Carlton. Dining is an experience to be savored and exquisite settings are surpassed only by their distinctive cuisines. The Five Diamond Ritz Carlton on the magnificent Hawaiian Island of Maui is a must for any visitor to the islands. The view is breathtaking. To one side, the rugged peaks of the West Maui Mountains and opposite, the sparkling Pacific. Patterned pineapple fields and emerald golf courses seem to go on forever. It is a beautiful haven for both man and nature.

Afternoon Tea is served in the Lobby Lounge handsomely appointed with dark wood paneling, oriental carpets and fine antique furnishings. You may also choose to take tea outside under umbrella tables on the breezy terrace which is colorfully accented with potted plants. Always elegant, Afternoon Teas at Ritz Carlton Hotels are quite wonderful with fine china, fresh flowers and most attentive service. Please be aware that there is a reservation cancellation policy for Afternoon Teas, so be sure to ask about it.

$18.00 Afternoon Tea... Finger sandwiches, fresh baked scone served with Devonshire cream, assorted tea pastries, and a pot of brewed tea.

TEATIME: 2:30pm To 4:30pm • Seven Days A Week
• May Accommodate Some Dietary Needs With Advance Request
• Low Caffeine Tea Available
• Watercloset: Same Floor
• Wheelchair Accessible
• **24 Hour Advance Reservation & Guarantee Required**
• Valet & Self Parking
• Credit Cards: MC,V,DIS,DC,CB,AE&JCB

L'autograph
duConcierge _____*Date*_____

ARMSTRONG MANOR

2426 Armstrong Street
(College Hills)
Honolulu, Oahu, Hawaii

808-949-7875

New Addition...Private Tea Parties At..Armstrong Manor. Armstrong Manor, on the Hawaii Register of Historic Places, is an elegant and peaceful private gathering place located just minutes from Waikiki. Enjoy an espansive view of Diamond Head & Waikiki from this 1938 Mediterranean/Art Deco stone manor. Leave the hustle and bustle of Honolulu behind, and enjoy.

Afternoon Teas feature the talents of some of the great bakeries of Hawaii, as well as a fine selection of International Teas and Pure Hawaiian Kona Coffee to tantalize your senses. A host or hostess will graciously help you design a personalized menu and attend to your tea party needs. Afternoon Teas with linens, fine china, and fresh flowers will no doubt delight your guests. Ask about live instrumental music ranging from Classical to Hawaiian. Private tea parties are available for up to 80 guests. Please book your date early. Mahalo! E-Mail: themanor@juno.com

$25.00 Afternoon Tea... Assorted finger sandwiches, scones and croissants served with island jams, petit fours, a seasonal fruit dessert created by Armstrong Manor's fine pastry chef, and a pot of brewed loose tea.

PRIVATE TEA PARTIES: Please Call To Plan
• May Accommodate Some Dietary Needs With Advance Request
• Non-Caffeine/Herbal Tea Available
• Watercloset: Same Floor
• **Book Your Date Early**
• On-Site Parking Area Available
• Cash Or Traveler's Cheques
Host Or Hostess's
Autograph _____*Date*_____

ASTON WAIKIKI
Beachside Hotel
presents A Special Tea Affair

2452 Kalakaua Avenue
Honolulu, Oahu, Hawaii

808-623-1030

New Addition...It's Teatime On Saturdays & Sundays At...The Aston Waikiki Beachside Hotel. "British influenced Teas, with the flavors of Hawaii." If you have the good fortune to vacation in Hawaii, visit The Aston Waikiki and reserve your date for Afternoon Tea with Sherri, the proprietor of A Special Tea Affair. Step back to an era when the friendship between Britain's Queen Victoria and Hawaii's monarchs influenced Hawaiian culture. Taking Tea was very much a part of the Hawaiian lifestyle back in the 1800's.

Tea is presented from a three tiered caddie in The Lobby or Palm Court at tables set with centerpieces, lace tablecloths and cloth or paper napkins in floral rings.Sherri serves her signature Teas in period-influenced attire. Some outfits are reminiscent of the 1800's while others, the Edwardian period or the 1920's. She uses lovely antique tea accoutrements from her personal collection. Ask her about "Crafts of the Victorian Era." P.S. Bring along this guide and receive $1.00 off an Afternoon Tea!

$15.00 Afternoon Tea... Assorted finger sandwiches, scones, Devonshire cream & preserves, dessert, brewed loose tea.

TEATIME: 3:00pm To 6:00pm • Saturday & Sunday
• Non-Caffeine/Herbal Tea Available
• Watercloset: Same Floor
• Wheelchair Accessible
• **24 Hour Advance Reservations Are Required**
• Parking: $3.00 W/Validation At Waikiki Beach Tower Next Door
• Credit Cards: All Majors

Proprietor's
Autograph _____*Date*_____

HALEKULANI
On The Beach At Waikiki

2199 Kalia Road
Honolulu, Oahu, Hawaii

808-923-2311

New Addition...It's Teatime At...Halekulani. You're in for a treat when you visit the Halekulani, the only Five Diamond property in Honolulu. In fact, the word Halekulani means "House befitting heaven." Afternoon Tea at the opulent Halekulani takes place in a tranquil setting on The Veranda which opens onto the Living Room of the hotel's main building. The historic hotel was built in 1917, and in 1932 the "main building" was added. Restored and reopened in 1984, the Halekulani is quite a beautiful hotel.

Tea is presented from rolling rattan tea carts by servers attired in crisp blue hostess dresses. Afternoon Tea is served at tables set with linens, imported white Bauscher, Weiden fine china & fresh flowers The decor has a comfortable residential feeling with cushioned rattan chairs. This is a popular spot for business oriented "Power Teas" as well as friendly social teas. F.Y.I. While you're at the hotel, catch a glimpse of La Mer. It's the only Five Diamond restaurant in all of of Hawaii and features neo-classic French Cuisine. Enjoy a spectacular ocean front sunset, and a view of Diamond Head too, from "House Without A Key."

$15.50 Afternoon Tea... Assorted tea sandwiches, black currant scones, Devonshire cream & preserves, assorted cakes & pastries, Harney & Son's brewed loose tea or Halekulani blend.
$4.50 Scones... With Devonshire cream & preserves.

TEATIME: 3:00pm To 5:30pm • Seven Days A Week
• May Accommodate Some Dietary Needs With Advance Request
• Non-Caffeine/Herbal Tea Available
• Watercloset: Same Floor
• Wheelchair Accessible
• **Reservations: No**
• Validated Valet Or Self Parking
• Credit Cards: V,MC,DC,JCB&AE

L'autograph
du Concierge _____Date_____

HAWAII PRINCE HOTEL
Waikiki
100 Holomoana Street
Honolulu, Oahu, Hawaii

808-956-1111

New Addition...It's Teatime At Hawaii Prince Hotel. The Hawaii Prince is the only all ocean front property in Waikiki overlooking the picturesque Ala Wal Yacht Harbor. This Four Diamond hotel is dedicated to gracious hospitality. The hotel caters to both business travelers and vacationers. William is the delightful Afternoon Tea manager, be sure to say aloha. Afternoon Tea is served in the open, airy casual Marina Front Lounge. The Lounge is appointed with pastel colored couches, low glass or marble top tables and pots of vibrant island plants and flowers.

Afternoon Tea is served at tables set with linens and Westchester china by the very friendly staff. Remember to plan a couple of days in advance for the Hawaii Prince's Afternoon Tea. F.Y.I. Arnold Palmer designed the 27 hole championship golf course here. Tea & Tee anyone? Please note, credit card guarantee is required for Afternoon Tea reservations. And, a cancellation penalty is imposed. Be sure to ask for the specifics.

$15.50 Marina Front High Tea... Assorted finger sandwiches including watercress, seafood, chicken and cucumber, and seafood, scones served with Devonshire cream, petit fours, chocolate dipped strawberries, and a pot of brewed loose Taylor's of Harrogate Tea, and Harney & Son's Herbal Teas.

TEATIME: 4:00pm To 6:00pm • Seven Days A Week
• Non-Caffeine/Herbal Tea Available
• Watercloset: Same Floor
• Wheelchair Accessible
• **24 Hour Advance Reservations & Guarantee Required**
• Validated Valet Parking
• Credit Cards: V,MC,DC,AE&JCB

L'autograph
du Concierge _____*Date*_____

SHERATON MOANA
Surf Rider
2365 Kalakaua Avenue
Honolulu, Oahu, Hawaii

808-922-3111

New Addition...It's Teatime At...The Sheraton Moana Surf Rider. Taking tea at The Banyan Veranda was an early century Moana tradition. Patrons from near and far found a respite from the afternoon sun in the comfort of the Veranda's lounge chairs fanned by cool ocean breezes. Guests sipped tea while observing the action on Waikiki, or they just became absorbed in the day's conversations.

Today, Afternoon Tea is served on the open, airy Banyan Veranda of the newly restored Sheraton Moana Surfrider. Tea is elegantly presented on a two tiered caddie by servers in pink and white attire and, white gloves! Tablecloths, wicker furnishings, fresh flowers, even a fan to borrow is part of the picture here. They invite you to "re-live those wonderful times past by taking tea with us again and sharing with us these glorious memories of kinder and gentler times." Enjoy!

$17.00 Afternoon Tea... Finger sandwiches, scone served with Devonshire cream & preserves, sweet pastries, and a pot of freshly brewed selected Twinings Teas.

TEATIME: 3:00pm To 5:00pm • Seven Days A Week
• May Accommodate Some Dietary Needs With Advance Request
• Watercloset: Same Floor
• Wheelchair Accessible
• **Reservations Are Highly Recommended**
• Valet Or Self Park For Approximately $3.00-$4.50
• Credit Cards: V,MC,DIS,AE&JCB
L'autograph
du Concierge _____Date_____

About The Author

Linda R.Wexler resides in the Foothill community of Altadena, California with husband Howard, and rescued doggies Chelsea and Barney. Originally from Buffalo, New York Linda graduated with a degree in art & art history from The State University of New York at Buffalo, where she also attended graduate school. She taught all levels of art in the Buffalo public school system for almost a decade. Linda has now lived and worked in Southern California for nearly 20 years in the book industry.

When not writing books or enjoying Afternoon Tea, Linda works on artistic projects of one sort or another. Many of her creative projects are inspired by fabulous flea market finds. Often mistaken for dealers, Linda & Howard have been spotted hunting for teapots & treasures at the "fleas" with walkie-talkies...at dawn!

The welfare of animals has always been of passionate concern for this author. Recently, upon hearing the plight of a local Black Bear, Linda embarked on a fundraising quest. She was instrumental in raising over $10,000 in funds plus product donations for the "celebrity" known as "Samson The Hot Tub Bear." He now resides in a new habitat at The Orange County Zoo.

Linda has several new *tea theme* titles on the way, along with a line of *tea* jewelry and apparel. There's new artwork on the drawing board too. Linda is a popular guest speaker at conferences and seminars on the phenom of the very civilized, Afternoon Tea.

To animals everywhere! Samson at the Orange County Zoo.

Buffalo & Vicinity

The author's first Teddy Bear Tea in Buffalo, New York

469

A memorable family tea party!

DELAWARE PARK CASINO
Lincoln Parkway
Buffalo, New York

716-882-5920

New Addition...Seasonal Teas At...Delaware Park Casino. The Delaware Park Casino is a historic landmark in Buffalo. Originally built in 1874, the structure was replaced in 1901 in time for the Pan-American Exposition. It was the vision of a number of businessmen & city planners in 1992 to renovate the property and again put it on the map as a venue for weddings, special events and most important... a spot for Afternoon Teas! The Casino is situated in a National Historic Landmark Park overlooking Delaware Park Lake, across the street from the nationally renowned Albright Knox Art Gallery-one of my favorites!

Afternoon Tea is served at tables set with linens & cloth napkins. The dining room is bright & airy with creamy colored walls, maple pillers, light wood trim, and hand-stenciled ivy & lattice. Please call for the dates of the Summer Teas which take place daily in August. Holiday Teas take place daily from mid-November thru mid-December, and Spring Teas daily during the month of May. F.Y.I. This park was designed by Frederick Law Olmstead the designer of Central Park in New York! P.S. Ask Jim the events coordinator for more history; it's actually quite fascinating.

$5.95 Afternoon Tea... Assorted finger sandwiches, scones with creme & preserves, suprise dessert, and a pot of tea.

SEASONAL TEAS: 2:00pm To 5:00pm • Call For Schedule
• May Accommodate Some Dietary Needs With Advance Request
• Non-Caffeine/Herbal Tea Available
• Children's Tea Parties Welcome
• Watercloset: Same Floor
• Wheelchair Accessible
• **Reservations Are Appreciated But Not Required**
• Street Parking, Please Call Re: Handicap Parking
• Cash Or Check

Event Coordinator's
Autograph _____*Date*_____

471

THEODORE ROOSEVELT
Inaugural National Historic Site

641 Delaware Avenue
Buffalo, New York
(The Wilcox Mansion)

716-884-0095

New Addition...The Annual Mother & Daughter Tea At...Wilcox Mansion. A wonderful way to welcome in the Spring season is to attend The Mother & Daughter Tea at the Wilcox Mansion. Janice, the events coordinator arranges special exhibits such as a vintage fashion shows & children's activities. Please call to see what's brewing!

Afternoon Teas are graciously served by attentive volunteers in starched white organdy aprons, at tables set with lace tablecloths, fine china & fresh flowers. Lovely silver teapots and authentic Victorian era recipes will enhance your Afternoon Tea experience. Visitors are invited to browse in the gift shop which is full of beautiful Victorian inspired treasures as well as books such as *Bully Fare* or *Emily Spinach.* Take home a memento of a lovely day! This is a wonderful spot to tour and learn more about the life & times of our president Teddy Roosevelt. If you're a Teddy Bear fan, do not miss the exhibit of Teddy Bears nicknamed after Mr. Roosevelt!

$14.00...Mother & Daughter Tea... Assorted tea sandwiches, freshly baked scones with preserves, sweet surprises and a continuous cup of brewed tea. Children under twelve-$7.00.

ANNUAL MOTHER & DAUGHTER TEA: April 25 & 26, 1998 & May 2, 1998 At 1:00pm & 3:00pm • Please Call For 1999 Dates
• May Accommodate Some Dietary Needs With Advance Request
• Non-Caffeine/Herbal Tea Available
• Watercloset: First Floor, Tearoom Up One Flight
• **Reservations Are Required**
• Free Parking Behind The Site, Off Franklin
• Credit Cards: V&MC
Special Events Coordinator's
Autograph _____*Date*_____

To think I sat were Teddy Roosevelt might have sipped!

ASA RANSOM HOUSE
Country Inn
10529 Main Street
Clarence, New York

716-759-2315

New Addition...It's Teatime At...Asa Ransom House. "In 1799, the Holland Land Company offered lots 10 miles apart in what is now Clarence, to 'any proper man who would build and operate a tavern upon it.' The first to accept this offer was a young silversmith by the name of Asa Ransom." This is one of the most popular spots for Afternoon Tea in the Buffalo vicinity. In fact, consider spending a night away from the city at this lovely & relaxing spot. When you go for tea, ask Judy & Bob for a tour.

Afternoon Tea is attentively presented by servers attired in black & white with pinnies & dust mop hats in the dining room at tables set with colored tablecloths, cloth napkins, special pattern white & green Syracuse china & fresh garden flowers. More than 20 years ago, this spot was known as the Mill Road House Tearoom. And, my mother remembers their famous squash soup & pumpkin muffins when she came here as a little girl! Weather permitting, Afternoon Tea is also presented on the lovely veranda overlooking the gazebo and gardens. Advance reservations are required for Afternoon Tea in the romantic gazebo. F.Y.I. Private tea parties are available for 20-40 guests. P.S. Allow time to browse in the gift shop which carries teapots & tea accoutrements too. Don't miss December when the Inn is really dressed-up!

$11.95 Afternoon Tea. Finger sandwiches, fruit garnish, two scones, Devonshire cream & jam, dessert, a pot of brewed tea.

TEATIME: 2:00pm To 4:00pm • Thursday • Closed January
• May Accommodate Some Dietary Needs With Advance Request
• Non-Caffeine/Herbal Tea Available
• Watercloset: Same Floor
• **Reservations Are Recommended, Summer...A Must!**
• Free Parking Area
• Credit Cards: V,MC&DIS

Proprietor's
Autograph _____*Date*_____

474

Tea is served!

OHLSON'S HOME BAKERY
& Tea Room

10681 Main Street
Clarence, New York

716-759-7199

New Addition...Victorian Theme Teas At Ohlson's Home Bakery. *Friday Victorian Teas Are Brewing.* What a pleasant surprise to hear about Lisa Ohlson and her tearoom. It took a while to track her down, but the effort was well worth it. Lisa presents lovely Theme Teas in the bakery's Victorian Tea Room. Ohlson's is a full line bakery, but when the tearoom is open you can also drop by for light lunches, tea & scones, and decadent sweets. The Double Chocolate Creme Fudge Torte created by Lisa's husband Marvin sounds like a *death by chocolate* must. The diet starts tomorrow!

Victorian Teas are served at tables set with tablecloths, mismatched vintage teacups & teapots, and fresh flowers. The tearoom is decorated in rosy tones with green accents and lacey curtains. At Christmas, Ohlson's has a little gift basket boutique. How about a Victorian Tea gift certificate? Ask Lisa about Friday Victorian Teas.

$9.95 Victorian Tea... Assorted finger sandwiches, scones, Devon cream & preserves, sweet surprise & a pot of tea.

VICTORIAN TEAS: Sweetheart Tea: Feb. 14, 1998 & Feb. 13, 1999
- Spring Tea: April 4, 1998 & March 27, 1999
- Mother's Day Tea: May 9, 1998 & May 8, 1999
- Leaf Peeper's Tea: October 3, 1998 & October 2, 1999
- Christmas Tea: Dec. 12 & 19, 1998 & Dec. 11 & 18, 1999
- Tea & Scones Etc. 10:30am To 4pm • Wednesday Thru Saturday
- May Accommodate Some Dietary Needs With Advance Request
- Non-Caffeine/Herbal Tea Available
- Watercloset: One Flight Up • Children's Tea Parties Welcome
- **Reservations Are Requested**
- Free Parking Area
- Cash Or Check

Proprietor's
Autograph _____*Date*_____

476

McFARLAND HOUSE
Tea Garden
15927 Niagara Parkway
Niagara-On-The-Lake, Ontario, Canada

905-468-3322

New Addition...It's Teatime At...McFarland House Tea Garden. A lovely drive along the lake will lead you to McFarland House Tea Garden. This 1800's historic Georgian House was the home of John McFarland and descendants for 150 years. John and his sons built the house from bricks which were made in a kiln on the property. A wing was added later to accommodate their growing family. Interestingly enough, the house survived The War of 1812 because it was used as a hospital and occupied alternately by British or American troops depending upon who had advanced to the house and was in control at the time!

Afternoon Tea & Tour is presented "no frills" style by delightful period costumed servers on the garden patio. We were here in July when the lawn & gardens were really lush and colorful. Allow time to tour the house as it is charming and will provide a wonderful history lesson. P.S. The period furniture & tea sets were quite wonderful. Peek around, a few gifts & tea accessories are tucked into nooks & crannies. F.Y.I. Niagara wine & wine coolers also available. This spot is a wonderful little teatime surprise. Enjoy!

$4.99 Afternoon Tea & $1.75 Tour.."Served in the true Georgian tradition." Half sandwich, freshly baked scone served with jam, sweet, and choice of tea.

TEATIME: Open From Victoria Day Weekend Thru Labor Day
- 11:00am To 6:00pm • Closed Monday In May & June
- 11:00am To 6:00pm • Seven Days A Week In July & August
- May Accommodate Some Dietary Needs With Advance Request
- Non-Caffeine/Herbal Tea Available
- Watercloset: Rear Facility, One Step Up
- **Please Drop In**
- Free Parking Lot
- Cash Or Check

Curator's
Autograph _____*Date*_____

PRINCE OF WALES HOTEL

6 Picton Street
Niagara-On-The-Lake, Ontario, Canada

416-468-3246   800-263-2452

New Addition...It's Teatime At...The Prince of Wales Hotel. You're in for a treat. The Prince of Wales Hotel at Niagara-On-The-Lake...what a spot! Although I grew up in the area, I feel as though I've just discovered this wonderful boutiquey tourist treasure. The Prince of Wales is a splendid hotel with ornate gingerbread trim and colorful summertime flowers everywhere.

Afternoon Tea is served in the Queen's Royal Lounge, or a few steps away in the sun room with a view of the main street. Tea is presented on tiered caddies at either love seat groupings with low tables or at traditional dining tables set with English china. The room is decorated with comfy tropical pattern emerald green tapestry loveseats and warm rust colored chairs and carpet. The modern faux-finish walls, potted plants and twinkle lights are a nice touch. The servers and staff are very gracious. But then, not every hotel accommodates the Queen and Royal Family! The Prince of Wales is quite special, you may want to consider vacationing here. Be sure to ask about the romantic room packages.

$9.00 Afternoon Tea... Interesting finger sandwiches, scones, sweet surprise desserts, and a pot of tea.

TEATIME: 3:00pm To 5:00pm • Seven Days A Week
• Non-Caffeine/Herbal Tea Available
• Watercloset: Same Floor, Bit Of A Hike
• Wheelchair Accessible
• **Reservations Are Not Taken**
• Free Parking In The Rear, Enter On King
• Credit Cards: V,MC&AE
L'autograph
du Concierge _____*Date*_____

ARABELLA'S TEA ROOM
at Port Colborne Museum

280 King Street
Port Colborne, Ontario, Canada

905-834-7604

New Addition...Tea & History At...Arabella's.
Thanks to the efforts of dedicated volunteers and the Port Colborne Museum Auxiliary, visitors to this Ontario historical site are in for a treat at Arabella's Tea Room. Allow time to meander about, there are a number of interesting buildings on the grounds reflecting life in the mid to late 1800's. The Tea Room was built in 1915 and remains true to the era as much as possible. In fact, a 1915 Eaton's catalogue was used as an historic reference. Lighting fixures of the era have been authentically restored, and many of the furnishings have been painstakingly collected by the auxiliary members.

Tea is served at tables set with vintage pink linens & tea cloths, and all of the pretty teacups and accoutrements have been donated. Your volunteer waitresses are ready to serve and answer questions. They are properly attired in circa 1915 floor length skirts or those no more than 3 inches above the ankle, and scalloped white half-aprons. Covered elbows were the norm. Be sure to find the circa 1879 New Haven 30 Hour Time & Strike Gingerbread Clock.

$2.50 Tea & Biscuits... Biscuits are served with butter and a variety of homemade jams & a pot of brewed tea with a cozy.

TEATIME: 2:00pm To 4:00pm • June 1 Thru September 30
• And One Week During Christmas, Tea & Christmas Pudding
• Usually The First Week In December, Please Call For Dates
• Non-Caffeine/Herbal Tea Available
• Watercloset: Same Floor
• Wheelchair Accessible
• **Reservations Are Recommended For Large Groups**
• Cash Please

Curator's
Autograph _____*Date*_____

THE MERCANTILE
Gift Shop & Cafe

230 West Street
Port Colborne, Ontario

905-834-5813

New Addition...It's Teatime At...The Mercantile. Described as "the little shop filled with gifts & good food from the heart," The Mercantile is a sweet comfy spot for Afternoon Tea. Rebecca & Larry lovingly designed this wonderful Victorian tearoom which is above the gift shop. Historic rounded windows trimmed with ivy, and pink flowers, Battenburg lace, matching valances & pretty wreaths are picture perfect! From this vantage point, The Mercantile offers a relaxing, almost hypnotic view of the ships going through the Welland Canal.

Afternoon Tea is presented from tiered caddies at tables set with doilies, linen napkins, Royal Doulton Tiverton pattern fine china, lemon squeezers, tea bells, and other sweet tea accessories. Rebecca wants her guests to feel at home and comfortable. The tearoom is artistically decorated with pink & green floral wallpaper in three patterns and many of her personal treasures. Allow time to browse, the shop carries beautiful gifts, tea accessories, books, packaged tea, teapots & teacups & more. Private tea parties are available for 15 to 38 guests. F.Y.I. Larry restored the beautiful oak staircase and renovated the tearoom himself, pretty talented guy!

$9.99 Afternoon Tea... Homebaked cheese scones with preserves & creamery butter, tiny tea sandwiches, tarts & treats, and choice of tea from the tea box. ($6.99 Children under 8 years.)

TEATIME: 11:30am To 2:00pm • Monday Thru Saturday
- May Accommodate Some Dietary Needs With Advance Request
- Non-Caffeine/Herbal Tea Available
- Children's Tea Parties Welcome
- Watercloset & Tearoom: One Flight Up
- **Reservations Are Encouraged**
- Free Street Parking
- Credit Cards: V&MC

Proprietor's
Autograph_____Date_____

480

THE TEA COZY
12377 Big Tree Road
Wales Center, New York

716-655-3304

New Addition...It's Teatime At...The Tea Cozy.
This is a cozy little country spot for Afternoon Tea. Maureen the proprietor, introduced Afternoon Tea to the area a number of years ago and is waiting for the tea spirit to catch on! Built in 1929, this converted garage has its own rural charm & ambiance. Light and airy, it has white walls, pink curtains, green carpet and hand-crafted floral wreaths.

Afternoon Tea is casually served at tables set with layered tablecloths, a collection of mis-matched English bone china, teapots with tea cozies...of course, and fresh flowers. Nearly everything here is homemade, the herbs are fresh from Maureen's herb garden. Maureen doesn't brag much about her tearoom...but then again, maybe that's part of the charm. Private tea parties are available for 20-30 guests, please call to plan. F.Y.I. Lunch is offered in addition to Afternoon Tea. Peek around for the knitted tea cozies, herb sachets and dried flowers. Many of the gift items are handcrafted. The muffins & scones are also available for take home.

$7.90 Afternoon Tea... Finger sandwiches, scones served with clotted cream & butter, dessert and a pot of brewed tea.

TEATIME: 11:00am To 4:00pm • Year Round • Closed Saturday
• Non-Caffeine/Herbal Tea Available
• Watercloset: Same Floor
• Wheelchair Accessible
• **Reservations Are Appreciated**
• Free Parking Lot Next Door
• Cash
Proprietor's
Autograph _____*Date*_____

Children's "Dress-Up" tea parties are fun & memorable!

Easy to Spy
Geographic Index
page 485
Alphabetical Index
page 492
& Recipes page 484

Recipes

California By Geographic Vicinity

NORTHERN CALIFORNIA   PAGE

City of San Francisco-continued

Alameda County

San Mateo County

Solano County

Contra Costa County

Santa Clara County

Santa Clara County-continued

Marin County

Wine Country

Monterey Peninsula & Vicinity

Central Coast Between Monterey & Santa Barbara

SOUTHERN CALIFORNIA

San Fernando Valley Area

San Fernando Valley Area-continued

Los Angeles-West Side

Los Angeles-Downtown Area

Whittier-Norwalk Area

Whittier-Norwalk Area-continued

Pasadena & Vicinity-continued

Inland Empire

Orange County & Vicinity

Orange County & Vicinity-continued

San Diego & Vicinity

CALIFORNIA   PAGE

California-continued

Nevada

Oregon

Washington-Seattle Area

Washington Alphabetical Index

British Columbia-Vancouver

British Columbia-Victoria

British Columbia Alphabetical Index

Let's Go Shopping!

Introducing...Linda Wexler's line of "A Spot of Tea" ™ original *sterling silver* tea-theme jewelry!

These limited edition collector's pieces are signed and numbered, and offered here for the first time anywhere. "I've designed these unique pieces to be part of my personal jewelry collection. They are truly conversation pieces and I am quickly identified as someone who is "into" tea...as you will be too!"

"Teacup" Ring...Here is the "teacup" ring you've been asking for with a wide band declaring "A Spot of Tea." A synthetic amber colored stone shows your cup full of beautiful tea! The tiny spoon has a drop of "tea" too!

Cufflinks....I needed cufflinks, so here they are for your favorite French cuff blouse or shirt too!

Please call for current prices. We may have to ask you to allow up to 6 weeks for delivery.

"Tea Set Necklace"....Now you can wear a sterling "tea-set"!
The center teapot says A Spot of Tea. This piece is available as
a brooch too. Please call toll-free to order: 800-SPOT OF T

Purse Hook...Our authentic reproduction in sterling silver. I was intrigued by this Victorian photograph and looked for a purse hook for the longest time; only to discover that they are extremely scarce. Most antique dealers had no idea what I was talking about. They thought I meant a chatelaine. I finally found one at around $1,000. Determined, I continued my search. I am pleased to present a sterling silver reproduction of my newly found purse hook. Please call for our fashionable price.

Tea Cozy Patterns!...Sized for a two or three cup pot. Order your cute pattern today and start knitting your gifts. They are especially charming when knitted to match your teacups!

Tea Signs!...Our uniquely designed wooden tea signs are painted with a teapot & sweets portrayed on *both* sides. A chain on each side holds the sign open, yet folds for easy storage. Too cute! "A Spot of Tea" or your favorite tea-line. 12"x13" each surface.

Let's Go Shopping!

New!....“A Spot of Tea” ™ “T”-Shirts & “T”-Bags!

Short Sleeve “Teas”....Beautifully detailed 100% cotton, preshrunk T-Shirt. Elegant black. A teacup is on the back too!
Long Sleeve Mock Turtleneck....For cooler climates. Ribbed-cuff. Elegant black. A teacup is on the back too. M&XL
Sweatshirt.... Comfy black sweatshirts. Back teacup too. M&XL
“T”-Bag...Black cloth tote says “T” Bag in metallic lettering.

Prints...Unframed, numbered & signed print inspired by our cover with only the phrase, A Spot of Tea.” Size is approximately 12x16. Please call for price & delivery information. Beautifully matted & framed prints may be available for quantity orders. Call 800-SPOT OF T for prices.

Are you a tea spotter?

If you've discovered a new tea spot please let us know. We'll be sure to let the proprietor know that it was you who referred us and mention your first name in the write-up if you'd like. Also, we'll send you a little gift to boot! We very much appreciate your taking the time to let us in on your "find." If you're able to pick-up a business card & send it to me, super! If you prefer, call **800-SPOT OF T**, or photocopy this page and fill it out over tea! Thanks again.

New Tearoom: _____

Proprietor(s):_____

Phone: ( )_____

Address:_____

City:_____State/Province:_____

U.S.A.   British Columbia   Alberta   Ontario   Canada

Referred   by: _____

Date:_____

Phone: ( )_____

Address:_____

City:_____State/Province:_____

Country:_____ Postal Code/Zip:_____

Autographed gift copies

To order an autographed gift copy of "A Spot of Tea" ™ please mail a photocopy of this page along with a check or money order for $31.50 U.S. Your autographed, gift-wrapped in "teacup" paper book will be sent via Priority Mail with an enclosure card. Or, you may fax this completed form and call with your <u>Mastercard, Visa or Discover Card.</u> **1-800-SPOT OF T** or **626-797-4TEA.**

Ask about our Deluxe Gift Package: An autographed copy of both **"A Spot of Tea,"**™ and **"My Tea Journal"** to record your tearoom experiences, plus a beautiful "TEA" Shirt. Deluxe packages are wrapped in "tea" gift wrap paper and sent with a gift card.

Chelsea Street Productions
1920 N. Lake Avenue, Suite 108-200
Altadena, California 91001

Recipient: _____
                              please print

Address: _____

City:_____State/Province:_____

Sent From: _____

Greeting:_____

_____

Visa/MC/DIS#_____ Expires:_____

Card Holder's Name:_____

Address:_____

Phone: (   )_____

510

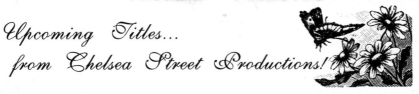

Upcoming Titles... from Chelsea Street Productions!

Children's Teatime Journal...A child's journal for recording her or his early teatime experiences. Geared to youngsters, there are wonderful vintage children's photos & more! A great gift.

Five O'Clock Tea... We've brought back a Victorian classic. A must for Afternoon Tea enthusiasts.

Now That's A Hat!...A one-of-a-kind photo collection featuring fabulous Victorian hats. Interesting hat facts too. A really fun book!

Mrs. Raccoon's Wondrous Tea Room.. This is the delightfully charming illustrated teatime storybook that your young children are sure to enjoy.

A Spot of Tea At Home...Host A Tea Party With Style You've been asking for some of my most creative tea party ideas. Here they are.

Life's A Tea Party!...A little cartoon gift book that is sure to make you and your friends smile. Particularly if you're really "steeped" in tea!

A Spot of Tea & Teatime Recipes... The *best of the best* recipes from many of your favorite tearooms, and the author's secret recipes too.

Tearoom Etiquette For The New Millennium... The book on *polite & power*, tearoom etiquette...for the next...turn-of-the-century!

Memorable Tea Rooms Throughout History... Learn about the famous tearooms of the past and how they may inspire tomorrow's memorable tea spots.

The Lost Art of Reception Chocolate... Learn the history of this one time fashionable hot cocoa service, and how to properly prepare & serve hot chocolate today. Be at the forefront of a trend! Photographs of lovely hand-painted vintage chocolate sets too.

A Taste of Celebrity-The Galactic Guide To Celebrity Owned Restaurants...A unique treat of a dining guide!

And of course...**My Tea Journal....**Tailor-made to record your many teatime memories, experiences, choices & impressions. A must for all true *tea-travelers*.

*An unfilled teacup will be placed
at our table, in memory of
Princess Diana*